Eagle Dreams

*To David — Your dad was
a friend of mine. Good
luck.
Enjoy!
[signature]*

Herman Son
With Foreword by James D. Hughes, Lt. General, USAF (Ret.)

JMT Publications ● *Shirley, Indiana* ● *http://jmtpubs.tripod.com*

Photo credits:

Ch 1 - Pen and ink drawing of Frank Luke and 27th Fighter Squadron Logo
http://www.geocities.com/Athens/Acropolis/7133/index.html
Used by permission of Daniel Conover
Spirit of St. Louis
http://wwww.charleslindbergh.com/plane/index.asp
Used by permission of Patrick Ranfranz, webmaster
Ch 2 - author's personal collection
Ch 3 - Maps from *Ebb and Flow, November 1950 - July 1951.* Used with permission of the United States Army, Washington DC. Posted on the web page http://www.koreanwar.org/html/maps
Ch 4 - all photos from author's personal collection
Ch 5 & 6 - Reprinted with permission of USAF Museum
Ch 10, 11, 12, 13, 16 - author's personal collection
Ch 17 - The "Frisco" Used with permission of the St. Louis Steam Train Association, web page http://www.thetrainmuseum.org/things/htm
Ch 18 - Roscoe Turner, used with permission from website http://www.geocities.com/CapeCanaveral/Lab/4515/turner.htm
USS Arizona after Japanese attack on December 7, 1941, used with permission from website http://www.history.navy.mil/photos/images/g30000
Ch 19 - author's personal collection
Ch 20 - author's personal collection
Ch 21 - author's personal collection. Cartoons excerpted from high school class year-book.
Ch 22, 23, 27, 28, 34 - author's personal collection
Ch 37- author's personal collection. Photo of F84-F reprinted with permission from USAF Museum
Ch 39, 41, 42, 47, 48, 50, 51 - author's personal collection

Song lyrics:

Memories Are Made Of This and *I've Got The World On A String*, used by permission of ASCAP
That Old Black Magic, from the Paramount Picture *Star-Spangled Rhythm*
Words by Johnny Mercer
Music by Harold Arlen
Copyright © 1942 (renewed 1969) by Famous Music Corporation
International Copyright secured. All rights reserved.
Used by permission of Hal Leonard Corporation, Milwaukee, Wisconsin

Contents

Foreword

James D. Hughes
Lt. General, USAF (ret)

"If it hadn't been for the Fifth Air force, we'd have been pushed off this peninsula."
- Lt. General Walton H. Walker
- Commander, Eighth Army

"Without question, the Air force definitely blunted the initial North Korean thrust to the southward. Without this continuing air effort in support of the courageous combat soldiers, spread thinly along the line, we could not have withstood the onslaught of the vastly numerically superior enemy."
- Major Genral William F. Dean
- Commander, 24th Infantry Division
- (Before his capture by the NKA)

In 1948 I was assigned ot the 8th Fighter-bomber Group at Itazuke Air Base in Southern Japan for what turned out to be one of the most professionally rewarding assignments of my Air Force career. It was here that I met Herman Son and got to know and respect him as a professional officer and as a first-rate fighter pilot. Herman's reputation as a "real stick and rudder guy" was well established and his fighter gunnery scores were a source of envy. In today's parlance, he was definitely a Top Gun! But, he was also a very nice guy and our friendship has endured the passage of many years. And so, it was a pleasure to serve with him and it is an honor for me to introduce his autobiography.

Life at Itazuke during the occupation years was sweet indeed! We flew Mustangs - and later, F80 Shooting Stars - almost as much as we wanted, and our missions were more fun than work. Our air-to-air and air-to-ground gunnery ranges were close by and we happily expended a lot of 50-caliber ammunition, many practice rockets and tons of bombs on a rock in the ocean. Formation flying was the name of the game: the formations varied in size from routine two and four-ship flights to squadon-size or, on special occasions, the entire group of three squadrons would form up. The group effort was affectionately known as a "JOCK-HANG"; 72 fighters (plus 3 spares) provided spectacular viewing for the crowd but it generated much cold perspiration, hard breathing and colorful profanity among the crews.

And then there was the unofficial, but highly popular, freestyle awareness training program that simply meant that any airborne single ship or flight of two was fair game for anyone who chose to bounce and engage in aerial combat. The stated purpose was to train pilots to keep alert constantly for the "bandit" out of the sun. But it was also great sport, and invaluable in honing fighter techniques and building experience. It also established an unofficial ladder of real hotshots, which, in turn, resulted in unofficial competition to be the top stick-and-rudder guy in the group. In this connection, Herman's name comes to mind, along with Bill Samways, Jim Gasser, Joe Rogers and Bob Wayne, to name a few.

And so, for the next two years, Air Force life at Itazuke went on at a relaxed and pleasant pace. If bad weather prevented gunnery, air tactics or formation training, the group stood down and most of the pilots had free time. These were the salad days!

But all that changed in a heartbeat. In early 1950, Secretary of State Dean Acheson had issued a policy statement that excluded the Korean Peninsula from America's defense permieter. This diplomatic blunder apparently encouraged the North Koreans to launch a full-scale attack against the Republic of Korea in an effort to reunite the peninsula under

Communist rule. On Sunday, June 26, 1950 North Korean Army tanks rolled into South Korea.

America was at war again, and the 8th Fighter-Bomber group was at the tip of the spear. The fun-and-games-days were over; instead of standing down in bad weather, we launched into torrential monsoon rain, wind and violent turbulence with an overload of Napalm, bombs, rockets and jerry-rigged oversize fuel tanks. Our lack of weather training and failures of the hastily improvised tip tanks caused several fatal accidents. Another factor of great concern was the number of recent graduates from pilot training who were thrust into combat with little practical fighter background. Here, the leadership and professional skills of Herman and the other experienced flight commanders were invaluable in the accelerated development of inexperienced crews. It was on-the-job training at its best!

The Korean War has been called "the forgotten war," possibly because it was sandwiched between World War II and the agonizing decade of the Vietnam War. But the toll of 58,000 American dead and the fact that the Korean Peninsula today is not under Communist rule militate strongly against that war being forgotten. Moreover, a common misconception is that the war in Korea consisted principally of two events: the Inchon landing and Mig Alley.

Inchon was an audacious stroke of military genius by General Douglas MacArthur that was executed superbly by the Army, Navy and Marines. Mig Alley was an air superiority campaign fought brilliantly, valiantly and victoriously by American fighter pilots flying F-86 Sabrejets and achieving a dazzling 10 to 1 kill ratio over the Soviet Mig-15.

While Inchon and Mig Alley are definitely pivotal events in this war, the successful defense of the Pusan Perimeter by UN forces was clearly decisive and a turning point that deserves equal recognition in military history.

During the summer of 1950, the North Korean Army easily overwhelmed the South Korean and American forces and occupied almost all of South Korea. The 8th US Army rallied near Taegu and established a last-ditch defensive position known as the Pusan Perimeter. It was here that American tactical airpower became the decisive factor in the fighting, striking hard at the overextended NKA supply lines and providing crucial close air support to the tenuous lines of defending troops.

Fifth Air Force fighters, some staging from the forward air base at Taegu, pounded the NKA troops entrenched in the "Bowling Alley" just a short distance from the runway. At the peak of the battle, twenty-minute missions from Taegu were the norm. Combat sorties flowed through an assembly line system for aircraft repair, refueling, rearming and launch. Tactical air delivered a steady, deadly rain of napalm, bombs rockets and 50-caliber bullets on the enemy engaged in close combat with our friendly forces. And it worked! The perimeter was stabilized. The enemy was exhausted and overstretched logistically. The port at Pusan was secure and American reinforcements, supplies and equipment poured in. And a much-needed victory gave a tremendous boost to Allied morale and confidence in Korea and the free world.

In the months following the Pusan Perimeter victory, the 35th and 36th Fighter-Bomber Squadrons of the 8th Group, with the appropriate project name of "HOBO", moved from Tsuiki, Japan to Suwon, Korea to Kimpo, to Pyongyang, North Korea. Here, after a few days, the intervention of some 60,000 Chinese Communist "volunteers" caused a rapid withdrawal to K16 in Seoul City, followed by a final move back to Itazuke to reform the group and re-equip the 35th and 36th with F80s. HOBO was home!

By now, most of the original 8th Group pilots had completed a full combat tour of 100 missions and were going home. Herman was among them, having flown 107 missions in the F-51 and the F-80, and having distinguished himself as a premier combat leader. His commanders, his squadron mates, the wingmen he led into battle, and especially the "new guys" whom he shepherded, mentored and developed into combat veterans, will bear witness to his reputation.

This book will acquaint the reader with a unique fighter pilot - one who is passion-ately in love with fighter flying and who is capable of communicating all elements of this passion with eloquence, clarity and humility tempered by the requisite cockiness that is the hallmark of the fighter profession. He offers a rare insight into the hard and dangerous realities that exist beyond the stereotyped facade of glamour and fun that is the public perception of the fighter pilot image.

James D. Hughes
Lt. General USAF (retired)

Tactical Air Unites in the Pusan Perimeter Campaign
8th Fighter-Bomber Group
18th Fighter-Bomber Group
35th Fighter-Bomber Group
49th Fighter-Bomber Group
51st Fighter-Bomber Group
Marine Aircraft Group 33
Task Force 77 Naval Air
3rd Light Bombardment Group
American-Korean Fighter Unit, Major Dean Hess, Commanding

Preface

Flying fighter planes is dangerous business. "Well, DUH," a teenager might say. Everybody who has even a nodding acquaintance with flying knows that it is dangerous. My insurance company certainly knew; they charged me a 40% loading on my life insurance because, statistically, my widow had a good chance to collect. I knew it, too. In the over 8,000 hours spent in God's firmament, shoehorned into the cockpit of a fighter, I came to understand at flying one is like handling a tiger. Breathtaking beauty is pierced with spine-tingling danger. Respect for the rules is, for the most part, obligatory. Occasionally, rules can be bent. On the other hand, the laws of physics - not the same as rules - cannot be flouted. For example, one can fly under the Golden Gate Bridge, clearly against the rules. With luck, one may be able to get away with it - if one doesn't hit the bridge. Hitting the bridge, however, won't work. Obviously! Fighter aircraft can wreak mind-blowing destruction and they can be mercilessly unforgiving of mistakes. Finally, fighter craft are seductive, offering awesome power, unleashed with the nudge of the throttle, guided with a gentle, sometimes forceful but skilled, touch on the controls, enabling mere man to go to places and do things that only the gods can do.

It's a little like flying with the angels. And, to think, I got paid for it, too!

Many times my life hung by a slender thread. The difference between safety and disaster was often only an inch or two, a fraction of a second or a few gallons of fuel. Every pilot who has flown professionally knows the truth of this.

Why was I spared so many times? Was it my skill and experience? Perhaps. There are times, however, when skill alone is not enough. Was it sheer luck that decided the issue? Maybe. But I've seen enough close calls to make me wonder, "Who, or what, stood the law of probability on its head?" One can presuppose that perhaps there is a higher power that decided these things - possibly a "guardian angel"?

It was at this point in my thinking that I decided to create a fantasy character to help me tell my story. What could be better than a guardian angel? Allow me to introduce Frank Luke. He has a rank of "Senior Guardian." Some of you may recognize the name. Frank was a fighter pilot in France during World War I. He was a member of the Eagle Squadron, the 27th Fighter. It is a part of the storied First Fighter Group, now active in the Iraq war. The First Group also included the famous 94th "Hat In The Ring" Squadron. Eddie Rickenbacker flew with the 94th. When Luke died on his final mission, September 19, 1918, he was America's leading Ace. Later, Rickenbacker would surpass Luke. Because of the circumstances of his death, however, Luke was awarded the Congressional Medal of Honor. Subsequently, during World War Two, Luke Air Force Base in Arizona was named after him.

Now, listen to some strange parallels: In 1947, after a short period in civilian life, I returned to active duty and was assigned to the 27th, the Eagle Squadron. World War Two was receding into history. Based at March AFB, Riverside, California, the 27th had just received the first operational jet fighters n the Air force. If Frank was looking down on me he must have been smiling, because I pounced in the F-80 like a robin on a June bug. I flew the F-80 for about a year before going to Japan in time to participate in the Korean War. When I came home, my new stateside duty station was - you guessed it - Luke AFB in Arizona! There, staring down at me from a painting hung on the wall in base headquarters was my "guardian angel," Frank Luke!

So, Frank has become the part-time narrator of my story. Most of the time, he will carry the narrative in third person. Occasionally, when things get tight, he will lapse into

first person to comment directly. When he does lapse into first person, his comments will be highlighted with an italic typeface.

The reader(s) of this book - I hope there will be many - may ask, "Why? What kind of book is this?" Let me say first what kind of book I hope it is not. My aim is to avoid an exercise in narcissism. This is a memoir so it skates close to that self-serving swamp. By definition, it deals with my subjective memory, my recall from early childhood into my old age. In covering over eight decades, I make liberal use of flashbacks and fast-forwards to relate my childhood and early youth to my adult life. I believe, and I think readers will agree, that there are connections. But memory is tricky, often a tool of self-deception. I have chronicled events as accurately as I know how. A number of them, particularly my military activities, can be documented, but many of them cannot. They simply arise from the recesses of my subjective memory. So the reader is free to take these words as simply the musings of an old man engaged in what is a favorite activity of the old: living in the past. My goal, however, is for more - the emergence of an outline of a life well lived. It is a life containing the normal ingredients: joy, sadness, grief, hope, faith, trust and betrayal, feat and courage, frustration and anger, victory and defeat, resolution and satisfaction. There are problems, there are solutions. Some of them are effective, some not. My story carries the reader back to my childhood and also to many parts of the world, where I was fortunate to have a seat on the 50-yard line of history's game. I am no pundit, but I am an amateur student of history. In my travels to various parts of the world, I will serve up a dollop or two of history. As a career military man, I have had many opportunities to observe the interplay of power between nations and cultures. I have seen war up close and personal. I have also had a full life and career as a civilian. That part of my life has not been as exciting or intense as my life in the Air Force, but still, it is part of my life experience. I hope that my views may offer some perspectives and insight. I can only say, "It's been a helluva ride!" If you think that is narcissistic, so be it.

Dedication

This book is dedicated to my wife and the love of my life for 32 years, Marilyn Joy Son. Since 1973, I literally owe my life to her. She has truly been my guardian angel.

It is also dedicated to my comrades in arms. There were / are many, both in combat and in peace. But we all had something in common, a love of the air and a willingness to cover our friend's tail. Without that, many of us would not have survived.

It is also dedicated to my two children, Emelle and Randal, in the hope that in reading these pages they may know something more about their father and what he was about. I have three stepchildren who form a part of my nuclear family: Holly Westlake Rumph, Carol Westlake Hassebrock and Robert H. Westlake. This book is also dedicated to them, their spouses and their children.

Finally, it is dedicated to the memory of those who have not survived. That list, of course, grows longer each day. Soon, we will all be a part of history. That fact, perhaps, is the final reason for writing this book now - to capture and preserve that small bit of history that I lived before I pass from the scene.

Acknowledgements

My thanks and appreciation go to Thomas Gordon, Patricia Treacy and Ellen Feinstein for their invaluable help in reading and editing my manuscript. Lt. General James D. Hughes has graciously provided a foreword, for which I am honored. I also thank Jean Fritz of JMT Publications for her many suggestions, not only about the manuscript but also on packaging and marketing. Without her help the production of this book would have been difficult, if not impossible.

CHAPTER 1
The Dream Is Born

*"A Passion for Flying - a Love of Music-and Boyhood Dreams ThatBecame Reality.
This Is The Story of a Fighter Pilot's Life."*

    Hello! In my life on Earth my name was Frank Luke. I was a World War I fighter pilot, a member of the 27th Fighter Squadron, killed on September 29, 1918. I was brave enough to win The Congressional Medal of Honor and have an Air Force Base named after me. After my passage through the pearly gates, I trained for another set of wings. Now I'm an angel with the rating of " Senior Guardian." As you have probably heard, guardian angels are sent by a "higher power" to look after the welfare of selected persons on earth. Several years ago, I'm not sure how many because we angels don't think of time the way earth people do, I was assigned a rather unusual case. It concerned a young boy who wanted to fly. I suppose my boss thought that along the way he might need some help. He was right. I monitored him from his beginning. As an angel, of course, I was aware of the boy's every thought, spoken and unspoken. Angels do not manifest themselves to earth people in the normal, "flesh and blood" sense of the word; but draw near and I will reveal to you his story.

In the beginning . . .

    His mother and father called him Herman Franklin. Late one May afternoon in 1927, the boy, not yet six years old, stood with his father in the barnyard behind the small, mid-Missouri home where he had been born. He and his father listened intently to the sound of an airplane, not a common sound in those days. Flying low, it was hidden behind the trees but coming closer from the west, throbbing louder. Suddenly, it burst into view — shimmering silver, a high wing monoplane moving through a cloud flecked light blue sky. Flying eastward at no more than 500 feet, it was so low that

The Spirit of St. Louis

the numbers on the wing could be seen . . . NX-211. There was some writing on the nose. . . ."St. Louis," it said. It disappeared as quickly as it came. It left behind an awe struck little boy. He felt his skin tighten up in goose bumps, all the way to his scalp as his father told him that the pilot was Charles A. Lindbergh. "Lindy", they called him. Lucky Lindy! He was

on his way from California, where he had picked up his brand new airplane. He was going to St. Louis, where he would refuel for the long trip to New York. His final destination was . . . .Paris!

"Paris, France? All the way across the ocean?"

"Yes, Herman Franklin. He will be flying from New York, across more than 3,000 miles of the Atlantic Ocean. No one has ever done it. It will be a miracle if he makes it!"

A miracle?? The boy wasn't sure about the meaning of the word, but he knew from his father's tone of voice that it was something grand.

He had heard his father tell stories about his adventures in France during The War. There were stories about the trip over on a troop ship, the great city of Paris where every-body spoke French and stories about "The Boche," as the French called the Germans. He had seen pictures and souvenirs his father had brought back buttons from a French soldier's uniform, a piece of shrapnel, his "overseas" uniform cap. France was a romantic land, so far, far away. The boy resolved that afternoon that someday he, too, would fly. Just like "Lindy."

Soon after that momentous afternoon, the boy went to bed in the upstairs loft of the small bungalow where he and his parents lived. During the night, he quietly climbed out of bed and went to the bedroom window looking out over a porch roof. Quietly, he raised the window and climbed out onto the roof. He walked to the edge of the roof, spread his arms outward and jumped. Yes! He flew, he did not fall - out over the back yard and out into the pasture behind the barn! He had perfect control, soaring and banking gently, just as he had seen airplanes do. Gently, he touched down in the pasture.

Just as gently, he swam up from his dream sleep, and found himself in the darkened room, warmly tucked into his bed. It was wonderful. He wanted to go back to sleep and do it again!

Over the next several years of his boyhood, the dream would recur. It was always the same, always so easy and wonderful.

During those ensuing years, Herman Franklin would grow through childhood, adoles-cence and young manhood. Then he was a pretty big frog in a very small puddle. Centertown was, to put it charitably, a "burg."

He was a leader in high school, editor of his high school paper and top student aca-demically. He completed his senior year in the spring of 1940 first in a class of twenty-one - not a particularly big deal, but in that environment it was. That fall he began his first year of college, majoring in music and education. By this time, he had become a modestly accom-plished classical pianist winning honors at state and national high school music contests. When he started college, his goal was to become a high school music.teacher. Still, the recurring dream floated in his mind, like an eagle borne aloft on the air currents of a sum-mer afternoon. Coming to the surface it tantalized, but there was little hope that it would ever come to fruition.

Toward the end of the first semester of his second year of college at Central Missouri State University a historic event that would change his entire life occurred. In the blue gray dawn hours of December 7, 1941 planes from the Royal Imperial Japanese Navy at-tacked Pearl Harbor, America's bastion in the Pacific. Violent explosions and greasy orange fires ripped through the American fleet, tied up in port, and American planes parked in neat rows at Hickham Air Base. It was a crippling blow, not only to our naval and air power and American lives, but also to American pride.

The next day, December 8, 1941, President Roosevelt went before a joint session of congress and in his famous ". . .a date that will live in infamy," speech asked for and received a declaration of war. Ever since Lindy's flyover, Herman Franklin had wanted to fly, but how could he, a poor farm boy ever hope to afford that. It was not likely.

On that "infamous" date, everything changed. The size of the puddle suddenly ex-panded - exponentially!

CHAPTER 2
The Dream Comes True

Twenty-three years after that dappled blue-sky afternoon in which he and his father stood transfixed he was no longer awe struck, no longer a little boy. He was a competent young fighter pilot. He was a flight commander, leading a flight of four F80-C "Shooting Stars," a modern jet fighter plane. Since June 26th 1950 he had been flying combat missions over Korea.

Frank, Herman Franklin's guardian angel, picked up on his charge's peril (note: when Frank has something to say in first person it will be italicized.)

Just like "Lindy" was in 1927, Herman Franklin, now the jet pilot in 1950, was in need of a miracle.

Today, August 20th, he and the other three members of his flight were returning through monsoon weather to his home base. It was 120 miles to the south on the north coast of Kyushu. They were dangerously low on fuel.

"*Frank,*" I said to myself, "*you are going to have to pull off a major miracle. To begin, you will have to control Son's thoughts and emotions.*"

Son would not, could not, think the unthinkable - that he and the three other members of his four plane flight would run out of fuel and crash into the Sea of Japan. The thought was there, hovering on the periphery of his consciousness. But to contemplate it head on would be to allow his fear to take control, to render him incapable of doing what he had to do, concentrating on the task at hand. Son was "in a zone," focusing with the intensity of an NFL wide receiver going deep for a pass, seeing the laces on the incoming ball, looking it into his outstretched hands, touching then gripping the ball with his fingers, unaware of the crowd noise or double-teaming defense men about to take him apart but only of making the catch.

A technical note from Frank, the Guardian Angel

You should know that pilots, particularly fighter pilots, are different. Yes, they really are different from earthbound people! They perceive, think and act in a three-dimensional world. Earthbound folks think and live in a two dimensional world where for the most part everything is flat. They deal with things that are ahead, behind, to the left or to the right. They can go forward, stop, back up, turn right or left. Pilots, on the

other hand, have learned to deal with a three-dimensional world that is bounded by the earth's surface, the upper limits of the earth's atmosphere and the horizon in all directions. They navigate through this universe applying six degrees of freedom. What does that mean, six degrees of freedom? It means that when they are flying they can bank left, bank right, yaw to the right or left around a vertical axis, pull the nose up, push the nose down around a horizontal axis, accelerate or decelerate. They can apply these freedoms singly or in an infinite number of combinations. They think globally with freedoms that earthbound folks don't deal with. As you follow the story of Herman and his flight mates you should try to think globally as though you are suspended at the center of a huge sphere, thus offering infinite possibilities of movement, just as they do. Oh, by the way, music, which is another of Son's passions, has many of the same multi-dimensional qualities. Now, let's get back to Herman's story.

Fuel was always a problem. The F80-C's with which his squadron was equipped had a maximum radius of action that barely extended from his home base to the target area a few miles south of Seoul. After no more than 15 minutes at the fuel gulping low altitudes necessary to attack their targets, the pilots of the 8th Fighter Bomber Group had to break off their attacks and return home. To tarry too long would have meant running out of fuel over the Sea of Japan with consequent fatal outcome.

Mission success in this situation was the first concern. Safety, as practiced in peacetime, was not.

Survival was . . ,well,. . .survival!

For reasons that will become clear, he had cut things much too close. That he knew.

Being privy to his thoughts, I, his guardian angel, knew that he knew.

He had more experience flying in bad weather than any member of his squadron, but he had never experienced weather that was this bad. Heavy, rain-sodden clouds of the monsoon season flopped over the Japanese Islands and its approaches to the north like a wet mop. How, under such conditions, could he possibly lead his flight to safety, to that small obelisk (shaped like the Washington Monument lying on its side) that was home base, the runway, hidden in the dense fog, before their fuel was gone? How, indeed! He checked his fuel counter. It showed that he had a mere 90 gallons remaining. "Not enough," he thought. Moments later, as if to emphasize his thought, the red fuel low warning light flashed on. This meant that he had only a few precious minutes to find the runway or, out of fuel, crash into the sea, taking Jim, Al and Russ with him.

How did Herman Franklin Son, First Lieutenant, United States Air Force, and his flight-mates find themselves in such peril?

"*It's appropriate that you should ask,*" said Frank, the guardian angel.

CHAPTER 3
Playing "Catch up."

The 8th Fighter Bomber Wing and the 24th Division, United States Army, was part of the post World War Two occupation force in Japan. Based on the northern coast of Kyushu, looking across the Japanese Sea to the Korean peninsula some 130 miles to the north, their mission was simply to provide a presence in Japan - in a phrase, to "show the flag." None of our diplomats, politicians or even our generals and admirals thought there would be a need to fight.

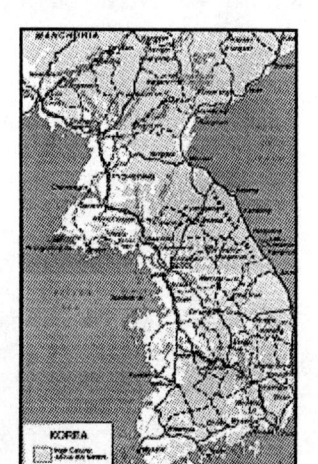

Nevertheless, as South Korea's ally, America was committed to defend South Korea. It was part of America's natural strategic defense perimeter around the Pacific Rim. The U.S. had made formal, diplomatic promises to come to their assistance if they were attacked. The conventional wisdom held that there was little chance of an attack from the North Koreans.

In that relaxed, post WWII reverie, it therefore made perfect sense to some, though not all to avoid a waste of resources preparing for war! Pell mell demobilization and budget cutbacks were the order of the day. Still, Friday nights meant 20-ounce steaks sizzling at the Officers Club. Settled with their families at Itazuke Airfield in western Japan, airmen of the 8th FBW flew the Lockheed F-80C and felt that they were a showcase for the newly independent U.S. Air Force. If they were not the Air Force elite in their new, fast jets, they came close. Was there overconfidence? Complacency?

Yes, and the facts were ominous. The U. S. Secretary of Defense, Louis Johnson, assured the public that only "the fat" would be trimmed. The muscle, he said, would not be touched.

But the 8th Wing and the 24th Division were woefully under equipped, under manned, and under trained. The 24th had barely 50% of their authorized equipment. What they had was obsolete and/or poorly maintained. The same was true of the 8th Wing. Although they had recently begun receiving new F80-C jet aircraft, they had only 15 aircraft, barely half the number authorized. Pilots flew with parachutes that were 10 years old. For crash helmets, they used football helmets that were discarded from the football team. The 35th had only 12 combat ready pilots instead of the 30 pilots that they should have had. To the Federal Government and the American public military folk were the scullery maids who

ate in the kitchen. There was no budgetary "main dining room" for them. As Ruyard Kipling, famous poet during the halcyon days of the British Empire, said:

> "Yes, makin' mock o' uniforms that guard you while you sleep
> Is cheaper than them uniforms, an' they're starvation cheap..."

Many books have been written about the diplomatic mistakes that were made, leading up to The North's decision to invade South Korea. In the light of history, however, it seems likely that the critical event was a public speech by the U.S. Secretary of State, Dean Acheson. Paraphrased, Acheson said that the U.S. was committed to defending a natural perimeter in the Pacific which led from the Aleutians, through Japan to the Philippines.[1] This error of omission excluded the Korean Peninsula and amounted to a default on a publicly stated promise. North Korea's Premier, Kim Il Sung, interpreted it as a green light to attack. Kim, taking Acheson's public statements at face value, thought that the U.S. would not become involved. When the attack came, President Truman went before the United Nations and asked for sanctions. Because The Soviet Union was boycotting the UN Security Council at the time, the Council authorized the U.S. to conduct military operations. If the Soviet Union had not boycotted, they could have vetoed the Council action. By such slender threads of chance often hang the outcomes of history.

Initially limited to extracting American civilians and families from South Korea, operations were soon expanded to stop the North. Significantly, it wasn't referred to as "a war." It was called a police action.

It has been forever thus. On the 26th of June, 1950, there was, for certain, "trouble in the wind, my boys . . .". The North Koreans launched their war of aggression against South Korea. Left to their own devices, the South Koreans would have been no match for the superior numbers and firepower of the North. But with America coming to their rescue, said the conventional wisdom, it would be "a walk in the park." Little did America's little band of South Korea's defenders know what the future held.

Ahead of the 8th FBW lay 37 months of very dangerous ground-attacks, with most of the flying taking place in a narrow box of air just above the heads of enemy soldiers, whose guns kicked up a storm of flying steel around them. The men of the 8th FBW were to spend most of the war flying at low level in miserable weather over mountainous terrain while being shot at. Many pilots did not come home because it was a killing zone at ground level where the guns were.

CHAPTER 4
Not The Best Way To Start A War

On this hot, miserably wet and muggy day, July 20, 1950, barely three weeks into the war, Son and his three flight members were in the middle of an assigned mission.

Flying four blue-nosed F80-C jet fighters of the 35th Black Panthers Squadron, they were preparing to strike their target. The 35th was one of three squadrons belonging to the 8th Fighter-Bomber Wing, commanded by Col. "Big Jack" Price. In an all-out attempt to overrun the entire peninsula, large numbers of North Korean troops, supported with Russian built tanks, were attempting to cross the Kum River Northwest of Taejon. The 24th was in mortal danger. The air was full of clipped chatter between the pilots of the jets and a ground forward air controller whose job was to coordinate air support for elements of the U. S. 24th Infantry Division. Major General William F. Dean commanded the 24th. General officers aren't usually found at the front lines, but because the 24th was in trouble he was there with his jeep and driver, attempting to steady his troops in the face of withering fire. In the confusion of the battle, he became separated from advance elements of his troops. He avoided enemy troops, living off the land, for approximately 35 days, trying to get back. He was finally captured. General Dean spent the rest of the war in a series of North Korean prison camps. His experiences are contained in his book, "General Dean's Story." It is a harrowing tale, for those interested in getting a worm's eye view of ground combat and prison life.

Elements of the 19th Infantry Brigade were deployed along the south bank of the Kum river. They were attempting to slow the advance of the North Koreans, who, in the early weeks of the war, had already taken nearly half of the South.

As an American two-star, General Dean was a prize catch for the North. If he could be induced to defect or to participate in communist propaganda, it would be a major coup for their side. He was to endure heavy physical deprivation and hardship as well as psychological torture, as they attempted to bend him to their will. His continued diabolical mistreatment, contrary to all the articles of the Geneva Convention, lasted for most of the war. But he resisted them. He survived month after month of solitary confinement, alternating with physical torture, including near starvation, until the end of the war. After the war and his release, General Dean was awarded The Congressional Medal of Honor, America's highest

decoration for bravery. He not only spoke the words, "duty, honor, country," he lived them - the highest values of military ethics, integrity and morality. Although he, himself, denied it, he is one of America's truest heroes.

The 24th was home based at Camp Brady, on the North Coast of Kyushu. Camp Brady was only seven or eight miles north of Itazuke Air Force Base, near Fukkuoka, Japan, home base for the 8th Fighter/Bomber Wing and its three fighter squadrons. Every time the jets of the 8th FBW took off to the north, they passed low over Camp Brady.

The 35th Squadron was commanded in the beginning by Major Vince Cardarella, a cheerful, cigar smoking Italian with a prizefighter's nose, in the mold of a Fiorello LaGuardia. In the War's second week, Vince tore off an external fuel tank while pulling up from a strafing run. The tank was observed to hit the tail of his aircraft. He was killed in the ensuing crash.

Major Rayburn D. Lancaster, a soft-spoken Texan, replaced him. Ray was friendly and easy to know in spite of his wry way of speaking. When Ray said something in that Texas drawl, his pilots knew it was from the heart, and that he meant what he said. Everybody respected and liked him. Next in command, was Captain Ray Schilleriff, Squadron Operations Officer. Ray was an experienced fighter pilot, one of the better ones in the squadron. He had a shy, ingratiating way about him and made friends easily.

(AUTHOR'S NOTE) As of this writing in February, 2004, my close friend and old boss, now in his 85th year, is dying of cancer. His doctors have told him it is terminal. Other than pain medication, he has decided to forego any treatment to prolong his life. Under hospice care at his home, the objective is to make him comfortable. Ray, my friend, you will be sorely missed, not only by your family but by all of us who served with you.

Ray passed away at 8:00AM, February 28, 2004. Shown below is e-mail correspondence between Ray's friend and Herman and Marilyn, as Ray's time dwindled down:

I just asked Herman if I could forward a letter he wrote to Barbara McMahan, Ray's ladyfriend, today after she wrote that "the end" was now very near and she wanted his friends to write something that could be read at his funeral. This is what he wrote....and cried....and tried to read to me when I came home....we cried. It's hard to lose good friends - especially one's you've known over 50 years....even when you know it for the best.

————————————

Forwarded Message:
Subj:
Re: Latest on R. D.
Date:
2/25/2004 2:38:22 PM Central Standard Time
From:
HSONSAN
To:
barmac@our-town.com

Barb, thanks so much for keeping us posted on Ray's condition. We are sad beyond telling to hear that his time is short. In view of the pain he is suffering, let's hope for a quick and merciful end.

If he can still hear and understand, please tell him that Herman and Marilyn love him.

I have e-mailed Don Hughes so I would expect that you will be hearing from him shortly.

Here are some thoughts that I have about Ray. If you or perhaps Mark could read them at his service we would be honored:

Ray. . .you were my boss, my comrade in arms, my close personal friend. What can I say that will tell the world what a champion you were? You were, first of all, a man who was most alive in the kingdom of the sky. You were a pilot's pilot who had the respect of every other pilot in the Black Panthers. But you had more than just flying skills. You had courage. You never flinched in combat against our enemy. You were loyal, always ready to cover our tails when necessary, just as we would cover yours. You had integrity. You said what you believed, and we knew that we could believe what you said. There was no spin, no deception. What we saw and heard from you was genuine, the real "McCoy." And, of course, you were lucky, just as all good fighter pilots are. Shortly before the Korean War you took off in a Mustang for some night flying. Climbing out to the east of Itazuke the Stang's engine suddenly quit cold. You didn't have much altitude, but you did the only thing you could do. You bailed out! Subito!! (Which means immediately! as they would say in Japanese.) No sooner had your chute opened than you landed in some trees, with your parachute thoroughly entangled in the trees branches. There you were, suspended above the ground. But it was so black you could not see whether you were sixteen feet above the ground or six inches! What to do? Hang there. .until the sun came up. Then you could see that you were only inches above the ground.Slipping out of your parachute harness, you walked a short distance to a farmer's house where you asked to be taken to a police station. Was your escape a matter of skill? Somewhat, perhaps. Training? You bet! Luck?? Yes, in spades!! As you often said, "Fighter pilots are the most interesting people!"

So here's to you, Colonel Lanc: As you top the windswept heights "Where never lark, or even eagle flew,/And while with silent, lifting mind, you trod/The high untrespassed sanctity of space,/Put out your hand, and touch the face of God."

May your next set of wings be those of a guardian angel?

Goodbye, old friend.

Herman Son (& Marilyn too)

Now, back to the story:

The four flight commanders in the squadron were First Lieutenant Herman Son, the commander of "A" flight. He was probably the best and most experienced pilot in the squadron, with the exception of the Group Commander, Colonel Bill Samways.

First Lieutenant Robert Wayne, a "gung-ho" West Pointer who played varsity football as a West Point cadet, was in charge of "B" flight. Bob, who still had a little growing up to do, was nevertheless an intrepid and aggressive pilot.

First Lieutenant Donald Sirman headed up "C" flight until he was shot down during the first week of the war. Don who was fly-

ing Son's personal airplane that day, bailed out, and was seen waving by his flight mates

after he hit the ground. He was quickly captured. Don also spent the rest of the war in POW camp, surviving until the very end. He was forced to make propaganda statements and sign his name to statements that were obviously not his. Two weeks before the war ended, according to reports from fellow prisoners, a trigger-happy prison camp guard shot Don, as he went outside the building where they were kept. Said his

friends, "All he did was go outside to take a p - -!"

"D" flight belonged to First Lieutenant Al Boyce. Al was a good pilot, as witness the fact that he scored a confirmed kill of a Mig-15 jet, while flying a prop driven F51 Mustang. He was a good commander in the air and a good teacher.

36th Squadron, known as "The Flying Fiends", was commanded Major James McNees,

a tough and capable pilot with lots of WWII experience. Jim was also one of the early casualties of Korea. He was shot down, and was not seen to have bailed out. As was the case with many pilots, Jim's remains were discovered at the crash site, well after the war. The author is not sure who replaced Jim.

Major William Sluder, also an early war casualty, commanded the 80th squadron, known as "The Headhunters". It is believed that Sluder ran into a trap, in the form of some cables that were strung across a narrow valley in the north.

This brief accounting of some of the key personnel of the Group would be incomplete without mention of the 8th Group's Commander, Lt. Col. Bill Samways. Son said of Col. Samways, " He is absolutely the finest pilot I have ever known. He is a rare 'natural' pilot, born to fly. What average pilots work hard to achieve, Bill Samways does effortlessly." "User friendly" would describe Col. Bill in today's techie talk. Everybody liked him.

Col. Samways had only recently been assigned to the 8th from stateside. Initially, he took over the 35th squadron, but that was only temporary, awaiting the return to the States of his predecessor. Col. Charles C. Chitty was sometimes referred to behind his back as "C cubed." Colonel Chitty was a bit of a martinet. Short of stature and always with a close-cropped "GI" haircut, Chitty was, in most ways, the opposite of Col. Bill. "C cubed" was cold, aloof, and for most of the pilots, hard to know. One could call him "professional," but one got the feeling that he flew only because it was expected of him, that it was in his job description. Everyone respected him, but that was about the end of it.

Col. Bill, on the other hand, was a pilot's pilot. He flew because he loved to fly. Those who flew with him soon discovered that he was a true virtuoso, without doubt, the best pilot in the entire Group. They not only respected him, they admired him, liked him and followed him willingly. They sensed that he cared about them. So when Col. Chitty left for the states and Col. Samways became the Group Commander all the pilots approved.

Another Message From Frank:

As may be gleaned from the previous two paragraphs, dear reader, there are two kinds of respect that are operational in military society. One is based primarily on fear and a disparity in power or authority. It is given because the giver doesn't have much choice. It's more common than one might think. The other kind of respect is based upon true admiration. It takes into account the entire personality of the receiver, his skill, his integrity and his ethics. It does not rely entirely upon authority, though authority is always present in military (and for that matter, civil) organizations. This kind of respect is freely given, and may and does apply in upward (subordinate to superior), downward (superior to subordinate) and lateral (peer to peer) directions. The latter kind of respect is probably the less common of the two, although eminently the more valuable. All kinds of organizations have operated for centuries, using both kinds. However, the true leader works to achieve and foster respect that is based on capacity and character, not authority alone. The strongest organizations are based on this second kind of respect. The events and the personalities of the Korean War can best be understood, if one has an understanding of how this organizational glue works.

CHAPTER 5
Fearsome Weather

Luckily, for the 24th, the weather in the target area was, if not completely clear, at least flyable that July morning. Such was not the case in Japan. Soggy clouds lay over the islands like a wet mop. For Contour Red, the weather from home base to only 30 or 40 miles south of the target area was worse than terrible. That morning, Col. Jack Price called Headquarters, Fifth Air Force and reluctantly had asked for a "stand down" because of the bad weather.

"General, we'll lose some of our pilots and aircraft if we send them out in this."

General Partridge, denied the request, telling Col. Price that, "Those boys in the 24th are dying, Jack. It is imperative that our fighters get through to help."

Son and his flight prepared for the mission, awaiting a launch order from Wing. Lt. Jim Tidwell peered apprehensively out the window at the rain coming down.

"Aw, Herm, they aren't gonna send us out in this, are they?"

" Don't know, Jim. We'll just have to wait and see. We gotta brief for it anyway."

Son told his pilots that major portions of the flight would be in weather. He stressed the importance of keeping tight formation during all weather penetrations. Then they dressed for the flight. Over flight suits they zipped themselves into Anti-G suits, looking like cowboy chaps. Then they donned and adjusted shoulder holsters for the Model 1911 Colt .45 caliber automatic pistols. The 45's were most uncomfortable. They were like wearing a claw hammer, when covered over with the rest of the gear, such as canary yellow Mae West life preservers. The pistols were worn only to be used if a pilot was shot down and was forced to evade capture on the ground. It was earnestly hoped that there would be no need to use the pistols. A backpack parachute topped off the ensemble.

Now sitting in the ready room, sipping coffee from individualized squadron coffee mugs, emblazoned with Black Panther icons, they only had to wait a few minutes. The phone rang. Russ Rogers jumped, startled by the ring. It was unlike Russ to be jumpy. Capt. Ray Schilleriff, Squadron Operations Officer, took the call.

"O.K., Red flight, get going! Contact Carrot Control on "C" channel in the vicinity of The Kum river. Good luck!"

Half full mugs were left on the counter. Contour Red Flight was out the door of the Quonset hut, running to the van that would take them to their aircraft. This was the most anxious time of all. There was nothing to do but wait or try to deal with the nervousness with banter and jokes.

As soon as they sat down in the van, which would carry them to their aircraft, Jim broke out in song, not too enthusiastically:

"Cigareeets an whuskey, an wild wild wimmin. . .
They'll drive you crazy, they'll drive you insane!"

Bravely, he was trying to keep everybody in a positive frame of mind. But he couldn't remember the rest of the words, and trailed off, tapping his foot and humming an approximation of the melody.

"You need to practice that a little more," said Al, dryly, as the van trundled out across the asphalt ramp.

First out of the van was Son, as the vehicle pulled up in front of his aircraft. He walked to his aircraft and started his visual inspection. The other three pilots were dropped off in turn.

The butterflies in the stomach began to subside. Now they were busy, doing their walk around inspections. When they sat down in the cockpit, they hooked their parachutes to inflatable rubber dinghies. Each dinghy carried an Escape and Evasion Kit, consisting of emergency rations, a signal mirror, fishing line, an American flag and gold coins. Again, it was hoped that there would be no occasion to use these materials. Even more ardently, it was hoped that, if one was downed in enemy territory, that they would be able to escape the tender mercies of a North Korean POW camp. Now the shoulder harness and seat belt connections were secured. G-suit hoses were plugged in. Helmets were slipped on, adjusted and connected to the radio cords. A kneepad holding the maps they would use was strapped to the right leg. Thin kidskin gloves were slipped on. An oxygen mask went over each pilot's face and was hooked to the helmet. The masks, tightly pressed against their faces, made them look like aliens from outer space. Each pilot began his pre-start cockpit check. Radios were snapped on and crackled to life.

"Contour Red . . .check in!"

"Two, OK!"

"Three!"

"Four, OK!"

"Let's start 'em up!"

Each jet emitted a low-pitched rumble as fuel ignited in the combustion chambers. Slowly, the engines gained rpm. When they had stabilized at idle, auxiliary power units were disconnected. As they came up on ground control frequency, Contour Red Leader asked for Taxi instructions.

"Itazuke Tower, this is Contour Red Leader with four chicks for taxi."

"Roger, Contour Red Leader, This is Itazuke Tower, you are cleared to taxi, Runway 35 Current ceiling 400 feet, visibility one eighth to one quarter mile.. Altimeter, two-niner point seven eight. Winds, West, Northwest at five miles per hour. Advise when you're ready to take the active. Over."

"Roger, tower. Will advise."

Frank said to himself, "*Even for guardian angels this is not good weather for a stroll across the Sea of Japan, to a target area on the peninsula, and then, worst of all, a trip back to Japan and a runway that almost certainly will be hiding in the fog. A major miracle will be needed here.*"

CHAPTER 6
"Thumbs Out!"

Each pilot gave a "thumbs out" signal to the ground crewman. It meant he was to pull the wheel chocks. Throttles advanced, and the ramp was awash in hot jet blast. The noise reached decibel levels guaranteed to damage hearing, but they didn't know very much about that sort of thing then. Slowly, they maneuvered out of their parking spaces. The ground crewmen and their pilots exchanged salutes. They turned their backs and leaned against the hot kerosene smelling wind as it whipped against their fatigues. One crewman lost his cap. Contour Red was on its way.

As they turned down the long taxiway leading to the end of the takeoff runway, the wheels and the jet wash of the aircraft kicked clouds of spray from the puddles that had accumulated in the rain. Short of the runway, they pulled into an arm-disarm area, to have their guns charged. Armament crewmen ran from their trucks, field jacket collars turned up against the rain. They opened the gun bays, and charged all six guns in each aircraft. The guns were now "hot", meaning that there was a live round in the chamber of each gun, and that they were ready to fire in full automatic mode, when the pilot turned on the arm switch in the cockpit and squeezed the trigger on his control stick.

Nose wheel struts bobbed up and down, as the pilots pumped their brakes.

"Itazuke Tower, Contour Red here. Permission to take the active, OVER."

"Itazuke Tower here. Contour Red you are cleared for takeoff."

"Roger tower."

The flight took the runway in fingertip formation, Tidwell on Son's left wing, Wimer on the right, followed by Rogers on Wimer's right wing. Lining up, Son braked to a stop as his brakes screeched in protest. He checked to see that everybody was in position. Checked also, flaps were set for takeoff. Shimmering heat waves issued from the tailpipes of the four jets. Contour Red Leader held one finger above his helmet, and twirled it. That was the signal to begin the runup to full power. Nose wheel struts compressed to the maximum. Now, holding both hands aloft on either side of his helmet, he pointed crisply forward, and released the brakes. In unison, four blue noses came up like the heads of four sprinters coming out of the starting blocks at the bark of the starter's gun. The jets began their takeoff roll, slowly at first, as they were heavily loaded with rockets, ammunition and fuel. Gradually, they picked up speed. They passed the 2,000 feet acceleration check point . . .Son's airspeed read 85 KIAS, barely enough. If it had been less than 85, he would have aborted the takeoff, with still enough asphalt in front of him to stop.

"Stick with these guys, Frank. They're going to need all the help you can give."

"O.K. Red flight, sock it in tight! I'm going to be on the gages from the git-go...just hang tight and we'll be on top in a few minutes!"

Gathering momentum, the F80's struggled to reach takeoff speed. The runway was 8,500 feet long, with markers along the sides that told pilots how much runway remained. The 8,000 foot marker flashed by. Airspeed was hovering at 128 knots. As the end of the runway approached, they had accelerated to 130 IAS, barely enough for liftoff. Straining to get airborne, they broke ground with no more than 300-400 feet of runway to spare. Immediately, they were in the clouds, skimming over now unseen rice paddies below, landing gears retracting, and airspeed slowly building. Son concentrated on his instruments, making sure that he maintained a positive rate of climb, while continuing to accelerate to climbing airspeed of 300 KIAS (knots indicated airspeed). The butterflies were completely gone now. Son talked to himself (or so he thought). Half a dot nose up! Steady! Cross check! Airspeed 200! Wings level! Rate of climb, 700 fpm! O.K Then, depressing the mike button on his throttle grip:

"Contour Red, flaps up . . .now!!" Son began a slow left turn to heading 340 degrees, pointing directly toward Pusan on the southern tip of Korea, 127 nautical miles away, across a rain swept Sea of Japan. They were suspended — inside a great, white ball, with no horizon. No up . No down.

Only Son's instruments told him his attitude and other vital flight information. Absolute focus and concentration on the task at hand was imperative.

"Contour Red Leader, this is Itazuke Tower, you are cleared to switch to tactical frequency. Good day, and good luck!"

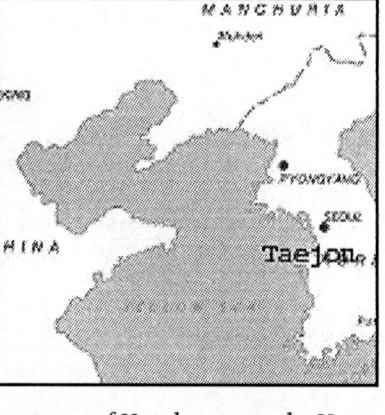

"Roger Tower, thanks! Break, break. . . Red leader to flight. . .come up "C" Charlie and check in!"

"Two!"

"Three!"

"Four!"

"Red Leader, Rog!"

At 300 KIAS, and at a climb rate of 3,000 feet per minute, they would soon top the clouds, reported to be at 25 thousand feet

Cheju-do was the site of the 618th AC&W (Aircraft Control & Warning) radar site. Call sign, Camel Control. They provided major navigational assistance, particularly during bad weather conditions. The distance from Itazuke AB on the northern coast of Kyushu across the Korean Strait to Pusan is approximately 127 miles. Another 100 to 200 miles is often required to reach targets to the north. The Kum River is located on Korea's West coast, approximately 100 miles northwest of Pusan.

Formation flying in the weather is tough work. The leader controls his airplane by reference to his own instruments. Wingmen, however, do not use their own instruments. They simply fly tight formation on the leader close enough, and sometimes that means very close, to keep him in sight. It is similar to the kind of flying that the Air Force Thunderbirds or the Navy's Blue Angels do when putting on their aerial demonstrations. That would be easy, except for the fact that human physiology, and perhaps psychology as well, interferes. While the leader may be maintaining a perfectly straight and level course, a wingman may get the overpowering feeling that his leader is turning into him, or away from him, that he may in fact seem to be rolling into an upside down position! There is no visual reference, only a shroud of impenetrable white. Under these conditions, the human balance mechanism in the inner ear is not at all reliable. It can tell a person that he is upside down when he is right side up. The signals that are sent by the inner ear are extremely compelling but they

must be ignored at all costs. To yield to these feelings is to risk disaster. All pilots have experienced this. It is called vertigo, or "the leans." A few minutes spent fighting it, can leave a pilot feeling like a wet dish rag!

"Oh, man! Look at that sunshine!"

"Roger, two. . .let's cut the chatter!"

Contour Red had popped out on top of the clouds, now spread out below them at 24 thousand feet. The sun was high in the sky now, coming from the right. It reflected upon the clouds and shone against the aluminum skins of the four fighters as they streaked north-ward against a backdrop of an intense cobalt blue sky. The clouds, now well below them, had turned into a brilliant, undulate white carpet. Now the flight could spread out and relax a bit. . .for a few minutes. They continued to climb to 30 thousand feet, before leveling off. At this altitude the outside air temperature was 40° below zero.

Red Leader contacted an important radar site, located on the island of Cheju-do, ap-proximately 75 miles north, and only slightly left of Contour Red's course to Pusan. This was the home of the 618th AC&W (Aircraft Control and Warning) squadron, which pro-vided radar coverage of the area. Col. Paul Jacobs, who, at 45, was the "old man" of the wing, commanded the 618th. Now retired and in his nineties, he and his wife, Frances, own and operate a small ranch in Southern Utah. But that day, and during the entire war, he provided a crucial life saving function to our pilots.

"Hello Camel, this is Contour Red Leader, with a flight of four, over!"

"Contour Red Leader, Camel here!"

"Camel. . .off the ground at Itazuke at five past the hour. Climbing on course for Pusan VOR."

"Roger, Contour Red, squawk 34."

"Roger, Camel. .squawking 34."

"Contour Red, I have you in radar contact. Do you need any assistance?"

"Not at this time, Camel. We'll be coming home in a bit, though. At that time we'd like a handoff to GCA, straight in at Itazook!"

(GCA, Ground Controlled Approach, is a precision ground based radar system that is used to direct aircraft to a landing runway under conditions of very low visibility.)

"Roger, Contour. . .give us a call at Pusan on your return!"

"Thanks, Camel. .Contour Red, out!"

Over the Pusan VOR (navigational fix), Son turned left 15 degrees to a heading of 325, throttled back and began a slow descent into the target area , south east of Taejon, approxi-mately 80 miles southwest of Seoul.

"O.K., Red flight, close it up. We're gonna let down to 9 thousand and hope we break in the clear. *footnote: The highest mountains in the area were 7,000 feet, thus letting down to 9,000 feet would provide 2,000 feet of clearance.

Approximately 50 miles south of Taejon, it was time to start letting down.

"O.K. here we go, down the chute. Hang tight!"

Fuel was always a problem. There was never enough. Jet engines are prodigious fuel hogs at low altitude. They consume fuel five to seven times as fast at low altitudes as they do when cruising at 30 or 35 thousand feet. Since the jets were based in Japan, they had to travel 250 - 350 miles to their targets, then let down to low altitude where fuel gushed through their engines. Finally, they had to stay in the area long enough to find, and suc-cessfully attack the target. Then came the climb back to high altitude for the return home.

Son had budgeted approximately 525 gallons of fuel to cover the flight from the time they took the runway at Itazuke, until the time they completed their attacks and started home. Starting with approximately 804 gallons of fuel on board each plane, there should be approximately 350 gallons left for the return trip and landing. Precious little. Even though

the aircraft were much lighter now, and much of the return would be at high altitude, it would be extremely tight - even if the weather were clear back at Itazuke.

Clear the weather was not. It was forecast to hold at 300 - 500 feet indefinite 1/4 to 1/2 mile for the rest of the day. Son didn't have time to worry about that now, other than to set "Texaco", which was to be called out by the first pilot to reach 350 minimum fuel on his fuel counter.

Now, he and his flight had work to do. At about 10,000 feet, they began to break out of the clouds. By 9,000 feet they were in the clear. A patchwork of verdant green hills and rice paddies were separated by roads, which were raised above the paddies. A few small, thatch roofed villages completed this panorama that scrolled past under Contour Red Flight's wings as they approached the river.

The river, which ran roughly East to West, was wide, shallow and meandering. They intercepted the river close to its mouth on Korea's West Coast, and turned right to follow it inland. It was very shallow, with numerous sandbars, easy to spot from the air. It was easy to wade across on foot in several places.

"Carrot Control. . .Contour Roger here . . . 20 miles south. . .inbound with four . . .50's and rockets."

"Roger, Contour . . .go to coordinates X-ray one-three, foxtrot one-two . .We're on the south bank of the river."

"Roger that . . .I see the river. Whatta you got for us, Carrot?"

"Roger, Contour. Think I have you in sight to the South West. We have enemy troops crossing the river. They're wading across and then using a large sand bar in the middle of the river. They're attempting to turn our right flank. We are trying to hold a defense perimeter along the south bank. Turn east at the river. As soon as I get a visual, I'll direct you."

"Roger that, Carrot! Contour, stack left," Son ordered. Al Wimer, flying Son's right wing, dropped down and slid easily over to the left side, slightly behind and to the left of Tidwell. Rogers slid under Wimer and to his left. Throttles back to idle, in loose, left echelon formation and letting down rapidly, the jets whistled in at 375 knots. Son picked up the target visually, ahead and slightly to his left. As Carrot had said, they appeared to be troops in the open. Their numbers were hard to estimate, certainly many hundreds, perhaps a thousand or more. They were wading and/or walking across, taking advantage of the wide, smooth sandbars in the middle of the stream. As he flashed across them, not more than 200 feet over their heads, Son waggled his wings and called,

"Carrot, . .this it?"

"Roger, Contour, go get 'em!"

But Son had seen something that disturbed him on his identification pass. Mixed in with the green camouflage uniforms of the North Korean soldiers, were numerous civilians dressed in traditional white.

"Carrot, Contour Red . . .there are civilians with those troops. They're dressed in white! Are you sure you want me to hit them?!"

"Contour Red, this is Carrot . . roger that!! Those Mama sans in the white coats have burp guns and grenades under their skirts. We don't know whether they're Mama sans or North Koreans in disguise. But we do know that they are firing at and killing our troops. They are hostile! So, I say again, go get em!"

Son thought about what was at stake. . .American soldiers, fighting for their lives.

"Oh, shit!" he thought. "Gotta, gotta!"

"O.K. Carrot. Red Leader, here. I'll report off target!"

Son pulled up on an easterly heading, roughly paralleling the river. Starting a wide, 270° turn to the right, Son commanded:

"O.K. Red flight, take your spacing. Check your switches. Fifties first! We'll go in from South to North. Keep each other in sight. If we have time, we'll make a second pass and get rid of our rockets. Pick your targets. Make it count!"

Son pulled his turn tight. Each successive member of the flight allowed his turn to loosen, in order to take spacing. For a brief instant, Son thought about his childhood, his first experience with his Uncle Carl, hunting rabbits on his Grandfather's farm.

No time for that.

Completing his turn, Son rolled into a shallow attack dive of approximately 25 degrees. He picked out a large concentration of troops in the middle of a large sandbar. He flipped on his gun switches. With slow deliberation he brought the cross in his optical gun sight down on the middle of the troops. As he approached firing range, he smoothly squeezed the trigger on his control stick and held it for approximately three seconds. Six 50 cal machine guns in the nose of his aircraft hammered and shook as his aircraft slowed perceptibly from the recoil. White hot tracer bullets lashed out toward the target like angry laser beams. The sulfurous smell of cordite gunpowder permeated the cockpit. Son lightly touched his rudder pedals, first, left, then right, moving the sight across the target. The ground lit up with the flashes of Armor Piercing Incendiary shells. Sand, water and human body parts erupted in one churning muddy bloody mass. The flight swung around for another pass, this time firing their rockets. As Red two was making his pass, four called out,

"Contour Red Four, 'Texaco."

"Red Leader, here. . .roger that, Four. Leader to flight, complete your rocket pass. I'll be pulling up and to the left. Let's go home!"

"Carrot, this is Contour Red, we gotta go. We're off target. Hope that helped!"

"Contour, this is Carrot. Good job! You have saved our lives. . .for the moment! Thanks!"

"Anytime, Carrot!"

"Red Leader to Flight. Let's form up. Turning left to climb out heading of One-Six-Zero. Cut me off. Close it up quickly. We've got weather ahead!"

Thou shall not kill. . .Son thought briefly.

Quickly, they were back into the clouds.

Frank The Guardian Angel Watched:

For certain, I was in the air that morning, in the skies over South Korea and Japan. How else can one account for the things that Son and his flight mates were able to do. How else can one account for the divine winds that blew at high altitude from the Northwest. Without them, Contour Red Flight would not have had enough fuel to carry it home. Without me, his angel, Son's flight mates would have broken contact with him in the weather and crashed into the Sea. Without such power, how could Son have flown a precision radar approach to the runway under such weather conditions? It was as if Son were a blind man with a white cane and a seeing eye dog, crossing the street and feeling gingerly for the curb. Call it God, call it a Divine Power, call it a Guardian Angel, call it what you will. Something was protecting Contour Red and its pilots that morning. Something was helping them to achieve the impossible.

"Turning left now to heading one - six zero, climbing. Now at heading 210° , continuing turn. 300 KIAS, rate of climb 2500 fpm. Rolling out of turn now. Steady on heading 160°. Everybody tucked in tight now. With fuel down to 300 gallons, and ammo gone, less power needed to climb. Throttle back smoothly to 97% power." Son always talked to himself in situations like these.

Was it his voice, or was it the voice of his Guardian Angel?

The flight broke out on top this time at 22,000 feet, but continued to climb to 35,000, where fuel consumption would be lower and the winds even more favorable. When they reached Pusan, they had leveled off and had throttled back to 89%. It was time to ask Camel for that favor.

"Hello, Camel. . .this is Contour Red, over Pusan with four. Do you have us?"

"Contour Red, this is Camel. Squawk 77 for identification. Over."

"Roger, Camel. . .parrot squawking 77. Over." (NOTE) This caused his aircraft to emit a distinctive radar code that Camel could use to identify him and his flight.

Camel Control responded, in a clipped, matter-of-fact emotionless tone.

"Roger Contour Red, I have you in radar contact. I understand that you wish a steer to Itazuke, with a handoff to GCA for a straight-in precision approach to runway one-seven. Correct?"

"Roger that, Camel."

"We didn't have fancy radars like this when I was flying in WWI," says Frank. *"For the uninitiated, the term, 'GCA,' stands for 'Ground Controlled Approach.' This is a precision technique for landing aircraft in bad weather. By use of precision radar equipment located close to the landing runway, the operator of the radar is able to determine the precise position of an approaching aircraft, in both azimuth and elevation. This allows the operator (controller) to issue instructions to the approaching aircraft. The aircraft is directed in both azimuth and elevation, thereby holding to a runway centerline and a glide slope that is projected into space. It is imperative that the pilot of the approaching aircraft:(1) trusts the controller without reservation, and (2) that he follows his instructions precisely. If the pilot is skillful, and these conditions are met, landings can be accomplished under near zero/zero conditions. If more than one aircraft is involved, not only must the flight leader be skilled, the three wingmen must stick to their leader like glue and trust him utterly. If Contour Red Flight was to complete its mission successfully, this would have to happen."*

"Contour Red, this is Camel. Current Itazuke weather is ceiling indefinite, obscured. Visibility is one-eight of a mile in light rain and fog. Winds are calm. Altimeter is two-niner point seven-two."

"Contour Red, roger, the weather."

"Contour Red, this Camel. Turn left, heading one-five-zero. Range from touchdown is one-one-five nautical miles. You may start your descent at will. This will be a hand off to GCA at a range of seventeen nautical miles. At that time you should be at an altitude of five thousand feet, coming up to the glide path from below, slowing to two hundred knots. Over."

OCA Unit
(Precision Radar)

"Camel, this is Contour Red. Roger. Turning left to new heading one-five-zero." Leader to flight, fuel check."

"Two, 90 gallons."

"Three, 90 plus."

"Four, 85 gallons."

"O.K. guys, we're goin' home now. Stay cool!"

Son throttled back to idle and began a long glide toward home, minimizing fuel expenditure. Just before entering the overcast, he set throttle at 75% to make it easier for his wingmen to keep position in formation.

Son thought, "This is going to be tighter than Aunt Mildred's corset!"

"Contour Red, Camel here, your range to touchdown is one-hundred nautical miles. Continue heading one-five-zero."

"Roger, Camel, understand. Contour Red steady on heading one-five-zero."

Now descending at 4,000 feet per minute without dive brakes, Contour Flight was accelerating like a car cresting the top of a roller coaster ride and heading steeply down , down, . . 300 . .350 . . 400 . .450 KIAS (Knots Indicated Airspeed). The altimeters were

unwinding rapidly. . .twenty thousand. . . .Fifteen-thousand. . Ten thousand. As his flight approached 10,000 feet he began to level off. Holding level at eight thousand feet, he let the airspeed bleed off to 250 KIAS. The cockpit air conditioning system, working overtime in the high humidity, suddenly "coughed," spitting out a couple of ping-pong ball sized balls of frost, startling Son with a blast of cold air from the vents at either side of his feet.

"Camel, this is Contour Red, we're level at eight thousand feet, slowing to two-fifty knots."

"Contour Red, roger. I have you at five-zero miles from touchdown. Turn right now, new heading one-seven-zero."

"Camel, Contour Red, Roger. Right to one-seven-zero."

In his mind's eye, Son could visualize the runway. It was a tiny obelisk, (shaped like the Washington Monument lying on its side and studded with high intensity runway lights that twinkled like diamonds.) The sides of the obelisk were almost parallel, the base only slightly wider than the top. It was dead ahead, on the horizon, but shrouded in the rain and fog.

The image of the runway existed clearly in Son's mind. Its shape and location, relative to Contour Red, would change with inputs Son received from his own instruments and the data given to him by his ground controllers.

Were they Guardian Angels, too?

"Dear God . . .give me strength . . .give me the strength and skill to bring this flight home safely. Help me to keep fear and panic at bay. Help me to do what I have to do...."

Contour Red's airspeed continued to slow . . .225. . .210. . .200. Son continued to descend to 5,000 feet. He sneaked a look at his fuel gauge.

. ."25 gallons! Enough for one approach, that's it. No room for error. Breathe . . .stay relaxed. Keep your cross check goin'. Don't over control."

"Contour Red, this is Camel, your range from touchdown is two-zero nautical miles. You should be at five thousand feet, slowing to final approach speed. Switch to GCA final approach frequency, channel "E" easy at this time. You're lookin' good, Contour. Good luck!"

"Camel, this is Contour Red. Roger. Thanks a lot, friend! Out.!

"Flight leader to flight, go "E" easy channel and check in!"

"Two!"

"Three!"

"Four!"

"Roger, lead, here. . ."

"Itazuke GCA, Contour Red Leader here. . ."

"Contour Red Leader, Itazuke GCA here. I have you in radar contact, fifteen miles from touchdown. This will be a precision radar approach to runway 17. Continue your present heading of one-seven-zero. I have you at five thousand feet, on the runway centerline, approaching the glide path from below. Extend your landing gear now, and assume landing configuration. Over."

"Roger GCA. . . Red to flight, gear down. . .NOW!"

With that command, four sets of landing gears came out and down, clunking with a gentle jolt into position. In the cockpits, landing gear warning lights winked from red to amber to "3 green", meaning down and locked.

"Two, I'm down and locked!"

"Three, gear down and locked.!"

"Four, got 'three greens'!"

"Roger Red flight. Power to 85%!"

Airspeed continued to slow down now. . .200. . .190. . .170. As the airspeed hit 170KIAS, Son called for full flaps.

"Contour Red, full flaps. . .NOW!"

The airspeed bled off rapidly . . .150 . . .140. . .130.

"Contour Red flight, this is Itazuke GCA. I have you now at nine miles from touchdown. Your landing gear should be down and locked, flaps set... at or near final approach speed. You are on the runway centerline, approaching the glide path from below... seventy feet. . .fifty feet. . .twenty feet. . . begin your initial rate of descent at 700 feet per minute. Over."

"Roger, GCA! Leader to flight, dive brakes down. . .NOW!"

With the extension of dive brakes, Son dropped his aircraft nose down by 1/2 dot on his attitude indicator. He "tweaked" his elevator trim button on top of his stick to account for the change, eliminating any pressure on the stick.

"Hold it gently," Son thought.

The airspeed stabilized at 120 knots. Rate of descent went from zero to 500 fpm down, to 700 fpm down.

So far, so good. . .stay loose. . .speed up your cross check. . .don't over control!"

"Contour Red, this is Itazuke GCA, I have you beginning your descent. You are on the glide path. . .on runway centerline, heading one-seven-zero, seven miles from touchdown."

Son could see his virtual runway clearly now in his mind's eye. The obelisk was much larger. It had moved from a position on the horizon to just over the nose of his aircraft. The base, relative to the top of the obelisk, was wider and widening . .widening. .

"Contour, Itazuke GCA, you are five miles from touchdown. You need not acknowledge further radio transmissions. On glide path. . .drifting slightly right of centerline. . .turn left two degrees, heading one-six-eight." Son eased his left wing down only slightly, about one-half an index mark on his attitude indicator. He held it for a count of three. "Heading indicator turning left. . .one-six-nine. . . . start to level wings. . .cross check. . .wings level. . .heading indicator steady at one-six-eight."

"One-six-eight . . .bringing you back to centerline. . .turn right heading one-six-nine. You are on glide path, on centerline. Assume original heading of one-seven-zero. Four miles from touchdown. . .going slightly high on the glide path. .Increase your rate of descent. . continuing to go high on glide path .10 . . .20. . .40 feet high. . ."

Son applied a small amount of down elevator trim and pushed the stick forward slightly to move the attitude indicator down about one-half dot. Airspeed increased to 122 KIAS.

"See you increasing your rate of descent now. . .coming back to the glide path. . .30 feet high. . .twenty feet. . .ten feet. . .resume your original rate of descent. Three and one-half miles from touchdown. . .on glide path, on centerline. . ."

Contour Red's pilots were hanging on now, literally, for their lives. What they did in the next ninety seconds would spell the difference between success and disaster. Was the Guardian Angel standing by?? Certainly, the crash crew was.

"On glide path. . . .on centerline. . . .On glide path. . . .on centerline. . .range two and one-half miles from touchdown. Drifting slightly left of centerline. . .right one degree. . .heading one-seven-one. . .back on centerline. . .resume heading one-seven-zero . . .on glide path. . .on centerline. . .range one mile from touchdown. ..on glide path. . .on centerline. ."

"Cross check. .cross check. . cross check!"

The virtual runway loomed dead ahead. . .the base of the obelisk was broad as a barn now and starting to pass under Red Leader's nose. Son knew it was there, burned into his consciousness, just as a blind man with his cane, tap taping, knows that the curb is there. With the help of his "Seeing Eye Dog," would Son the blind man find what he sought? Would his wingmen still be with him? He dared not look away from his instrument panel to check!

"Contour Red Leader, GCA. You are approaching GCA minimums of ceiling 300 feet, visibility 1/4 mile.. If you do not have the runway in sight, you may continue the approach at your own discretion. You are one-half mile from touchdown, on glide path, on center line. . .over the airport boundary... "

"There!!", Son caught a glimpse of the ground. . .

"Stay on your instruments. . .cross check, cross check, cross check.. bring the outside into your cross check."

These self-commands were non-verbal, occurring within nanoseconds within Son's brain.

"Approaching runway threshold. . .you should have the runway in sight. . ," said GCA.

Through his peripheral vision, and partially obscured by ragged wisps of fog, Son caught glimpses of the ground. It was so close he could almost reach out and touch it!

"Yes!! . . .the threshold lights flash past. . .Runway!!!. .. .. .center stripe . . .two more seconds. . .ease left, just a hair!! O.K!! back on the throttle!!. . .hold it off. . .steady. . . steady. . .hold it. .we're on the ground!!!"

Son felt his main landing gear make contact with the rain slick runway, skipping noise-lessly along at first. Then came the reassuring undulations of the asphalt as his aircraft, as though it were a giant migratory bird, settled down with its full weight on all three wheels, slowly decelerating and folding its wings. He quickly looked left ... then right. Everybody was there!

"Thank you, dear God!" He took a deep breath and exhaled.

"Stay relaxed Son?. . .sure. . .in a pig's eye!"

The Guardian Angel smiled...

Four Plexiglas canopies slid open. Oxygen masks were unhooked and pushed aside, revealing the pressure marks around each pilot's face where the masks had been sealed. Each man was smiling broadly. It was raining, but they didn't care. They looked up and felt the rain upon their faces. It felt good.

"Itazuke GCA, Contour Red. . .you are a genius! Thank you, thank you!!!"

"You're not bad your self, Red leader! Glad you're back!"

"So are we!"

"You are clear to ground control."

"Roger, GCA. Leader to flight, go "B" bravo and check in."

"Two. . I think I just shit my pants!"

"Three. . . Heavy duty!"

"Four, Wow!!"

"Thanks, guys. Great job!"

"Yes, great job," said Frank, "if I do say so myself!"

Turning off at the end of the runway, the flight pulled into the disarm area to have their guns cleared. Each pilot put their arms outside the cockpit, signifying that there were no fingers on or around gun or armament switches. Armorers approached. They opened the gun bays and cleared the guns and insuring that the aircraft wouldn't be taxiing into the ramp area with hot guns.

While waiting, Contour Red Four flamed out. His engine quit, out of fuel!

"Four here. Guess what? I just flamed out!"

"Well, whattaya complaining about? You got home, didn't you?! O.K., we'll send a tug for you!"

"Tower, this is Contour Red, in the disarm area. Taxiing to ramp area. Red Four just flamed out. Could you send a tug to bring him in?"

"Contour Red, this is Itazuke Tower, Roger, tug is on its way!"

"Thanks Tower. Contour Red, let's go home and get out of these wet suits, O.K.?"

"click."

"click."

The flight suits of all four pilots were soaking wet. It was though they had been in a sauna, but it really came from the tension and the hard work that they had just completed. Contour Red pulled into the parking area, and followed the ground crew men's directions,

guiding them into their individual spaces. At the "cut" signal from the crewman, throttles were pulled back, "around the horn" and the screech of the engines, like chalk on a blackboard, subsided into a descending moan, grinding and finally clicking to a stop. It was quiet except for the pattering rain, coming down steadily. There followed the unhooking, unsnapping, unstrapping, unplugging and turning "off", in reverse of the steps that had been performed 2 1/2 hours earlier at the beginning of the mission. This time all the tension was drained, all the anxiety gone. Only bone deep fatigue and relief remained. Flight forms were filled out as crew chiefs hooked ladders to the side of each aircraft. Each pilot got out of his aircraft and was greeted by his chief.

Sergeant Billy Buster wore a worried smile. Ahhh, Lieutenant! How'd you ever find the runway?!"

"Dunno. Guardian angel, I guess. It was hairy."

"Well, glad you're home, sir!"

"Yeah. . ." Son's voice trailed off. He was too tired to talk.

They waited to be picked up by the van.

Back in the squadron Quonset, flight gear was discarded with the personal equipment technician. Ray Schilleriff was there to greet them with a bottle of standard issue straight rye whiskey. One shot to each pilot went "down the hatch." Even Jim Tidwell, "our backslidin' Mormon", and Son, who had a Baptist upbringing, didn't refuse.

"How'd it go, Herm?" said Ray.

"Pretty good, I guess. We got some troops crossing the river, out in the open. By the way, why don't you go out to my bird and drain the fuel out of the fuselage tank and see if you can fill your Zippo with it!"

"Pretty tight?"

"We had to send a tug for Russ. He'll be here in a few minutes. He flamed out at the end of the runway, said Al."

"Yeah, ha, ha!" laughed Jim, nervously, "but I knew ol' Herm would get us home alright!"

"You're kiddin!" said Ray.

"Nope."

"Well, here. . .have another shot!"

"Nah, that's O.K.."

Then, they were off to debrief the mission, with Lt. Fletch Meadors, Squadron Intelligence Officer. Fletch got all the particulars from each pilot while the details were still fresh on their minds, and got it off in a mission report to Wing. Little did they know that fifty years later information from their mission reports would be in the national news and on the Internet. By the time they had finished debriefing, they could feel the warmth of the Rye in their stomachs as it loosened the knots that were there. Minutes later, Son was ready to leave for Kasuga, the family housing area located six miles south of the airstrip where his wife, Arretta, and their 3 $\frac{1}{2}$ year old daughter, Mary-Lynn were waiting.

"See y'all around noon, tomorrow . . .unless friend Schilleriff, here, has something for us sooner," Son said.

"See ya!"

"See ya tomorrow, Herm."

"Call us if you need us, Ray."

"O.K."

With that, they were out the door, headed to their cars.Son fished his car keys out of the zippered breast pocket of his flight suit, unlocked the door to his nearly new 1948 Olds 66 two-door coupe and slid in behind the wheel. He produced a pack of Pell Mells and a zippo lighter from his left shoulder pocket, tapped a cigarette from the pack and lit up. He took a deep drag, absorbed in thought.

"Why? Why do you do this??"

He took another drag. It didn't taste good. He snubbed it out in the ashtray. He leaned forward, putting his head on the steering wheel and encircling it with his arms

"Yeah, why do you smoke? Gotta quit that. . . someday. . .but not now. That's not what we're talking about here. Why did you do what you did today?"

A voice answered. Was it his conscience?

Was it Frank, his angel?.

Probably.

"Why, indeed?? Why do you think you do it?"

"I don't know. Why should I go out there every day, where I'll probably get my ass shot off! Why don't I just do what Chris H. did . . .walk into Col. Bill's office, salute and lay my wings on his desk? Now Chris is a motor pool officer . . .no more sweat, no more facing down that fear every day."

"You haven't answered the question. . .what motivates you to go out there and do it?"

"Because if I didn't do it there wouldn't be anyone else to do it. And, I believe what we're doing for South Korea is right - we're fulfilling our promise to them."

"Go on."

"Like, it's my responsibility. . . my job. It's what I'm supposed to do."

"Yeah. . . you were always a sucker for that."

"Well, I guess I do it because those guys trust me."

"Hmmm. . .Tell me more."

There was no doubt in Son's mind that America was acting in good faith in supporting South Korea. The U.S. had treaty obligations to come to the aid of the Koreans if they were attacked. South Korea had every right to self-determination. This fledgling democracy was being attacked by a ruthless communist dictatorship. We had to come to their aid. That was one reason he did what he did. But there was an even deeper reason.

Son thought about his friends, the guys he depended upon, who depended on him:

Although Rogers was the youngest in the Flight, Son soon came to recognize that Russ was the best natural pilot of his fledglings. Sometimes, Son thought of Russ as a young Bill Samways. He was instinctive, like Bill. He was friendly, somewhat shy, always upbeat.

Son's other two pilots were converted bomber pilots. Only another "from birth" fighter pilot knows the significance of that assertion. Bomber pilots are sometimes referred to by their more agile friends as "drivers - as in 'truck'." Bombers take off, climb to altitude, set course to the target when told by the navigator, fly straight, usually with the assistance of an automatic pilot, until they reach the target, drop their bombs, return home and land.

This is not to denigrate bomber pilots but to point out that they are different. The bomber crews of the 8th Air Force, flying out of England against the Nazis made the supreme sacrifice, sustaining terrible losses in the skies over Germany. The same can be said of the B29 crews who helped to bring The Empire of Japan to its knees.

So what's different about fighter pilots? Well, their mission requirements are different for one thing. Fighter pilots are constantly on the move. They are required to maneuver, climb, turn, dive, shoot, bomb and, yes, navigate all on their own. Because of their mission, their aircraft are generally faster and less stable by design. Some people say that they can tell the difference between the two types in their personalities. Personality does seem to correlate with profession. Accountants and salespeople, for example, are quite different by temperament. Fighter pilots tend to be more aggressive and outgoing, while bomber types tend to be more passive, phlegmatic. Major Lancaster, the 35th CO, had a motto, which he kept on his desk after "C cubed" left: Fighter Pilots are The Most Interesting People. That statement seems to sum up the differences.

So, when Wimer and Tidwell arrived in the Squadron nearly two years previously, and were assigned to Son, Son knew that he had his work cut out for him. Wimer, Jewish, and from Salem, Oregon, flew B29 Superfortresses during WWII. He was college educated, but

he didn't know what the term "trail dragger" meant. He was alert, very articulate and out-going, all of which didn't seem to fit the bomber pilot profile. He was ahead of Son on the permanent quarters list. Al's wife, Jeanette, had just joined him from stateside, and Son, who was still living in the BOQ (bachelor officers' quarters) appreciated being invited to dinner regularly where he got to know both of them quite well. Al and Herm (as they called him) just hit it off. They played gin rummy, talked politics and, of course, flying. Herm began to sense that maybe there was fighter pilot potential in Al.

Jim Tidwell flew B24 Liberators during the "Great War." That was not much different from Al's experience. In personality, however, Jim , a Mormon from Salt Lake City, Utah, was quieter, more introspective than Al. Where Al was sophisticated and worldly, Jim was guileless, almost innocent. He had a cherubic smile, all of which seemed to go with his Mormon faith. Jim's wife, Gladys, was still in the States, as was Herm's. He, too, was a denizen of the BOQ (Bachelor Officers' Quarters), and would occasionally go to the "O" Club and hoist one or two. Hence, we called him our "backsliding Mormon." Jim would get red in the face and say,

"Aw, you guys. . .cut it out!"

In retrospect, the other pilots weren't being very nice to Jim in teasing him this way, but he was a good sport, and seemed to take our good natured ribbing quite well. All of us predicted that when Gladys arrived, she would march to the club, get him by the ear, and restore him to the straight and narrow. As it turned out, they were right. Nevertheless, Herm thought he could make a fighter pilot out of Jim Tidwell. He was right.

Fortunately, during the early months of 1948, the Black Panthers were on detached service at Miho, Japan, a remote air base in western Honshu. Without the presence of "C cubed," there was less pressure, a more relaxed atmosphere at Miho. Although Son didn't know it at the time, he had nearly two years to work with Al and Jim before war was to begin. Son wanted to teach them and they wanted to learn, so the project was begun. Some-one, not Son, said, "that trying to teach a bomber pilot to be a fighter pilot was a little like trying to teach a nun how to be a harlot." Well, it was difficult.

Son set up his own little fighter pilot school. First, he put them in the AT6 "Texan", a single engine advanced trainer. Gradually, they learned the basics. They learned how to take off and land in the AT6 without ground looping. Then they soloed in the P51 Mustang. They learned fighter formation flying — the tactics and the techniques of fighterdom. By the time the war started, they were good, solid fighter pilots. In the process of this peda-gogy, and the war that followed, strong bonds of trust and friendship were formed that last to this day.

"I taught Al and Jim everything they know about fighters. They believe in me. What they did today was the ultimate expression of what they have learned. One of the most important things they learned was that when the occasion requires it, you must be able to put your life in someone else's hands. Sooner or later, it'll be your turn. You'll have to depend on them."

"*Interesting,*" said the angel, "*. . .anything else?*"

"They didn't give that trust blindly. They gave it only because they know me. They know my skill and they know what I stand for. I earned their trust."

"*O.K., that's good reason. . .what's the other half of that . . .what's the other side of trust?*"

"Loyalty?. . .I guess I am pretty loyal, if by that you mean, giving your best to another, supporting them, defending them."

"*Loyalty is pretty important, isn't it? What would happen to loyalty if you went to join Chris at the motor pool? What would Al and Jim think? They trust you. Do you trust them?*"

"Yes, of course I trust them! And to quit would be betrayal. . . .not just of them, but of myself. I don't think I could do that . . .it would be. . . .betrayal??? Yes. My father taught me

that trust, once earned, is precious. Months, even years of effort may be put into building trust, but it can be destroyed in an instant, and once lost it is almost never regained."

"O.K. That's correct. . . *A man's true character is who he is to himself. . .no secrets. It's not what you pretend to be to others. It's who and what you are. How do you feel now?*"

Better, I guess. . . just hope I can measure up. It's hard. I always thought I had a brave heart, but . . ."

"*But you've never been tested???*"

"Not like today!"

"*Well, how do you think you did?*"

"I'm not sure. . ."

"*Not sure?! What do you want?*", said the voice, incredulously. "*You faced your fears, didn't you?*"

"Well, I sure didn't throw my fears out of the airplane! Somebody once told me that anyone who flies combat and says he's not scared is either a damn fool or a damn liar."

"*Of course you were scared. . .but did you continue to function, to do what had to be done?*"

"Uh huh. O.K."

"*You're not going to go see Col. Samways tomorrow?*"

"No. . . . But it ain't easy!"

Again, Frank smiled.

Son turned the key in the ignition, started the car and drove slowly off toward Kasuga, his wife and daughter. During the five mile drive, he thought about his wife and daughter and what had happened since they had arrived in Japan. It was bizarre. After a somewhat fitful sleep, Son awoke the next morning, thinking about the war and the events that preceded it.

CHAPTER 7
Family Pressures

Arretta and Mary-Lynn had joined him the previous October, only after much controversy. Arretta really didn't want to come. In fact, their marriage nearly broke up because of it. Son had been in Japan for almost a year, and was aching to be with his family again. After much arguing, exchange of angry letters, and a couple of overseas telephone calls, he finally convinced her to come. As it turned out, the following 18 months would be extremely difficult, stressful for all of them. If he had known what was to come, he might have decided to let them stay in the ZI (zone of the interior to those not familiar with military acronyms).

Mary-Lynn didn't take well to the travel and change of environment. By the time she arrived, after a 12-day voyage across the Pacific aboard a slow U.S. Army troop ship, she had severe digestive upset. The usual Kaopectate treatment didn't work. She went into severe dehydration, and had to be placed in the Army Hospital in Fukuoka. The Sons, as parents, were not allowed to stay overnight with her, per Army regulations. It took a full week to get Mary-Lynn stabilized. By the time she returned home, she was a frightened and nervous little girl. Gradually, however, she seemed to return to normal. But there was to be more stress.

The 8th Group participated in the Far Eastern Air Forces fighter gunnery competition, held at Johnson AFB near Tokyo. Son was on the team from the 8th, and was on temporary duty at Johnson for nearly a month. Then, as luck and skill would have it, the 8th won top honors and was selected to go to Nellis AFB at Las Vegas, Nevada to participate in the USAF worldwide meet scheduled to be held the following Spring. So, after all the problems involved in getting his family to join him in Japan, Son found himself aboard a C-54 transport, winging his way across the Pacific to the States. He was to be gone for nearly six weeks. After placing second in the worldwide meet, the team returned to Japan.

Upon his return, Son asked for two weeks leave, beginning May 1st. He got reservations at an Army rest hotel, The Aso Kanko, located in the mountains of southern Kyushu. The Japanese originally built the facility in the 1930's, as the primary site for the Winter Olympics. There were hot mineral baths, a beautiful pool, breath taking scenery, and a kimono clad staff that waited on them hand and foot. They walked in the mountains. They enjoyed their daughter. They lounged by the pool and watched Mary-Lynn dance and play. She was unbelievably cute! They ate Japanese food, soaked up the surroundings and just plain relaxed. What a welcome change it was. They had time to talk, and repair their somewhat tattered personal relationship. Little did they know of the events looming on the horizon.

After returning from leave, Son reported in to the Squadron, and settled into the normal rhythm of occupation duty in a foreign land. The duty schedule was easy and relaxed. The flying involved checking out the Squadron's pilots in new F80-C jets. Son had previously flown them, and therefore was designated as the Squadron IP (Instructor Pilot). He gave instrument check rides and busied himself with writing a manual for instrument flying in the F80. The latter activity was particularly important, he thought. Instrument proficiency among the squadron pilots was low, and Son felt that something needed to be done about it. Major Ray agreed.

There was talk, of course, about the North Koreans. There were incidents at the border between North Korea and South Korea. There were threats. There was plenty of evidence that the North was armed "to the teeth." They had the support of The Soviet Union, which had given them their arms. They were being trained by Soviet personnel. The U.S. military knew that if South Korea were attacked they would be bound by treaty to come to their aid. There was no great concern, however. Taking a page from national leadership, it was thought highly unlikely that North Korea would be stupid enough to attack. So the good life of occupation duty continued. All of this was about to change.

The Korean War's first casualty was the good life of the 8th FBW. During the occupation of Japan, Friday nights meant 20-ounce steaks sizzling at the Officers Club, cheap drinks and a Japanese band which supplied a rough approximation of American dance music. Settled with their families at Itazuke Airfield in western Japan, airmen of the 8th FBW flew the Lockheed F-80C and felt they were a showcase for the newly independent U.S. Air Force. If they were not the Air Force elite in their new, fast jets, they came close.

The watchword was, "shempainai", roughly translated from Japanese, it meant, "no sweat!" And so it was on Sunday afternoon, June 25. Herman and Arretta put Mary-Lynn in their car and drove to nearby Fukuoka to look for some cloisonné table lamps for their apartment. They shopped for quite awhile, found what they wanted and made a purchase. Then they browsed, looking over thousands of items carried in the stores at prices that were too good to pass up. They bought a couple of other things and headed back to the base. As they pulled up in front of their apartment, Sumiko-san, their Japanese maid, came out to meet them, talking and gesturing excitedly. Finally, they understood her. The Squadron had called.

"Caru Base!," said Sumiko

By now, it was early evening. Ray Schilleriff answered the call. What would he be doing at work at that time of the day? The answer came quickly. The North Koreans had just crossed the 38th parallel, dividing the North from South Korea. It was no border incident dustup this time. It was an invasion in force.

"What?!"

That is how Son learned that come morning, he would be in a war.

He was told to report to the Squadron at 5:30 A.M., June 26th, 1950; Son called Al Wimer and Jim Tidwell to tell them. It was a little hard to get to sleep that night.

The morning of the 26th brought rainy weather with middle clouds at about 8,000 feet - - not too bad but not good. After Picking up Al and Jim, Son headed out the main gate at Kasuga and turned left . . .onto the left side of the two-lane asphalt road leading to the airstrip. It was still dark. About a mile down the road, a single, yellow headlight appeared, its beam flickering up and down through a thin ground fog as the vehicle carrying it bounced over holes in the road. As it approached, he could see that it was a three-wheeled hybrid that looked like a curious blend of motorcycle on the front end and a pickup truck in the rear. What appeared to be a large wooden tub was loaded onto the bed of the vehicle. Strapped to the rear of this contrivance was something that looked similar to an oversized garbage can, topped with a large, inverted funnel. An acrid, yellowish smoke came from

the top of the inverted funnel. This arrangement permitted the gases from the burning char-coal to be used as fuel for the wheezing, one lung engine. Passing this thing on the left side, Son was assailed with a blend of strange smells . . . that of charcoal and honey bucket. The driver of this "farm vehicle" was on his way from a centrally located honey pit. He was carrying a load of "honey" for his rice fields. "Honey", briefly explained, is human excre-ment, properly aged. It is collected in the pits and then spread on the fields. So, now, dear reader, you know. It makes the rice grow like crazy! It also makes the eyes water and the nose burn. It is a smell with muscles.

Major Ray Lancaster,(The 35th Squadron Commander, and referred to as Major Ray, to distinguish him from Cap'n Ray Schilleriff) the Operations Officer) briefed the mission. They would be providing top cover for transport aircraft that were engaged in evacuating American civilians and dependents of military personnel. These folks were mostly diplo-matic personnel and dependents of KMAG (Korean Military Advisory Group) people. The transports were collecting and flying them out from Kimpo and Suwon Air Bases. Pilots were cautioned to not, repeat not, shoot at anything on the ground. Their job was just to protect the transports. The UN had not yet authorized engagement in ground operations. That restriction, which annoyed fighter pilots, was to be lifted shortly. In the meantime, three squadrons of F80-C"s , totaling no more than 30 to 35 combat ready aircraft, had to provide constant cover over Kimpo and Suwon from sunup to sundown. That meant that each aircraft in the group had to fly nearly four times on average each day! That meant that each aircraft had to be maintained in flyable condition(in this situation rules were bent). "Flyable condition," did not mean "combat ready" in the normal sense of the word. If a bird could fly, and if it could shoot and drop bombs, it was called in to operations as "flyable". The maintenance people — mechanics, electronics people, armorers and crew chiefs like Staff Sergeant Billy Buster — worked literally around the clock to support operations. They would be among the many unsung heroes of the war.

Now, consider the pilots. Each squadron had approximately a dozen combat ready pilots, plus a few others, mostly group and wing staff people, who were assigned to one or another of the squadrons for flying duty. It meant that they had to fly every available pilot, those who were combat ready and those who were not. Calculating on a mission average time of slightly over two hours, It meant that each available pilot was in the air nearly seven hours each day!

In the "Catch 22," of the day, it was said that, "you couldn't fly combat until you were combat ready, but the only way to get combat ready was to fly combat!" Go figure! They did. The answer that they came up with was obvious. If you wore a pair of wings, and if you had been checked out in the aircraft, you were "combat ready!"

"Put him on the schedule!" said Major Ray, firmly, as the flight board was being filled in.

The weather, while not critical, meant that the fighters would have to "bust through" a layer of clouds whose bases were approximately 8,000 ft, and which extended up to 20 or so thousand feet. No "big deal."

The Black Panthers' share of the mission required that flights of four aircraft would take off at approximate ninety minute intervals. Interleaving the three squadrons of the group yielded a flight taking off every thirty minutes throughout the day. The first flight would fly out to the target area, arriving on station at one of the designated air bases in Korea — Kimpo or Suwon. They would descend to and maintain an altitude of eight to ten thousand feet and begin an orbit, keeping the airfield and its approaches under surveil-lance. From their intelligence reports, they knew that the North Korean Air Force was sparsely and poorly equipped. Their first line fighter aircraft was the YAK-9, propeller driven and capable of speeds in the 350 mph range. The NKAF was reported to carry an inventory of about 50 such aircraft. They also had an indeterminate number of IL-2 "dive bombers." These open cockpit craft resembled the old Stukka JU-88 which the Luftwaffe used to

support Hitler's "Blitzkrieg" tactics at the beginning of WWII. Their armament consisted of two .30 caliber forward firing machine guns, coordinated to fire through the propeller. A gunner, facing toward the rear, manned twin, flexible small caliber machine guns in a style reminiscent of WWI. Of course, they were capable of carrying two 500 pound bombs. It was thought that the NKAF had no more than twenty or twenty-five of these.

Our job Major Ray said was to, "Shoot those puppies down if any of them are dumb enough to show themselves!"

They did show themselves.

And we did shoot them down.

By the end of the first ten days, the 8th FBW had accounted for most of the NKAF flyable inventory. Some were destroyed in the air. Ray Schilleriff (Cap'n Ray), Al Boyce, Bob ("Slick") De Wald and Bob Wayne scored victories in the air. The NKAF had their aircraft dispersed to several small fields, which they kept well camouflaged. However, they located some of these sites and destroyed a number of aircraft on the ground. This type of "ground target," not being associated with the ground battle, was OK for us to attack.

During this period of the war, Son and his flight were never in the target area at the right time. Twice, they were letting down into the area, and once were going home, they heard the radio chatter indicating that a fight had broken out but they had no chance to get into the action. The fights were pretty one-sided, usually started and finished within a couple of minutes. The 35th's pilots all returned home, unscathed. Unscathed? Well, there was one incident. . . .

CHAPTER 8
"Honey Bucket" Bob

First Lieutenant Bob Wayne, "B" flight commander, and his flight, had just been relieved on station from their top cover responsibilities. Things had been quiet. There were no Yak-9s or IL-2's to play with. Bob thought, "How boring." They hadn't reached minimum fuel, which would have forced them to return home. Bob thought maybe he could get a little action if he took his flight down to ground level and looked for some "targets of opportunity."

"Seek, and ye shall find," was Bob's motto. Long story short, he found a target that shot back. Bob's plane was hit. When his fire warning light came on there was only one thing to do. Eject. Bob's flight mates saw his parachute blossom and lower him safely to the ground. He landed on a roadway which separated the rice paddies in the area. There were concentrations of enemy troops nearby who also saw Wayne's descent. Immediately, they began to converge on Bob. They were held off, however, by Bob's flight mates, now led by element leader Captain Ray White, who kept a covering fire going until they were relieved by the next flight.

Bob, meanwhile, had one thing in mind. He had to hide. Hearing the approach of North Korean soldiers, he dove off the road into the thick brush that surrounded a rice paddy. He slipped into the foul smelling water and all but submerged himself. There were a number of thin, hollow reeds sticking out of the water. Bob pulled a couple and tested them to see of he could breathe through them. Yes, he could.

As the North Koreans approached his hiding place, Bob placed one end of the reed in his mouth and completely submerged himself in the honey bucket muck. The soldiers passed within only a few feet of his hiding place, but never found him. He knew, or assumed, that we would try to get an ASR helicopter, based at Taegu, in to extract him. He waited. Nearly two hours passed. He cautiously raised his head out of the water so he could breathe a little easier and hear better. He could see our fighters circling overhead and occasionally diving down to attack some target which he could not see. All of this told him that a rescue attempt would be made. He just needed to be patient.

Meantime, the ASR had taken off from K-2 (an airfield designation) at Taegu. The top cover flight was notified. As the chopper swooped in, the fighters laid down covering fire. Bob, with his head barely out of the stinking water, heard and saw what was going on. As the chopper slowed to a hover, Bob jumped out of his hiding place and scrambled up the bank onto the road, waving frantically to the chopper. As soon as he had struggled into the chopper it was up and away! There was no fire from the ground during this operation, thanks to our covering fighters.

After a short flight back to K-2, Bob was airlifted back to Itazuke.   F o u r hours after the incident began, Honey Bucket Bob walked into the 35th Squadron Ops Quonset. Several pilots were there, doing what pilots do while waiting to go fly: Al Boyce and Jim Tidwell were perched on stools at the coffee bar. The perpetual pinochle game was going on around a low table. Cap'n Ray was working on the schedule blackboard.

"For God's sake, who's that?", exclaimed Fletch Meadors.

Bob stood there, in the middle of the room, his face still covered with mud. Then his face split from ear to ear in a grin,showing a mouthful of white teeth. "Yep, I'm back!, he said, still grinning.

"You sure are, and you smell like s - - -!"

"Hey! Who drug in that dead animal?!"

Cap'n Ray dropped his chalk and turned from the schedule board: "Bob,- - -go get in the shower!" he growled.

Bob headed back to the shower, as everybody stood up, laughing and holding their noses.

"Get outta here. . .and burn that flight suit!" somebody yelled.

Minutes later, Bob returned in a clean flight suit, showered, shaved and liberally doused with Mennen After Shave.

"Hey. . .there's Honey bucket. . . Pheeeew!!!. . .what kind of honey bucket did you fall into this time!?"

Actually, he didn't smell so bad now. All was forgiven as Bob told and retold his harrowing adventure. But the next morning, at Squadron briefing, when Bob took his seat, the pilots on both sides of him got up and moved away from him. When Bob looked puzzled, everybody laughed. He really didn't smell bad, so clearly it was a "put up job." It took him some time to wear down his sobriquet of "Honey Bucket" Bob!

CHAPTER 9
The Journey Begins

Son continued to fly missions - two, sometimes three a day. When he was in the air, he was all business, focused on doing his job, getting himself and his flight mates to the target and home again. In between, there were moments, albeit few, when Son had time to think about his life. Centertown and the little farm of his birth and childhood seemed light years away. How did he get here, in this foreign land, flying combat in jets? Son let his mind relax and wander:

Frank thought, *"I'd better stay with this guy and see what he gets into."*

Son ruminated: All journeys begin. . . .at the beginning. It was a time of "Easy Come, Easy Go."

The year was 1922, in the middle of that post World War I cultural turbulence called The Roaring Twenties. It was the age of the flapper, skull-tight hats and short skirts. Prohibition, enacted into law after the war, helped to create an environment in which the bootlegger sold illegal spirits in spite of the law. In the big cities, New York and Chicago, particularly, nightclubs called "Speak Easies" thrived. They were supplied with alcohol from the outlaw producers and protected in their illegal activities by corrupt police who were "on the take" from gangsters such as Al Capone and others. If the mob didn't own the clubs outright, they took "protection" money from them, which they used to pay off the cops.

In this cozy arrangement all the participants understood the rules. Most of the Speak Easy operators observed them. Those who didn't got punishment that was swift and bloody, administered by the goons of the mob. Sure, it was corrupt with a capital "C", but who cared? Not many. After the war, the public was in a mood to let its hair down. It was the age of fast cars, fast women and all around loose behavior. The popular music of the time was "hot" jazz. In this "golden age" for jazz, musicians found that there was a ready market for their talents. Some of the stars of this period in our musical history, created music that lives on in Jazz's standard repertory. Hoagie Carmichael, gave us "Deep Purple," and, "Stardust," A true American classic. "Fats" Waller contributed "Two Sleepy People". Trumpeters Bix Biederbecke, and Louie Armstrong were musical giants. Musically, the legendary Duke Ellington did it all. He was a world-class composer, arranger and performer. His works are too numerous to list. But who can forget "Take The A-Train," "Black and Tan Fantasy," Sophisticated Lady," and the ethereal and spiritual, "On Sunday". His works are part of the life-blood of American music. There is Oscar Peterson, Ray Brown and the greatest

piano player of them all, the late Art Tatum. Books have been written about each of these musical geniuses. They, and many others of equal or almost equal stature, gave us America's truly original art form.

Early in his life, Son began to absorb this music, along with a classical repertoire that came with years of piano lessons. The feeling for music and the feeling about flying seemed to merge in his heart. The dance crazes of the time were The Blackbottom, The Lindy Hop and The Charleston. In the stock market, The Bull was king. "Hot tip" speculation was rife, fortunes were made and lost, literally, overnight. Stocks could be bought on "margin" with as little as 10% down. As long as the market was going up, things were great. It was "easy come, easy go." This cultural and financial binge continued in the big cities through most of the decade. But in October, 1929, this volatile mixture crashed headlong into the social and economic debacle of The Great Depression. People who had been financially ruined, victims of their own excesses, jumped out of skyscraper windows on Wall Street. What seemed to be a never-ending prosperity evaporated. Unemployment became a plague upon the land. In the cities, bread lines and soup kitchens replaced the speak easy night clubs. Long before the creation of the "Misery Index," a popular song of the times, "Brother, Can You Spare A Dime," spoke eloquently of the public's misery.

The excesses of the period reached beyond the big cities. In the hinterland, sometimes currently referred to by the east and west coast people as "flyover country," the gang wars of New York and Chicago echoed but faintly. There was the occasional bank robbery, committed by criminal celebrities such as "Pretty Boy" Floyd and "Bonnie and Clyde". And, yes, bootleg hooch could be had, even in small town America. But when The Depression hit, it struck rural America just as hard as the big cities. True, there weren't bread lines in the villages. The pain was softened somewhat because country folk could grow their own food, but unemployment and grinding poverty were everywhere. Those who lived in small town America were lucky if they had any kind of job. If one was a schoolteacher, worked for the railroad or the U.S. Post Office, he/she was indeed fortunate with a job that produced an income ranging from $50 to $150 per month! Most of those not in this category were in serious financial straits. Many, who lived on small family farms scraped out an existence off the land. Families helped each other by trading labor and bartering their produce. Folks still got married, went to church, had children and reared their families.

CHAPTER 10
A Family Takes Root

Herman and his Mother

In this social milieu, in the year 1920, in small town, rural America Son's mother, Effie Grace Garnett, 31, and his father, John Herman Son, 32, met, fell in love and were married.

John Herman was a railroad telegrapher. He took a job as station agent for the Missouri Pacific Railroad in Centertown, Missouri, population three hundred fifty souls. His salary was $120 per month. It was a princely sum for the times.

They bought a small, four-room house on the edge of town. There was no plumbing, no electricity and no heat, unless a wood-burning stove furnished it. The property had 32 acres of rolling, partly wooded land, a barn and a nice outhouse, better known by country folk as a privy. It was a perfect fit for them.

As a farm girl, Grace was familiar with all things agricultural, a background that would come in handy during the hard times that were ahead. Then came an event from out of the cosmos.

Sometime during the middle part of February, 1922, a modest couple of years after Son's Mother and Father were married, two elemental and microscopic bits of protoplasm, one male and one female, found each other. They joined and the cosmic spark of life was ignited. In the safety and warmth of the womb, Son would spend the next nine months preparing for entrance into the world.

Thus, in this decade of the roaring twenties, in small town, rural America, his journey began: On October 16, 1922, Herman Franklin Son arrived. His mother gave birth at home, without benefit of a hospital, without benefit of anesthetic, attended by Dr. Aufderheide, the only doctor in town. Conventional wisdom says that adults do not normally remember events prior to age 4 or 5. Perhaps, in a few cases, individuals may remember things that happened as early as 3 years of age. Son maintains, however, that his experience differs radically from this norm. He says at the outset that he has absolutely no way to prove that he can remember his birth. Nevertheless, he says he can. If he cannot prove it, neither can anyone else disprove it. It is not, he says, something that his parents told him that he has internalized as memory. It is his own experience. It is not verbal. It is a feeling, as in a

dream - coming from a dark and safe place into the light of the world apart from his mother. Jim Carey, a famous Hollywood comedian, recently interviewed on TV, was asked, "How soon after you were born did you know that you were this talented?", "Oh, right after I came out!" he said, " I started telling jokes and doing routines immediately!" Well . . .if Jim Carey can do it......????

"As an angel who not only believes but understands things extraterrestrial, I cannot disagree."

Herman Franklin's first person stream of consciousness follows:

"I can remember nursing at my mother's breast, which I did until I bit her, convincing her that it was time to wean me. I remember the anxiety (anger?) that I felt at being deprived of what by now had become so comforting and familiar. Apparently I survived this early, mild trauma. I have no specific memories of this after being placed on the cup.

"How old was I when I was weaned?" Son says, "I would guess 18 - 20 months."

"There are a few other early memories, going back to about age 1. I remember being fed in a high chair by my mother and playing vigorously in my oatmeal, which I spilled into the tray of the high chair when my mother's back was turned. I remember being put into a stroller (my mother has told me about this, so it is possible that my memory is partially a recounting) and paddling around the kitchen as my mother did her chores. We had an old fashioned, cast iron, and wood fired kitchen range with water tank on the side. It was used to cook, bake, heat water and the room. I can specifically remember pulling up to the front of the stove while sitting in my stroller and grasping the handle of the oven door. The next thing I knew was that my left hand was pinned between the very hot oven door and the top of the stroller. The back of my left hand was burned severely. Nearly 80 years later I can still remember, and I have the scar to show for it.

"There were three other incidents from my infancy that I can remember quite clearly. All three involved my father. The first two of them produced feelings of fear, the third a sense of sadness and foreboding.

"I was out of my stroller, playing on a linoleum floor. I was eating a cracker or crust of toast, I'm not sure which. Some of the food went into my mouth, the rest was scattered on the floor. My father told me to pick up the crumbs.

"What??" I started to crawl away. He stopped me, placed me back in front of the crumbs, and made me stay there "until you pick up that mess." I was trying to obey my father, but couldn't. Finally, after dampening the crumbs with an appropriate amount of tears, my mother intervened.

"A few months later, I was playing outside near our house. My father was working in the yard and wasn't paying close attention to me. I wandered away, up the alley toward a neighbor's house. My father came to get me. He told me not to do that again, on pain of corporal punishment. A short time later, headstrong little character that I was, I was gone again. This time he came after me with a small switch, cut from the limb of a budding peach tree. He headed me down the alley and motivated my progress with stings from the peach tree switch. When I got home, my pants were wet. I didn't venture up that alley again unless my father was with me or he had given me permission.

"Later, I was probably about 4 years old, I had a little dog named Bobby. Our house fronted to the main highway through town and there was a fair amount of traffic. I was warned never to go out on that street alone. The danger of it was sufficiently impressed upon me, and I never transgressed. Perhaps I also had the peach tree switch in the back of my mind. I was also told to watch Bobby closely, and that he could be 'run over' too, if we weren't careful. But Bobby, being a resourceful little dog, didn't let the fence around our

yard stop him. He crawled under the fence several times, but sooner or later he would come home unharmed. One day, however, he didn't come home.

"That night and all the next day until Daddy came home from the Missouri Pacific Depot where he worked as a station agent, I was apprehensive. I wanted to know, and I didn't want to know. Daddy said that he thought maybe "an ole hoot owl got him.""

"Where? How do you know?"

"I found his bones in the woods. We'll walk over there tomorrow, and I'll show you."

"That evening, after my father had milked the cows (more about that later), we walked across the pasture toward the woods. A few yards into the woods, Daddy stopped and pointed. "There," he said, pointing to the skeletal remains of a small animal of some sort. I supposed that it was Bobby's bones, and that was that. Bobby was gone. I accepted it as fact that, "An ole Hoot Owl got him." If he was run over by a car, and my father didn't want to tell me, didn't matter. To this day, however, I cannot hear the hoot of an owl at night without thinking of little Bobby."

Mama and Daddy Were A Team.

"My mother was a big, strong woman of 5 feet 9 inches, certainly capable of heavy, physical farm work, but that was not all she wanted from life. A graduate of Missouri Normal College (now known as Central Missouri State University), she obtained her teaching certificate and became a school teacher in a small, one room country school near Marion, Mo. It was there that she met my father, the railroad station agent at Sandy Hook, and a stop on the Missouri-Pacific river route from St. Louis to Kansas City.

"When she married my father, she left her teaching position to become a full time wife and homemaker. That is what women did in those times. Her goals were to be a good wife and homemaker, to have children, love them and teach them her rock ribbed Christian values. She would teach them to appreciate the beauties in the world that surrounded them - music, art, literature and nature.

They would learn to play a musical instrument, most probably the piano, which sat in our living room. She would teach her

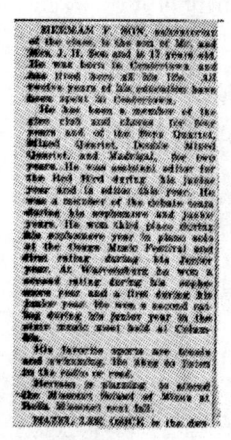

children about the larger world, of strange and exotic lands. We would travel. Daddy had a lifetime pass on the Missouri-Pacific that was honored by other rail lines. We took advantage of this to take trips to Mexico, going all the way to Mexico City. We took in the World's Fair in Chicago, where I learned about the first automatic transmissions for automobiles. In 1936, television was only a gleam in the eye of a few visionary scientists, such as David Farnsworth, who worked on "far out" projects for RCA(Radio Corporation of America). The fair had an exhibit of a labo-

ratory model that could transmit pictures over the air from one point to another!

"Wouldn't that be something!" Daddy said. "Yes, it certainly would," Mama agreed. To Mama, everything was an opportunity to learn and teach.

"She also taught us the Ten Commandments as they applied to everyday life. Education and learning were high on her list of priorities. All her children would go to college. Truth and honesty, hard work, keeping one's promises and religious faith were cardinal points on her moral compass. Finally, she placed great importance on rearing her children to become productive, and patriotic American citizens. She believed that you got out of life what you put into it. If that's true, and I believe it to be, then Mama lived a full life.

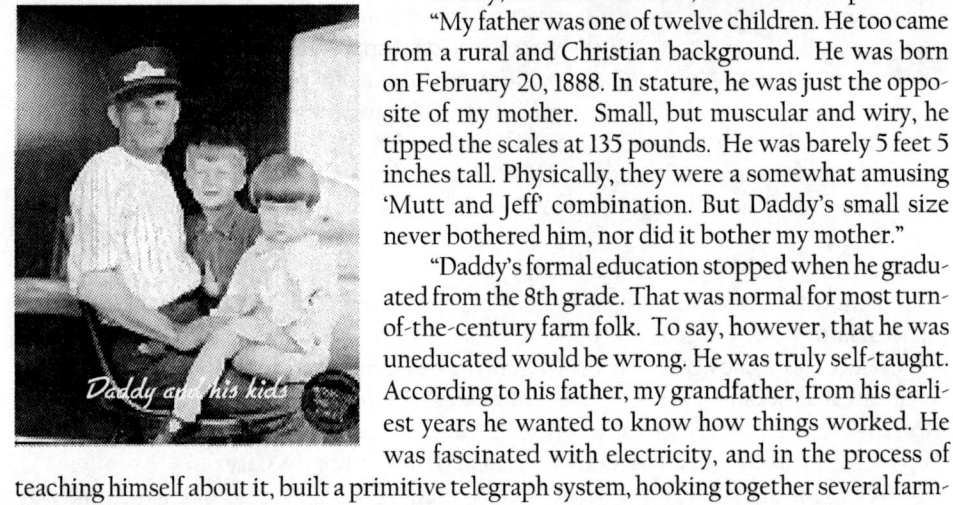
Daddy and his kids

Daddy, on the other hand, was small but powerful.

"My father was one of twelve children. He too came from a rural and Christian background. He was born on February 20, 1888. In stature, he was just the opposite of my mother. Small, but muscular and wiry, he tipped the scales at 135 pounds. He was barely 5 feet 5 inches tall. Physically, they were a somewhat amusing 'Mutt and Jeff' combination. But Daddy's small size never bothered him, nor did it bother my mother."

"Daddy's formal education stopped when he graduated from the 8th grade. That was normal for most turn-of-the-century farm folk. To say, however, that he was uneducated would be wrong. He was truly self-taught. According to his father, my grandfather, from his earliest years he wanted to know how things worked. He was fascinated with electricity, and in the process of teaching himself about it, built a primitive telegraph system, hooking together several farmhouses in Miller County. He taught himself and two of his younger sisters Morse code. Then he taught some neighboring farmers. Soon he had a network of telegraph keys and clickers up and running, connecting several farms. His efforts paid off with his first job as a railroad station agent-telegrapher in Olean, Mo. in 1908. It turned out to be his lifetime vocation. He worked for The MOPAC (Missouri Pacific Railroad) for over fifty-five years, and was their longest service employee when he retired in 1963."

"During the 1920's his interests turned to 'wireless.' At first, it was just Morse or International Code, transmitted and received between stations without benefit of any wire connection! That seemed truly miraculous. He played around with crystal sets, sending and receiving messages to and from other 'amateurs' such as himself. He wanted to learn more, so he sent away for a three-foot shelf of technical reference books published by ITT. Gradually, as he learned more about the subject, he bought more sophisticated equipment, finally getting into radios that could receive the human voice."

"The equipment that he bought during those days, as one could imagine, was primitive. Since there was no public electric power in Centertown his radios were battery operated. The front controls featured not one dial to tune in stations, but three! Each dial controlled, 'A variable capacity condenser,' Daddy said, expecting me to understand. Starting from the left, each condenser must be tuned to the desired frequency. The first one was used to set a "rough" frequency, the second one refined the adjustment and the third was used for final and fine adjustment. Sound was transmitted through a headset that was plugged into the front panel of the radio. Later, headsets were replaced with large speakers,

shaped a little like a large question mark, with a large tuba-sized bell on the end. Radio Corporation of America, (RCA), built these early radios."

"In the late 1920s, circa 1928, Daddy decided that they had to have electricity in our house. It looked as though Missouri Power and Light Company would never run power lines to Centertown from Jefferson City, nearly 15 miles away. He researched the problem and found that the Delco Corporation made and sold a 'farm light plant.' It consisted of a gasoline engine driven, 32-volt direct current generator and a bank of about a dozen big glass jars containing lead-acid batteries. The batteries, when fully charged by the generator, could store enough power to run electric lights in the house and in the barn. Daddy would crank up the engine on the light plant every evening and let it run until bedtime, which generated enough power to last until the next evening. It was direct current, not alternating and it was only 32 volts, not 110 volts like public power, but it was better than kerosene lamps. Daddy still hoped that someday they would get public power. It happened sooner than he expected. Early in the Roosevelt Administration, the Rural Electrification Administration (REA) was established with the goal of providing electric service to the country. Soon, Missouri Power and Light Company began planting light poles and stringing power lines from Jefferson City. When 110 volt, alternating power became available, it made a lot of things possible that weren't before."

"In addition to better radios Daddy bought a new General Electric refrigerator to replace the old ice box. It had a sealed motor, compressor and condensation coils sitting on top of the box, which gave it an ungainly appearance, but it worked beautifully. We were the first family in town to have such a luxury. Daddy also bought a new Emerson Electric 12 inch oscillating electric fan to make July and August heat more bearable. We were fast becoming a "high tech" family in the thirties.

"Next Daddy became an agent for Atwater-Kent radios, which by now were much improved over the early primitive radios. These radios operated on normal house current, and were housed in handsome cabinets done in console and table model styles. The company gave him a beautiful console model, which Daddy installed in the living room. It had one dial that glowed with a yellow-orange light that was used for tuning. A big, 12 inch speaker was hidden in the cabinet behind a woven louvered screen. The tone was beautiful."

"So lifelike!" Daddy exclaimed.

He invited Herman Miller and Vic Witthaus over to listen. They were amazed and promptly ordered one for themselves. When the radios came in, via Railway Express, Daddy delivered them and set them up, including a "properly designed" antenna. Herman and Vic immediately became Daddy's best word-of-mouth advertisers. From that point, Daddy built a substantial business, not only in original sales of the radios, but in repairing and adjusting them. He set up a small repair shop in an alcove of the second floor of our house, which we also used for sleeping. After all the chores were done, and after supper, Daddy would go to his little shop to work on a radio. Sometimes it was his own, sometimes a neighbor's and sometimes he would be "just experimenting." I kibitzed regularly during these sessions, asking questions, which I'm sure, could have been called "stupid" or "naïve." But if Daddy saw them that way, he never let me know it. He would always answer, talking to me about electrons, vacuum tubes, magnetic coils and power transformers. I wanted to know how things worked. I asked endless questions, and Daddy would patiently continue to explain.

"In 1918 he was drafted into the Army and sent to France, not as an infantryman, but as a member of the Signal Corps. As a railroad telegrapher, his skills were at a premium. He worked behind the lines, helping to maintain the communications network for the Allies. After the war, he was discharged and took a short-term job with The United States Food Administration. As I write this, a framed and yellowing certificate hangs on our kitchen wall, which says,

"To John H. Son: This is to certify that you have served as a Member of the United States Food Administration, engaged from December, 1918 to August 1919 in the American relief of the liberated peoples of Central and Eastern Europe.

Your work has been done voluntarily and unselfishly, without thought of personal reward. You have well served your own country in its humane task of mitigating the misery, starvation and economic distress consequent to the Great War."

The certificate is signed in original pen and ink by:

Herbert Hoover
United States Food Administration
Director General of Relief

"And, of course, everybody knows who Herbert Hoover was. Don't they?

Daddy had lots of stories to tell about his time in France. He told us about the long boat ride from New York to Brest aboard the George Washington, about getting seasick for the first but certainly not the last time in his life. It was an ongoing problem for him. He told us about how the ship traveled in convoy to minimize vulnerability to German U-boats. Fortunately, he was not in the infantry and didn't have to endure the horrors of trench warfare, but he was close enough to it to be able to describe much of it. He brought home lots of souvenirs and pictures. He told us about the French countryside and Paris, the Eiffel Tower and the French people. He learned to speak a little French, enough to get by with shopkeepers and restaurateurs.

"Soon after they were married and moved into their little house and farm, Daddy bought a new car! It was a Model T Ford coupe. Of course, it was black. As Henry Ford said, when someone questioned him about color(s) for his mass-produced product, "They can have any color they want, as long as it is black!"

"They also bought a couple of milk cows and some chickens. Rhode Island Reds and Plymouth Rocks were my mother's favorite breeds. They set in to transform their little 32-acre spot into a garden place. They prepared the soil for two plots. One fairly large one was for potatoes and corn. Another smaller one was reserved for tomatoes, green beans, carrots, lettuce, onions, radishes, rhubarb and strawberries. If a plant variety could be had, whether seed or sapling, Mama would order them from Stark Nurseries and try them out. They planted fruit trees in the side yard next to the house - cherry, peach, apple and pear, all ordered from Stark. Within a couple of years, the trees began to bear fruit. The amounts were small at first, but increased steadily each season.

"As their labors began to pay off and the harvest was brought in, my mother, in order to preserve all of this bounty, referenced the Sears-Roebuck Catalogue, probably the second most important book in our house, the Bible being first and Compton's Encyclopedia being third. Most things we needed were ordered by mail. She ordered Ball and Mason glass jars by the score. Everything was canned. Nothing was to be wasted. In the hot, mid-western

heat of May through July she would labor. I can still see her, working in the kitchen, packing cherries, pears or peaches into the jars, adding sugar or spices, then screwing the lids on tightly. After placing the jars in wire racks, she would lower them into large, flat-bottomed pans, cover them with water and bring to a boil. It was hard to tell which was hotter, the canning kettles or my mother as she sweated profusely in the summer heat and humidity. Air Conditioning was a long way away.

"As they could afford to pay for them, more milk cows were added to their modest herd. As milk production increased, they started bottling it and selling it to our neighbors. It was real, whole milk, not homogenized and unpasteurized. Real cream rose to the top of real glass bottles. They sold it for ten cents per quart and made a few pennies on each bottle. Later, they added a cream separator. It had a big, gleaming, metal bowl on top, into which the raw milk was poured. A large hand crank, hooked to a series of gears, drove a centrifuge, which was the heart of the machine. By turning the crank, which was difficult at first, because of the gearing, the centrifuge could be spun at a very high rpm. When it reached the proper speed, Mama or Daddy would turn a valve, releasing the raw milk into the centrifuge. Then, as if by magic, the separated milk would start to flow from two spouts - the top one gave cream, and the bottom, skim milk. Now, they could sell the rich cream for twenty-five cents per half-pint, or they could churn it into butter. The skim milk was made into cottage cheese or it could be used to feed the chickens.

"Daddy had the cows tested for tuberculosis, and Mama was a fanatic about sanitation. Used bottles were subjected to a rigorous scrubbing with soap and bottlebrushes, then rinsed in boiling hot water. After every use, the separator was taken apart, piece-by-piece, and subjected to the same treatment. They didn't come up to today's sanitation standards. But the risk of contamination was probably quite low. Not only did we sell the product to our neighbors, we consumed it ourselves without ill effects. We also delivered them. Thereby hangs another tale. There will be more about that later."

CHAPTER II
The War Continues

Ray Schilleriff's voice penetrated Son's reverie. Son and the three other flight commanders in the squadron had just been promoted - temporary combat promotions to Captain. Big deal, they thought. It was about time.

It was time to brief his flight for another mission. This time, again, it was close air support, attacking targets under the control of a Forward Air Controller and an airborne spotter aircraft, nicknamed "mosquito." It looked pretty routine, except for the weather. It was not as bad as it was on August 20th.   Ceilings at Itazuke were forecast to remain at 5,000 feet or more for the period of the mission. Still, it was bad enough to require major

Major Raymond Schilleriff

portions of the mission to be flown in the clouds. Again, Son went over the techniques of formation weather flying, including procedures to be followed if visual contact with the lead aircraft (Son) was to be lost.

"If you lose me in the clouds, don't panic. Quickly get on your own instruments and establish that you are in level flight. Turn left or right 30 degrees, depending on what side you are on, to diverge from our on-course heading. Hold that heading for 45 seconds. Turn to parallel our on-course heading and proceed normally. There's a good chance that you will be able to re-establish visual contact. If you cannot regain visual contact, abort and return to base on your own."

Son was a little concerned about one member of his flight on this mission - 2nd Lt. Leon Pollard, a brand new pilot, fresh out of flight school for less than one year. He had little or no weather flying experience. He was "checked out" in the aircraft, and therefore considered "combat ready." He put Leon on his left wing and told him to hang close. Son hoped there would be no need for Pollard to "go it on his own."

The outbound portion of the mission went as planned. They climbed up through the overcast, broke out on top of the clouds, flew to the Pusan VOR navigational fix, descended through the overcast again and broke out in the vicinity of the target area. A call to "Volleyball", the mosquito aircraft in the area, yielded target location and instructions for an attack.

"Volleyball to Contour Roger, yes, I have a target for you - vehicles, including trucks and possibly a tank, camouflaged in wooded area. Do you have me in sight, Contour?"

"Roger, Volleyball. I have you."

"I'll mark the target with smoke rockets."

Leon "Billy" Pollard

The mosquito marked the target, after which Contour Roger flight positioned itself to attack, this time with napalm, a jellied gasoline firebomb that was probably the most effective weapon in the Air Force arsenal. Three minutes later, the target area was a blazing inferno, marked with several secondary explosions. If there were any enemy forces or equipment hidden in those trees, they could not have survived.

"Contour...wow! You got 'em for sure!" Good shootin'. Volleyball here, thanks a lot!"

"Any time, Volleyball. We aim to please! We'll see you next trip."

Son formed up his flight and set course for home. "So far, So good."

After a brief period on top of the overcast and leaving the Pusan VOR southbound Son began his descent, soon to take his flight back into the clouds. He wasn't worried about breaking a 5,000 foot ceiling at Itazuke. That would be a piece of cake. Then, suddenly:

"Contour Lead . . .I've lost you!" It was Pollard, panic in his voice. Son could hear him hyperventilating, gripping the microphone button on his throttle. Seized with fear, he was blocking Son's attempts to calm him.

"Leon...take it easy. Get on your instruments." As soon as Son finished his transmission and released his microphone button, the air was again filled with Pollard's frenzied breathing. As soon as the air cleared, Son tried again to contact him. There was no answer.

Within a matter of a minute or less, it was all over. . .no more sounds, no more breathing. 2nd Lieutenant Leon W. Pollard would join the ranks of the "missing in action" in this war. What happened? He was a victim of vertigo, the overpowering feeling of confusion and disorientation coupled with an inability to trust and use his own flight instruments. This would lead his aircraft to enter into an out of control spiral, ultimately crashing into the sea.

Son was numbed. Could he have done anything to have prevented this loss? Probably not. Was Pollard ready to fly combat? Under normal standards he wasn't. Under the "standard" that prevailed in this war he was considered ready. Anyone who could fly the airplane was "ready."

Yeah.

How do pilots who are flying combat deal with death, with the possibility or probability that they will meet a sudden and violent death? Paradoxically, they accept it and they deny it. How does that work, you ask? They accept the fact of death in combat for they see it happening all around them. How could they deny it? Easy. Most pilots, Son included, believe in their own immortality when they are in combat. They all firmly believe that it will happen to "the other guy" but not to them. Psychologists call it denial, and for most pilots, it works. It's a shield erected to protect them from a storm that would otherwise blow them away and render them incapable of doing their job. Does that mean that they believe in guardian angels? Maybe so. Maybe so.

Over the next couple of weeks, Son and his flight mates continued with a heavy schedule of missions, still flying the F-80 Shooting Star. During the first six weeks of the war,

Son logged 69 missions in the F-80. Notwithstanding, the war on the ground was not going very well. American and ROK troops fought valiantly, but they were forced inexorably back. Eventually, the battle line stabilized along the east bank of the Naktong-gang River on the west and along the mountains north of the city of Taegu along a line extending east to the port city of Pohang. Within this small perimeter, in the Southeast corner of the Korean peninsula, the U.S. and South Korea made its stand. We had to hold here or be swept into the sea. The outline of this perimeter was clear to see from the air. Within its confines there was a beehive of activity. Everywhere there were troops, vehicles, tanks, artillery pieces and what turned out to be one of the world's busiest airfields located at Taegu, and known as K-2. Scraped out of the bare earth and overlaid with pierced steel planking, (PSP) the runway at K-2 was rough and uneven. A takeoff run or a landing rollout was like riding a roller coaster. Pilots, somewhat cynically, called it "Rollicking Runway." The dirt under the PSP and the taxiways was not stabilized. Combining that with airplanes constantly taking off, landing and taxiing yielded an atmosphere that was beyond choking. The dust got into everything, human and mechanical. It was a hard environment for both men and machines.

Flying west or north beyond the confines of this postage stamp small enclave with all its activity led one over land that at first glance looked to be completely uninhabited. There appeared to be no activity because during daylight hours, the NKA pulled in their horns and did everything possible to camouflage their positions. At night, however, they moved in supplies and did their fighting - probing our lines. Firefights erupted all along the front. Artillery duels were constant, lighting up the night sky, the flashes reflecting strobe-like off overhanging clouds. The air rolled and reverberated to their thunder. The NKA made repeated attempts to establish beachheads on the east bank of the Naktong, but all were thrown back.

During daylight hours, it was time for American airpower to do its thing. Constant attacks were launched against the enemy's dug in positions using our full arsenal - strafing, rockets, bombs and napalm. These attacks were very effective, not only in creating casualties but in keeping the enemy off balance. However, the U.S. Army wanted more. Ideally, they would have liked to have fighters orbiting overhead constantly during the hours of daylight. With jet aircraft flying out of Japan, time over target was quite limited which meant that there were gaps in our coverage. The answer, some said, was to go back to the old WWII prop driven fighters such as the P-51 Mustang. So in late August, there occurred what Son considered to be a retrograde move. His squadron was about to go back to flying P-51s.

Ah, but where to get them? There were precious few Mustangs in the theater. Most of the P-51 inventory was in the ZI (zone of interior), assigned to national guard units. It was decided to ship these aircraft to Japan. They were flown to California ports and hoisted aboard U.S. aircraft carriers such as the USS Boxer. Lashed to the deck and exposed to sea and salt water during the trip, they were off loaded in Yokahama. From there, they were ferried to Itazuke. There were enough aircraft to equip two squadrons. It was decided to create a new Wing, with the 35th and 36th squadrons re-converting from F-80s back to P-51s. On August 11, 1950, the new wing was relocated from Itazuke to Tsuiki, a old, abandoned Japanese airfield on the east coast of Kyushu. A new wing commander, Colonel Charles F. Stark, was assigned to the wing. He was noisy and vociferous. He insisted on leading his wing from the cockpit, which was all very commendable except for the fact, that will become apparent, his flying style was erratic and unpredictable. He soon earned the nickname of "Ravin' Mad" Stark.

The move to Tsuiki meant going from an established base to field conditions. A tent city sprouted and for the rest of Son's time with the squadron, he would live in a tent, eat

his meals from a mess kit, use an outdoor latrine and sleep on a cot. Separated from his family and his apartment at Kasuga, no longer did he have the comforts of home.

Most of the pilots in the two squadrons had flown the Mustang before, so checking out in the aircraft presented no particular problem. However, the condition of the aircraft was another matter. They were loaded with salt and corrosion. The guns were in terrible shape. Most would not fire reliably and were subject to constant jams. Nor were the guns "harmonized," meaning that they had not been adjusted to fire where the gunsight used by the pilot to aim the guns said they should point. This threw an additional workload on our already overworked maintenance personnel. They did the job without complaining, well, almost without complaining.

As soon as the move to Tsuiki had been completed both squadrons resumed flying missions again. This time our efforts were concentrated almost entirely on close air support of our ground forces defending the Pusan Perimeter. We flew a lot of "first light" missions. Because the NKA would "hole up" during the day, ceasing all supply movements and hiding their vehicles, we tried to catch them at "first light," just as the sky was starting to get gray. This meant taking off from Tsuiki at around 4 o-clock in the morning in order to arrive over the target area at first light. Takeoffs were of course made into a sky and ocean that was pitch black. There was no visible horizon. Although we were not in the clouds, we may as well have been. There was no visible horizon so everything was done on instruments. This placed a premium on good formation flying.

After finding and hitting a target on a first light mission, flights would not return to Japan. Rather, they would land at K-2 (Taegu) on "rollicking runway." Taxiing to the end, they would join a queue to await refueling and rearming. They would then be placed on "strip alert," ready to be launched to attack another target. Since the "bomb line" (a line demarking the front line, beyond which everything was considered enemy and therefore free game) was only a few miles away, a flight could take off, be assigned a target, attack it and return again to K-2 within 15 to 20 minutes. On one particularly active day, Son and his flight flew six missions. Except for the "first light" from Japan and the last flight back to Japan, flown after dark, no mission was longer than 20 minutes. The weather was stifling hot and the dust was choking. Pilots sitting in the queue would snap on their oxygen masks and set their regulators to 100% oxygen to escape the dust, but they couldn't escape the heat. If you were unlucky, after such a day of this, your flight got tagged to stay overnight at K-2, to be placed on strip alert for immediate takeoff the next morning. Having been so tagged, pilots might say, "Fine, let's go to the BOQ (bachelor officers' quarters), have a drink and go to dinner." Ha!!! There was no BOQ, no officers' mess, etc. Accommodations were limited to canvas cots on the flight line. Here, pilots were treated to an all-night fire-fight only miles away, just across the river. Battle casualties were brought in on stretchers to await airlift to Japan and rear area hospitals. The groans and cries of the wounded combined with the sound of cannonading to make sleep all but impossible. It served to impress on us, however, that if we had to fight a war, the way we were fighting it in the air was much to be preferred to what the GIs at the front had to endure.

A word must be said here about the 618th AC&W Squadron (Aircraft Control and Warning) and the radar site that the squadron manned on Chedu-do Island. Located halfway between Japan and the southern tip of the Korean peninsula, they were able to maintain surveillance of all air traffic between Japan and Korea. A take-off from K-2 at last light in the evening meant a flight over the ocean after dark. The 618th, call sign Camel Control, was always there to give pilots a "steer" back to base. It was a comforting feeling.

By late August, early September replacement pilots from the ZI were beginning to arrive. Son was glad to receive one of these new pilots. First Lieutenant Patteson Gilliam was a "Pointer", a graduate of the U.S. Military Academy. "Pat", as he was called, was an exceptional young man. He was a friendly, likeable guy and every inch a professional of-

Patteson Gilliam

ficer. In addition, Son soon found that he was a good pilot and an officer with unlimited potential. He fit right in to "A" flight and started flying missions on a regular basis.

It was on one of those Tsuiki-Taegu rearm/refuel missions that Pat was lost. Son's flight was attacking a truck convoy about 25 miles north of Taegu. As individual members of the flight pulled up after their first pass at the target, Pat called to say that he was hit.

"Contour Lead - Contour Four, here - I'm hit."

"O.K., Contour - - head south. Form up and let's get back across the bomb line."

By now, Pat was losing speed and altitude. It was obvious that he had lost power.

"My prop's running away. I can't control it."

This meant that he had taken a hit in his prop governor assembly, causing his propeller to go into flat pitch, like a car put into neutral, lots of rpm but producing no thrust. The flight was in enemy territory, approximately ten miles north of the bomb line. It became quickly evident that Pat would not be able to make it back to friendly territory before running out of altitude. Son pulled up on Pat's right wing.

"Pat, get out. Get out now. Get rid of your canopy."

They were no more than two thousand feet above the ground.

Again, Son said, "Pat! Get out!"

As Son said this, he observed Pat's canopy fly off. He saw Pat stand up in the cockpit as his plane began to nose over into a dive. Son was still yelling for him to get out when Pat's airplane hit the ground. It exploded in a greasy, orange and black fireball.

As with all of those lost in this war, those who will remain forever young in our hearts, one wonders how Pat's life would have unfolded. We shall never know.

CHAPTER 12
End Run

The stalemate in the Pusan perimeter was beginning to wear thin on most of those participating in it. How long, everyone wondered, will this go on?

Suddenly, on 15 September, American forces pulled an end run with an amphibious assault at Inchon Harbor, just west of Seoul. It was a complete surprise, catching the North Koreans off guard. The thrust would quickly cut off NKA supply lines to the south. NKA pressure at the Pusan Perimeter melted like snow under a hot shower. American troops burst out of the perimeter and dashed north to join up with elements of the amphibious operation at Inchon. Now the NKA in the south was completely cut off. Within days, the NKA had retreated all the way north past Seoul, now again occupied by the Americans.

Shortly after Inchon and the run to the North, the wing moved from Tsuiki to a base in Korea known as K-13, located at Suwon, approximately 50 miles south of Seoul. No longer did we have to endure that long flight across and back across the Sea of Japan. Nor did we have to land or take off on a PSP (pierced steel planking) runway that made our airplanes behave like bucking broncos. We also had range, now, to penetrate deep into North Korea, interdicting lines of communication and transportation. We still attacked troops and did close air support, but the character of our operations changed significantly. Life in the squadron was still in field conditions. But as we prepared for cold weather, our tent city took on a degree of permanence. 8-man squad tents were insulated and "tricked out" until they were almost like a small bungalow. Tarpaper and insulation was added to the sidewalls of the tents. Wooden floors were constructed from the lumber scrounged from 5-inch rocket boxes. These boxes were made to order. Originally used to ship and store 5-inch HVAR rockets, each box was made of oak and measured approximately 6 by 6 inches and was about 8 feet in length. They were perfect for flooring. An oil-burning stove was added to provide heat. A pot of acidic black coffee simmered on the stove until it tasted like paint remover and, viola`! - - we had all the comforts of home.

Colonel Stark (Ravin' Mad), our peripatetic wing commander, continued his some- what overactive leadership of the wing. He would write himself in on the schedule, always as the flight leader, and fly missions regularly. The other members of the flight were always on guard, never quite knowing what to expect from Ravin' Mad. One day, returning from a mission, Stark brought his flight into the landing pattern at Suwon. He was cleared to land as he turned on base leg. Pulling his airplane into a tight turn onto final approach, he squeezed the stick. However he had neglected to turn off his gun switches and to remove his finger from the firing trigger on the stick, so that as he turned on final, his guns erupted, spraying .50 caliber slugs up and down the runway and ramp. Bullets zinged but somehow missed hitting anything. Yes, our Ravin' Mad commander had done it again!

After Inchon, the battle lines surged northward. Seoul, the capital city of South Korea, changed hands again. By now, it had sustained major battle damage. Most of the buildings in downtown Seoul had either been destroyed or had sustained major battle damage. Most South Korean civilians who lived in the city had fled. Those that remained took shelter anywhere they could find it. In October outside temperatures were dropping. Little children covered with sores, many with no shoes, some clothed only in flimsy shirts, roamed the streets, scrounging through the battle debris for food. This was the pitiful detritus of war.

5th Air Force moved its operations management activities to the Seoul University campus, one of the few areas of the city that had not sustained major damage.

CHAPTER 13
Reassignment

Herman is awarded the DFC by Brig. Gen. Edward F. Timberlake

Soon after the wing arrived at K-13 (Suwon), Son was reaching the end of a normal combat tour of 100 missions. After his 107th mission on September 30th he was reassigned to the Combat Operations Center at 5th Air Force Headquarters for duty as an operations duty officer. The COC was the nerve center for all air operations. He moved from K-13 to K-14, Kimpo airport, just west of Seoul. Again, it was tent city. Winter was fast approaching. The tents weren't winterized. Above all, Son remembers the cold. His feet were cold, all the time. When bedtime arrived, he would prepare for the cold night ahead, where temperatures would drop to 10 to 20 degrees below zero. He would start with thermal underwear. On top of that would go a winter flight suit, then a winter flight jacket. Wool socks and boots remained on. A towel would be wrapped around his head. Then he would slip into his down filled sleeping bag. With all this, he still felt cold. There seemed to be no escaping it. However, when he started to feel sorry for himself, he thought about the GIs fighting at places like Pork Chop Hill and Hungnam. Compared to them, Son felt warm as toast.

Son's job as Operations Duty Officer at the COC was routine, basically a clerical operation keeping track of air operations and issuing "frag" orders to squadrons in the field. His flying switched from the P-51 Mustang to a C-47 transport aircraft. There were four of these attached to the support wing at Kimpo, and since Son had extensive C-47 experience going back several years, he was afforded the opportunity to fly as aircraft commander. He flew occasional supply and support missions back to Japan, ferrying personnel and supplies. Sometimes referred to as "beer runs," these flights gave Son an opportunity to spend the night with his family, still located at Kasuga.

He also flew combat missions to the north, supplying advance Air Force elements working with the Army in communications and forward air control activities. He remembers a couple of these flights which involved carrying heavy loads into short, primitive fields close to the Yalu River demarking the boundary between North Korea and Manchuria. Takeoffs and landings under these conditions were scary. Everything had to be "just right" and on the hairy edge of maximum performance for the aircraft. Short field landings

into a 2,500 ft dirt runway meant "hanging it on the props" with full flaps and approach speeds that were just above stalling (75-80 KIAS). Aiming for the extreme short end of the runway, throttles would be chopped, the airplane would land in a three-point attitude and maximum brakes would be applied. The airplane could usually be stopped in around 2,000 feet. Takeoffs were equally hairy. Flaps would be up until airspeed reached about 70 KIAS, then extended to "Full", thus popping the airplane off the ground. These procedures worked as long as the airplane continued to perform optimally. Any loss of power would have been disastrous.

By now, Son was beginning to think of going home, all the way home, back to America and the land that he loved. He was basically marking time until ZI reassignment orders would come through. Where would he go? He hoped that it would be a fighter assignment, something that would make use of his combat experience. All he could do was wait ...December, January, February.

At last, his orders arrived. He was to be assigned to Headquarters, Tactical Air Command, based at Langley Air Force Base in Virginia. "Wow! This should be a good assignment," Son thought. He took advantage of another C-47 flight back to Japan. At home that night, he broke the news to Arretta.

"Guess what, Honey! We're going home. Next month! We're being reassigned to Langley Air Force Base in Virginia. Isn't that great!?"

Son thought that Arretta would be overjoyed. She smiled weakly, but her response was less than enthusiastic.

"What's the matter? Aren't you happy? We'll love it at Langley. It'll be a fat assignment for me. I'll be working in the Operations Directorate of a major Air Force Combat Command. That'll be fast track for me and an opportunity for rapid promotion. Langley is a beautiful base and it's in a beautiful part of he country. What's not to like about that?"

"I was hoping we could get an assignment in Arizona, maybe Phoenix, somewhere close to my folks. You know how frail Daddy is,." Said Arretta in a pouting voice.

"I don't know. The only place I could think of would be Luke Air Force Base. I think that The Air Training Command has a wing there. I don't know exactly what they do. But that wouldn't be a very good assignment for me."

"Couldn't you ask the Air Force for a compassionate reassignment, based on my father's illness?"

"Dunno if the Air Force would do that."

Son was crestfallen. Why couldn't Arretta see how important this next assignment, coming directly from a combat unit in Korea could be to his career? "Arretta's father? He was in his seventies and a lifelong smoker - smoked camels right down to the butt. He had severe emphysema. But what could Arretta do if she were there? Not much in Son's opinion. Arretta had used this ploy before, anytime they were stationed away from Phoenix. Son wondered what the attraction was. He hoped that they could come to some sort of understanding before they left for the ZI. He was afraid that it would spell trouble on the domestic front if the assignment to Langley remained firm.

CHAPTER 14
Time to Pack It In

The last week in February Son's assignment in Korea was terminated and he returned to Japan. During the six months that he was flying combat, he had logged 107 missions and had been awarded the Distinguished Flying Cross, the Air Medal with 8 Oak Leaf Clusters and the U.S. and Korean Presidential Unit Citations.

It was time to start packing up for the return to America. He sold his Oldsmobile to a Staff Sergeant at Kasuga. The Noritake china, the cloisonné lamps, the rattan living room furniture and other artifacts they had accumulated were all carefully packed and crated for shipment. Son, his wife, Arretta, and their daughter Mary-Lynn, by now nearly four years old, boarded a C-47 at Itazuke for the flight to Haneda Air Base near Tokyo. The next morning they boarded a Pan American DC-6 for the long flight across the Pacific. The first leg took them to the Island of Guam for a brief refueling stop. Then it was off to Hickham Air Force Base in Hawaii. They were there for about 3 hours, long enough to get off the airplane, walk around the terminal and have something to eat.

The final leg, over 2,000 miles, took them to SanFrancisco, the Golden Gate and Fairfield AFB. Looking down as they approached San Francisco, they could see The Golden Gate Bridge, crossing the strait that was the mouth to San Francisco Bay and the harbor. Tears welled up in Son's eyes as he thought about the last time he had seen that bridge. It was more than three years ago, when he had boarded a U.S. Army troop transport, The General Blatchford, for the 14 day trip across a storm tossed Pacific to Yokahama. What an unbelievable three years it had been. What a "Wizard of Oz", down the yellow brick road kind of journey his life had taken to this point.

CHAPTER 15
The Past is Prologue

Son, his wife and daughter checked in to the VOQ (Visiting Officers' Quarters) for an overnight stay awaiting a commercial flight out the next day for Phoenix, Arretta's hometown. Son had a built-in leave in the form of a 14-day delay enroute to Langley AFB. They were tired from the long trip across the Pacific and the 8-hour time change. They were able to order dinner sent to their room that evening, which pleased Arretta. She suffered from anxiety attacks whenever she had to go out in public. The technical name for it was agoraphobia, an unreasoned fear of going out in public. Son hoped that she would be able to get some effective professional help for her problem once they were settled in their new assignment, wherever it was. He had promised Arretta that he would look into the possibility of a compassionate reassignment once they got to Phoenix. Maybe that would help, although he didn't hold out much hope that the Air Force would look kindly on his request. He would give it his best shot but secretly he hoped that they wouldn't.

After dinner, they talked for awhile, put Mary-Lynn to bed and then went to bed themselves. Son thought about their stay in Japan, drifted into and out of sleep a couple of times, then he went to another place.

CHAPTER 16
Learning To Drive

"Herman Franklin, do you want to go with me to deliver the milk tonight?"

There was only one answer to that question. A vigorous, affirmative nod of the head said that of course he wanted to go. Herman Franklin hoped that soon, his father might let him drive the car.

After the fresh milk and cream had been bottled, it was placed in wire racks for easy carrying and then loaded aboard our bottle green, practically new, Model "A" Ford for door to door delivery. The Sons began this service in 1930. Son was eight years old.

The Angel read his thoughts:

Cousin Vernie Wilson, Herman, Cousin Henry Holliday, Sister June, and Cousin Rosemary Cartwright.

" I had already been behind the wheel, sitting in Daddy's lap, and learned how to steer the car. I was intensely interested, and for sometime had been watching Daddy's every move. After he had started the car, backed it out of the garage and put the milk in the car, we backed out of a long alley out to the street. Then, headed down the street, Daddy would depress the clutch pedal, shift into low gear, apply some throttle then smoothly let out the clutch. Away we would go down the street. As our speed increased, he would depress the clutch again, simultaneously letting up on the throttle and, while holding the clutch in, shift into second gear, again coordinating increased throttle with clutch engagement. Shifting into high gear would be a repeat of the process. I watched all of this repeatedly until it was burned into my brain. Then, after finishing our route and parking the car in the garage, Daddy would go in the house, but I would stay, sliding behind the wheel. Then I would practice. Clutch in, shift into low, apply throttle and let out clutch. "Brrrrm!" Depress clutch and let up on throttle. Shift into second, apply throttle and let out clutch. "Brrrm!" Now into high gear. Steer . . left , right, back and forth. "Brrrm, Brrrrm,!" I knew I could drive!"

This evening, as we were driving along a straight street, and I had been sitting on Daddy's lap, I said, "Daddy, I can drive! I know I can. Please! Can I drive?" Daddy stopped the car.

"O.K., Herman Franklin, (That's what my parents always called me) lets try it."

I was so excited and scared at the same time, that I nearly wet my pants. Daddy got out of the car and left me behind the wheel. The car was in neutral, and the street was perfectly level, so there was no need to apply the brake.

Daddy said, "O.K., we've got three more houses down this street. I want you to put it into low gear, then let out the clutch very slowly. Just let it idle slowly down the street in low gear. Keep it straight down the road, now. I'll run ahead with two quarts, one for Millers, the other for Hutchinson's. Then I'll meet you before we get to Schwerangan's in case you need help in getting stopped. Now, go ahead. . . push in the clutch. . .put it in low. . ."

Daddy didn't have to tell me. I knew what to do. I put it into low and let out the clutch, ever so s-l-o-w-l-y. The car began to move! My heart was pounding. I was really driving!!! Daddy took two quarts of milk and walked ahead, leaving me with that wonderful car. I was doing it!. . .all by myself!!

Daddy left the second quart on Hutchinson's front porch and came out to meet me. He opened the door on the driver's side and, walking along beside the car, said,

"Mama! Guess what?"

"Now, do you know what to do to stop the car?"

"Push in on the clutch and the brake at the same time and put the gearshift in neutral."

That's right. You know how to do it. Stop when we get to the next house."

That night, when we had finished the route and came home, I ran into the house and exclaimed, "Mama! Mama! Guess what?! I drove the car tonight, all by myself!"

"You what!?"

"Yes!" I drove the car!" Daddy came in behind me, smiling that sheepish little grin he used when he was proud of me.

"But he's so little! He can hardly see over the steering wheel." Mama wiped her hands on her apron and looked concerned.

"Don't worry, Grace. He did fine. He only drove about a block, and there weren't any other cars around. It's good for him to learn."

Well, don't you ever let him drive without you, Mama said, a hint of a smile flickering across her face. When I went to bed that night, I was so excited I could hardly go to sleep.

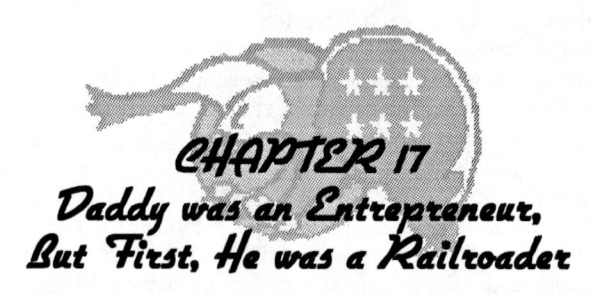

CHAPTER 17
Daddy was an Entrepreneur, But First, He was a Railroader

Daddy loved The Railroad, pure and simple. I am sure that he held a feeling inside of him that was very close to the feeling that I have for flying. Why else would he stick to it for fifty-five years, through thick and thin, until he retired in 1963 at the age of 75? He never said that much about how he felt about it, but he did have lots of stories about what happened to "Ole Number 11." Today she got a hot box (wheel bearing trouble) and had to pull into the siding at Centertown. There was only a single track from St. Louis to Kansas City, with side-tracks, located periodically along the main track. It was necessary, under this system, for a central dispatcher to keep track of every train's location, direction and schedule. As eastbound trains approached westbound trains, one train would have to be pulled into a siding track to wait for the other train to pass.

Daddy told about talking to the Engineer on Number 11. He handled the big, throbbing beast of a steam locomotive. Daddy explained how he got up in the cab and saw the Fireman shovel coal into the red-hot inferno of the engine's firebox. I felt goose bumps on my arms as Daddy talked about it. Then he told about talking to the blue serge suited Conductor with his little pillbox cap adorned with its Missouri Pacific red and gold insignia above the bill. He was boss of the train, and, my, how he clucked and fretted about the mechanical delay! Daddy also talked to the porters, and the white hatted chefs in the dining car area, looking as though their pictures should be on the front of a box of Cream of Wheat! He talked to the crew that manned the mail car. He even talked with some of the passengers. It was romantic, almost as if an alien space ship had landed in Centertown! There were people on that train, Daddy said, that lived in big cities, like St. Louis, Chicago, or even faraway places like New York and San Francisco!

When the Conductor said that the hot box had been repaired, Daddy called the Dispatcher in Jefferson City, for orders to the train that Daddy took down in writing. After reading them back verbatim to the Dispatcher he delivered to the Conductor. The Conductor pulled his gold, 21-jewel pocket watch, attached to a gold chain that ran across his vest, from its vest pocket-hiding place and checked the time. He looked first to the front,

then to the rear of the train. He slipped his watch back into his vest pocket. He mounted the steps of one of the passenger cars. Then, leaning out so he could be seen, he waved a signal to the Engineer and the Brakeman that meant, let's go! He bawled, in a voice that was uniquely railroad, "Alllllllaboooooard!" The big, black beast that was the locomotive, gave a couple of short toots on its whistle acknowledging the Conductor's signal. The Engineer then slowly cracked the throttle. Super heated, high-pressure steam from the boiler began to move into the big pistons on either side of the engine. They began to push the huge driver rods that were attached to each of the immense, driver wheels. Slowly, slowly they began to turn, moving the dead weight of the locomotive itself plus pulling the fifteen or so passenger cars that were coupled behind it. For several seconds, it seemed like longer, the only sound was a harsh creaking, grating and scraping noise as the wheels began to move all of that dead weight over the steel rails. It was as if the big engine, like a champion weight lifter, was attempting to do a snatch and press of 800 pounds of bar bells. Holding its breath and trembling under the extreme exertion, it pulled and pulled. As the weight of the train began to move, little hisses of steam erupted from around the pistons attached to the driving wheels. Finally, as the pistons drove to full extension, the beast emitted an other worldly, "Whooouhff!," as hot steam mixed with coal smoke was blown out the smoke stack. It was as though a weightlifter exhaled all the breath he had been holding in one tremendous snort. As the wheels began to turn faster and faster, the beast's breath picked up speed accordingly, gradually changing to a rhythmic, "chuffa-chuff, chuffa-chuff" and laying down a dense cloud of steam laden coal smoke, as the train disappeared around the curve at the east end of town.

How could Daddy not be in love with such a romantic business?

One day, when I was about five, I was spending some time with Daddy at the depot. An eastbound freight train, carrying a load of cattle destined for the Stock Yards in St. Louis, pulled into the siding at Centertown. The freight was waiting for a westbound passenger train, which had priority. Daddy picked me up with one arm, and started walking down the right-of-way toward the locomotive that was at the head of the freight train. The cows in the cattle cars, as we passed by them on the way toward the front of the train, were bawling and thrashing around. It smelled like a barnyard. After a short trip to St. Louis, they would all be turned into hamburger.

As we approached the engine, Daddy said, "Let's ask the engineer if we can climb up into the cab and take a look!" "What!? I thought. That's scary!" But I trusted Daddy, so I didn't say anything.

Up we went. Daddy easily climbed the long steel ladder extending down the side of the engine. We arrived at the level of the cab, which seemed like a long way from the ground to me. We clambered on to the steel floor of the cab, and Daddy put me down. I could feel the tremendous heat of the firebox. Daddy introduced me to the Engineer and the Fireman, who were dressed alike, wearing blue denim shirts and blue and white stripe Oshkosh overalls. Their outfits were topped off with matching, high-crowned, billed caps. The fireman, however, was wearing a huge, red bandana handkerchief around his neck, and his face was blackened, as though he was ready to play a role in black-face vaudeville! Daddy told me later that that was because of the black dust that came from the coal that he shoveled into the red hot maw of the firebox. The Fireman asked me if I would like to see into the firebox. I shook my head, first up and down, then from side to side! I wanted to see it, but I was scared! The Fireman reassured me.

"Here" he said. "This is how I do it."

He scooped a big shovel full of coal from the coal tender, right behind the cab. Holding the shovel low, he wheeled smoothly toward the firebox, and pressed a pedal on the floor. The big, clam shell doors of the firebox opened, letting out a tremendous blast of heat. I

ventured a sideways look. It looked like what I would later imagine the inside of a volcano would look like. I turned to Daddy and asked him to pick me up. I was thrilled and terrified at the same time. We stayed another minute, Daddy talking to both men while holding me on his shoulder. He thanked them. Then we climbed back down that long ladder to solid ground. Very excited by the experience, I wasn't to feel quite like that again until years later, when I soloed a J-3 yellow cub for the first time.

CHAPTER 18
The War That Changed Everything

Still in a dream, the vision of that canary yellow, J-3 Cub airplane put Son's memory into fast forward. In the Fall of 1941, he was just beginning his second year of college at Central Missouri State University in Warrensburg, Mo. He hadn't decided on a major field of study, but it was beginning to look as though it would be music and education. 12 years of private piano study under his mother's watchful eye had turned him into a modestly accomplished classical pianist. He enjoyed music, jazz as well as classical.

Roscoe and his lion's cub

But something was missing. He didn't have the recurring dream anymore, at least not in the same form as he experienced in early childhood. But he thought about flying while he was awake. A lot. He remembered how he felt that afternoon in 1927 when he saw The Spirit of St. Louis fly over the farm. He remembered trips to Jefferson City to see air shows that featured pilots like Wiley Post and Roscoe Turner.

On December 7th, 1941, an event occurred that was to change his life. In fact it was destined to change the lives of hundreds of thousands and millions of people all over the world. On a Sunday morning (Son found out about the Korean War on Sunday, too), a major air strike force of the Japanese Imperial Navy, with complete surprise, attacked the U.S. Seventh Fleet while it was berthed at Pearl Harbor in Hawaii. Hickham Army Air Field was also struck. As a result, American power in the Pacific was critically wounded.

USS Arizona after Japanese attack on December 7, 1941

The shock effect on the American public was total. As the enormity of the event began to sink in, consternation turned to anger. The next day President Franklin D. Roosevelt spoke to the Nation in an address to both houses of The Congress.

"Yesterday, December 7th, 1941, a day that shall live in infamy," our president began. He then proceeded to outline the details of the attack and the damage that had been done. He then

called for a declaration of war against "The Empire of Japan."

In reaction to the President's words, the amorphous anger that was felt at the beginning coalesced into an unshakable national resolve. We gave our unqualified support and commitment to our Commander in Chief, our President. We knew the war would be long and arduous. Just how arduous we were soon to find out, but there was no doubt in anyone's mind that we would triumph in the end.

College was not what he expected. In fact, it was a drag. His grades, except for piano and English Composition were barely passing. Chemistry? Right then he was barely holding on with a "D". Algebra II? Fuggetaboutit! There was nothing wrong that a little attention and motivation wouldn't have cured, but it just wasn't there. What motivated him was playing the pin-ball machine and talking to girls down at Riggles, a popular college student hangout. That afternoon, after FDR's speech, the campus was abuzzz with excited talk. So much of thoughts about dull chemistry and Algebra.

"I'm going to enlist! What about you?"

"Maybe. If I don't I'll probably be drafted anyway. They're going to be calling up millions of men."

"But if you enlist, you can choose your branch of service!"

"Yeah? Who sez?"

"A guy at the recruiting station."

"Well, I'll believe it. . ."

"You guys are all nuts. I'm going to volunteer for Aviation. I hear the Navy is looking for pilots," Son said.

The next several days, attendance at college classes and lectures was down. The recruiting offices in Kansas City were full of young men clamoring to enlist!

Skipping over a mass of detail, Son did enlist. He did get into a flying program, but it was not Naval Aviation, his first choice. Nor was it the U.S. Army Air Corps, his second choice. He applied for both programs, and was fully qualified, passing the mental and aptitude tests with flying colors. But color proved to be his undoing. The Navy and Army medical examiners both said, "Son, go home. You're color blind."

Son couldn't believe it. Color blind! How could they say that? He could tell colors all right. He knew what red was. He could point out green and blue and yellow and. . . .! Still, there it was. They had asked him to read a bunch of numbers that were described by colored dots on a page. The Ishahara color test, they called it! What was that? He had never seen anything like this before.

Crestfallen, Son went back to college and tried to collect his thoughts. He could see his lifelong dream fading into a bunch of colored dots. He knew he could fly. He would prove it if they gave him the chance! A week or so went by. Son's anger, about which he could do nothing, was beginning to depress him, when an angel appeared. The angel took the form of some comments by a college friend.

"I hear that the U.S. Army just announced a new program for college students," said the friend.

"What?"

"It's called The Enlisted Reserve Program with CPT." They let you stay in college while you train."

"What kind of training?"

"Flight training."

"Flight training?" Son's ears pricked up. Then he thought. No, he couldn't pass the physical. But just to make sure, he promised himself that he would check it out with a recruiter tomorrow.

CHAPTER 19
Glider Pilot Training – Is This a Joke?

"Yes," the recruiter said. "If you sign up now in the Army Enlisted Reserve, you can stay in college and receive basic flight training leading to a private pilot's license. Then, when you are called to active duty, probably in 6 - 9 months, you will go directly into the Army's Glider Pilot Program. Of course, you have to pass the physical."

Son's heart sank. "But," he thought to himself, "It'll give it one more try. I'll try anything, if it means I get the chance to fly!"

He walked through the tests with no problem until he heard the examiner ask, "How's your color vision?"

"O.K., I guess," Son fibbed, feeling anxious and a little guilty.

Imagine his surprise when the examiner hauled out a shoe-sized box that was full of small skeins of colored yarn! There were reds and blues and greens and yellows . . .the examiner asked him to separate the skeins in to four like colored piles. Son knew he could do that!

After getting his parent's written permission, he signed up in the Army Reserve-CPT program. Now he would get to fly, even if it were only a J-3 Cub and an Army Glider. About the latter, he didn't know much, but he figured he'd find out soon enough.

Flight training, under the auspices of the college, began in January, 1942. The dream, so long cherished and nurtured, had become reality. He soaked up everything his instructor, a young commercial pilot named Bill Bruton, told him. He even enjoyed ground school, although he now wished he had been a little more attentive when he was in college algebra! He hadn't realized that there was so much math involved in flying! He worked extra hard and eventually mastered it.

Finally, there came the day when he would solo. He has logged a total of 8 hours of dual instruction with Bill, and had passed all the basic skills, stalls, both power on and power off, spins, s-turns across a road, etc. Now he and Bill were sitting in the little yellow Cub at the take-off end of the field. Bill had gone over everything with him. Bill climbed out of the back seat and secured the safety belt. This was the moment.

"Go. You know what to do, Herman!"

Yes. He did know what to do. Pointing the airplane down the takeoff strip, he slowly opened the throttle. Before he knew it, the airplane took advantage of a slight bump in the field to launch itself into the air.

Herman's first plane, a J-3 Cub

He was flying. By himself! This was no dream. He felt just like he did that evening years ago when his father had let him drive the Model A Ford for the first time.

The landing was easy, uneventful. So was the rest of the 40 hours of training he would receive before getting his private pilot's license. Again, Son's memory went into fast forward.

CHAPTER 20
You're In The Army Now!

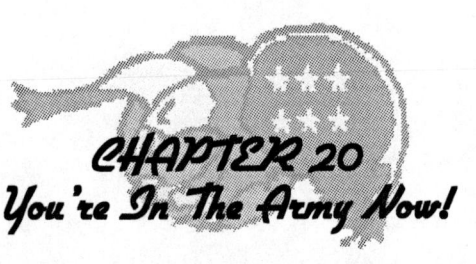

Back in 1942, A "troop train" didn't always carry troops. Sometimes it would carry green, young civilians on their way to their first military assignment. Such was the case that fall day in mid-September when Herman Franklin, the boy, left his parent's home to begin his first day of active duty in the United States Army. The train, which apparently began its westward journey in the eastern part of the country, was comprised entirely of day coaches. As it wended its way westward, additional coaches were added as needed. By the time it arrived in Warrensburg it was a long train indeed. Young men were hanging out of the windows, waving, yelling and singing. Mama and Daddy were there, of course. As the train pulled in it was time to say our goodbyes.

Mama's eyes were full, but she smiled and told me to, "take care of yourself."

" Of course, Mama. Don't worry about me." She gave me a hug.

We were not a demonstrative family. Daddy looked at me with that funny little cross-eyed look. His lips were tight, as if to keep back his emotions. He grasped my hand and shook it firmly.

"Good luck, Herman Franklin. Write."

"I will, Daddy. I will."

With that, I turned, placed my foot on the first step of the rail car, and grasping the handrail with one hand, and my small suitcase in the other, pulled myself up into the car.

As I reached the top step and opened the door to the car, I was cast precipitously from my warm, stable, predictable small town and small family environment into tumultuous and unpredictable culture shock. Who were these men/boys who spoke in such strange accents and behaved in such strange, out of the ordinary, even outlandish ways? One spoke as if he had hot marbles in his mouth.

"Eey, muthah fucker, whatcha name?"

"What?"

"Eey, man! I axed yo yo name!"

"Herman."

"Hummin? What kinda muthafuckin' name is dat?"

"Well, it's my name and it isn't what you said."

"Yeah?"

"Yeah!"

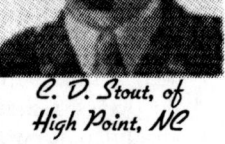

*C. D. Stout, of
High Point, NC*

Son walked away, down the aisle and stepping around a floating crap game that was holding forth in the middle of the aisle. He found out later the guy with marbles in his mouth was from The Bronx, dark, Italian, profane. There were others, strangers all . . . a big, blond Dutch fellow from Pennsylvania (His last name was Versteeg, Son would find out later) with an unfamiliar accent, and a wiry guy with sharp features who turned out to be from South Carolina. Friendly, he had a soft southern accent. He said his name was Cody - Cody Stout. His hometown, he said, was High Point, North Carolina. Son took an instant liking to Cody and the feeling was obviously reciprocated. There was an empty seat and Cody invited Son to sit down. They became instant friends.

Over the next 36 hours, the train lurched and jerked its way westward. Its final destination was that city in New Mexico with the unspellable name, Albuquerque. The train offloaded its human cargo at Kirtland Field southeast of town. As they got off the train, they were loaded onto a number of "Six-By" trucks, the standard issue two and one-half ton truck for the Army in WWII. Still not knowing exactly where they were going, they jounced and bounced their way from the railroad station to the base, and then out across the desert to a vast tent city. There were thousand of tents! Amid shouting and yelling from guys in uniform, these civilians soon to become soldiers were herded into tents, issued sheets and blankets and told to pick out a cot and make their bed. This, they were told would be their home until further notice.

There were real airplanes at Kirtland, AT-11 twin-engined Beechcraft advanced trainers that were used to train navigators and bombadiers. Son heard that one of the AT-11 pilots was a First Lieutenant named Jimmy Stewart. It was the real Jimmy Stewart allright. Later he commanded a B-24 Liberator Bomb Group in the 8th Air Force in England and retired with the rank of Major General.

After going to the mess hall for his first GI meal, ladled out onto a stainless steel tray, neatly divided into compartments for potato, vegetable, meat, bread and desert, Son ate heartily. After that long train trip, he was hungry indeed. The food wasn't fancy but it was good and there was plenty of it.

Marched back to their tents by a guy wearing two stripes on his sleeve, somebody said he was a corporal, they were all in bed by 9:00 PM. Here they were introduced to the 24-hour clock. It wasn't 9:00 P.M., it was 2100 hours! O.K., whatever it was, it meant lights out. The wind blew that night, as it did every night for the rest of Son's stay there. The next morning at 0500 hours he was awakened by the sound of the wind, sand on his bed and in his mouth and a bugle, blaring out reveille. Out of bed! Fall out in front of the tent. Get in formation! Roll call! Son could hear the AT-11s being warmed up in preparation for the day's flying. He wondered what it would be like to fly one of those airplanes.

"Smith." "Yo!"

"Sorenson." "Hup."

"Son." "Here."

"Stankowski." "Yo!"

"Stout." "Heah!"

So it went. After roll call, they marched in formation (Son was to find out that this was the only way they got from point A to point B.) to the mess hall for breakfast. Here he learned about a favorite Army entrée for breakfast known colloquially as "SOS" or S— on a Shingle. Actually, it wasn't bad . . creamed chipped beef on toast.

Next, they marched to the supply squadron to be issued their uniforms and equipment. Son got two pair of heavy GI brogan high top shoes, two heavy olive drab wool pants, two khaki summer pants, a winter blouse, shirts - both winter and summer, two

square tipped cotton ties, two "overseas" caps, a winter overcoat that must have weighed 40 pounds, underwear, socks, toilet articles, a duffel bag and a foot locker in which to store all his new found riches.

Son spent the next month and one-half doing close order drill, pulling KP (kitchen police) and guard duty and waiting anxiously for reassignment to primary glider pilot training. It seemed like much more than six weeks before he got his orders but eventually they arrived. He an over one hundred other "aviation students" were packed onto a troop train to begin the long journey to a place called Ft. Morgan, Colorado.

Located in the northeastern part of the state not far from the Nebraska line, it was famous for sugar beets. The town itself was no more than 8 to 10 thousand people, a small farming community. There was not a lot to get excited about on weekend pass there. The flying was pretty simple. Called "dead stick", it consisted of flying light planes such as Taylorcraft and Aeroncas which Son had already flown in college CPT. The difference was that this time, all landings were made with a dead engine, hence the name, "deadstick." Son learned how to use the slide-slip maneuver to lose excess altitude on approach to landing without building up excess airspeed. Presumably, the tactics we learned simulated the flying characteristics of a glider which we would be flying in the next stage of our training. In late November 1942, we completed this phase. Most of us were reassigned to a place called 29 Palms, California for basic glider training.

Again, it was back on a troop train, taking us this time to a drop off point near the town of Banning, California. It was 2 AM. Most of us were at least partially asleep. The train jolted to a stop and someone yelled, "O.K., everybody off!"

It was a beautifully clear, moonlight night. In that light, the terrain looked like the surface of the moon, the silhouetted twin peaks of San Gorgonio and San Jacinto loomed in the darkness. It was bone chilling cold. We stood around waiting for some "6-by" trucks to pick us up and take us on the final leg of our journey. Son stood there shivering in this crowd of GI's and, for the first time since he left home, he felt alone, lonesome and homesick. It must have been the mountains, so massive and ominous, so different from his midwest home.

The trucks finally arrived, and after a bone-jarring ride northeast across the high desert for some sixty miles they arrived at Norton Flight Academy, near the town of Twenty-nine Palms, CA and under civilian contract to the U. S. Army to provide basic glider training. The day was just dawning as they piled out of their trucks. Son hoped that the coming day would lift his spirits, and it did. They spent the morning checking in, getting organized and being assigned to their living quarters.

For the next 7 months, Son flew small gliders including some high performance sailplanes at "29." First, he went through the training program. When he graduated after about 2 months, he would have normally been scheduled to go to advanced glider school at Victorville, CA where he would have flown the big CG4 cargo gliders. Instead, he was promoted to the grade of flying staff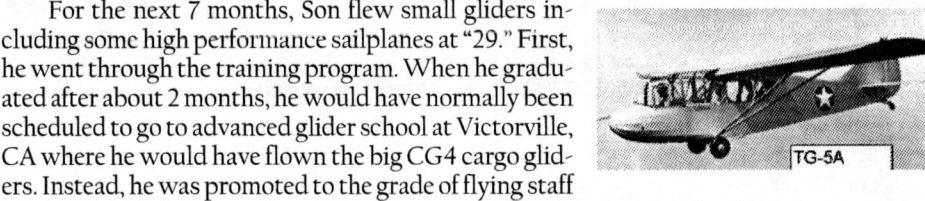

TG-5A

sergeant and held over to become an instructor. His salary increased to $144 per month and he was having fun. In May, 1943 everything changed. Word came that the glider training program was to be eliminated!

What?!

Everybody not in advanced glider training was to be reassigned.

Where? To what?

These were all disquieting questions. He had already failed to qualify for cadet training because of his color vision deficiency. What else was there — cooks' and bakers' school? The infantry? He was sent back to Kirtland AAF to await reclassification and reassign-

ment. It was back to tent city, KP and guard duty. His morale hit a low point, but another strange twist of fate awaited.

When he wasn't pulling duty of some kind, Son had lots of free time. He would go to the Post Exchange (PX) where most of his fellow soldiers congregated. There a big, colorful Wurlitzer Jukebox had been installed. He was now a private again. Privates we were on salary of $21 per month, which didn't leave room for much discretionary spending. But 3.2% draft beer could be had for 25 cents for a large pitcher. Lucky Strikes were ten cents per pack. The jukebox was constantly being fed with the GI's nickels and the songs were typical pop top 40 for that time - "String of Pearls", "Boogie Woogie", "My Ideal", "Chattanooga Choo-Choo" and many others. There were lots of tables and chairs and a big, pine floor great for dancing. The only trouble with that was there were no girls. So we just sat there, sipped our beer, smoked our Luckys, told stories, tried to act like men and got to know one another.

In that big, casual pool situation where Son found himself, rumors abounded. Most rumors were exactly that - rumors. A few were based on fact. The problem was separating fact from fiction. One "rumor" in particular caught Son's ear. He had been talking to one of his friends about his problem with color vision. The friend told him that he heard there was an ophthalmologist in Albuquerque who was involved in a research project to determine if so-called color blindness was really incurable. It was his theory that with training in color perception it could be cured. He was looking for volunteers to participate in his research project, the friend said. Son thought,

"Wow! If this is true, I want to be part of his project!"

CHAPTER 21
There Is a Chance

It was true. Son contacted the doctor and was included in his research. The doctor gave him the standard Ishahara color test, which Son could not pass. He then worked with Son on a daily basis for one month. None of the exercises he did involved any memorization of the test. At the end of the month, the doctor gave Son the test again and he passed.

Son flew out of the doctor's office, went straight to the cadet recruiting office and applied for cadet training. This time he passed the physical and was accepted. Now he would be a cadet and he would fly! Oh happy day! Now, instead of cook's and baker's school, he would be going to preflight training in Santa Ana, California. The site was the Orange County Airport, now known as John Wayne Airport. Son was not aware until many years later that his parents had received a personal letter from the Commanding Officer at Santa Anna, notifying them that their son had been accepted for aviation cadet training as a pilot. The Colonel told them of the rigorous training that their son would undergo and of the responsibilities he would assume as a commissioned officer and airplane pilot. Son found the original letter, yellowed with age, in his father's papers after he had passed away.

During the next 8 1/2 months, Son was involved in one of the most massive, accelerated training programs that had ever been attempted. To this day, it has not been surpassed. In 1941, soon after Pearl Harbor, President Roosevelt called for a massive arms buildup to meet the challenge of a worldwide war, a war for our very survival. Among the things that he called for was a program to train 50,000 pilots per year! Yes, that's right — 50,000. It wasn't enough to just build lots of airplanes. We had to have pilots to fly them — lots of pilots. Stephen Ambrose, the well-known military author, cites in his book, "The Wild Blue Yonder," some interesting numbers:

Total number entering pilot training = 317,000
Killed in Training:

Completed training	= 193,000	Primary	= 439
Washed out	= 124,000	Basic	= 1,175
Advanced 1,888			
Total: = 3,502 [1]			

Most "experts" thought that it could not be done.

The Army Air Forces, under General Henry H. (Hap) Arnold, developed a training program to train pilots, navigators and bombardiers in an 8 1/2 month time frame. The standards were high. First came physical and mental testing. The objective was to screen for I.Q. scores of 120 or better. On top of that came a battery of mental, medical and physical dexterity tests designed to identify those most capable of success in either one or all of the three categories - pilot, navigator or bombadier training. Those who passed this tough screening process were continued in training. Son scored very high on all tests, fully qualifying for all three categories. This meant that he could have his choice. Did he want to be a pilot, a bombadier or a navigator? The answer to that question was, of course, a no-brainer. Son chose pilot training.

After two more months in pre-flight training, devoted to military subjects with lots of "spit and polish" things like barracks inspections, subservient kow-towing to upper classmen by lower classmen, demerits for minor rules infractions, close order drill and big pass in review parades, Son was ready for reassignment to Primary Flight Training.

In due time there was another train ride. . . .(naturally!)

And time to say hello to Norton Flight Academy, a civilian contract school, where Son was to spend July and August learning how to fly the PT-22 primary flight trainer. Norton was located near Blythe, California on the west side of the Colorado River, approximately 120 miles north of Yuma, Arizona. Because the river afforded water for irrigation there was a strip of green roughly corresponding to the river flood plain. Cash  crops were fruits and vegetables. Beyond the reach of irrigation, however, the desert dominated the landscape, stretching north into Death Valley. Average high daytime temperature was 120 degrees Fahrenheit. The barracks buildings were arranged in a quadrangle around a flag pole and parade ground. The upper class which was one month ahead of Son's lower class lived in the buildings on the west side of the quadrangle. Son's class occupied the east side. Individual buildings were sized to accommodate a dozen other cadets, and were quite nice by war time standards. They even had air conditioning of sorts, "swamp coolers" which worked quite well as long as the humidity was low.

The bugler blew "Reveille" at 0500 hours. That's 5:00 A.M. in civilian talk. All the cadets, both upper and lower classes, sprang out of their bunks, put on the uniform of the day, khaki pants and uniform shirt and, of course spit shined high top GI shoes. Within five minutes of the bugler's call they poured out of their barracks and fell into formation. The squad leader of each barracks took roll call and gave his report to our class cadet Captain,

"All present and accounted for, SIR!!"

Class Captains, in turn, reported to our Wing Officers. Within five minutes, our Wing (both upper and lower classes) had been reported and we were commanded to "fall out." We now had 30 minutes to return to our barracks, shower and shave and get dressed again in time to be marched to the mess hall for breakfast. Breakfast also was a thirty-minute affair. From there we marched to the flight line and reported to our flight instructors. Because of the extreme temperatures, flight operations were conducted from 0600 hours to 1200 hours. After that the airplanes were too hot to touch!

PT-22 Ryan Primary Trainer
(cou Cy USAF Museum)

Six cadets were assigned to each flight instructor. The one to which Son was assigned was a hard-nosed individual who believed in intimidation. There were other instructors, Son found out, that were less vociferous but just as demanding. All cadets got 8 hours of dual instruc-

tion in the PT-22 before soloing. The airplane was a low-wing monoplane with dual open cockpits. The student took the front cockpit while the instructor rode in the rear. Both pilots wore cloth aviator helmets that were connected by plastic tubing similar to that used in stethoscopes. The instructor could talk to his student using a "gosport." The communication was all one-way from instructor to student. The student pilot could not talk back to his instructor, signaling only his understanding by nodding of his head.

We were told that 40% to 50% of our class would "wash out" in primary training, a prediction that proved to be true. This knowledge created a lot of pressure on all of the students. All of them wanted to succeed. Son had little or no trouble flying the PT-22. It was a simple airplane and he enjoyed flying it when he was solo. However, he dreaded those flights when he was scheduled to fly with Mr. Kowalski. In addition to yelling his instructions to Son over the gosport, Mr. Kowalski would occasionally grab the stick and shake it from side to side, beating Son's knees. Another cute trick was to hold the gosport out into the slipstream. The sound that then assailed Son's ears was deafening. These tactics did not improve Son's ability to fly. After one of these sessions, Son feared the worst, that he might be "washed out." Two cadets of the six assigned to this instructor did wash out. One was chronically airsick. The other failed because of "lack of aptitude." But Son survived.

Afternoons and evenings were devoted to ground school and physical training. The ground school was easy, the physical training was not! The physical training area consisted of a 1/4 - mile track, scraped out of the desert sand, and an area set aside for "PT" or calisthenics. Today, this form of human torture would be called aerobics. Led by a "TAC" officer, First Lieutenant "Iron Mike", we did pushups under the hot sun and in the hotter sand! We did "The Randolph Shuffle." We did sit-ups, side-straddle hops, squat-thrusts, running in place, deep knee bends and other contortions too numerous to mention! After the "warm-up" we would run around the track in the loose sand until we were breathless. The routine would have killed an average, sedentary civilian in his 30s or 40s. But we were all under 21, and indestructible!

One morning, a couple of weeks after we had arrived, the bugle blew as usual. Suddenly there were cries of consternation within the under class barracks.

"Somebody swiped my shoes!"

"They're gone! Versteeg, you bastard, did you take my shoes?!"

Then, someone looked out the window. There, piled around the flagpole, were scores and scores of shoes! Someone had sneaked into our barracks and had stolen all those shoes, at least tied them together in pairs, and piled them around the flagpole! Who would pull such a stunt!?

While Son and his lower class cadets on the east side of the quadrangle were struggling to get into formation and make their reveille formation and report, someone looked across the quad, where the upper classmen were standing in resplendent formation, choking with laughter!

"Why, those!!!!!"

Two days later, several upper class barracks reported some "creative" vandalism. Someone had slipped into their barracks when they were gone and taken several mattresses, drug them to the latrine, put them in the shower and turned on the water!

The perpetrator(s) were never found, however it was assumed that it had to have come from the lower class. The writer of course denies any knowledge or responsibility.

It was behavior worthy of a college sophmore, not "officer material" in the United States Military. Accordingly, both incidents were investigated and a cadet honor court was held. But since no individual or individuals could be identified, a group punishment was meted out. The entire lower class was placed on restriction for the duration of their stay at Norton. There would be no weekend passes. What a bummer! The upper class got off "Scott Free"

BT-13 Basic Flight Trainer
(Courtesy USAF Museum)

since by the time the court investigated and convened the upper class was within a week of moving on to basic flight training.

The balance of Son's time at Blythe passed all to quickly. He had survived the first hurdle toward becoming a pilot. The washout rate in basic flight training, the next step, was less than 10%. Son's view of the world was bright.

Soon Son would fly a "real" airplane. At Lancaster, California, a few miles west of what is now Edwards AFB, Son was introduced to the BT-13. Nicknamed the "Vultee Vibrator" for the noise of its 450 horsepower radial engine, it sported a fancy paint job - canary yellow wings and robin's egg blue fuselage. It had a fixed landing gear, a two position propeller, full panel instrumentation and two way radio.

"Wow," Son thought when he first saw it, "This is a real airplane."

This time, Son drew a different kind of instructor, one who was very "user friendly." Son thrived under his coaching, adding to his repertoire of skills. Night flying and formation flying were introduced. Acrobatics continued and were easier to perform with the added power of the BT-13.

Instrument flying was a real challenge. On his first instrument ride, Son climbed into the rear cockpit, which was equipped with a hood that could be pulled over Son's head, blocking any view of the outside. After takeoff, Mr.Crump, his instructor, told Son to climb to 6,000 feet altitude and level off. When this had been accomplished, he was told to pull the instrument hood forward and over his head, snapping it to the top of the instrument panel. Son had logged some instrument training in the Link trainer. He knew what he was supposed to do. The instrument panel told him what the airplane was doing. The airspeed indicator showed his airspeed. The altimeter read off his altitude above sea level. The rate of climb indicator registered his vertical speed, both up and down. The directional gyrocompass gave aircraft heading in degrees, clockwise from north (ZERO DEGREES). The flight indicator or attitude gyro displayed the attitude of the aircraft, wings level or banked; nose above or below the horizon.

Simple.

All Son had to do was integrate the information being presented from five different sources into a whole concept in his mind. Then he had to take the appropriate actions on the aircraft controls to make it do what Mr. Crump asked him to do.

"Hold this heading and altitude," Mr. Crump commanded.

"Easy," thought Son. His right hand gripped the stick, his left the throttle. His feet performed isometerics on the rudder pedals. 6000 feet read the altimeter. Then it started to read higher - 6050, 6100, 6150, it read. Son, noticing this, pushed forward on the stick, while watching the altimeter. It suddenly reversed itself, moving downward now - 6100, 6050, 6000, 5900, 5800! Son gripped the stick and pulled it back.

"Easy does it, Mr. Son, you're over controlling. Watch your heading. You're turning left. Keep your wings level."

"No," thought Son. "I can't be. I'm not turning!" A quick glance at his turn indicator confirmed that he was, in fact, turning left. His attitude indicator showed that he had allowed his left wing to drop and that he was in a 20 degree left bank.

He applied right stick (aileron) until the attitude indicator showed that his wings were level. But every sense in Son's body told him that he was now banking and turning to the right! His instructor had told him that it might be difficult to trust his instruments at

times, that his own central nervous system would betray him. Now for the first time he really knew what Mr. Crump meant. He looked again at his instruments. They told him he was straight and level. With a supreme effort of will, Son tried to ignore the powerful feelings of his inner sense of balance and movement and concentrate on his instruments. Gradually, he got the hang of it but it was hard, hard work. He felt like he was in a dark room trying to balance a broomstick on the end of his nose. Every muscle in his body was tense. He gripped the stick as though he was trying to choke it.

After twenty minutes or so, Mr. Crump told Son to come out from under the hood. He unsnapped it and moved it back behind his head and shoulders.

Back on the ground, they talked about the flight.

"What did you learn?"

"I learned that instrument flying is hard work! Is it really possible to fly an airplane that way?"

"Oh yes. In fact, with practice you should be able to fly on instruments with even greater precision than you are able to do using your normal visual references. For example, you should be able to control your altitude within plus or minus 50 feet and your heading within plus or minus one degree."

"What was I doing wrong?"

"You were over controlling. Remember this: If you trim the airplane properly and set it on a straight and level course, you can take your hands and feet off the controls and the airplane will almost fly itself! Very little pressure on the controls is needed to make it do what you want it to do. But the main thing you need to do is relax. You were choking the stick, weren't you?"

"Yes, I guess I was."

"What do you do when you go to the latrine, stand and unzip your pants? Do you choke it or do you hold it gently?" Son almost lost his proper military demeanor, but he got Mr. Crump's point.

"Hold the stick the same way," Mr. Crump said.

On his next instrument flight, Son took Mr. Crump's advice. It was a breakthrough. He progressed rapidly in his instrument flying skill. Even the feelings of vertigo that bothered him so much on the first flight gradually faded away. To this day, Son has never forgotten Mr. Crump's advice: "Relax and hold it gently." That applies to many things besides instrument flying.

There were more new flying challenges. Flying at night was the next item on the basic flight training agenda. After the evening meal Son's cadet squadron, consisting of about 30 student pilots were all scheduled to fly that evening. 22 of them were put on a bus, yes, a bus. They drove east into the desert for about 50 miles, finally coming to a big dry lake called Rosamand. Flat as a billiard table, and probably just as hard, it was a perfect place from which to fly airplanes. The eight students who didn't ride the bus got to fly, along with their instructors, to the lake. After they made one landing with their instructors, the first group soloed, staying airborne for about an hour. The process was repeated until everybody had logged his dual checkout plus one hour of solo nighttime. Son thought this was fun. A lighted runway, marked by portable runway lights, made approaches and landings easy.

Son was scheduled to receive 60 hours of flight time during his two-month stay at Lancaster, including instrument, night and formation flying. Formation flying? It was somewhat like driving a car down a crowded freeway, maintaining clearance between your vehicle and all the others on the road. The only difference was that flying introduced a third dimension. By the time he had completed his assigned hours, Son was doing well in all phases of the program. Of course, ground school subjects including map reading, navigation, meteorology and the physics of flight and military "spit and polish" continued.

One day all the cadets were told that a "very hot pilot", named Tony LaVere, was coming to Lancaster to demonstrate the capabilities of the P-38 Lightning twin-engine fighter. In 1943 the Lightning was among the world's fastest airplanes. It was doing spectacular things in the Pacific. Major Richard Bong was a leading "ace" with multiple kills of Japanese Zeros to his credit. In Europe, the Luftwaffe pilots called the Lightning "The Forked Tailed Devil."

LaVere was the chief test pilot for Lockheed, builder of the P-38. Rumors had it that he could make the Lightning do tricks that the engineers who built it said it could not do! On the appointed day all the cadets marched down to the flight line where temporary bleachers had been set up at the edge of the tarmac. As the cadets took their seats they could see Tony's sleek, silver P-38 parked on the tarmac in front of them. The greatest pilot walked out, climbed the ladder and lowered himself into the cockpit. A public address system introduced him and told briefly what he was going to do.

"Mr.LaVere will take off and immediately after retracting his landing gear, feather (shut down) his left engine. Then he will start a slow aileron roll to the left, into the dead engine! Following that, he will restart the left engine and climb out to a position to do the rest of his demonstration, which will need no further explanation."

A whisper ran through the audience. "He can't do that! That's impossible!"

With that, Tony engaged the starter for the right engine. Slowly, the big, three-bladed, twelve foot diameter propeller began to rotate in a counter-clockwise direction. After a couple of turns a large puff of blue-white smoke belched from the turbine exhaust outlet behind the 1650 horsepower, twelve-cylinder engine. Already the left engine was cranking, this time in a clockwise direction. Because of the opposite rotation of the engines the tremendous torque that they generated was cancelled out. Son had read about this feature of the airplane and knew that it was an important factor in the docile handling characteristics of the airplane.

The wheel chocks were removed and, as Tony advanced the throttles, the engines emitted a low-pitched, almost throaty growl that bespoke of the power, which the pilot held, literally, in the palm of his throttle hand. No other airplane, before or since, sounded quite like the P-38. Nearly 60 years later, Son would be able to recognize that sound, unique to the Lightning. Tony turned the P-38 and quickly and smoothly taxied out to the end of the takeoff runway.

All eyes were riveted on the airplane as it began its takeoff roll. It didn't make a lot of noise - just that low pitched growl, almost purr-like. As soon as it became airborne LaVere retracted the landing gear. As it passed abreast of the audience, not more than 50 feet off the runway, the prop on the left engine slowed and came to a complete stop, fully feathered! Smoothly and simultaneously LaVere began a left aileron roll into the dead engine! Before the cadets could recover their breath, he completed the roll, continuing to climb out on only one engine! No other pilot had ever attempted, much less accomplished, such a maneuver! He restarted the left engine and continued to climb. His show continued to be equally mind boggling - loops, immelman turns, vertical rolls, both up and down, slow flying with gear and flaps down, hanging the airplane, almost literally, on its props. After about twenty minutes during which he held the audience spellbound, the announcer said that Tony would attempt to land the airplane with both engines off and feathered. Again, this sounded all but impossible to the assembled cadets. How could he do this?

From an altitude of several thousand feet, Tony dove the Lightning toward the end of the landing runway at maximum allowable airspeed (475 KIAS), feathering first the left, then the right engine as he came. Streaking down the runway only a few feet off the ground with neither engine operating, he began to pull up into an egg shaped loop. At the top of the loop, he extended the gear. The G forces involved in the loop helped to extend the gear. Diving back toward the ground to complete the loop, he leveled out in time to make a

smooth landing with neither engine operating. With his remaining momentum, he rolled toward the stands, tapping the brakes to make the airplane bob and bow, coming to a stop only yards in front of his audience!

There was a standing ovation. Wow!

There were no guarantees, but each cadet was asked to state his choice of airplane type, bombers, transport or fighters, he would most like to fly before going to advanced flight training. Those who chose fighters would most likely go to single engine advanced to fly the AT6 Texan. If ever there was any question about what type of airplane Son wanted to fly when he graduated and won his wings it was eliminated with that stupendous demonstration. He wanted to fly fighters, preferably the P-38! When his orders came he was assigned to Williams AFB, near Chandler, Arizona. There, he understood, he would be prepared to fly fighters. He might even get a few hours in the P-38 before graduating. He could hardly believe his good fortune!

CHAPTER 22
The Goal Is In Sight

Two weeks later, he was making his bunk in a cadet barracks at Williams AFB, Arizona. He was about to begin the last two intensive months of his flight training. At the end of it, he would be commissioned a Second Lieutenant and would receive his coveted silver wings.

It has been said, life is a series of choices, each choice leading to consequences. Son's first choice went all the way back to that fateful day in May, 1927, when he saw The Spirit of St. Louis flying over his home in Missouri.

"Someday," he said to himself, "I'm going to fly, just like Lindy!"

Then, at Lancaster, California, after being "blown away" by the dazzling flying of Tony LaVere, there was the decision to opt for fighters.

Now, he found himself about to realize the import of those decisions. He eagerly embraced it,

The AT-6 "Texan"

thinking of what was about to happen. He would get his wings and move on to the next phase, transition training in combat fighter aircraft, probably, he hoped, P-38s. Then, along with his friends and fellow pilots he would go overseas. It could be Europe. It could be the Pacific. He would know shortly.

The rest of his flight training went smoothly. He had little trouble mastering the AT-6 Texan advanced single engine trainer. There was the usual dose of transition, formation, night and instrument flying, all of it very similar to what he had learned in Basic Training. There were some additional challenges, however. First, he learned to shoot and drop a bomb from an airplane. After all, that's what his training was all about - combat. Gunnery camp at a god-forsaken place in the southern Arizona desert called Ajo, represented, it turned out, a cross-roads for Son. Out of his class of over 600 cadets, Son achieved the top gunnery scores in his class. It wasn't that much different from what he had learned about guns and shooting from his father and uncle when he was a boy.

O.K., fine. He'd be effective in combat.

Back from gunnery camp, Son licked his chops in anticipation of the final phase of his training, a

The AT-9 Curtiss Jeep Advanced Trainer

check out and time in the P38! It began with 10 hours in the all metal, twin-engine Curtis AT-9 trainer. Flying an airplane with two engines was, after all, different from flying a single engine bird. The AT-9 also had some characteristics that were useful from a training standpoint. It was heavy and it was "hot." Son's instructor told him, only half-joking, that the airplane took off, climbed, approached and landed at only one speed: 120 MPH. Emergency procedures on single engine flight were speed critical. But never mind. The 9 was the last remaining obstacle between Son and the nirvana of flying that delicious P38! This close to the final goal, Son was not to be denied. He negotiated the AT-9 requirement and went on to the next step. P-38 training involved a stiff dose of ground school. He had to learn about all of the systems/sub-systems in a very complex airplane including hydraulic, engine and electrical. He had to become intimately familiar with all the instruments and controls in the cockpit. He had to pass a blindfold cockpit check. While sitting blindfolded in the cockpit with his instructor perched on the ladder, he had to point/touch each control or instrument in the cockpit when named. He had to be able to recite, verbatim, all emergency procedures.

When he flew this airplane, solo, for the first time it would be without the benefit of any dual flight instruction with an instructor. This airplane had only one cockpit, only one set of controls.

When the appointed day to solo arrived, it would be "sink or swim."

That day came soon enough, though Son, in his anticipation, thought it would never come. In the briefing room and under questioning from his instructor, Son went through all the steps one more time. Then it was time to slip into his parachute and walk out to the airplane.

Yes, of course, there were butterflies.

He climbed up the ladder, his instructor behind him, and eased himself down into the cockpit. It was time to show his instructor what he had learned. After strapping himself in, he smoothly and quickly went through his pre-start checklist. His instructor nodded, go ahead. First, he would start the right engine. The crew chief gave his O.K. signal. Son responded with a twirling of his finger as he engaged the start switch. The big, twelve foot, three blade prop began to rotate in a counter clockwise direction. The cylinders fired, emitting a cloud of blue-white smoke through the turbine behind the engine, the three blades becoming a blur. The start procedure was repeated for the left engine, turning its prop in a clockwise direction. Both engines now settled into a smooth idle. Son's instructor said very little as the big fighter came to life. At this stage, he was there more for reassurance than anything else, Son having demonstrated his competence several times. There was a final pat on the shoulder, and he climbed down the ladder that was then pulled away. Son called the tower for taxi instructions. He gave the "chocks out" sign to the crew chief. Wheel chocks were pulled. Son slowly advanced the throttles and the big Allison engines responded. The airplane moved slowly out of its parking space.

Nervous? "Who, me??" Son thought. "Naah."

Taxiing toward the takeoff end of the active runway, Son felt a sense of power and mastery that was hard to describe. He was cradled between those two big engines, now purring like jungle cats and capable of producing over 3,000 horsepower. That was more

than that produced by a half-dozen locomotives like the one whose firebox he saw when his Daddy took him up into the cab of "ole' Number 11" in Centertown, years ago!

Now, for the big moment . . .after being cleared for takeoff, Son taxied carefully onto the active runway, lining up directly over the center stripe. Clamping his feet firmly on the brakes, he slowly pushed the throttles forward to full takeoff power. Son's knees were shaking a little now as he noted quickly manifold pressures, engine RPM and temperatures. The noise from the turbines had risen to a full-throated roar. Everything O.K. . . he released the brakes. The acceleration pushed him back against the seat. Keeping the nose pointed firmly at the runway  dashed line center stripe, Son watched the airspeed . . . 80, 90, 100, 120. The dashes were whipping, almost blurring, under his nose Time to fly! Easing back on the control wheel, he lifted the airplane off the runway.

"This is no AT-6!" he thought. The power, the speed and smoothness was in a word, awesome. For now, he didn't have time for any thoughts beyond what the mission called for. Retract the landing gear when safely airborne. Reduce power and RPM from full takeoff to climb settings. Monitor all temperatures, oil and coolant. Keep your head on a swivel, looking for other airplanes. Climb to 500 feet, make a left turn and leave the traffic pattern. Continue to climb and head for the transition area. Become familiar with the handling characteristics of the airplane. Continue climbing to 10,000 feet, noting a rate of climb in excess of 2,500 feet per minute!

Cheez!

Try a couple of barrel rolls, first left then right. Wow - easy as pie!!

45 minutes later it was time to return to base. Son followed his pre-landing checklist to the letter. Turning onto the downwind leg he slowed to 180 knots and extended the landing gear. He extended half flaps just before turning onto the base leg. Turning to final approach, he extended full flaps. Keep the airspeed at 120 and adjust throttles as required to stay on the proper glide slope. As the runway threshold flashed under his wings, Son eased the throttles to idle and held the airplane off until it touched the runway, its tires making a sound like tennis shoes on a gym floor.

Taxiing back to the parking area, Son saw his instructor standing there with the airplane crew chief like they were a welcoming committee!

After debriefing by his instructor, Son had time to think a little about what had just occurred. In less than 8 months he had learned to fly, starting in primary training, flying the open cockpit Ryan PT-22, then on to basic training in the BT-13. Finally, in advanced training it all came together with his checkout in the P-38. There were nine more hours to log in the P-38, but failing an accident of some sort, it was all downhill from there.

Graduation day was set for January 7, 1944, almost three weeks away. There was the usual nervous waiting for orders. Where would Son's class go next? A good number of the graduates from the class just ahead were sent to Santa Rosa, California for further P-38 training prior to being assigned overseas. It was assumed that class 44-A (The first class to graduate in 1944) would follow that same road.

Also, there were uniforms to buy. As cadets, all uniforms and clothing was government furnished. As commissioned officers, that would no longer be the case. Each graduate was given a $300 uniform allowance to cover the cost of one standard Army officer's uniform consisting of a dark green blouse, two pairs of "pink" twill pants, one dark green pair and two dark green shirts. The winter overcoat was a handsome twill, belted trench coat in a

color that matched the "pink" pants. A Luxembourg officers' cap topped off the ensemble. Most of the cadets bought their uniforms at Goldwater's department store in Phoenix, owned by Barry M. Goldwater, later to become a famous politician. Believe it or not, in those days, $300 just about covered the cost of everything.

CHAPTER 23
Another Fork In The Road

While Son was still working on his P-38 total hours, a Saturday arrived, and it seemed an appropriate time to go into town and celebrate a bit. One of Son's classmates, Pete Webb, by name, mentioned to Son that he had a date, but that she had a girl friend that needed a date for the weekend.

Would Son be interested?

"Sure", he said, thereby changing the course of his life for many years to come. Tall and willowy, with shoulder length auburn hair, full lips and a shy smile, Arretta captivated Son almost immediately. The electricity was almost overwhelming. That night, they went to a dark and inviting cocktail lounge at the Adams Hotel in Phoenix. It was crowded with cadets and their dates. They had drinks, cuddled in a booth, and danced on an overcrowded dance floor to 40's big band music on a five plays for a quarter, kaleidoscopic, red and yellow jukebox. He asked her for another date.

In the meantime, the machine that spit out military assignment orders continued to grind. Shortly after Son's first date with Arretta the orders were issued. Yes, most of 44-A was being assigned to P-38 transition training at Santa Rosa. Yes, most of the class drew Santa Rosa . . .but not Son. Because of his grades in advanced, particularly his gunnery scores at Ajo, he was being assigned to Williams AFB as an instructor — again! He and his friend, Cody Stout, were already talking about the adventures that awaited them in California and beyond that in a combat unit overseas. Now Cody would be going ahead without Son. He was disappointed, but his friend, Cody, said not to worry, that it was probably all for the best.

Little did they both know. Months later, Cody was flying P-38's in Italy and was killed in a mid-air collision. The other pilot, "R.R. (Railroad) Thompson, also a friend and classmate of Son's was also killed.

Before graduation there were a couple more dates with Arretta. She was ecstatic on hearing the news that Son would be staying at Williams.

January 7, 1944, dawned clear and bright. The sun was shining brightly, twinkling off the more than 650 pairs of gold, second lieutenant bars now pinned on the shoulders of each graduate. A pair of silver wings was pinned precisely just above the left pocket of each new officer's blouse. Shoes were shined to an unbelievable brilliance. Pants were creased. Hats were positioned on each officer's head precisely as they should be. The entire class stood at attention on the north side of the huge parade ground. The military band was ready. The parade began. First, the band passed in review in front of the reviewing stand. Following that each squadron, carrying its own flag, passed in review. Following this, there

was a speech by Colonel Herbert Grillis, the base commander. Finally, the class roll was called. Each newly commissioned officer heard his name called. Then it was over. He had done it in just over $8 \frac{1}{2}$ months!

CHAPTER 24
Married Life Begins

On March 18, 1944, Herman and Arretta were married. Son's first duty assignment after graduation from Flight School was as an instructor at the gunnery camp for Williams AFB located at Ajo Air Base. A more remote and primitive site can hardly be imagined. Ajo is a small copper mining town, owned, to this day, lock, stock and barrel by the Phelps Dodge Corporation. Located only 40 miles north of the Mexican border and half way between Tuscon and Yuma, it was an ideal place for gunnery training. Thousands upon thousands of acres of uninhabited desert stretched to the west toward Yuma and the Colorado River. Here fledgling pilots could practice shooting, bombing and rocketry with minimum risk of hitting anything except perhaps a gila monster or a sidewinder rattlesnake.

Herman and Arretta rented a small, two bedroom FHA wartime housing apartment for $32.50 per month. It provided the basics, barely. Little, straw colored poisonous scorpions were regular visitors, crawling down the walls and sometimes into shoes and articles of clothing. There was no refrigerator and the kitchen stove and hot water heater were fueled by kerosene. There was an ice box for food storage, but ice was hard to come by. They found they could rent a refrigerator, but there was a waiting list. It took 9 months for their name to reach the top of the list. During wartime everything was rationed - meat, sugar, coffee, clothing, shoes, tires and gasoline. No cars were built then for civilian consumption. They bought a 1939 Oldsmobile 98 with unknown mileage and a set of tires that had been re-treaded several times. They made do with this bucket of bolts because there wasn't anything else available.

In the fall of 1944, The United States Army Air Corps held a fighter gunnery competition.

The competition involved all pilots in the U.S. Army Air Corps Training Command, divided into East Coast, Gulf and Mid-west and West Coast Commands. Each training base (I'm not sure of the total number of bases), of which Ajo was one, conducted its own competition (elimination) to select base team and individual representatives. Teams consisted of three students and their instructor (me). We flew North American Texans (AT-6) equipped with a single fixed, 30-caliber machine gun firing through the propellor. Rounds were fired just after a prop blade had passed through the gun's line of sight, so we couldn't shoot holes through the prop! My team and I won the Ajo competition and then went on to win at the national level. The national meet was held at Ajo because of our range facilities and weather. As I recll, we flew six missions — three against air-to-air targets, shooting at a banner being towed by a B-26, and three air-to-ground firing at a 10 x 10 panel target. One hundred rounds were fired on each of the six missions. Scores were recorded on each mission. With four airplanes firing on a single 6 x 30 banner target, scoring was accomplished

by using bullets that were tipped with a special colored paint. Hits made by an aircraft firing blue ammo would leave a blue smudge on the bullet hole, for example. Air-to-ground scoring was easy as each pilot fired at an individual panel. A perfect score for the six missions would have been 600. I don't remember the break-out of my scores for air-to-air vs. air-to-ground, however I know that I scored somewhere in the range of 275-290 on air-to-ground. That was easier than air-to-air which involved deflection shooting at a moving target. In order to hit the target it was necessary to aim well in front of it, particularly at high angles of deflection. In a curve of pursuit, a good pass would involve starting to fire at an angle off of approximately 45 degrees down to perhaps 15 degrees. As the angle off decreased, the apparent lead also decreased so that at 15 degrees the apparent lead was less than half of what it was at 45 degrees.

Anyway, Son and his three students won. Son won the instructor's trophy and his three students, Cooney, Caruthers and De La Luz, won trophies also. Son still has his, even though one of its pot metal wings has been broken.

40 miles to the south was Mexico and another 40 in the same direction would lead to the Gulf of Lower California.

The flying and instructional duties were easy. He enjoyed working with students. Most of them were young American pilots, much like he. Some, however, were foreign students - French, Dutch and Chinese. Of these, only the Chinese posed serious problems. They came from an ox cart culture, not a high-tech, mechanical one. Although they were highly motivated, as pilots they were clumsy. There is no other way to put it. The main problem, however, was language. Only a few students in each class could speak and understand English. Training had to be given in small groups in English through use of an interpreter. Son would brief his flight of perhaps three or four students by speaking a couple of sentences that would then be repeated by the interpreter. There was no way for Son to be sure that his instructions were being understood.

One day, after briefing his Chinese cadets on an upcoming aerial gunnery mission, Son took off, leading his flight upward and westward toward the aerial gunnery range. He and his flight rendezvoused with a B-26 tow ship that was towing a white banner target. Per briefing instructions, Son led his flight through a series of passes, shooting at the target. When the tow ship reached the western limit of the range it did a procedure turn and set course again, this time in an easterly direction. As the tow ship began its turn, the fighters, again per Son's briefing, were to pull up and circle until the tow ship was established on its reciprocal course. His students should have been following behind him in follow the leader fashion. When Son looked behind him, however, his students were nowhere in sight. He started trying to contact the only English speaking member of the flight, but all he got in return was in Chinese! Finally, Son spotted them, three tiny specks to the south, now flying toward Mexico! He had to chase them all the way to the Gulf of Lower California before he caught them and got them turned around, back "under his wing."

Shortly after their arrival at Ajo, Son received an invitation from the base commander, inviting he and "Mrs. Son" to join the commander and his wife at the officers' club for cocktails and dinner. Son was pleased that his presence at the base was being recognized. He took the invitation home and told Arretta. She blanched and said she couldn't go.

"Why?"

"I just can't. I'm too nervous."

"What? That doesn't make sense. You're attractive, witty and charming. What's to be nervous about?"

"You don't understand!"

"No, I guess I don't!"

"If you go, you'll have to go by yourself!"

"I can't do that - I'd look like a fool!"

"Well, I can't help that!!"

With this exchange, Son began to realize that he and Arretta were marching to different drummers. He didn't know it then, but Arretta suffered from agoraphobia or extreme anxiety whenever she found herself in social situations. In other words, it was difficult for her to go out of the house! There were reasons for this behavior that were very complex, going all the way back into Arretta's childhood. Son was to find out as the months and years slid by that she had been abused. She was the product of a dysfunctional family. Some of the abuse she suffered was physical. Some of it was psychological. Cutting to the bottom line, she had married Son for all the wrong reasons. Although she probably couldn't admit it, even to herself, the main reason was to escape from the anger and hostility of an intolerable family environment. Her father was an alcoholic, a philanderer and a wife beater. Her mother, understandably perhaps, was a man hater. Arretta's unconscious road map of life, laid down in childhood, painted "man" to be like her father. Her mother was her feminine role model.

What about "man?" He can't be trusted.

Woman? Mary did what she had to survive. If her life had been a book it would have been titled, "Suppressed Anger." This psychological road map was what she unconsciously bequeathed to her daughter.

Herman didn't understand Arretta. Afraid to go out in public? Ridiculous! Didn't she know how important it was to him to have a wife who supported him? Refusing to attend a "command performance" was certainly not the way for Son to get ahead in the Army. He had already made up his mind that he wanted to make the service a career. But now what, he wondered?

If Arretta married Herman for all the wrong reasons, the obverse was also true. Herman married Arretta because he was immature and homesick and because as he has often said since, "all my brains were below my belt buckle!"

Nevertheless, Herman had a strong sense of values about marriage. Simply put, divorce was more than an admission of failure, it came close to being a sin. He therefore put everything he had into trying to make the marriage work. He tried praise. He didn't lie to her. He truly felt that she was an intelligent and beautiful woman and he told her so. It didn't work. For Arretta's part, she constantly tried, emotionally, to put her father's face on Herman. For obvious reasons, that didn't work either.

At times they were happy. There was a strong physical attraction and when Arretta's demons were asleep, they got along very well. But always, in the background, the 800 pound gorilla of Arretta's emotional problem threatened to reassert itself.

CHAPTER 25
The Great War Grinds On

Six months after he graduated from flight school and took up his instructional assign-ment at Ajo, American, Canadian and British forces launched "Operation Overlord." D-day was June 6, 1944. Launched from England, it was the most massive amphibious and critical operation of World War II. Unbelievable in its complexity and scope, its objective was no less than the defeat of the Nazi War Machine on the continent of Europe. Over 200,000 soldiers, sailors, marines and airmen participated. An armada of more than 5,000 ships of all sizes and types carried and supported the invasion forces. The full resources of the 9th and 8th Air Forces provided air support. Many of Son's classmates were involved, flying P-38s, F-51's and P-47's. Many, including his close friend, Cody Stout, were killed. His feel-ings were ambivalent. On the one hand he was grateful for his cushy stateside assignment, but on the other he felt a twinge of guilt for not being a part of the big show.

The outcome of the war hung in the balance. If Overlord succeeded the end of World War II was in sight. If it failed, what then? It was hard to contemplate. The invasion had to succeed. The first 48 hours were critical. The entire Western World held its collective breath as Allied Forces stormed the beaches at Normandy. The surf turned pink from the blood of our young men as they faced withering fire from the German guns. It was a titanic struggle. Ships and tanks were impaled on steel and concrete barriers that the Germans had erected. Their rusted skeletons now litter the sea bed along the Normandy coast. Total allied KIA (killed in action) was in excess of 9,500 in the first 24 hours. But with tenacity and courage we established a beach head secure enough to allow for the landing of addi-tional troops and supplies. The next step was to take the high ground atop the bluffs that rose behind the landing beaches. This also was accomplished and the German guns that were able to inflict such devastating losses on our forces were silenced. [1]

Most of those who lost their lives in that battle are now interred in the military cem-etery atop the bluffs overlooking the English Channel thousands of white crosses marking their graves.

This is the only territory we ever asked for from the French.

It is hallowed ground.

After the initial successes at Normandy American British and Canadian troops and material poured onto the continent through the major ports of Cherbourg and Le Harve. Hard and bloody battles were ahead - The Ardennes, The Hurtgen Forest. In December, 1944 the Germans, realizing that they were losing, launched a major counter offensive. In bitter sub-zero temperatures the Battle of the Bulge came close to success for them. But our forces prevailed. Then there was the crossing of the Rhine River. It was, then, only a matter of time. General Patton's Third Army was poised for a dash to Berlin. But following a major

political decision, Patton was told to hold and allow the Russian Army to take Berlin. There is little doubt that Patton, if allowed, could have reached Berlin first. One wonders how post war history would have been affected if that had happened.

Hitler and his mistress, Eva Braun, committed suicide in their bunker in Berlin and on May 2, 1945 the war was over. Thousands of lives were lost on both sides in this titanic struggle. Ultimately the German forces were caught in a giant pincers. The allies closed in on Berlin from the west, Russia and the Soviet Union from the east. Hitler and Mussolini were dead and the Allies were victorious. America then turned its attention to the Pacific and what we assumed was our remaining enemy, The Empire of Japan.

In August, 1945 the face of war was changed forever. The world, for better or worse, entered the nuclear age. Two atomic bombs were dropped, one at Hiroshima the other at Nagasaki. The two nuclear detonations resulted in 250,000 civilian deaths.[2] While they were undoubtedly instrumental in forcing the Japanese surrender, they did not kill as many people as the B-29 fire bomb raids on the nights of June 9th and 10th. On these two nights the B-29s created firestorms of unprecedented fury in Toyko, Yokahama, Osaka and Nagoya. Total deaths were over 400,000 for these raids alone. The impact of these raids, combined with the two nuclear attacks broke the will of the enemy. Japan surrendered. For those who might wonder about the morality of deliberately targeting civilian populations, a reading of a recent book by James Bradley is recommended. "Flyboys," is a true story of what happened to nine young U.S. Navy flyers who were shot down during air attacks on Chi Chi Jima, a forlorn pile of rocks located just north of better known Iwo Jima. Of the nine airmen, eight were captured. The ninth was rescued by an American submarine after he survived 3 days in his raft. His name was Lt. JG George Herbert Walker Bush. The other eight were all brutally murdered by their captors on Chi Chi Jima. Their bodies were then dissected and cannibalized. What this story reveals about the Japanese character during that war is shocking. The ethic of the "spirit warrior" held that glorious death in defense of the Japanese Nation was preferable to surrender. To the Japanese, Americans were sub-species, animals that deserved no mercy, no dignity. The book documents this ethic that permeated all of Japanese society If we were to defeat such an enemy, he had to be crushed. That is the rationale and justification for the air war that brought Japan to its knees.

In the morning of 2 September 1945, more that two weeks after accepting the Allies terms, Japan formally surrendered. The ceremonies, less than half an hour long, took place on board the battleship USS Missouri, anchored with other United States' and British ships in Tokyo Bay.

For a brief, historic moment the world was not at war. That is not to imply that the world was at peace. It was far from it. The Soviet Union deployed 40 divisions in Eastern Europe. From Finland in the north to Yugoslavia, Albania and Hungary on the south, as Winston Churchill warned, "an iron curtain had descended on Europe, dividing East and West." It was here that the Cold War, destined to last for the next 50 years, began. The Soviet Union, formerly our ally, had now become our enemy. It was difficult for America to recognize the nature of this struggle. We wanted nothing more than to go home, throw down our arms, shuck off our uniforms, go back to school, get married and have families. We did all these things with a vengeance, and our economy took off like a rocket. All that pent up civilian demand exploded into an industrial capacity that grew rapidly to meet the demand.

In the meantime, things were brewing in Europe that demanded our attention. Almost reluctantly, we responded to the Soviet threat.

Now World War II was really over. Pell Mell demobilization began.

As a nation we could not get away from the war and things pertaining to it fast enough. Millions of soldiers, sailors and airmen were discharged. The huge war production machine that had been churning out the munitions of war did an abrupt about face. It stopped

military production and began shifting gears to meet pent up civilian demand. Brand new airplanes were flown from the production line to "the bone yard." One such depository was Kingman, Arizona. In a matter of a few months over 10,000 airplanes, P38s, P51s, P47s, B17s and B24s with less than 10 hours of flying time on them, were flown there, and simply pulled out into the desert. Eventually they were turned over to the War Surplus Administration for disposition. Individuals could buy P51s for $500 and P38s for $1,000. WSA eventually decided to put the entire block of over 10,000 airplanes up for competitive bid. They were to be sold "as is." The winning bidder, Martin-Wunderlich Construction Company, was a penny ante contractor prior to the war. They made millions during the war, building bases, roads and other things for the war effort. But their big killing came when they won the bid for the 10,000 airplanes. For this cache they paid $ 5,000,000, a pittance when one considers that the fuel and oil in the tanks of those airplanes alone was worth more than the purchase price! First, instruments and communications gear, all valuable commodities, were removed. Then almost new engines, over 30,000 of all sizes and types, were removed and packed. Propellers and other parts were stripped. Finally, the aluminum carcasses were cut up and melted down into ingots and recycled. Everything was sold on the O.E.M. market. No one knows exactly what all this treasure yielded or what M-WC's eventual return on its initial $5M investment was but it must have been eye-popping.

Early in 1946, the Army announced that it would take applications from those who were interested for regular army commissions. A regular commission could be compared, roughly, to tenure in the academic world. Reserve or wartime temporary commissions were just that - temporary. They could be cancelled at any time whenever the need expired. A regular commission, on the other hand, was permanent. It could be cancelled, but not without serious reason such as malfeasance, crime or treason. If one wished to make the military service a career a regular commission was therefore most desirable. Son made application and was ordered to go to Biggs Field, El Paso, TX where he spent three days in taking tests, physical and mental. Although he felt that he did well he had no idea of how many commissions were being handed out or how he stood in the competition. When he finished the Army said, "Don't call us, we'll call you." Son went back to Ajo and forgot about it. In August, 1945 two atomic bombs dropped on Hiroshima and Nagasaki ended the war with Japan.

"Now what?" thought Son.

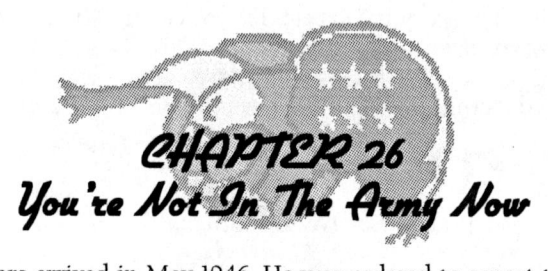

CHAPTER 26
You're Not In The Army Now

Discharge orders arrived in May 1946. He was ordered to report to Ft. Mac Arthur California near San Diego for out-processing. In two days he became a civilian and an unemployed one at that. He and Arretta returned to Phoenix and Son began looking for work. Of course, he wanted to continue to fly, but landing a flying job was not going to be easy. His goal now was to become an airline pilot. He mailed his resume to every airline. He received very polite, form letter rejections:

"Thank you for your interest in Around The World Airlines. We have reviewed your resume and qualifications and find that they do not meet our current requirements. However, we will keep your resume on file and will blah, blah, blah . . ."

Sure.

The airlines were looking for pilots with multi-engine experience, lots of it. Son was a fighter pilot, mostly single engine. There just wasn't much of a market for fighter pilots in 1946. But Son was persistent. There just had to be some company that would give him a flying job. If they would just give him a chance, he thought, he would show them. He knew that flying transport aircraft could not be that difficult. There were a lot of small, start-up airlines that popped up like mushrooms in a damp spring after the war. Some of those war surplus C-47 aircraft shed their olive drab paint. Sporting new shiny aluminum skins and colorful paint jobs. They epitomized the ebullient can-do spirit of their new companies.

One such company was Arizona Airways, based at Sky Harbor Airport in Phoenix, Arizona. They owned three (count 'em) DC-3's, the civilian version of the military C-47. The airplanes had been converted to passenger configuration, with plush airline seats, felt headliners and galleys. AA's business plan was to fly regular intra-state, scheduled service without airmail subsidy. They filed an application for interstate routes and airmail subsidy. The Civil Aeronautics Board had lots of applications on its docket and they moved very slowly. In the meantime, AA flew from Phoenix to outlying points within the state, such as Tuscon, Yuma, Nogales, Bisbee-Douglas and Globe. Passenger traffic on these routes was sparse indeed. As long as they stayed within state borders for their scheduled service they did not have to be approved by the Civil Aeronautics Board in Washington. However, without subsidy, it was doubtful if the company would be able to stay afloat for more than 18-24 months.

"Well, they're local," Son thought. "Maybe, if I'm persistent, I can get on with them."

In the meantime, Son used some of his GI Bill entitlement. He enrolled in instrument training classes with Southwest Airways. He got his commercial and instrument license, flying in a High-wing Fairchild 24. An instrument ticket was a minimum requirement to fly with the commercial airlines.

Bill Moore was the chief pilot for Arizona Airways. He was a retired MATS (Military Air Transport Service) pilot with thousands upon thousands of hours of multi-engine flying time.

To get a job with Arizona Airways it was necessary to get past Bill. He was gruff, a bit intimidating, but he had a soft spot.

"What makes you think you could fly for us?"

"Well, why not? I've flown fighters, and I've flown twin-engined, B25s and B26s too."

"I'll give you "E" for effort, Son. I expect that you could learn to fly the gooney all right. Maybe we could use you if we were a little larger. Who knows what will happen. If we get an airmail contract, we may need some more pilots."

"Bigger? What did he mean by that?" Son was over 6 feet tall and weighed 175 pounds. "Oh well," he thought:

"Can I keep in touch?"

"Sure."

This conversation repeated itself weekly until one day, Bill said, "O.K. Herman, we'll give you a chance."

Herman found himself flying right seat for a monthly stipend of $225 per month, barely enough to pay the rent and buy groceries. But at least he was flying. His captain was a guy named Frank Halloran, an ex-TWA, American Airlines pilot and a very friendly man who took Herman under his wing. He was a good teacher. Herman soaked up what Frank had to offer like a sponge. The gooney was easy to fly, just a double breasted Cub, really. Frank was generous, letting Herman fly left seat on a regular basis. He was logging 70 to 80 hours per month with lots of night and instrument time. This experience would be invaluable to him later.

One night he and Frank took a scheduled run from Phoenix Sky Harbor to Prescott, Arizona. It was a night flight but the weather was clear. After the stop at Prescott the flight was scheduled to proceed westward to Kingman in the extreme western part of the state. Son flew left seat on the way to Prescott. Frank took the left seat on departure for Kingman. Taxi out and take-off was normal. As luck would have it, we had eight or ten passengers. Half the time we would have no more than one or two. Sometimes we were empty. Just as we were clearing the airport boundary at an altitude of perhaps fifty feet, the flight attendant came rushing to the cockpit.

"Fire!"

The attendant didn't have to tell us. The right engine (on my side) was on fire. Orange-red fire streamed from the cowl flaps behind the engine. We immediately went into our fire emergency procedure - cowl flaps closed, shut down the right engine and feather the prop, activate the fire extinguisher. Call an emergency to the tower and request immediate landing in the opposite direction. The fire coming from the cowl flaps diminished to only sparks.

We climbed out to perhaps 300-500 feet and did a big, looping turn. We had taken off to the north, now we were on approach to land to the south, all on one engine. I was glad Frank was sitting in the left seat. He handled it masterfully. We landed without further incident. I learned a lot about flying from that incident. Someone once said that, "flying is simply long, interminable periods of utter boredom, punctuated by occasional moments of stark terror!"

When those moments present themselves survival absolutely depends on keeping stark terror at bay. Sometimes keeping it at bay isn't enough. But doing so at least provides a ticket to play. That night Son was glad that Frank was sitting in the left seat. He was a consummate professional. Emotionless. He went through the procedures without any evidence of panic or excitement. Afterward he asked Frank,

"How could you be so cool?"

"Focus, Herman. You must stay focused on what you are doing. Don't think about what might happen. If you do things correctly, it will probably come out O.K. In any case, you can't give in to fear. It will only paralyze you. You must be able to focus in the same way a big league ball player in the batter's box would when facing a 100 MPH fast ball . . focus so intently that he can see the seams on the baseball as it comes toward him."

Focus. Son never forgot that lesson in flying. Could it apply to other life situations? Certainly.

Frank called Bill Moore. There was no way we could continue with our scheduled aircraft and flight. Bill said they would dispatch another airplane, but it would take a couple of hours. We all repaired to the coffee shop at the airport to wait. One of our passengers was the movie actor, Robert Young, a nice guy. We ordered hamburgers and coffee and sat around and talked. He was going to Kingman to check out a movie location. As soon as the other airplane arrived we all boarded it and continued on to Kingman, then back to Prescott and Sky Harbor. It was a long night.

About the time this was happening, another important event in Son's life was developing. In the late summer of 1946, soon after he was discharged, Arretta told Herman that she was pregnant. They were both very happy and looked forward to the blessed event sometime in the middle of the following March. The pregnancy seemed to help Arretta with her emotional problems. Son hoped that this would continue after the baby's arrival. If AA was successful in its pending application before the CAB (Civil Aeronautics Board), allowing for expansion of its service to out of state, Son's flying job would be secure. Herman and Arretta kept their fingers crossed.

Later, Herman was scheduled to fly with another AA captain, Bill Bradley. Bill was ex-air corps with all of his experience in C-47s, C54s and C-119s. He was a superb pilot. He taught Son a lot of things about flying the DC-3: How to handle it in a cross wind in both landing and takeoff situations and how to do short-field takeoffs and landings; what to do when flying with only one engine. They flew into and out of places like Clifton and Globe, the latter a dirt strip of no more than 2500 feet, bulldozed into the side of a mountain. Normally, one lands into and takes off into the wind. At Globe, that rule was modified. One always landed uphill, regardless of the wind, a little like a fly landing on a wall. Conversely, takeoffs were always downhill. Even though the weather in Arizona was rarely bad, Son got plenty of practice flying on instruments using a hood to block out the outside view. With Bill acting as observer, he made many, many approaches to landings using his instruments. Bill always critiqued his performance. As a result Son steadily improved his instrument flying technique. As will be seen, these were lessons that literally saved Son's life and the lives of members of his flight in Korea.

Son flew for Arizona Airways for one year. During that time he logged nearly 800 hours and gained invaluable flying experience. The pay, however, was terrible - - only $225 per month. Even when calculated in 1946 dollars it wasn't much. But the job gave Son what he wanted even more than dollars. He was flying! As the first year came to a close, however, the fates were about to deal what at first seemed like a cruel blow. The little fledging airline was hemorrhaging financially. Just before the company declared bankruptcy Son was laid off.

CHAPTER 27
Life Gets Complicated

What now? Son was presented with a double challenge. First, at about this time he became a father. On March 16, 1947, Arretta gave birth to a beautiful baby girl. They named her Mary-Lynn. Even in her infancy she was graceful. He enjoyed feeding her and rocking her to sleep. He loved her, and the realization dawned. Now Son had to support not two but three people. It was imperative that he find employment soon. As a stopgap, he took a job with Holsum Bread Company that paid $200 per month. That certainly was not enough.

No more than two weeks later a Western Union Telegram arrived. It was from The War Department in Washington, D.C. With trembling fingers, Son opened the yellow envelope and tore out the telegram. His eyes took in the words, "You have been nominated by the President for appointment in the Regular Air Force. . . . . . with the initial rank of second lieutenant, date of rank January 1, 1948. Conditioned on your acceptance, your regular Army serial number will be 0-57626. Your first duty assignment will be the 1st Fighter Wing, March Air Base, CA., reporting not later than 1 September, 1947. Wire your acceptance to the above address within 48 hours of receipt."

He was flying again. Arretta heard Herman exclaim the news. She wasn't happy. That fact tempered Son's joy.

"Arretta, please! Try to understand. This is an opportunity, not just for me but also for us! For me, it's what I want to do. Fly professionally. For us, it's security. I can't support you and Mary-Lynn on $200 a month! It's a regular commission! The pay, ($327 per month) while certainly not exorbitant, is a lot better than what I'm doing now. It offers a career, and (don't laugh) retirement with full medical care. Would you like to see the world? We would travel, see the world that tourists never see!"

Son sat down. He could hardly believe his good fortune. The three days that he spent over a year ago at Biggs Air Base in El Paso had borne fruit.

"Yippee!!!"

The die was cast. Son telegrammed his acceptance to the War Department. On September 15, 1947, Son resumed his military career. He reported to the First Fighter Wing and was subsequently assigned to the 27th Fighter Squadron. The Wing, has three squadrons - the 27th, 71st and 94th - assigned to it. It has a long and storied history going back to World War I. Eddie

Rickenbacker, famous ace of World War I, belonged to the 94th. All who are members of the fighter pilot fraternity recognizes its emblem, the famous Hat in the Ring. Son met the squadron commander of the 27th, Lt. Col. Loren G. McCollum. The 27th, known as the Eagle Squadron, had a storied past also. Lt. Frank Luke, Congressional Medal of Honor winner had Luke AFB named after him. He flew with the 27th in France during WWI. Col. McCollum introduced him to other members of the squadron. Son sensed that there was something special about McCollum. He was right. When he retired it was with the rank of Lt. General.

"Well, well," said Frank. *"Son is certainly getting in with the right crowd. He couldn't be in a better outfit. I was a member of the 27th Eagles when I was killed on my last mission in France in 1918. He'll get the best kind of training in this outfit!"*

The 27th was a friendly, high-energy group - just what one would expect. Herman felt right at home. In 1947 this was the elite fighter outfit in the Air Corps, soon to become the separate and independent United States Air Force. They were the first to be equipped with jet aircraft. This was the dawn of the jet age. It began, experimentally, right after the end of WWII. We learned from the examples of the German Luftwaffe who flew the Me-262 at the end of the war. Based largely on the German design, Bell Aircraft built and flew the first American jet, the P-59. It provided a test bed for a lot of engineering development, ultimately resulting in the P-80-A, Lockheed Shooting Star that was the first truly operational jet fighter.

The first P-80-A airplanes were assigned to Williams AFB in Chandler, Arizona, where Son graduated from flight school. Williams mission was to build a base of experience with jets and then transfer this knowledge and skill to other pilots who were assigned to units scheduled to be equipped with jets.

Son could hardly wait to sit down in the cockpit. This would be an experience that would outshine his checkout in the P-38 when he was a cadet at Williams. However, he was counseled to have patience. He would have to go to Williams AFB for transition training.

"The 27th squadron cannot check you out." So said his flight commander, Captain Frank Mertley.

"You will have to go to Williams AFB. There is a waiting list right now, but we'll get you in as soon as possible. In the meantime you can get your flying time on the AT-6."

"O.K., and since I am current in the C-47 I can fly that too."

"Great! We're going TDY (temporary duty) to Ft. Hood, TX on 1 October for a joint exercise with the Army. We'll be moving a lot of stuff down there and we could use your gooney bird skill."

Son wished he could have been checked out in the 80 so he could participate in the exercise at Ft. Hood. But he did fly the wing C-47 with a couple of loads of personnel and cargo, so he didn't feel useless. He also was appointed as an instrument instructor and check pilot in the AT-6 and C-47. In this role he gave a lot of dual instruction to other pilots in the squadron, teaching them ways to improve their instrument flying skills. It has been said many times that the best way to improve one's own skills is to teach them to others. Certainly that was true for Son. He appreciated and took advantage of the opportunity. His flight and squadron commander took note of his initiative and motivation, much to Son's satisfaction. Months later, in combat in Korea, he found his skills were crucial to his and his flight mates survival.

Decent housing was in short supply in Riverside. Son couldn't afford more than $100 per month out of his $327 monthly pay. Until he could find something suitable Arretta and their baby daughter, Mary-Lynn stayed in Phoenix with Arretta's parents. Not a good situation, Son felt. It took about two months of searching before he found a small house in West Riverside. A squadron friend, Russ Talliferro (pronounced Toll-iver) told him about

a small house next door to where he and his wife, Kay, were living. Son checked it out. It was perfect. The rent was $85 per month. He signed a 6-month lease and called Arretta immediately. She was full of questions:

"What kind of neighborhood? What is the rent? How about utilities? Is there any furniture? Kitchen?"

Finally, she agreed to come. Son took 3 days leave and drove immediately in his rattletrap '39 Olds to Phoenix to help Arretta pack and prepare for the move. He bought a cheap 2-wheeled trailer and a hitch to hook it to his car. They packed up all their worldly possessions - a bed, baby-crib, dishes and cooking utensils and clothing. They set out for the long drive back across the hot summer southwestern desert from Phoenix to California. Of course, the car was not air-conditioned. Son threw a couple of 5-gallon gasoline cans filled with water in the trailer. He knew that the Olds would probably overheat, and with a leaky radiator it would never make it without stopping for extra water. Every fifty to seventy-five miles they would have to stop, let the car cool off, then, carefully loosen the radiator cap to let the steam blow until it was safe to remove the cap and give the old lizzie a drink. All of this made for a very long, uncomfortable trip, particularly for Mary-Lynn. Fortunately they didn't have any tire trouble. The old tires on the Olds were in terrible shape, having been re-treaded several times.

27th Fighter Squadron, 1948, March AFB, California
(Son fourth from right, second row)

On the way back Son told Arretta excitedly all about his new assignment and their new house. It was one of four small houses located on a short residential street, located near the western edge of the city. A very nice old gentleman, a semi-retired farmer, owned them all. He rented exclusively to families from March. All of us were military, and he knew that we didn't make a lot of money. In fact we called the street "Poverty Row." The important thing to our landlord was that we take good care of his property. The other families on the street were all assigned to Son's squadron, the 27th. That meant they could carpool to work, a big saving. The guys and their wives were all nice, Herman said.

He told Arretta that she wouldn't have any trouble making friends. That thought didn't register with Arretta. The very thought of having to make friends with people outside her immediate family panicked her. All of the husbands, Russ Talliferro, John Hancock and myself, were Lieutenants except for Captain "Pinky" Harold. All the wives were friendly and welcomed Arretta, the newest member of "poverty row." Arretta responded with her usual case of terminal shyness.

Now that he had his family together, Son enthusiastically focused his daytime energies on his job with the squadron. He was anxiously waiting for his name to come up for P-80 transition training at Williams when suddenly it was decided that he could do his checkout locally.

"Wonderful," Captain Frank Mertley, Son's flight commander, said. "Now we can get on with the business at hand. There's no reason I can't check you out. This bird is not that different from most other fighters, except for the fact that it does not respond quickly to throttle changes when going from idle to full power. You just have to anticipate a little more and be farther ahead of the airplane. If you remember that, you won't have any trouble."

After an appropriate amount of ground school and cockpit checks, including a blindfold test administered by Frank, the moment arrived. Son was about to enter the jet age. Sitting in the cockpit with Frank standing on the ladder outside, he brought the shoulder harness straps over each shoulder and hooked them into the seat belt buckle.

"Go ahead and start," said Frank.

Son gave the signal to the ground crew and flipped the start switch. The turbine engine began to turn – two percent, four percent, six percent. Finally, reaching eight percent on the rpm tachometer, Son flipped another switch (the I-16 pump) which injected fuel (JP-4 kerosene) into the burner chambers. As combustion occurred the airplane emitted a low, vibrating rumble, quickly fading as the engine gained rpm. As the rpm reached 18 percent, Son opened the throttle to idle. The engine quickly accelerated to 30%, the normal idle rpm.

Truncating detail, Son was finally ready to taxi.

"Just remember that on takeoff it will be slow to accelerate. Don't worry, it will happen. When your airspeed reaches 120, rotate to pull the nose-wheel off. As soon as you are airborne retract the gear and wait for the airspeed to build to about 300 KIAS (knots indicated air speed) before you start to climb. Then you'll feel like an angel is pushing you! After that, it's a piece of cake. Have fun, and I'll see you in about 40 minutes!"

The flight went just as Frank said it would. The main difference was the absence of immediate acceleration and lack of torque on take-off. There was no need for right rudder to compensate for the torque. Also he noted the complete absence of vibration. The only noise was from the wind, whistling around the plexiglass canopy. The approach and landing was routine.

Back in the squadron ready room, Herman sat down with Frank and critiqued the flight. Frank had watched his take-off and landing.

"It looked great from where I was," said Frank, who used a squadron jeep to station himself near the end of the active runway. "Did you have any problems?"

"Not a one."

After another four or five flights Son was ready to try his hand at flying in formation. He and Frank went up together. It was not difficult at all. In fact, the lack of torque and the smooth handling qualities of the airplane made formation flying very easy.

"You're really catching on to this, Herman. I am impressed at how quickly you're learning."

"Thanks!"

And so it went. Son was fitting in well with his squadron mates. They all liked him. He could tell and he reciprocated. There was only one cloud on the horizon. Since Son had never had an overseas assignment he was vulnerable to the next overseas quota placed on the wing. He told Arretta that their time at Riverside would probably be short. He also told her that most overseas assignments were, at least initially, unaccompanied. That meant no dependents. The supply of family housing at most overseas locations was tight. Depending on where he went, there would probably be a separation of several months up to a year. Her response was oddly non-committal.

"Well, I'll just have to go back to Phoenix and live with Mom and Dad."

"No, when it happens, we'll find a house or an apartment for you. You don't need to be staying with your folks."

"All right."

When Son's number came up, there were two possibilities. He could go to Europe or the Pacific. Which would it be. Whatever the assignment, he wanted it to be in fighters. His C-47 time, however, could make him vulnerable to another kind of assignment.

Things were happening in Europe that made it increasingly likely that he might go that direction.

Berlin blockade and airlift

An international crisis arose from an attempt by the Soviet Union, in 1948-49, to force the Western Allied powers (the United States, the United Kingdom, and France) to abandon their post-World War II jurisdictions in West Berlin. In March 1948 the Allied powers decided to unite their different occupation zones of Germany into a single economic unit. In protest, the Soviet representative withdrew from the Allied Control Council. Coincident with the introduction of a new Deutsche Mark in West Berlin (as throughout West Germany), which the Soviets regarded as a violation of agreements with the Allies, the Soviet occupation forces in eastern Germany began a blockade of all rail, road, and water communications between Berlin and the West. On June 24 the Soviets announced that the four-power administration of Berlin had ceased and that the Allies no longer had any rights there. On June 26 the United States and Britain began to supply the city with food and other vital supplies from outside by air. They also organized a similar "airlift" in the opposite direction of West Berlin's greatly reduced industrial exports. By mid-July the Soviet army of occupation in East Germany had increased to 40 divisions, against 8 in the Allied sectors. By the end of July three groups of U.S. strategic bombers had been sent as reinforcements to Britain. Tension remained high, but war did not break out.

Churchill was right. The Russian bear was hungry and not to be trusted. Still, America did not take the threat very seriously. We allowed our military forces to fall into serious disrepair. It took another war, this time in Korea in 1950, to awaken us.

To support the Berlin Airlift there was a great need for pilots with multi-engine experience, particularly C-47 and C-54 aircraft. Son didn't want to go to Europe, but his logbook seemed to be pushing him in that direction. He asked Colonel Perigo, the Group Commander, to use his influence if possible to get him assigned to fighters. It looked as though the best possibility for that was in the Pacific.

When his overseas assignment came, in September, 1948, it was to the 8th Fighter Wing, based in Japan. They were currently equipped with F-51s. That meant that his experience with jets would be interrupted. For that reason, he was mildly disappointed. But the rest of the assignment sounded O.K. As Son had anticipated, he would have to go unaccompanied. The wait for base dependent housing was forecast at 10 - 12 months. That was the hardest part. He didn't want to be separated from his wife and child for such a long time. This was the downside of a career in the military. Family separations were common, and apparently unavoidable. He and Arretta talked about it. His concern was that Arretta and Mary-Lynn would be O.K. while they were separated. She said that as long as she could find a comfortable house or apartment, they'd be all-right. She said that Bob Bachman, an old friend and neighbor, had said that she could call him if she had any trouble with the house. Bob was the brother of Delores, a friend of Arretta's, who had dated Pete Webb the night that she and H.F. had met. That's convenient, thought Son.

CHAPTER 28
A Long Road Ahead

Now the process of moving his family from Arizona to California was, except for the automobile involved, reversed. A couple of months before he got his orders, they decided that the old '39 Olds had to be retired. They looked at the new cars now showing up in dealer showrooms. They all seemed so expensive. Finally, however, they settled on a new '48 Oldsmobile Model 66, a small two-door hatchback, done in two-tone beige and brown. It cost $2,400 but at least it was new and dependable. They were both very proud of it.

Herman said goodbye to all his friends in the squadron, Frank Mertley, Jack Fallon, Bill Craig, Frank Culp, John Hancock, Russ Talliferro, Pinky Harold and the others. It was tough to leave these guys with whom he had already formed close friendships. That, as Son was to confirm many times in the future, was a part of military service life.

At home, he and Arretta packed everything into their trailer. This time, in their new car the trip to Phoenix was easy. Son had two weeks delay in en route before having to report to Ft. Mason, CA, the port of embarkation for the Japan and the Far East. He was able to find and lease a small two-bedroom house, not too far from Arretta's parents and get Arretta and Mary-Lynn securely in place. He arranged for most of his monthly pay to be deposited by allotment to a joint bank account in Phoenix. Arretta had the new car, although she didn't particularly like to drive. At least she could go to the grocery store and visit her parents. He made sure that his insurance and personal affairs records were set. But it was hard thinking about the months of separation that lay ahead. They both promised faithfully to write regularly. All too quickly the time ran out and Son had to leave. He flew to San Francisco and reported in at Ft. Mason.

Early on the morning of the next day he boarded a U.S. Army Transport, The General Blatchford, for the long trip to Japan. The Blatchford was a flat-bottomed "rust bucket" ocean going ship, capable of a top speed of close to ten knots in smooth seas. This would be Herman's first experience in travel on the high seas, scheduled to take 9 days. Weather forecasts for the trip were not particularly favorable. In fact, a major storm system was winding up in the mid-Pacific. It was nothing to worry about from a safety standpoint. Nevertheless, he was not looking forward to it. He just wanted to get there. Most of the ship's space below decks was devoted to cargo. Passenger accommodations were Spartan and space was tight. Son found his bunk assignment and settled in for what he knew would be a long and tedious trip.

By late afternoon everything was ready for debarkation. A pair of tugboats pulled up and attached lines to the Blatchford. Stevedores and vehicles on the pier scurried to carry out their assigned tasks. There were a couple of deep-throated blasts from the ship's horn. Slowly, the ship inched away from the pier and a trip of some 6,000 miles began. There was a cold, light rain falling, but Son pulled his trench coat around his neck and stood on deck to see what he knew would be his last view of his beloved America for a long time. The ship pulled out into San Francisco Bay. The tugboats disengaged and the Blatchford headed for The Golden Gate. As they passed under the Golden Gate Bridge, Son could feel the first great swells of the open ocean. Ahead and to the west, the sun was setting. Even through the mist its great red ball could be seen slowly descending into and below the horizon. Son thought, ironically - the big red ball of the sun was the iconic symbol of the land he was traveling toward: Japan. Looking back toward the stern, Son took a long look. Beyond the white wake of the ship the Golden Gate Bridge stood astride the mouth of San Francisco Bay. The San Francisco hills and city skyline stood as sentinels to an America that he would not see for three long years. He experienced a twinge of homesickness, such as he had not felt since that night near Palm Springs after he got off the train and looked up at the dark shapes of San Gorgonio and San Jacinto. After a short walk around the main deck, Son found his bunk and settled in for the night. He went to sleep to the strange amalgam of sounds that are produced by a big ship at sea - the low frequency thrum of the ship's engines, the creaking noises made by the structure as it plowed through a moderate sea. As he cleared his mind of the day's events and drifted into sleep his conscious thoughts faded. They were replaced by another set of images that welled up from deep within his subconscious. . . .

CHAPTER 29
The Owl and The Pussy Cat

"Tell me about the Owl and The Pussy Cat, Grandpapa!" Herman Franklin said to his Grandpa Son.

He and his father and mother were visiting at a home in Eldon, Missouri where Grandpa lived with his daughter, whom H.F. referred to as Aunt Gertrude, Daddy's sister. Grandpa was in his seventies and in the prime of his life, at least intellectually and as far as H.F. was concerned, physically. "Natty," in a word, would describe grandpapa Son. He always wore a spotless white shirt and tie, even in the most stifling summer heat. In the winter he matched the shirt and tie with neatly pressed wool slacks. In the summer, grandpa preferred blue seersucker, also sharply pressed. When going outside, he also wore a hat, either a snap-brim felt or white straw, depending on the season.

During his "productive" years, Grandpa had been a farmer and a school teacher. He (and his family of 13) farmed for physical survival. He taught school for intellectual survival.

Herman Franklin always enjoyed talking with Grandpa, who had a talent for, among many others, for poetry. On call, he could recite verbatim from dozens of poems, suitable to the occasion. He could do the heavy stuff by Milton, Keats and Rudyard Kipling. Herman Franklin didn't fully understand the abstract meaning of some of these, but he always felt the emotional impact. What he really enjoyed, at age 5 or 6, were some of the whimsy poems.

He had an incredible memory, at least so it seemed to him. He didn't read children's stories and poems, he recited them . . . verbatim, with all the emotion that made them come alive. For example:

The Owl and The Pussy-Cat

The Owl and the Pussy Cat
Went to sea
In a beautiful pea-green boat
They took some honey and plenty of money
Wrapped up in a five-pound note.

The Owl looked up to the
Stars above,
And sang to a small guitar,
"O lovely Pussy, O Pussy,

my love,
What a beautiful Pussy you are,
You are,
You are!
What a beautiful Pussy you are!"
Pussy said to the Owl, "You elegant fowl.
How charmingly sweet you sing!
Oh! Let us be married;
Too long we have tarried:
But what shall we do for a ring?"
They sailed away for a year and a day,
To the land where the bong-tree grows;
And there in a wood a Piggy-wig stood,
With a ring at the end of his nose,
His nose,
His nose,
With a ring at the end of his nose.
"Dear Pig, are you willing to sell for one shilling
Your ring? Said Piggy, "I will."
So they took it away, and were married
Next day
By the Turkey who lives on the hill.
They dined on mince and slices of
Quince,
Which they ate with a runcible spoon;
And hand in hand on the edge of the sand
They danced by the light of the moon,
The moon,
The moon,
They danced by the light of the moon.

or:

Two little kittens
They lost their mittens and they began to cry…".

H.F. was a young fighter pilot in Japan when Grandpapa Son died in 1947. He was 96 years old. He was and still is a hero of Herman Franklin's.

CHAPTER 30
Grandpa Garnett

Grandpa Garnett's death, in 1937, wounded H.F. deeply, more so than Grandpapa Son's. Not because he was any closer to him that Papa Son, but simply because he was so much younger. Grandpa became ill with what H.F.understood was the flu. He took to his bed in the big, old stately farmhouse where he and Grandma had lived for more than 30 years. That was a house that was filled with many childhood memories for Herman Franklin. As a little child, he remembered Grandpa picking him up, then sitting down in his old rocking chair. There he would just rock H.F. until he fell asleep. Sometimes, he would put him astride one of his shoes and bounce H.F. up and down in a game of "Trot, Trot to Boston." He always wore brown, corduroy trousers that had a unique feel and smell. He had a mustache that was just right, long enough and wide enough to cover all of his upper lip, with a little wisp extending down both sides of his mouth. When he talked, his mustache moved, in unison with his words. It may have been possible, with practice, to read his mustache!

When he became ill, H.F. was very worried, because, somehow, he sensed that it was no ordinary flu that had felled Grandpa. Mama, Daddy, Grandma, Aunt Jane and Uncle Carl were all there. The conversations were guarded and quiet. H.F. couldn't follow everything that was being said. But he knew.

Three days later, Grandpa died in his sleep. When Mama told H.F. he felt like he was drowning. He wanted to cry, but all he could do was choke. There was a big, horrible knot in his throat that wouldn't go up or down. Mama held him and comforted him, even though she was grief stricken too, until he began to relax. But the pain was still there.

H.F. asked Mama, "Why?"

Mama said, simply, "It was God's wish."

That really didn't answer his question then. He just knew that Grandpa was gone, and that he wasn't coming back.

The funeral was held at the old country church, New Hope Baptist, where both his grandparents, uncles and aunts were all members. Mama taught Sunday School there as a young woman, before she met H.F.'s father. Officiating was The Reverend R. L. Hood. His hair was almost totally white. Ten years before, he had been the preacher at Centertown Baptist Church.

Herman Franklin has another, very early childhood memory associated with that, but he will save it for now.

"Mama, Daddy, Aunt Jane, Grandma and Uncle Carl all sat on the front pew. I was so close to Grandpa's open casket I could almost reach out and touch it. Reverend Hood's grave words floated through the air. I could hear them, but I didn't take them in. The horrible knot in my throat was back. My eyes filled with tears, and I was sure I was going to

cry. Finally, the sermon seemed to be over. The choir began to sing, "Rock of Ages," an old hymnal favorite. Reverend Hood concluded with a prayer. The congregation stood, and began to pass by the casket. There were muffled sobs from some of the women as they passed. As family, we waited until the others had filed past, then we went, first, Grandma, then Mama, Daddy and me, followed by Aunt Jane and Uncle Carl. I stumbled up to the casket and looked. It was then that I knew, for the first time, the finality of death. I saw his body, but Grandpa was not there. He was somewhere else. Again, I was struck with the finality of it all. I would never be with Grandpa again . . .never. . .never!!!

"But Grandpa is still here. In my heart. Every time I see a kid flying a kite, I think of Grandpa. . .every time I see a young boy or girl playing with their grandpa. . .every time I hear a song. It was a popular song of that year, not notable for its staying power as a classic, but one that nevertheless stuck in my mind. It has never gone away. Every time I think of Grandpa I feel that old sense of loss, not as sharp as it was in childhood, but there. I can hear that song, playing in my brain, "It's Been So Long:" . . .since you held me tight . . .and you said good night. . .its been so long. . . ."

Why such a nondescript song from the middle thirties should be lodged in H.F.'s brain in such a manner is hard to understand, except to say that sometime the next day it was playing on the radio at home. H.F. was still in the throes of his grief when he heard it. Apparently, it formed an association in his brain that remains today.

CHAPTER 31
Comes a Little Sister

In October 1925, my mother became pregnant a second time. This time she went to the hospital in Jefferson City. She was gone a week before coming home with my baby sister. Her name is June. Now a wife and mother with three adult children (all boys) and nine (or is it ten?) Grandchildren, I have always felt a strong bond between us. I cannot recall ever having feelings of jealousy or competition between us. There was 3 1/2 years between us, and I guess I felt pretty securely established as the "prince" of the house. I assumed the role of big brother and June seemed to accept that without rancor. When I was about 9 or 10 years old, June and I were given joint responsibility for taking care of a couple of sheep that we had. We took care of cleaning and sweeping out their shed, fed them, curried them and petted them. Eventually, the sheep went off to market, but we were farm kids, and we had grown to expect that. If our parents had intended that project to provide a lesson in cooperative behavior and the importance of working to achieve something it was effective. I was pretty proud of my little sister, and I think she felt the same way about me.

June and I were given other cooperative ventures. Mama told us that the cherry trees were full of cherries and that they were about ready to pick. If we wanted, we could pick cherries. She offered to pay us, jointly, a nickel per half-gallon pail. The trees were loaded, the limbs sagging down, the bottom ones almost touching the ground. June picked from the low branches, since she wasn't quite ready to climb the stepladder. I picked from the ladder, going as high as I could. It was imperative that we get the trees picked quickly, for as the cherries ripened the birds would go after them. So Mama helped too, though her production didn't earn us any nickels. In the hot weather, picking a half-gallon pail full took longer than I thought it would. It was "not a bowl of cherries," it was considerably more! After a day of picking, our fingers, and sometimes our lips would be stained with juice. Mama said, "You can eat one now and then, but don't overdo it or you'll get a stomachache!" June and I smiled at each other almost as if to say, "I won't tell if you don't!" That evening, after supper (we had three meals each day - breakfast, dinner at noon, and supper in the evening), we would help Mama stem, pit, sort and wash the cherries before she would put them in Mason jars for canning. Then we were paid, probably 25 or 30 cents. June and I would cut the swag down the middle. It never occurred to either of us to count the amount of cherries each of us picked. We did the same thing with other "special" chores such as picking peaches or pears or digging potatoes. For these jobs, we were being paid, not bribed. Our regular chores, like helping with the milking, carrying in wood for the stoves or cutting grass we did simply because it was "our job". Don't misunderstand. We were not perfect little angels. Sometimes we would procrastinate or get involved in something else more interesting, such as roller skating or playing with friends. Then Mama

would say, "Herman Franklin, (as soon as she called me that way, I knew that we were about to get a short lecture) it's alright to play and have fun, but you do that after you have finished your chores. The wood box is empty. Why don't you go carry in some wood. June, I need some help here with the dishes."

Later, after I went into the service and married Arretta, my Sis and I didn't see each other much. Our lives diverged. Although I am much to blame for allowing it to happen, Arretta put a wet blanket on most communication with my family. In order to keep the peace, I went along with it. "Don't make waves," I thought to myself, "it'll change."

It didn't.

Sometime during the early morning hours Son awoke to the continuing sounds of the General Blatchford as it continued its progress westward. The seas were running much heavier with waves of six to eight feet. A mid-Pacific storm was in the offing. Although the pitching and rolling was not severe it was enough to make many of the passengers seasick. Fortunately Son was not among those who were afflicted. As the day progressed, however, the winds picked up and the rains began. The ship was heading directly into a major mid-Pacific storm. Each hour it got worse. By evening ten to twelve foot waves were breaking directly over the bow of the ship. The captain reduced speed to no more than three or four knots, just enough to keep the ship headed into the wind and perpendicular to the breaking waves. As the ship crested each wave the bow would come out of the water. Then driving into the trough, the bow would come back down, hitting the water with a tremendous boom. Again, water would pour over the bow. Passengers were told to stay inside, not that any of them really wanted to venture out on deck. Mealtimes were a disaster. It was impossible to keep dishes and meal trays from sliding on the tables. For those who wanted to eat, and there weren't many, sandwiches and coffee were available. The storm continued for two more days, finally abating on the fourth day out. The ship resumed its normal cruising speed - a brisk eight to ten knots!

CHAPTER 32
The Town We Called Home

Travel by sea gives one substantial opportunity to reflect. Over the next week Son engaged in extended self-dialog about his life and its beginnings:

I have said many times since leaving my boyhood home and going off to war that, although I didn't know it at he time, I was 'a big frog in a very, very small puddle.' Centertown, Missouri, located in almost the exact geographical center of the United States, could hardly be called a 'town.' The terms, 'village', or 'burg.' would be more accurately descriptive. Located on U.S. Highway 50, approximately fifteen miles west of Jefferson City, Mo., the state capital, Centertown today has a population of 350. That is about the same as it was when I lived there. A joke of my early adulthood goes, 'It wasn't until I grew up and went off to college that I found out that the name of the place wasn't 'Resume speed!' Yellow Pages? We were lucky to have a telephone system. In fact, there was a 'central' operator. Mrs. Pace manned the switchboard, a primitive, manual thing, which she operated out of her own house.

The Missouri-Pacific Railroad ran through the middle of town, as it did many little towns of the Midwest. I don't know where the term, 'from the other (or wrong) side of the tracks' came from, but it didn't apply to Centertown. We lived on the South side, about two blocks from the tracks. The MOPAC depot, where Daddy worked, was almost squarely in the middle of town. Painted yellow, with 'railroad' brown trim, and smelling faintly of creosote, it was typical of hundreds, perhaps thousands of depots scattered throughout America. There was a waiting room, furnished with a couple of Spartan, wood benches for passengers use. There was a little, pot bellied, coal burning stove, with which to heat the place in winter. The office area, adjacent to the waiting room, was where Daddy worked. That's where he kept his trusty L.C. Smith typewriter, on the desk, next to his telegraph receiver and high speed 'bug' which he used for sending and receiving Western Union messages. Whenever his station call letters came clicking in on the receiver, Daddy would drop whatever he was doing, rush to the desk, pull out a yellow Western Union Telegram form from the desk and insert it into the typewriter. All the while, the message would continue to come in. As soon as he got the paper adjusted, he would begin typing. He was the fastest 'hunt and peck' typist I have ever seen! He used only the first fingers from each hand. Before the message ended, he had usually caught up with the dots and dashes that were being transmitted over the wire. I was awe struck. How could he make sense of any of that? Daddy took advantage of my curiosity and began to explain and teach me Morse code (the letter 'a' is dit-dah, 'b' is dit dit (space) dit dit, etc.). Later, I learned International Code, slightly different from Morse, and used in the military. This knowledge and skill would come in handy later when I went into the service.

The rest of the depot consisted of a large storage area for storing and shipping freight, and a loading dock. There was a four wheeled, iron-tired Railway Express wagon which sat idle most of the time, but which could be used, I supposed for hauling things from freight cars to the depot.

Down the tracks to the East was a mail mast; a device on which mail sacks could be suspended, awaiting 'ole Number 11 or Number 12', east and west bound passenger trains, which did not stop in Centertown. 'Butch' Swearingen was employed by the Post Office ....his only job was to go to the post office in the afternoon to pick up outgoing mail which Mrs. Proctor, the Postmistress, had put into a special, heavy canvass bag. She padlocked it securely and attached a destination tag. Butch would then take it to the depot, where he would check with Daddy to see of the train was on time. He would then walk the sack to the mail mast, a distance of about 100 yards. Butch had a short right leg the result of childhood polio, and wore an orthopedic shoe with a sole and heel that extended his foot by probably four or five inches. Still, he walked with an exaggerated limp. Twice a day, though, Butch would make the round trip from the Post Office to the mail mast. Then he would wait for the train to come through. As the train approached the mast at a speed of 60 mph, two things would happen in quick succession: (1) one of the mailmen would take a sack of Centertown's incoming mail, and at the precise millisecond, heave it off the train. It would hit the dirt just before the mail mast and, in a cloud of dust, roll to a stop; and (2) the other mailman would extend a long steel arm with a crook at the end of it. As the train approached the mail mast, the steel arm would snag the sack of outgoing mail, which Butch had loosely tied to the mast. The mail would be pulled into the speeding train and the transaction was complete. Butch would then retrieve the dusty sack that had been dropped off. After a short stop at the depot for a drink of water and a fresh plug of Red Man chewing tobacco, (his lips and ample mustache were stained with tobacco juice) he would limp his way back to the Post Office with the day's mail. Like the old, mongrel dog that took his nap every afternoon in the shade of the depot, Butch was the ultimate in loyalty and dependability.

Another character who contributed to our town's social matrix was John "Barleycorn" (that's what Daddy called him) Dudley, the town drunk. Most of the time, John was sober. He would work at all kinds of odd jobs around town - minor carpentry; help with the harvest and other tasks. But about once a month, John would walk out to the edge of town to pay a visit to Roy Thompson, our resident bootlegger. Roy had a way with 'corn squeezins' that was apparently to John's liking. A pint of his white lightning was usually sufficient to render John incoherent and barely able to navigate up the railroad right of way toward the Depot. There, his head rolling on his shoulders as if it were about to fall, he would attempt to sit and or stretch out on one of the waiting room benches to sleep it off. Daddy, of course, would not tolerate this, and would promptly roust him out of the Depot. Most of the time John would go peacefully. Sometimes, however, he would get belligerent, whereupon Daddy would grab John's shirt collar, and lift him up from the bench. Then he would get a firm grip on the seat of John's pants, and unceremoniously throw him out of the depot. Later, John could usually be seen staggering across the town square and up the street that led toward the Baptist Church. Eventually, he would find a cool patch of grass and pass out until he sobered up. That would usually take care of the problem for a month or so, long enough for John to accumulate enough cash to pay Roy another visit.

Lest the reader think that our town was populated only by ne'er do wells, mention must be given to some of our town's entrepreneurs.

We had a general store, owned and operated by Vic Witthaus, the 'merchant prince' of Centertown. His store was stocked with the usual inventory of canned goods, specialty meats such as bologna, hot dogs and Kraft American cheese loafs. We rarely bought any of

these items. Daddy said they were too expensive, and besides, we raised our own. We did depend upon the store for staples - sugar, salt and bread. Vic also had an Orange Crush pop cooler, always filled with ice and pop of all kinds, Coke, Pepsi-Cola, Orange Crush, Nehi Strawberry and other flavored sodas. In the hot, barefoot time of summer, I would pad into the store. What a relief it was to put my bare feet on the wooden floor instead of the hot gravel outside. I would go over to the cooler, open the lid and just hold my hands in the ice-cold water. The pop looked so inviting, and I was so thirsty. "If only I had a nickel," I thought longingly. Vic saw me and said, "Do you want a pop, Herman Franklin?"

"Yes, but I can't pay for it, I said plaintively." June and I had put all our liquid cash in the bank in a savings account, and I didn't have any money to jingle in my pocket.

"Well, I could put it on your Dad's bill."

"What do you mean?"

"I will just write it down, that you bought a pop, and then when your Dad comes in, he can pay for it."

That sounded easy, so I told Vic that I wanted an RC Cola (they were the biggest) and maybe a Snickers bar. That would be five cents for the cola and five cents more for the Snickers. Vic said he would put both of them, 'on the tab.' It sounded OK to me. I reached in the cooler and fished out a big 12-ounce bottle of RC Cola. With the cold icy water dripping from it, using the bottle opener on the front of the cooler, I pried the cap from the bottle. It came off with a hiss, a tiny wisp of vapor rising from inside the bottle. Vic fished a Snickers bar from inside the glass case and handed it to me. I peeled back the paper and took a bite - all chocolaty and chewy — then washed it down with a long swallow from the RC. What bliss! I don't think I've ever enjoyed a soda and a candy bar quite as much as I did that one. At supper that evening, I thought about what I had done. I knew that I should tell Daddy, but I couldn't bring myself to say anything. But a day of judgment was coming. A couple of days later, as we were all seated around the circular, oil-cloth covered kitchen table for supper, Daddy looked up from a thin sheaf of papers that he had been shuffling. He fixed me with his, 'Uh-oh, trouble's coming,' look. Daddy was slightly cross-eyed, so we were never sure which eye he was using, but it didn't matter. When he fixed you with that gaze, you wanted nothing more than to fall through the floor.

"Herman Franklin," he said, pursing his mouth until his lips almost disappeared, and using his steeliest tone. "What's this?!"

He held up three or four yellow slips of paper.

June began to cry, because she knew what was coming. Herman Franklin was about to get a tonguelashing that was just as painful as if it were administered with a peach tree switch.

Herman Franklin tugged at the top of his bib overalls. There wasn't anything to say. That he knew.

"Herman Franklin, we can't afford this. This is too expensive. If you are thirsty, come home and ask Mama for a drink of cold water or some iced tea. We have to watch our nickels. I'm disappointed that you did this. Why didn't you tell me?"

"Disappointed? Why didn't you tell me?"

There was no satisfactory answer to such questions. H.F. simply hung his head in shame. He didn't want to disappoint his father.

"Don't do that again."

"Yes, Daddy."

Centertown also boasted that it had a four-year high school. Not many towns the size of Centertown (population 375) did. But Centertown had a mayor, a bank and a city budget. The school district was financed by county property tax money. For years Daddy was elected to the school board, functioning as its secretary. They issued bonds, again by vote of the populace, to raise money for construction of the school building and to buy a big yellow

International school bus that brought students in from the country. Son went from first grade through 4 years of high school there. In high school he was on the debate team, was active in music, piano and vocal, and during his senior year was the editor of The Red Bird, the high school newspaper. It goes without saying that at home a high emphasis was placed on education.

CHAPTER 33
The Empire of Japan Looms Ahead

On the morning of the tenth day the end of a long voyage approached. As the Blatchford entered the port of Yokahama of a set of strange new smells assailed Son's nostrils. They were not the smells of a seaport like San Francisco. This was "The Land Of The Rising Sun." Since he had never encountered these strange smells before they were hard to categorize. They were just different. Peppery? Oriental? Salty? Fishy? All of the above! The ship slowed to a crawl, finally stopped and waited for the tugs to appear and attach themselves. Finally the ship eased into the dock. Lines were secured and gangways lowered. For the first time, Son saw Japanese people. He compared the stevedores handling the ship with the stereo-typed caricature that most Americans held. He began to see that contrary to his precon-ceptions they did not all look the same. There were differences and similarities. He noted the funny characteristic billed caps, a Japanese version of a baseball cap he supposed, and sandal-like shoes called "tabis" which separated the big toe from the other four.

There was a Japanese band, playing or attempting to play "Stars and Stripes Forever." Processing through the port was rapid. Son boarded a bus that took him to a place called Zama, a replacement depot where all incoming personnel were checked in and transporta-tion to final destinations throughout Japan were arranged. Later that day he was aboard a C-46 Commando on a flight to the southernmost island in Japan - the Island of Kyushu - and a base named Ashiya. He looked out the right window and saw the snow-capped peak of Mt. Fjui, an icon in Japanese life. In the Shinto religion Mt. Fuji is thought to be the home of ancestral spirits. It was indeed a beautiful and stately mountain. Months later he buzzed across the top of Mt. Fuji in an F-51 Mustang, clearing the rim of the volcano by only a few feet. Fortunately, he was flying from west to east, the direction of the prevailing winds. As he crossed the eastern rim, his mustang was grabbed by the tremendous downdraft caused by the wind spilling over the edge of the mountain. His mustang was "lassoed" and pitched down so violently that Son's head hit the canopy. Because he had plenty of altitude once over the edge of the mountain, he was able to recover. After that he gave Fuji and its ances-tral spirits a wide berth!

Ashiya was the home of the 8th Fighter Wing, Son's new outfit. Two of the three squadrons, the 36th called the Flyin' Fiends and the 80th, known as The Headhunters, were based there. The third squadron, the 35th Black Panthers was on detached service at a remote base located on the north coast of the Island of Honshu. Son was ultimately as-signed to the 35th. Miho Air Base was to be his new home for the next several months. Because the 35th was the only unit on the base, the squadron had responsibility for all of the many base house-keeping functions normally carried out by specialized units in a larger base setup. The squadron was therefore augmented with base security, food service, base

and technical supply, communications, aircraft control and warning and air-sea rescue personnel. In a normal setup, officers in the squadron would be assigned primary duty as pilots. Here, however, each officer also had an additional duty. In addition to being a primary duty fighter pilot and flight commander, Son found himself being appointed Base Supply Officer as an additional duty.

"But Major Davis, I don't have any experience in supply. I've never been a supply officer."

Major Glendon V. Davis was both Squadron and Base commander. Son was to find that he was an excellent officer. He and his wife, Sally, later became personal friends.

"That's O.K., Lieutenant. You'll pick it up quickly. Lieutenant Lattimore has the job now, but he'll be going home in about a month. Just stick with him and pick his brains. He'll need to sign over the base supply account to you before he leaves."

"What does that entail? What will I be signing for?"

"Well, just about everything on the base - all the items in dependent housing, furniture and equipment, all the items needed to run the mess hall, vehicles and equipment in the base motor pool, the air-sea rescue crash boat and its equipment, the base dispensary, communications equipment and tech supply in the squadron."

"Is that all?" said Son

"I think that about covers it. If you have any questions, though, Lattimore can fill you in. Anyway, welcome aboard! We're glad to have you as a Black Panther!"

Son didn't expect this. He said to himself, however, that he'd just take it as it came and do the best he could. One step at a time, he thought. Within a month however Son assumed by signature on Memorandum of Receipt and Lattimore relinquished responsibility for just about everything on the base. He found that he had a very knowledgeable enlisted man, Master Sergeant John Winters. Winters had an assistant, Sgt. Bill Zook, who had spent his entire service career in supply. It became apparent to Son that Winters and Zook knew what they were doing so Son let them do it. Certainly he was not too proud to let the Sergeant teach him a few things about supply either.

Back in the squadron, Son was assigned as Flight Commander of "A" flight. He found that he had some very inexperienced pilots in his flight. Not fighter pilots, as he expected, but bomber pilots! Why did the powers that be make such assignments? It was hard to say, but it probably reflected an air force wide paucity of skilled pilots. This was certainly going to be a "make do" project, he thought. They had arrived at Miho only a month or so before Herman. They were not current in the P-51, in fact not even the AT-6 single engine trainer assigned to the squadron. Jim Tidwell had flown the B-24 four-engine bomber as had Bill Wetzel. Al Wimer was a B-29 pilot. Both of these large bombers featured tricycle landing gear, a far cry from the conventional tail-dragger landing gear of the F-51 and the AT-6. Herman knew he was going to have to start with some basics on how to land and handle these aircraft on the ground. Once that was accomplished they could go on to more advanced subjects such as formation flying and tactics in the air. They started with the AT-6. Both Jim and Al were avid students and Herman was a patient instructor. Within a couple of months they were checked out in the F-51 and were making progress in formation flying. Son also worked on their instrument flying skill, using the AT-6. It was a day-

to-day thing - each day a little better than the last. Eventually, they were all checked out in the P-51. That meant that at least they could get the Mustang in the air and back on the ground in one piece!

Part of the squadron's training requirement was to mount a full 16 plane mission, and in formation to circumnavi-

gate the entire island of Honshu. External drop tanks, carrying extra fuel, were necessary for this mission lasting over four hours. Wimer and Tidwell were not ready for this mission. Son lead one of the four, four ship flights. Lattimore, the erstwhile supply officer, flew on Son's left wing.   The morning of the scheduled mission arrived. Major Davis briefed all the pilots, outlining every aspect of the mission, including take-off and form up procedures, routes and navigation, communication and emergency procedures. We all got a "time hack," that is we synchronized our watches with Major Davis' watch.

"Start engines at Oh Nine Hundred hours," said Davis.

Each pilot had written details of the mission on a knee pad. This he carried with him, strapping it to his right leg so that he could make ready reference to it in the air.

"O.K., let's go!"

With that, sixteen pilots in full flight gear headed out of the squadron ready room and walked to their aircraft. At the appointed time, 0900, props began to turn and sixteen Rolls-Royce Merlins sprang to life. Momentarily, the ramp was awash in blue-white smoke. Radios snapped on and each pilot checked in. Major Davis asked the tower for taxi instructions. Major Davis with his four- ship flight taxied out first, followed in turn by the other three flights. All flights, with tower's permission, took the active runway. After run-up and pre-takeoff checks were performed, Major Davis began his takeoff roll. After a straight ahead climb to about 500 feet, he began a slow turn to the left. As each successive flight took off it cut inside of Major Davis flight, thus closing on him. After a 360 degree turn all four flights were in position, in trail and below Major Davis. As they set course for Misawa on the northern coast of Honshu, the flights loosened their spacing to a comfortable distance and settled in for what we all supposed would be a somewhat boring three or four hours. It was not to be. About an hour into the flight, Lattimore, who was flying on Son's left wing, issued a distress call.

"Contour Blue, Two here, I got a problem."

"What's the problem?

"I have to take a s ____!"

"What!"

"I got the runs!"

"Can't you hold it?"

"No!"

"Well try!" (Pause)

"Uh Oh!!"

"What's the matter?"

"Lost it!"

"What do you want to do? Do you want to abort?"

"No. Let me work on this."

With that, Lattimore moved out a hundred yards or so from the rest of the formation. Son noticed that he was flying erratically.

"You all right?"

"Yeah. I'm just trying to get out of my parachute and flight suit!"

"Sure you are. How you gonna do that?"

"I think I can do it. Just give me some time."

After about five minutes of continued drunken-like flying, Lattimore settled down and closed his spacing on Son. Son could see that he was rolling back his canopy. He could hardly believe what he saw next. Lattimore pitched his offending undies overboard!! Then he closed the canopy. Houdini couldn't have done it any better.

"You O.K.?" There was no response.

"Are you airsick?"

"Not if you mean am I puking into my oxygen mask! I'm just going to have to decontaminate this bird when we get home."

"You can break off and go home if you want to."

"Nah, I think I can make it."

Four hours later the squadron returned to Miho, entered the traffic pattern and landed. Back in the ready room, everybody laughed.

"Lattimore, you idiot . . go hose yourself down!"

After decontaminating himself and his aircraft, he was back in everybody's good graces. Somebody said that for that effort he should be awarded the French Croix De Peuw!

Meanwhile, Son got to know the people of this small base, really a small closed community. He and other members of the squadron were invited several times for dinner with Major and Mrs. Davis. Since Al Wimer had been at Miho for several months before Son, he was assigned a set of quarters in base housing. His wife, Jeanette, joined him. Jeanette, a strawberry blonde, was so glad to be there, their enforced separation ended. She was friendly and easy to know. Son and other members of the squadron spent a number of evenings at the Wimers. Although this eased somewhat Herman's feelings of loneliness it didn't completely eliminate the ache he felt in being separated from Arretta and his new baby daughter, Mary-Lynn. After he had been there for about six months, he was asked by the Wing at Ashiya to confirm his intention to bring his family to Japan. In his mind there was no question whatsoever. He wanted them to come. But letters from Arretta indicated that she didn't want to, in fact might refuse to come! That would mean a long two and one-half years before he would see them. Intolerable! He had to talk with her. He arranged for a long-distance overseas telephone call. The technology in 1948 was primitive. There were no satellites, only cable and radio. The communications were "simplex," meaning that when one party was transmitting, the other party could only listen. It was noisy and difficult to hear. Nevertheless, Son absolutely had to talk with her. He arranged the call by making an "appointment" with the receiving party. Arretta was told that a call would be coming from Japan at about 10:00 A.M., M.S.T. (Mountain Stqndard Time) In Japan, that meant that Son would have to be standing by the telephone at 2:00 A.M. The cost? — $50 for a five minute call. That was a lot of money then. But if he could convince Arretta to come it would be worth it.

"Hello! Arretta?" There was a pause for several seconds.

"Yes, I'm here!"

"I got your letter saying you don't want to come. I can't stand that, do you understand?"

"I know, but I just can't see leaving Phoenix, traveling all the way to San Francisco, uprooting Mary-Lynn."

"Once you get here, you will like it. Japan is a fascinating country. The housing is nice."

"I don't know - it just seems impossible."

"Arretta, do you want to stay married to me?'

"Of course."

"Then you must come. I can't stay married if I can't be with you for over two more years! What's it going to be?"

"I do want us to be together. Can't you come home?"

"Arretta, you know that's ridiculous! I'd have to leave the Air Force, and I'm not going to do that!"

"I just don't know!"

"Yes you do! It's time for you to make a decision. Are you coming or not?"

There was a long pause. Finally, Arretta said,

"I guess I'll come then."

"All right! I'll do everything I can to help you prepare for the trip. I want you to bring our car. If you can't drive it to the port yourself, then we'll get someone to drive it for you. You will be getting official orders soon that will authorize all your travel. I'll keep you posted on things from this end."

"I hope I'll know what to do."

"You will. Everything will be spelled out for you. I'll write you every day to make sure that you have everything you need."

"I'm nervous, just thinking about it."

"I know. But you'll be all right. Trust me.

"O.K., I guess."

"I'll be in touch, dear. Goodnight and I love you."

"I love you too."

With that the conversation was terminated. Son didn't know whether to feel relieved or not. He didn't feel entirely sure that he could trust Arretta to follow through on the decision to come. All he could do now was to wait and hope.

In the meantime he continued his duties at the squadron. His job as base supply officer was by now routine. The flying however continued to present a challenge. There weren't enough flying hours available to provide the kind of training that Wimer, Wetzel and Tidwell needed. He thought, "I'm glad there's not a war on right now. I love these guys but they aren't ready to fight."

In August, 1949 Headquarters, Fifth Air Force in Nagoya decided to close Miho and consolidate all three squadrons at another base on Kyushu. It was too costly to operate a single squadron in detached service with all the attendant base costs. The 36th and 80th squadrons moved from Ashiya and the 35th moved from Miho to Itazuke Air Base. Itazuke was located on the northern coast of Kyushu, near the industrial town of Fukkouka, Japan. The move made sense. From a personal point of view, Son was happy that housing and other facilities to support dependents was much better than it would have been at Miho. There was a large commissary and officers' club located at Kasuga, the main base that supported the fighter strip at Itazuke. There was a large general hospital located in Fukkouka. The move was completed without undue difficulty. Son wrote Arretta to tell her the news.

CHAPTER 34
Another Family Separation

Soon after the move to Itazuke was completed, Far Eastern Air Forces, located at Hickham Air Base, Hawaii announced a FEAF wide fighter gunnery competition. All operational squadrons would compete. Based on local squadron competition, each wing or base would nominate a team to compete at major command level. Finally, two teams, one in conventional class and one in jet class, winners at Air Force level, would be nominated to represent FEAF at Nellis Air Force Base in Las Vegas, NV to compete in a world wide fighter gunnery competition. The 8th Fighter Wing conventional class team, consisting of Captain Asa Adair, First Lieutenant Herman Son, First Lieu-

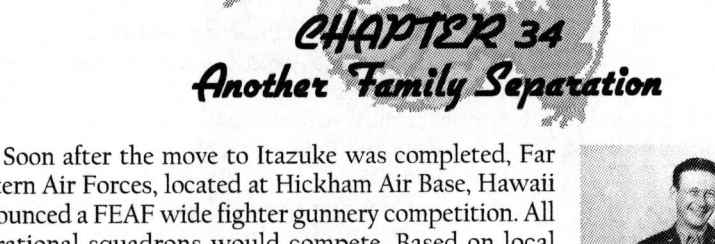

Front to rear, l to r:
Tabor, Adair, Son, Haggerty

tenant Chris Hagerty and 2nd Lieutenant John Tabor eventually won at Fifth Air Force and FEAF levels, thereby winning the right to go to Nellis. The team commander was Major James McNees, commander of the 36th squadron. Engineering and armament officer was First Lieutenant Joe Rogers, also of the 36th.

While this was going on, Arretta got her travel orders to proceed to Japan. She arrived in October. Son met them at the ship as it arrived in Yokohama harbor. It was an overnight train ride to Fukkoka. Permanent quarters were not yet available, so Herman, Arretta and Mary-Lynn moved into temporary housing. It wasn't the best situation. Two families occupied one building, with common bath and toilet facilities separating the families. We were told that a permanent apartment would probably become available before Christmas.

To add to the Son family's woes, Mary-Lynn was ill. The long trip, the change in routine, change in food and water, produced severe diarrhea. She was in danger of going into severe dehydration. There was nothing to do but put her in the Army general hospital in Fukkoka. Although the medical treatment was adequate, there were no provisions for a parent to stay with a sick child. Much as Son argued with the hospital staff, they would not, said they could not, permit it. Thus the physical ailment was compounded by the psychological trauma of being separated from her mother. After a week, Mary-Lynn recovered and was reunited with her mother and father. However it was some time before she recovered from the emotional upset.

Now, as Christmas approached, the Sons finally got an apartment. What a relief it was. They had two full bedrooms, full bath, a nice living room and a kitchen. There was enough furniture to get by, although their household goods from the States would arrive soon. They settled in, and in spite of what was going on in the fighter gunnery competition,

began to relax. They got a house maid, a very sweet and polite Japanese girl named Sumiko, who spoke fairly good English, knew how to cook and sew and clean house. The monthly charge, paid to the dependent housing office was $9.50! What a bargain.

As Christmas approached, they got a tree, decorated it and were prepared to have an almost normal Christmas. In March, however, another separation loomed, albeit a shorter one. Herman was a member of the FEAF conventional class fighter gunnery team. That meant that he would be packing soon to go to Nellis AFB, NV.

"How long will you be gone?"

"I don't know for sure. FEAF intends to fly our entire team, pilots, maintenance personnel, armament and communications people, the whole bunch, to Nellis. They'll put us on a C-54 and we'll grind our way all the way across the Pacific. I understand that we'll pick up our airplanes there. They will be flown in from the Virginia Air National Guard. They want to give us at least a month before the competition to get our airplanes tuned up, guns harmonized and to familiarize ourselves with not only our airplanes but the area where we will be flying. The competition itself will last a couple of weeks. My guess is we'll be gone at least six weeks."

"That's not fair," Arretta said petulantly. "I just get here and now you're going to be gone."

"I know. I agree, it's not fair! But try not to think about it. I'll be home before you know it, and then we'll have some time together. I'll take a couple of weeks leave and we'll go to the Aso Kanko rest hotel. It's up in the mountains south of here. It's a real spa. They have natural springs with hot water. They pamper their guests. The place was built for the 1936 winter Olympics I hear. I've heard it's really beautiful. We can relax and get to know each other again."

"Promise?"

"Promise."

On the day of the team's departure, Son kissed and hugged Arretta.

"Take care of yourself and take good care of Mary-Lynn. Sumiko will help you I know. Won't you, Sumiko?

"Yes, reutenant!"

Son chuckled. Sumiko could not pronounce the English sound for the letter "L".

"I'll write as soon as I get there and give you an address to write to me."

"I'll miss you!"

"I'll miss you too. I love you!"

With that, the black Plymouth staff car beeped its horn outside their apartment. Son gave them both a final hug, grabbed his B-4 bag and was out the door.

Later that afternoon the entire team, together with all its equipment, were on board a C-54, four-engine transport on their way to the United States. The airplane was not configured for passengers - no plush airline seats, just canvas bench seats. Cold and drafty, there was no soundproofing. There were a couple of bunks up front for the crew, but none for the passengers. The best place to sleep, or to try to, was atop a pile of parachutes in the back. There was a short stop at Guam for refueling, then the long over water leg to Hickham AFB, Hawaii. After 8 hours in the air, everybody welcomed the 3 hour stop. They went into the terminal and had a real meal, washed down with a beer or two. This did wonders for everybody's attitude.

Toward the end of the third long over water leg, the big transport airplane approached the California coast. They were scheduled to land at Fairfield in Marin County, just north of San Francisco. This time, Son saw the great bridge spanning the mouth of San Francisco Bay from above, not below as he had done when he left by boat for Japan. It was a beautiful sight from this angle too, thought Son - it's America, the land of the free! He hadn't ex-

pected to see it again so soon. After landing and a routine customs check, they were again on their way. It was a short trip this time, only a couple of hours.

After landing at Nellis, they were met by Colonel Deward E. Bower, commander of the training group which would act as host for the meet. Colonel Bower, incidentally, was Herman's old boss from many years earlier when he first became an instructor at Ajo right after he graduated from flight school. At that time, Son was a second Lieutenant and Bower was a Captain. It was good to see him again.

They checked into the BOQ (Bachelor Officers' Quarters) and unpacked. Dinner at the Officers' Club and relaxed chit-chat filled the rest of the evening. They were scheduled to meet with Colonel Bower and his people tomorrow for briefing on meet procedures. The six airplanes that they had been assigned and would fly had already arrived, flown in by Virginia Air Guard pilots. Joe Rogers said that he was anxious to see what condition the birds were in.

"I hope they're flyable. If they're in reasonable shape we can fix the guns. I know that they won't be anywhere close to proper harmonization. If we're going to have a chance in a gunnery competition these birds have to have a thorough checkout on their guns."

Joe was right. While flyable, the airplanes were in no shape to shoot accurately. To adjust the guns a somewhat involved procedure was required. Nellis had, as all fighter bases did, a "firing in" range. The guns, there were six of them, three on each wing, had to be pointed so that the trajectory of their bullets when fired intersected a point in space approximately 650 feet in front of the airplane. But first, Joe ordered all guns removed from the airplanes and brought to the armament shop where they were subjected to thorough inspection, cleaning and oiling. Most of them were dirty and could not be relied upon to perform. After putting them back in their wing mounts, each airplane was towed to the firing range. There it was placed on jacks and pointed generally in the direction of a bulls eye target at the other end of the range. The jacks were adjusted, using precision leveling equipment, to place the airplane in an attitude that it would assume if it were in the air and flying at an airspeed of 275 KIAS. The target was moved until it was directly in line with the plane's gunsight. Then each of the six guns was individually adjusted, using a special optical tool, until it also pointed at the center of the target. After that, test rounds were fired and scored on the target. Fine adjustments were then made until each gun was hitting where the airplane's gunsight said they should be hitting. Now the pilot could fly his airplane and point it at what he wanted to hit and when he pulled the trigger on the stick, expect to hit where he aimed.

As soon as harmonization and other maintenance work was accomplished, the four primary team pilots, Adair, Son, Haggerty and Tabor, began twice daily practice missions. Thanks to Joe and his maintenance personnel, the airplanes performed reliably.

Of course, everyone felt that, while in Las Vegas, they should pay their respects to the great god, Neon on that long street known as "The Strip." Most of the hotels and gambling joints that were there in 1950 are still there in 2002, albeit larger, brighter and gaudier.

The Sands and the Flamingo immediately come to mind. Downtown, there was The Golden Nugget, flashing its "c'mawn in!" with a two story high, animated neon cowboy sign. Vegas, sometimes referred to as "Lost Wages," is a monument to shallowness and to greed. The idea that one just might possibly "break the bank" seems irresistible to enough people that they keep coming back. Of course they keep losing their money. Winners did not build those big hotels. Losers built them. Low priced food and entertainment are the bait that brings customers in, but the gaming is the mainstay of cash flow and profit. Herman decided to put a roll of nickels in to a slot machine. It took him about half an hour, but as most gamblers do, he lost. The team took in dinner and a glitzy show at the Flamingo. Son remembers in particular the singer, Billy Daniels, and his treatment of "That Old Black Magic." That was a song that somehow reminded him of Arretta, now six thousand miles

away in Japan. He silently promised himself that he would make it up to her when he returned.

Back at Nellis, preparations for the gunnery competition proceeded. Thanks to the efforts of Joe Rogers and his team of armorers the guns were functioning perfectly. Daily practice flights, both air-to-air and air-to-ground, were honing the team's skills. They knew the competition would be stiff, but the felt that they had a good chance to win. The flying activities of the team did not interfere in any way with the normal training routines of the base. Nellis AFB, much as Luke AFB, had a combat crew training mission. They took pilots from a variety of sources and trained them in combat tactics in the F-86 and F-51. One day right after lunch hour, Son and his flight had just landed from a mission. At the end of their landing roll they pulled into a de-arm area at the end of the runway to have their guns "cooled." Then, executing a 135 degree turn to the left, they started taxiing down the long ramp and parking area to the south part of the field where they were assigned to park. About 1,000 feet long this journey, they passed Nellis Base Operations. "Base Ops", the control tower, base weather office and a snack bar were located in the building. Canopies were open and oxygen masks were unsnapped. Suddenly, Son heard the high-pitched snarl of a Merlin engine at near full power. Just as suddenly it stopped, then snarled again! This was the sound of some pilot in trouble. From the beginning, F-51 pilots have been warned about the powerful torque forces generated by that big 12-cylinder engine swinging a 12-foot four-bladed propeller. Looking forward from the cockpit, the prop rotates in a clockwise direction. This generates torque in the opposite or counter-clockwise direction. At slow airspeeds, as in a landing situation where the pilot bounces and attempts to correct with a sudden application of full throttle the ability of rudder and aileron to control it can be exceeded. The airplane can roll uncontrollably to the left. Son looked to his left and rear to see where the noise was coming from. There it was. An F-51 had just landed, or attempted to land on the same runway that Son and his flight has just used. It was now careening, like a wounded bird, off the runway to the left and across the grass infield. Each time he would attempt to correct a bounce with throttle, he would veer further left and start to roll. That would prompt him to cut the throttle, which would lead to another bounce and another application of throttle! Son could see what was going to happen. By now, he was almost directly behind Son's airplane, crossing the taxiway and ramp and heading for Base Operations! The last bounce was about 100 yards in front of the Snack Bar. He hit the building on the fly, driving the front of the airplane into the snack bar. No one knows why it didn't catch fire. Providentially, the lunch hour crowd had left. A cook and a waitress were the only persons in the bar. The waitress was killed. The cook and the pilot survived. He missed a collision with Son by mere seconds.

Finally, the competition began. Each team flew a total of twelve missions: four each of air-to-air, air-to-ground and bombing. The competition was close, but eventually the 27th Fighter Group team from Bergstrom Air Force Base, flying F-82s, won the conventional competition. The 8th Fighter Group team placed second. It was disappointing not to win, but considering that this was a USAF wide competition, a second place finish was nothing to be ashamed of. General Hoyt Vandenberg, the first USAF Chief of Staff, was there to present awards and to congratulate all participants. Congratulatory letters were also received from Lt. General Stratemeyer, CINCFEAF, and Major General Earl Partridge, Commanding General, Fifth Air Force.

Now it was time to return to Japan, 6,000 long miles back across the Pacific - Hawaii, Guam, Haneda and finally back to Itazuke. Son had been gone six weeks, although it seemed like a much longer time. Arretta, Mary-Lynn and Sumiko greeted him warmly. It was so good to see them again. Son promptly put in for two weeks leave and made reservations at the Aso Kanko Hotel. Two days later, they packed for a well deserved vacation. Driving in their new Olds, on the left side of the road, naturally, they soaked in the beauty of the lush

Japanese countryside. Arretta seemed to be in good spirits. Mary-Lynn was her most charming, impish self. Son was beginning to relax. After a 2 hour drive, they arrived. The Aso Kanko is located in the mountains at the upper end of a lush green blind valley in a jewel-like setting. They unpacked, ordered dinner in the room and really began to unwind. Maybe now, thought Son, we can have a normal family life for the rest of our tour.

Little did he know in those early weeks of June, 1950, what additional twists the fates were conspiring to bring about.

The Korean War began on June 26, 1950. Contour Red, his flight, and the 8th Fighter Group were among the very first American forces to be committed to a long struggle. 9 months later, with 107 combat missions in his log book, the Distinguished Flying Cross and the Air Medal with 9 oak leaf clusters pinned above his left breast pocket Son, with his family, was heading back home.

CHAPTER 35
By The Time We Get to Phoenix

Son was drifting, somewhere in space. He could hear the sound of a jet airplane some-where. He opened his eyes to see his daughter, Mary-Lynn, gently shaking him.

"Daddy, wake up!"

They had a flight to catch at noon.

Later, they were on a bus taking them from Fairfield to the San Francisco airport. After a two-hour flight, they touched down at Sky Harbor Airport in Phoenix. Arretta's father was there to meet them in his black 1941 DeSoto sedan, emphysema notwithstand-ing.

Son immediately drafted and sent a Western Union telegram to Headquarters, USAF, asking for a compassionate transfer to Luke AFB, located about 15 miles west of Phoenix. The base had only recently been reactivated after being closed right after the end of WWII. Son found out that they had two squadrons of F84-B and C airplanes and one squadron of F-80B's The Michigan Air National Guard had been transferred, and combined with the 127th Squadron of the Arizona National Guard. Together, they activated the 3600th Flight Training Wing, with a mission of training pilots before sending them to Korea. The Train-ing Command, based at Randolph AFB, was a support command, not a combat command. Son correctly assumed that it was not the best place to be for career advancement. But the flying would be good - tactical stuff in fighter aircraft. If the reassignment came through, Son thought, so be it. He would take it and give it his best effort. At least he would be flying fighters and supporting the Korean War effort.

He had fulfilled his promise to Arretta. Now all they could do was wait.

A week later an answering telegram came. Somewhat surprisingly, the reassignment was approved. That meant that they would have at least three years in the Phoenix area. He hoped that he had done the right thing. It was time to put down some roots.

They bought a house, a neat little all-brick three-bedroom ranch located in one of the many new subdivisions that were springing up in response to the many new families that were formed immediately after WWII. 7148 North 25th Drive was located Northwest about half way between downtown Phoenix and Glendale, Arizona. It was a straight shot down Glendale Avenue to Luke AFB, 10 miles to the West. The price was $7,450.00, which they financed with a VA nothing down loan at 4 1/2%. The monthly payments were $54.50 including taxes and insurance.

They bought a new car to replace the 1948 Olds that they sold in Japan. It was a really cool 1951 Mercury two-door that ran like the wind! They started working immediately to improve their little piece of real estate. Son built a basket-weave redwood fence. They prepared flower beds and planted them. They built a trellis around the carport and fes-

tooned it with red and blue morning glories. They planted flowering oleander bushes along the back side of their property, just inside the basket-weave fence. Son built a brick barbecue pit. In the hot Arizona summer all of this was back breaking work, but Son was young, in great physical shape and he didn't mind.

Things were "looking up." Arretta seemed to be relaxing, less prone to the anxiety attacks that plagued her in Japan. Son was fitting in well at the base. He was getting to know the personnel of the wing. He was assigned first to wing headquarters as an operations staff officer, attached to the 127th squadron, flying F-80s, for flying. Admittedly, Son had some politicking to do. At first everybody referred to him as "that regular officer." With the exception of Son, all were recently recalled National Guard officers, so-called "weekend warriors." As luck would have it, a couple of the National Guard guys, Captain Howard Ebersole from Michigan, and First Lieutenant Ray Silvius, from Arizona, bought new homes in the same sub-division as Son. They wound up carpooling together. They soon developed a mutual respect and friendship. Ebersole, "Ebe" for short, was a B-17 pilot from WWII, and a graduate MSEE. His technical knowledge impressed Son. "Ebe" was also impressed with Son's fighter and combat credentials. One day Son bet Ebe that he could do a double Immelman in a T-33 two-place jet trainer. This was a maneuver that involved diving to maximum KIAS of approximately 550 KIAS at low altitude, then pulling up steadily at 4-G's acceleration, rolling out of the first Immelman at approximately 300 KIAS and immediately going into the second Immelman. The second Immelman could be completed at about 120 KIAS, near stall speed at the top. Ebe said that it was impossible. Son said that he should get into the back seat of a T-33 with Son in the front and he would prove that he could do it. They did it and Son proved it.

Ray Silvius was also a great guy. In civilian life he was a staff reporter on the Arizona Republic, the leading newspaper in the state.

Son, Ray and Ebe were neighbors, fellow carpoolers, fellow officers and friends.

Arretta seemed to be happy with her new home and being close to her mother and father. When Son came home one afternoon with a "command performance" invitation to a party at the home of the Base commander, however, things on the home front took a turn for the worse. They had talked about this before. Son had tried to explain that it was expected that an officer's wife be an active participant with her husband in the social life of the base. Not to do so would put her husband at a distinct career disadvantage. Whether Arretta understood this or not, the bottom line was that the anxiety attacks returned.

What to do? Son urged Arretta to get professional help. But who? With no help or guidance, they finally selected a psychiatrist. Dr. Otto Bendheim was a classical Freudian, which meant extensive probing of the subconscious with the objective of bringing to light long suppressed conflicts and feelings, then, hopefully, resolving them. In the summer of 1951 she began her 55-minute hours with Dr. Bendheim on a weekly basis. They continued, off and on, for the four year duration of their stay in Phoenix. Son didn't know exactly what to expect. He hoped that the anxiety attacks would get better or disappear. After several months, however, there was no detectable change. Her agorophobia was strong as ever. Any attempt to go out in public, including trips to the grocery store, triggered panic attacks. She could go to visit her parents' house and the doctor. That was about it. Arretta's emotional problems had roots that went deep into her psyche. Son's efforts to talk to her about them were fruitless. He sensed that she had very low self-esteem, and he tried to do everything possible to bolster her feelings about herself. She was an intelligent woman, far beyond the average. She was talented and liked to paint. Son praised her for her talent and intelligence.

She was a voracious reader, although her reading was restricted to works of fiction, tending toward dark works from authors like Thomas Wolf and F. Scott Fitzgerald. Her behavior was unpredictable. At times she could be relaxed and charming, but with no

apparent reason that Son could discern, she would go into one of her dark periods. During these periods she was all but unapproachable. Something seemed to seize control of her personality. Son offered to see Bendheim too if he thought it would be helpful, but Arretta said, no, Dr. Bendheim said it was necessary to continue to work with her alone.

The more Son thought about it and the more he learned about Arretta's parents and their backgrounds, (from Arretta, significantly) the more convinced he became that Arretta had suffered severe abuse as a child. The abuse seemed to have come primarily from her father, Claude, but her mother, Mary, also played a role.

Claude Webb was a runaway from home at 15. Born in Gallatin, Tennessee, he left home ostensibly because he couldn't get along with his father. He landed in eastern Texas, taking a job working on the railroad tracks as a maintenance man, a "gandy dancer." There he met Mary Marcella Walker, daughter of a prosperous wheat farmer. Prosperous though Mary's father was, he was also (according Arretta's perception) a philanderer and a wife beater. Whether or not Mary suffered any physical abuse, she apparently did suffer emotional abuse. She hated her father. So, two lost souls, Claude and Mary, met and immediately "connected." Neither had any education beyond elementary school, but that didn't matter as much then. They got married and Mary left home to join Claude on the railroad. Their home was a railroad car, provided by the road for married employees. Here, in 1926, Arretta was born. Claude, now a teenage father now feeling his responsibility, said that they needed to go west. They gathered together their earthly belongings and together the three of them started west in Claude's model T Ford. They stopped in Phoenix, The Valley of The Sun. Claude found a job picking cotton. Mary worked in a field kitchen providing food for the itinerant field hands. Claude's boss took a liking to him and, seeing that he needed a job with a better long range future than picking cotton, helped them get a civil service job working for the U.S. Indian Service in Phoenix. They moved to a small apartment on the grounds of the U. S. Indian School where Claude took a job as a "Boy Supervisor" and Mary went to working the kitchen. By now, again according to Arretta, Claude also had a drinking problem. He would stay sober for a month or so, then he would go off on a two or three day drinking binge. Mary would not know where he was until he would come home, beat up on her and then slap Arretta around because she would cry. Eventually, Claude stopped drinking. Cold turkey, but by then, as far as Arretta was concerned, the damage had been done. By her late teens, Arretta had an attitude problem about men. She received inputs not only from her father but her mother as well. Moreover, she was looking for a way out of her dysfunctional family.

Claude and Mary worked for the Indian Service until they retired. This was where they lived and where Arretta grew up and met handsome, immature, uninformed and uniformed Herman Son in late 1943. A major segment of Son's journey through life was about to begin.

CHAPTER 36
A Three-Act Play

ACT I -"In the beginning," Son remembers, "there was hope and excitement. In the fall of 1943 I was a young cadet, just past my 21st birthday, when I first met Arretta. It was on a blind date, arranged by a cadet friend. His name was Pete Webb, strangely coincidental, but no relation to Arretta. He had a date with Dolores Bachman (familiar name? — she was the sister of Bob)."

Pete asked Son if he would like to double-date with him, Dolores and her friend.

"Sure", Son said.

Tall and willowy, with shoulder length auburn hair, full lips and a shy smile, Arretta captivated Son almost immediately. The electricity was almost overwhelming. That night, they went to a dark and inviting cocktail lounge at the Adams Hotel in Phoenix. It was crowded with cadets and their dates. They had drinks, cuddled in a booth. Son couldn't dance but on a crowded dance floor it didn't matter. 40's big band music pulsed on a five plays for a quarter, kaleidoscopic, red and yellow jukebox. Son asked her for another date. Curtain for Act I.

On a bright and sunny morning, January 7, 1944, Son joined over 600 of his fellow cadets in a full-scale formal parade and review and graduation ceremony.

This was a day for which he had worked and dreamed. Today he would be commissioned a Second Lieutenant and pin on his silver pilot's wings. Of course, Arretta was there to give him as hug and kiss and to pin on his wings. Son was doubly happy. First, he had made it through a tough, challenging 8-month training program. Secondly, he had his orders. 95% of his class received orders sending them on to "RTU" training, where they would be checked out in combat aircraft, then sent overseas and into combat with all it's uncertainties. But because Son had achieved the highest score in his class in gunnery, he was tagged to become an instructor. He had mixed feelings about this actually. He didn't want to see his classmates, particularly guys like Cody Stout and R.R. (Railroad) Thompson leave him behind. They were going on to a great adventure. But his new assignment introduced some relative safety and predictability into his life. His first assignment was at a gunnery base in southern Arizona, Ajo, AFB. What now? Son asked Arretta to marry him.

ACT II — Their life together began routinely enough. WWII, with all its perils and uncertainties provided a backdrop, but they were in love and were not concerned about "what if" kinds of questions. They were married in the base chapel at Williams Air Force Base by Army Chaplain Arlie McDaniel on March 16, 1944. In a simple ceremony, attended by Claude and Mary Webb and Dolores Bachman, their life together was joined.

Their first home was in a wartime FHA housing project in Ajo, Arizona, where they rented a small one-bedroom apartment for $32 per month, sharing it with nasty little straw

colored scorpions. They had a penchant for crawling into shoes overnight, so vigorous shaking was required before slipping them on in the morning. Truncating a mass of detail - enough for a book or two, really - it very soon became apparent to Son that Arretta was marching to a different drummer. To say the least, he was confused, often hurt by her double-bind (damned if you did, damned if you didn't) style of communication. Gradually, as he came to know more of her background, he began to realize that she was setting him up emotionally, trying to put her father Claude's face on him. It didn't fit him, but that didn't keep her from trying. Instead of realizing that their marriage was a mistake, Son kept trying, too, trying to love her, trying to get her to love him in return. At this point, they did not have children, and the marriage could easily have been terminated. But that would not have squared with Son's Baptist upbringing, which held that marriage was a contract for life, and that divorce was a travesty. In her defense, Son did get love in return, but it was often booby-trapped, set to explode in his face without warning. Four psychiatrists and many years later, Son came to understand the nature of her internal demons, to understand that much if not most of her behavior was compulsive and beyond her conscious control.

Act II, it was to turn out, lasted for over 25 years. How would Act III unfold? Time would tell.[1]

CHAPTER 37
The Sky Is Where The Heart Is

It has been said that interesting and challenging work and someone to love is all man needs to be happy. There was no doubt in Son's mind about the former. He worked doggedly to achieve the latter but it was often frustrating. He therefore tended to invest more and more of his emotional capital into his work. He was assigned to the training group as an assistant group operations officer, responsible for flight scheduling. He was getting all the flying time he wanted and it was the best kind, in F-84s (jet fighter) and almost all tactical, low level work with students who were being prepared to go to Korea. Son's recent experience there was very useful. Occasionally he would get a chance to do some cross country flying, picking up new aircraft from the Republic factory in Farmingdale, New York. For example,

Flight from Farmingdale

As the student load at Luke increased, it became obvious that the old F-84 B and C models that the Michigan National Guard was flying when that unit was activated and sent to Luke, were not going to hold up. Brand new F84-Gs were coming off the production line at Republic's plant in Farmingdale, New York.

The F-84 Thunderjet

Most of these new airplanes were going to tactical units in the U.S. and overseas. However, since Luke's mission was in direct support of combat operations in the Korean War, a portion of Farmingdale's production was diverted to Luke. One of Son's "additional duties" was taking delivery on some of these airplanes and ferrying them across the country to Luke. It was a nice change of pace from the routine of administrative chores and working with students. Checking in at Farmingdale's operations center, Son would sign papers receipting for the new airplane. He would then file his flight plan for the return flight to Luke. Taking off in early afternoon, he would schedule a refueling stop at Wright-Patterson AFB near Dayton, Ohio. Taking off to the southwest and climbing through 20,000 feet, Son saw through a thin layer of diaphanous clouds the great throbbing metropolis of Manhattan slide under his left wing. From four miles up it was hard to imagine that small, banana sized piece of real estate sold by the Indians for $21 to our colonial forefathers now held some 7 million people. The afternoon sun glinted on the "sky scrapers". Son could see commercial airliners flying into and out of JFK and LaGuardia. Up there he had only to deal with the elements,

a clear set of procedures and his aircraft. He was glad to be where he was and not down in that maelstrom of humanity.

In a little over an hour from his departure from Farmingdale, Son was letting down for a landing at Wright Patterson. He filed his next leg of his flight This was a long one, close to two and one-half hours from "Pat" to Luke AFB. His flight path would take him across St. Louis, Kansas City and then the great expanses of Kansas and Oklahoma. It was summer, and as usual there were thunderstorms brewing over the plains. "Tornado Alley" was well named. Some of the most violent weather anywhere could be generated by monstrous thunderstorms that would rise to altitudes of 60 thousand feet. Hail, lightning and violent updrafts/downdrafts that could tear an airplane apart were common. This evening the thunderstorms would be there, along a squall line. Like the defensive line of a football team, they would be working to block all comers, to prevent any penetration into their backside where suddenly everything would be clear sailing. "Stormy," the weather forecaster on duty, said that there would probably be holes and thin spots along this line where penetration could be possible. Son filed his flight plan and stopped at the snack bar for a quick hamburger. Then it was time to go.

Looking west from 45,000 feet

Climbing westward, Son passed through flight level 350 (35,000 feet). Son's airplane was still in the sunlight, but the lights of towns, villages and highways were beginning to appear in the darkly shadowed ground below. He had passed over St. Louis and had checked in with ATC (Air Route-Traffic Control) as he passed Kansas City. The Sun was almost on the horizon, setting slowly. Just as predicted, the line of huge thunderstorms loomed in the distance. They were backlit by a reddish Sun. They looked like huge billowy mounds of homemade peach ice cream.

Beautiful, almost beyond description, and at the same time menacing, their anvil shaped tops soared to an altitude of probably sixty thousand feet or more. The edges of their billows were lined with bright gold. As his jet surged westward, darkness edged its way into this fiercely beautiful painting. The clouds turned slowly from peach to purple. Son had now leveled off at an altitude of forty-five thousand feet and the exhaust from his engine was condensing into instant ice crystals, leaving a snowy white trail behind him. But the thunderheads towered well above him. As he drew closer, heavy, almost constant flashes of lightning came from the innards of these monsters, projecting stroboscopic images that remained for a fraction of a second on the retina. The effect was similar to what one might see, sitting in a movie theater and watching an old, silent film. But these were in full color, done in a surreal blue with traces of pale yellow. Son was flying through deep canyons of clouds, but was in clear air. Without warning there was a sudden, sharp jolt of turbulence foretelling the violence that churned within the interiors of these beasts. This was classic, summertime, and cold-front weather. The storms formed along a front of several hundred miles, making any sort of detour around them impossible. There were several cells in the immediate vicinity, but just as "Stormy" had predicted it appeared that there were thin spots between the cells where there was little or no lightning. Son asked Air Route Traffic Control (ATC) for a weather advisory. Upon hearing that ATC radar showed the line as almost solid, with some thin spots, Son asked ATC to give him a steer through the line. On instruments now, he was entering the cloud mass. There were sharp jolts of turbulence and almost constant lightning flashes but no hail. In about ten minutes he was through it, out the backside of the front. Now there was nothing between him and a friendly runway at Luke AFB. From a hundred miles away in the clear desert air he could see the rhythmical blinking of the Luke AFB light beacon, first white, then green. Several minutes later the main gear of his Thunderjet made contact with the asphalt, the tires making a staccato

"chirp, chirp!" and issuing puffs of blue smoke. He rolled to the end of the 10,000 foot runway, smoothly applying brakes to decelerate from his touchdown speed of 150 KIAS. Turning off and taxiing back to the parking ramp he looked up into the night sky. There, off his left shoulder, was the big dipper with the two stars forming the bottom of the cup pointing to the North Star. It hadn't changed since he was five and his father explained the heavens to him, and wouldn't change into an infinite future. He felt a sense of accomplishment being back on the ground, but at the same time he felt an uncanny urge to be back in the sky, with the music of the universe surrounding him, soaking into his heart and soul. It was a realm in which he felt truly at home.

Now, back at 7148 North 25th Drive, he grappled with that other part of his life, his relationship with his wife and family. He loved his wife and he adored hs daughter. Most of the time he felt close to Mary-Lynn. There were times, however, when he felt caught up in a strange dynamic involving his wife, his daughter and himself that he didn't fully understand. When he tried to play with or occasionally discipline her Arretta would intervene. If it was play, she would interrupt it with a message that said, "You don't have time to play now, you need to. . . .go clean your room, do your homework, etc." If it was discipline, which rarely happened, Arretta would come to the rescue, casting Son in the role of a persecutor. The message to Mary-Lynn was, "Mother won't let him treat you that way!" This made it very difficult for Son to establish a "normal" father-daughter relationship, and it was frustrating.

The desk duty at Luke was good enough, no question. The flying, however, saved his sanity. It was the one realm in his life where he felt mastery. It was challenging and exciting, always, but like an animal trainer working with tigers in the ring, Son was always up the to challenge, able to subdue the tigers.

Son & F-84-G
Luke AFB, 1951

In 1951, Luke Air Force Base was home for the 3600 Combat Crew Training Wing. With the Korean War generating thousands of combat missions and a "normal" combat tour set at 100 missions, there was an ongoing need for replacement pilots. Luke worked to supply that need. Brand new, "slick wing" pilots, just graduated from flight school, or in some cases Dutch, French and German pilots from NATO were sent to Luke to learn to fly and fight with the F84 Thunderjet. After logging 80 hours of tactical, mostly low level bombing, straffing and rocket missions successful USAF graduates were assigned directly to Korea. NATO pilots returned to their home countries.

During the first three years of Son's assignment with the 3600th CCTW trained over one thousand pilots, but not without cost. Luke's accident rate was high, in fact the highest in the USAF. There were reasons. A combination of mostly new, inexperienced pilots and a demanding, high-risk kind of flying mostly at low levels was a major reason. Also, as a result of the Korean War, the base had been reopened after being closed at the end of WWII. An Air National Guard wing, the 135th based in Michigan, plus elements of the Arizona National Guard provided the personnel and aircraft to staff the reactivation. The aircraft, particularly the old 84B's and C's belonging to the Michigan Guard, had not been well maintained. Combine questionable, poorly maintained aircraft with marginally skilled pilots and high-risk flying régimes with pressure from above for high productivity and a high accident rate was almost a certainty. Plumes of black smoke, rising from the southwestern Arizona desert were an almost weekly occurrence. As one can imagine, the "pow-

ers that be" wanted it all - demanding, high-risk training, high productivity and low accident rates.

Sometimes the accidents occurred right in front of us, on the runway. Herman and
Colonel Martin, Training Group Commander, had just walked out the door of group operations, on the flight line. Martin had his jeep parked nearby.

"Herman, let's pay a visit to runway control."

Runway control was a radio-equipped truck with a mini-control tower mounted on
its bed. Whenever training flights were going on, the runway control truck was manned
with a qualified instructor pilot. His job was to observe everything that was going on in the
air and on the ground within the scope of his vision. He looked for things that might lead to
trouble - flap settings, gear down and locked on approach, airplane attitude and airspeed
on final approach, anything out of routine. Warnings from runway control have averted
accidents or potential accidents many times.

Driving north across the ramp toward the active runway 210, we saw an F-84 in a left
turn onto final approach. It was obvious that the pilot was in trouble. Flaps fully extended
and gear down, the airplane was in a dangerous nose high attitude, but sinking rapidly. In
other words, the airplane was stalling and would almost certainly crash on the overrun
short of the active runway.

"God, look at that, Herman! Let's go!"

With that, Martin kicked the jeep into second and floor boarded it. We raced to the
end of the runway, just as the jet hit the ground. The impact drove the landing gear up
through the wings, probably rupturing fuel tanks. The airplane bounced and flipped upside down, skidding to a stop in a cloud of dust and smoke just short of the end of the
runway. The ambulance and fire truck were already on the way, sirens sounding and red
lights flashing, but Martin and Herman were the first to arrive. As the airplane skidded
upside down, the canopy was sheared off. The framework of the windshield and the crash
bar behind the pilot's seat was the only thing that kept the pilot from being decapitated.
His helmet had been knocked off and the top of his head had been dragged on the ground.
There was a space of perhaps 18 to 24 inches between the cockpit rail and the ground,
maybe enough to get the pilot out. He was still alive, gasping and making asthmatic snor-
ing sounds. Son reached up into the cockpit and released his seat belt. He and Martin then
struggled to pull the man out. They were afraid of fire. As the ambulance arrived, they had
extricated the pilot. The medics then took over and got the man onto a gurney and put him
in the ambulance. The fire engine sprayed the airplane with foam, suppressing any fire
danger.

"Let's follow the ambulance, Herman. I want to know who the pilot is."

At the base dispensary they found that the pilot was a Dutch student. His injuries
were critical. The doctor said that the frontal lobes of his brain had been destroyed and that
his chances of survival were less than 10%. Even if he survived, he said, he would be a vegetable. Amazingly, and perhaps mercifully, he lived for two days.

Later the runway control officer said that he started telling the pilot to hit the power
and go around. He said that it was obvious that the airplane was stalling. It was hard to
understand how the pilot could have been so oblivious to his situation.

Fighter flying is relatively safe if you know what you are doing and follow the rules. An
experienced pilot can bend the rules - maybe. However, if you don't know and if you disre-
gard the rules, flying can be terribly unforgiving.

As one can imagine, the "powers that be" wanted it all - demanding, high-risk training,
high productivity and low accident rates.

Non e' possible, mon capitano! What to change? - training regimes, output, hardware
(aircraft) or leadership???? All of these factors were examined.

Luke took pride in the high quality training that it provided. Col. Maurice L. Martin was the commander of the training group. "Maury," as he was called by his peers, was a principled West Pointer who believed that to send a pilot into combat without rigorous training in the type of flying that he would be required to do in theater was, to put it mildly, wrong. He resisted efforts by those up the chain of command to soften the curriculum. Maury said that to make such changes would simply push the accident problem overseas where it would show up as higher combat losses. Eventually, he was relieved and reassigned, going to Korea to take command of a fighter wing. After his departure the new Training Group commander made changes to the program that made it less demanding. The student load was reduced. Total flying hours required per month came down. Brand new F84-G's were added to the program, replacing the old, underpowered F84-B's & C's. These latter airplanes were derisively referred to as "lead sleds." On a hot Arizona afternoon when runway temperatures would reach 140 degrees, it took all of 10,000 feet of runway to get airborne!

In June, 1954, Luke AFB took delivery on 4 brand new F-84F Thunderstreaks, swept wing, supersonic aircraft. These early models had the so-called "split tail" horizontal stabilizer. At transitional speeds, going from sub-sonic to supersonic, the airplane had a sneaky tendency to become very nose heavy. Once the sound barrier of Mach 1 was penetrated, however, the airplane flew normally at supersonic speeds up to mach 1.2. Herman checked out in the airplane and found it to be a joy to fly. Care had to be taken, however, not to get into steep nose down position at medium to low altitudes. The airplane accelerated rapidly and required a lot

F84-F, Luke AFB, 1951 (courtesy USAF Museum archives)

of altitude to recover, particularly with the nose-heavy characteristic going through mach 1.0. Later versions of the airplane corrected the problem with a "slab" horizonal stabilizer. Luke never used the F-84F for training, only evaluation. The later version of the airplane was manufactured in limited numbers. Delivery priority went to tactical units, so Luke never received any.

In the meantime, a new aircraft maintenance group was created to centralize all aircraft maintenance. Training was compromised, maintenance was improved, new aircraft were added and output rates were reduced. All of these factors contributed toward reduction of the accident rate.

"Promotion - "Below The Zone"

In the fifties, USAF officer promotion policies set forth certain "time in grade" requirements for promotion. For example, five years as a captain was required for one to be considered for promotion "in the primary zone" to the grade of major. Each year quotas for each grade were established. Promotion boards evaluated all officers meeting the criterion and the top rated people were promoted until the annual quota was filled. In addition, provisions were made to allow exceptionally well-qualified officers to be considered for promotion who did not meet the "time in grade" requirements. Each year a small number of promotions were allowed "below the zone." In June, 1952 the boards met and made their selections for promotions from the primary zone and below the zone. At this time, Son had been a captain for only two and one-half years, not enough to place him in the primary zone. Therefore, when his name was included in those officers promoted to the grade of major it was a surprise. Apparently his combat record in Korea weighed heavily in the board's consideration. Gratefully, Son pinned on the gold oak leaves of a major. Did this mean that he would be on a "fast track" for future promotions? Time would tell.

A Movie Producer

Combat Crew Training Command Headquarters was located at Randolph Air Force Base near San Antonio, Texas. Continuing their search for ways to increase training efficiency and reduce the accident rate, they asked the Wing at Luke to develop proposals for training aids. Son wrote up a proposal for a training film designed to set forth principles of fighter gunnery for jet aircraft. His proposal was submitted and, somewhat surprisingly to Son, approved. A professional civilian scriptwriter from the Air University was assigned to work with Son to develop a movie script. Peter O'Crotty, yes that was his name, worked with Herman for about two months during the writing phase in which

F-86-F Aerial Gunnery

Herman described various principles and techniques relating to air-to-air gunnery and air-to-ground attacks. Son put O'Crotty in the back seat of a T-33 jet trainer and flew him through typical missions so that he would see, from the pilot's perspective , how different attack modes developed. O'Crotty took all of Son's inputs, flying and verbal, and broke them down into movie scenes and a script. Wilding Pictures, Incorporated, based in Chicago, was given the contract to produce the film. Son and O'Crotty were assigned to work with Wilding. Major segments involved actual film footage taken with gun cameras during actual gunnery missions. Most of this footage was taken during missions which Son flew, both at Luke for air-to-ground phases, and at Nellis Air Force Base near Las Vegas, Nevada for the air-to-air portions. The air-to-air portions were done with the F-86. Sabrejets. A gun camera was specially mounted on the vertical stabilizer of an F-86 focused so that it looked as though one was astride the F-86, riding it like a horse.

Other portions of the film involved animation, using model aircraft. This portion of the production was done at Wilding's studios in Chicago, with Son and O'Crotty supervising details of the production. Made in the nineteen-fifties, this training film is still available in Air Force archives, although new technology and new aircraft have made it obsolete.

Under New Management

When Colonel Maurice Martin left for an assignment with the 18th Fighter Group in Korea he left, in the opinion of Son, a large hole. He and Herman got along famously. Son was not Martin's "pet", far from it. It was just that the two of them saw eye-to-eye about the role of the Training Group. That was not the case with the new commander, Colonel Levi Chase. Without a doubt, Chase was a good officer, but he had an entirely different personality. He was gruff and hard to talk to, at least Son thought he was. As has already been said, he watered down the training curriculum, although in his defense he was certainly under orders from CCTAF headquarters in Randolph to do so. The relationship between Son and Chase was somewhat strained and Son really didn't know what to do about it. He continued to do his best on the job, but sometimes that alone is not enough. Son's promotion below the zone to the grade of Major occurred right after Chase took over. His comment when he heard about the promotion was something like,

"Well, duh! What the hell was that board thinking?"

No congratulations. His attitude was obvious. It became even more obvious when Herman's next O.E.R. (Officer Efficiency Report) was due. His immediate boss at the time, Colonel Dick Catledge (later the commander of the USAF aerial demonstration team - The Thunderbirds) gave Herman a very good report. All reports, however, were to be endorsed by the next officer up the chain, in other words, by Colonel Chase. Chase all but negated Catledge's favorable report. Paraphrased, he said that Son did not have sufficient force to his personality to be a successful officer. Furthermore, he said, in an attack on Son's family situation, that his lack of participation in social functions was detrimental. Yes, no doubt. There were other O.E.Rs in subsequent years that said essentially the same thing. Short of divorcing his wife there wasn't much if anything that Son could have done to change it. Combining that with a couple of "backwater" assignments after leaving Luke all but assured that Son's name would be removed from below the zone promotion lists in the future.

A Lot Can Happen In Four Years

A normal tour of duty in one assignment is three years. This may be extended or curtailed at the convenience of the Air Force or by special request initiated by a subject officer or by request of other persons or organizations. Officers may request extension or reassignment for compassionate reasons, subject to approval of appropriate authority. Son's initial assignment to Luke was through compassionate reassignment request when he returned from Korea. His initial orders called for him to go to Headquarters, Tactical Air Command at Langley AFB, VA. In view of Arretta's emotional problems and her family situation, Son asked the Air Force to assign him to Luke AFB. The request was approved. As the end of his three years approached, early in 1953, he again petitioned the Air Force to extend his stay at Luke by an additional year. Arretta was under the psychiatric care of Dr. Louis Bendheim, who attested to the fact that although she was making progress in her treatment she needed additional time.

The Air Force approved the requested extension, subject to future Air Force requirements. That meant that Son would have an additional year as long as the Air Force didn't have a priority requirement somewhere else that had to be filled.

"Arretta, we may have up to another year. We'll have to play it day to day, however. When the string runs out, there won't be much that I can do."

"Why don't you just tell the Air Force that you want to resign?"

"That's a no-brainer, and you know it. Don't you?!"

"I guess so."

"We'll take it a day at a time."

Besides routine desk and flying duty with the Training Group, other interesting things happened, including:

* The Great Flood
* Temporary duty at Holloman AFB at the White Sands Test Facility

The weather in Arizona can be unpredictable and times tempestuous. Normal annual rainfall amounts to no more than seven to eight inches. When spread out over a year, this is hardly enough to settle the dust. Occasionally, however, monster thunderstorms can develop in the hills and mountains north of Phoenix. When that happens, dry washes (creeks and rivers that do not flow normally) can become raging torrents. Flash floods can strike with little or no warning. In the spring of 1952 Luke was the victim of such a flood. There was little or no warning. It started to rain, however it was not the local rainfall that posed the problem. Rain on the watershed in the mountains came roaring down on the base. Over half the field including the runways and ramp areas were covered in a matter of minutes with 12 - 18 inches of fast moving water. There was no time to move aircraft. Fortunately it did not get deep enough to jeopardize the aircraft or ramp equipment. Odds and ends, the

strangest things, floated on the waves of this fast moving flood - a baby chair, anything made of wood, boxes, old tires and more. It lasted for perhaps an hour, and then, as quickly as it arose, it subsided. The water made its way to the Salt River, a major stream capable of handling this kind of volume. It was all over. A check of ramp areas and other areas of the base revealed no significant damage, but it was scary.

Holloman Air Force Base in Southern New Mexico is the Air Force support base for the White Sands Missile and Test Range. Since World War II, the test range has been the site for developmental testing for major weapons systems. The first test of the atomic bomb was conducted there. Over the years many systems and test projects have had their genesis there.

The Deceleration Project[1]

As far back as 1945, service personnel realized the need for a comprehensive and controlled series of studies leading to fundamental concepts that could be applied to better safeguard occupants of crashing airplanes. The initial phase of the program, as set up by the Aero Medical Laboratory of the Wright Air Development Center, was to develop equipment and instrumentation whereby airplane crashes might be simulated, and to study the strength factors of seats and harnesses, and human tolerance to the G forces encountered in simulated airplane crashes.

The crash survival research program was originally slated to be conducted near the Aero Medical Laboratory, but Muroc (now Edwards Air Force Base) was chosen because of the existence there of a 2,000-foot track, built originally for V-1 rocket research. That particular program had been completed and was taken over for the deceleration research program to save building a new track.

Designed to Aero Medical Laboratory specifications and fabricated by Northrop Aircraft Inc., of Hawthorne, Calif., equipment was maintained and operated on service contract by the Northrop Company.

The "human decelerator" consisted basically of a 1,500-pound carriage mounted on a 2,000-foot standard gauge railroad track supported on a heavy concrete bed, and a 45-foot mechanical braking system believed to be one of the most powerful ever constructed. Four slippers secured the carriage to the rails while permitting it to slide freely. At the rear of the carriage, 1,000-pound-thrust rockets provided the propelling force. Braking was accomplished by 45 sets of brakes, each consisting of two clasping pairs of brake surfaces installed on the road bed between the rails. These brake pairs clasped the 11-foot-long braking plates beneath the carriage chassis to apply the desired slowdown or deceleration. By varying the number and pattern of brake sets used and the number of carriage-propelling rockets, it was possible to effect the controlled decelerations to almost any G force.

The first run on the decelerator took place on April 30, 1947, with ballast. The sled ran off the tracks. The first human run took place the following December. Instrumentation on all of the early runs was in the developmental stage, and it was not until August 1948 that it was adequate enough to begin recording. By August 1948, 16 human runs had been made, all in the backward facing position. Forward facing runs were started in August 1949. Most of the earlier tests were run to compare the standard Air Force harnesses with a series of modified harnesses, to determine which type gave the best protection to the pilot.

One such project managed by Lt. Col Paul Stapp was designed to test various crew restraint systems to determine crew survivability under extreme conditions of acceleration/deceleration. A three-mile track was built to accommodate a rocket sled which carried a cockpit with seat and restraint straps. Stapp would strap himself into this contraption, wearing full gear including helmet and oxygen mask. The rocket would accelerate the sled to speeds of up to 650 mph. At about the two mile mark the sled would be decelerated with a system of water brakes. Stapp would be subjected to G forces of up to 20 Gs, that is, up to 20 times his normal body weight. One test was so severe that his eyes were forced

from their sockets. His face was bruised, not because he hit anything, but simply because of the tremendous forces he sustained. After each test, he was given an exhaustive physical to determine what damage, if any, his body sustained. As a result of Stapp's work cockpits, restraint systems and escape equipment were developed and incorporated in Air Force aircraft that have undoubtedly saved many pilot's lives.

Son was called in to support another test project called The Snark. Snark was an intermediate range, air breathing sub-sonic tactical missile that could carry either conventional or nuclear warheads. During the early period of the Cold War, it was designed to be deployed in Europe. It was a large missile, about the size of the B-47. It was also designed to be launched with rocket assist from camouflaged sites - no runways required. Son's part in the project was to fly a camera chase plane, in this case a T-33 2-place jet trainer. The cameraman of course rode in the back seat of the T-bird, behind Son. At the appointed time, Son and his camera man who had been circling about three miles away from the launch site, would start his turn toward the launch site, coming in from the rear and paralleling the intended flight of the missile. Missile countdown to launch was begun. Son's job was to arrive over the launch point at an altitude of no more than 50 feet, so that the cameraman could film the launch and subsequent climb out of the bird. It worked exactly as planned and Son got an opportunity to fly formation with an unmanned missile as it proceeded down range. The missile was destroyed at the far end of the range, but of course Son broke off the chase before that event.

During this period, Son was flying 40 to 80 hours per month, a fairly heavy schedule. He didn't mind, in fact he loved the amount of flying he was getting. However, it did produce one problem, a problem that turned out to be a blessing in disguise. He started getting headaches, regular everyday headaches. They would start each day after returning from a flight. They were excruciating, behind-the-eyes kinds of headaches that seemed to involve his sinuses. He went to see the flight surgeon. The flight surgeon told him that his sinuses were infected. He also told him that the infection was a function of several factors. First, Son was flying to high altitudes where breathing oxygen was required. The oxygen contained in the aircraft tanks was necessarily dry. The ups and downs of each mission with accompanying pressure changes were exacerbating the problem. Then the surgeon said,

"But if you really want to stop those headaches, why don't you stop smoking."

"What, how could that be a problem?"

"Smoking irritates the mucous linings of your throat, your sinuses and for that matter your lungs. It sets up the conditions that make infection almost a foregone conclusion."

"Well, maybe you're right. I'll try it for awhile and see if there is any improvement."

The next day, Son threw away his Pell Mells. It was tough at first. He really missed his smokes. He persisted, however, and within a few days he did notice that his sinus headaches were going away. Maybe the flight surgeon was right. After a month he still wanted to smoke. The urge would come and go. It would assail him unexpectedly. For example, a cigarette just naturally went with a cup of coffee or, strangely, when talking with someone over the telephone. One day someone lit up and blew a puff of smoke Herman's way.

"Lemme borrow one of those, O.K.?"

"Sure!"

He was back at it. He thought to himself, "Maybe if I only have five or six a day I'll be all right!"

Soon he was back at his old pack and a half habit. The headaches returned. "O.K., I guess the flight surgeon was right. I'm going to have to quit and stay quit." Again he threw away his cigarettes. When he got home he told Arretta that he was quitting for good, and that he wished that she would too. If they both quit they could reinforce each other's resolve. Arretta agreed to quit.

CHAPTER 38
Cotton Candy, Halos and Circular Rainbows

Some of the most beautiful things in the firmament are clouds. They come in all sizes, shapes and varieties. Meteorologists have assigned names to different cloud types: There are stratus, cumulus, cumulonimbus and cirrus. Viewed from terra firma they are a source of wonderment. Some of these are benign; some are fierce and life threatening. Man looks upward and sees in the clouds all kinds of things - rabbits, deer, fish and human faces. All are beautiful. One of the greatest privileges in being a pilot, however, is to be able to fly close to them, over them, under them and through them. Clouds have much to teach and show mortal humans. They can inspire and they can strike terror into the heart of the most valiant flyer.

Early in Son's flying career he was learning how to fly the F-51 Mustang at a transition school in Ft. Meyers Florida. There he absorbed a basic lesson about clouds. When flying around clouds caution should always be exercised. Why? Clouds can sometimes shroud hard objects, like mountains or the ground. Unpredictably, one pilot can have an idea about flying in or near clouds. Accepting that premise, therefore, why couldn't there be two or more airplanes in the same vicinity? If neither is aware of the other it may be an accident about to happen.

During the summer months in Florida, one can almost call out the time of day by the circadian rhythm of cloud buildup and dissipation. During morning hours they sky is usually clear with perhaps a few fluffy little cotton balls floating in a sea of blue. By noon, the cotton balls begin to expand, fueled by rising warm air. As energy from the sun continues to warm the earth the buildup continues. By mid-afternoon the little cotton balls have expanded to fill perhaps half of the sky. The bases of these clouds may be no more than 2,500 to 3,000 feet above the surface, flat on their bottoms and blue-gray in color. The tops of these mounds of brilliant white cotton candy may extend up to fifteen, twenty or more thousands of feet. Sometimes they develop into full-fledged thunderstorms with all their violent phenomena. Flying through a sky full of these buildups can be great sport. It can also be very dangerous, as Son found out one afternoon.

He and his flight had just completed an aerial gunnery mission, flown well out over the Gulf, off the Middle Western coast of Florida. Descending from 15 thousand feet or so, they were returning to their base, Page Field, near Ft. Meyers, Florida. Feeling frisky and full of testosterone, they decided to "rat race" on the way home. Son peeled away from the four-ship flight, with the other members following close behind. A little like hummingbirds that are trying to outdo each other, they twisted, turned and rolled in follow-the-leader fashion down toward the canyons of clouds. At an altitude of probably seven or eight thousand

feet, Son flew directly toward the right side of one of these cotton candy confections, intending to roll sharply to the left around the edge of the cloud, using it almost like a pylon. He felt a little bump of turbulence as he clipped the edge of the cloud.

In a nanosecond, he was face-to-face with a 4-engine B-24 Liberator bomber, coming around the other side! He was so close; Son swears that he could read the words, "Hamilton Standard" on the propellers of that big boxcar! There was no time to think. He simply continued his left roll past vertical to upside down and pulled hard on the stick as he flashed underneath, clearing the 24 by only a few feet. Yes, he was still alive. He missed, but he was afraid to look behind. What about the three other airplanes that were following behind him? Thankfully, they also missed. After that Son added a paragraph to his flying rulebook: When flying around clouds, unless you are under instrument flight rules, assume that someone else may be doing the same thing.

Cirrus clouds are one of the most beautiful things in the universe. They occur only in higher altitudes, generally above 15 - 20 thousand feet, where the air temperature is well below freezing. They are sometimes called "mares tails". They are thin, wispy veils, white and diaphanous when viewed from the ground. But when seen up close, preferably when flying through them, they take on an otherworldly character. They are composed wholly of ice crystals, millions upon million of them. There is a Beatles song, "Lucy In The Sky With Diamonds." That is what cirrus clouds are - a sky full of diamonds. Flying through them can sometimes create strange and almost mystical sights. Because ice crystals refract light, somewhat like a prism, they break up the visible light spectrum into its component colors, every color of the rainbow. If there are no other clouds, try this: fly through the middle of a deck of cirrus with the sun coming from over the shoulder. Look below and away from the sun. There, suspended in mid-air at two o-clock low, is your airplane shadow or silhouette, surrounded by a circular rainbow! Is that silhouette a guardian angel? Who knows?

Chapter 39
Another Son Is On The Way

In mid-March, 1952, Son came home from Luke to some exciting news.

"Herman, I think I'm pregnant."

"Oh, that's great! Are you sure?"

"No, but I'm over two weeks late, so I'm pretty sure."

"Well, let's get you to a doctor right away."

They made an appointment to see a pediatrician, who confirmed that she was, indeed, pregnant. Both prospective parents were quite happy.

"Herman, do you want a boy this time?"

"That would be great, but it really doesn't make any difference, Dear, as long he/she is healthy and you are O.K."

From what the pediatrician told them, and what Arretta knew, they calculated that the new arrival would be born sometime around the first to middle of October, 1953. Just as she had behaved during her first pregnancy Arretta became serene, her anxieties receded. Son hoped that maybe this time her improved mood would continue.

As she reached the eighth month Arretta said,

"This one sure is a kicker, a lot more active than Mary-Lynn was when I was carrying her. It must be a boy!"

"That's fine with me. Just as long as it's healthy!"

On the morning of October 7, Arretta began having labor pains. This time, also, was very different from Mary-Lynn. Instead of a slow build-up her pains came on quickly.

"Herman, I think we'd better go to the hospital. My pains are about 45 minutes apart!"

"Let's go!"

It was a 20 minute drive to St. Joseph's Hospital in North Phoenix. When Arretta was pregnant the first time, with Mary-Lynn, she had a difficult time, being in labor for almost 24 hours. They figured they would have plenty of time to reach the hospital, but they barely made it to the maternity ward. Richard Randal, a healthy rambunctious boy, was born only 45 minutes after reaching the hospital.

Randal Son
Age 6 months

Both kids were very intelligent and were absolute sponges of their environments. They walked and they talked very early. They were both "readers" who could read fluently well before entering first grade. "Randy", however, was completely different from Mary-Lynn. M-L was graceful, introspective and very feminine. Ran was all boy, very physical and rambunctious, in fact his parents almost thought of him as an accident waiting to happen. Early, he had

some digestive problems. He could not tolerate milk protein. He also had problems with orange juice. It took awhile to get a formula figured that he could tolerate. In the meantime, feeding times were pretty stressful. Either Herman or his mother would give him his bottle, and after a few minutes of feeding he would begin to cry. The crying increased in intensity until he would get red in the face and scream, obviously in pain. The doctor said, "Colic."

Mary-Lynn at 7 Years

Finally after several trial-and-error changes, a formula was found that Ran could tolerate. It was called Mull-Soy, a hypo-allergenic formula made from soybeans. It had a light brown color, almost like coffee with a good amount of cream. Once the switch was made, the colic went away and Ran thrived, much to everyone's relief. Mary-Lynn was almost 6 years old and had started kindergarten. The family soon settled into the routine of taking care of another infant. In fact, focusing on Randy, and perhaps regular appointments with Dr. Bendheim, her psychiatrist, seemed to keep Arretta's anxieties at bay.

In the summer of 1954, Herman made contact with a General Motors dealer who would allow him to go the factory in Detroit and pick up a new car for the invoice price. He was able to buy a new Oldsmobile 98 for only $3,000. He hitched a ride with a pilot friend who flew him to Selfridge AFB near Detroit. Then he went to the Olds new car pickup point. The delivery people there were very helpful, showing him the car that had been reserved for him and checking him out on all its features.

"Sure is a beautiful automobile," said Son.

You'll really think it's a beauty when you drive it. It's a long drive to Arizona though. When do you plan to start?"

"Tonight. I'll drive until I get sleepy. Ought to be able to make 300 miles."

"Well, don't stretch yourself too far. Good luck!"

With that, Son turned the key and pulled slowly out of the parking bay and headed west. It was a beautiful car, so responsive and quiet. He had wanted a 98 for sometime. The trip back to Phoenix was uneventful.

CHAPTER 40
Buon Giorno, Napoli!

No sooner had Son returned from Detroit with his new wheels than he was contacted by the Wing Personnel Office. They told him that they had an outstanding requisition for an overseas assignment to Naples, Italy. It was a mandatory requisition and Son was the most logical officer at the base to fill the requisition. He was (a) beyond his normal three-year tour of duty; (b) he only had 3 years overseas duty. Many officers had more; (c) the requisition required a major, rated, with C-47 experience.

"It looks like you're it, Herman," said the Wing personnel Officer.

Son thought to himself: "This is not a very good assignment for career advancement in operations, what Son had hoped for. In fact, it was "backwater." If he had someone of influence to go to bat for him, Son thought, it could probably be changed. But who could that be? Certainly it wasn't Levi Chase. Son was actually pretty naive when it came to Air Force politics, much to his disadvantage he would later come to realize.

Herman broke the news to Arretta. He thought that she would be upset, but strangely she wasn't. She began reading about Italy and its culture, particularly its art. Since returning from Japan, she had begun to paint, not very well at first. But that didn't matter. It was a hobby that seemed to consume her, so Son encouraged her. Also, Mary-Lynn had begun to take ballet lessons, and was enthusiastic about it. Arretta found out that Naples boasted an outstanding opera company and the San Carlo Opera House.

"Maybe Mary-Lynn could continue her dancing there," said Arretta.

"Headquarters, AFSOUTH?" Son asked himself. That, he found out was the air headquarters for Allied Air Forces, Southern Europe, a NATO assignment. This was definitely not a top-drawer career building assignment. It should be great for the family, however.

"I don't see why not!"

The more Son thought about it, the more he began to see some positive aspects to the assignment. There would be no separation this time. Arretta and the kids would travel with him. The living would be great. They would be living "on the economy" not on a military base. That meant a nice apartment somewhere in the city of Naples. There would be an extra cost of living allowance to compensate for the higher cost of housing. There would be opportunity to travel and see all of Europe. The AFSOUTH assignment would also probably mean opportunity to travel to Greece and Turkey, both countries being under the aegis of AFSOUTH. The headquarters, he learned, was comprised of about 50% USAF officers, 25% Greek Air Force officers and 25% Turkish Air Force officers. Working with officers from those countries should be interesting. This would be Son's first assignment where he would be "out of the cockpit," that is, not in a primary flying job. He was ambiva-

lent about that. He knew that eventually he would move from duty that primarily involved flying to desk duty. So be it.

The assignment also got Son to thinking about his education. The Air Force had been, since the end of the Korean War, placing increasing emphasis on education. The goal was to have an officer corps that was 100% college degreed. Son had two years of college at that point. Conveniently, The University of Maryland offered through their overseas off-campus program, the opportunity to take fully accredited college courses in the same headquarters where he would be working. He decided that he would take advantage of this.

So preparations for the move were begun. The first question was what to do with the house. They could sell it. The market was good, and Son thought he could probably make a thousand or two over what they had paid for it. After giving it some thought, however, they decided to keep it and rent it while they were gone. Did Arretta think that they might come back to Phoenix after a three-year tour in Italy? Maybe she thought that owning a house there would be an incentive to return. That, however, didn't figure in Air Force plans for personnel assignments. Son told her as much, but it was decided to rent the house. Son contacted a property management company and signed a contract with them to cover the next three years. They agreed to find tenants, lease the property at agreed upon rent, collect the rent, do necessary repairs and maintenance, subject to owner approval, and submit receipts together with regular reports. It sounded good. The rent would more than cover the mortgage payments and taxes. In three years, who knows, the property would undoubtedly be worth more than it was then and there would be some tax advantages.

The next item of business was to decide what to do with their new car. Actually, they now had two. They still owned the 1951 Mercury. After looking over an information packet from Naples, they decided to sell both cars. The streets and roads in Naples and in Europe, for that matter, were not really suitable for large American cars. So they sold both cars. Since they had only paid $3,000 for the Olds, and it had only the mileage from Detroit to Phoenix on the odometer, Son was able to sell it for what he paid for it. The Mercury sold easily also.

In October final orders arrived and it was time to go. Allied Van Lines came to pack their household goods. Everything went. Son thought about the old Air Force saying about moving: "Three moves equals a fire!" Well, this was only his second major one, so maybe he would be safe!

On the day of departure, they said "goodbye" to Arretta's mother and Father. Claude's chronic emphysema, brought on by years of deep inhaling the smoke from Camel cigarettes, was a concern, but other than that, Son told Arretta, that they would be fine.

A three hour flight on American Airlines took them to JFK in New York. There, they caught a connecting flight to Maguire Air Force Base where they would stay overnight in transient quarters awaiting a departing flight to Europe the next morning.

"So far, so good," thought Son. Arretta seemed to be in control of her emotions and both Mary-Lynn and Randy, now 7 and 1 years of age, respectively, were just excited to be going on a trip. The MATS (Military Air Transport Service) flight would take them to Prestwick in Scotland, and after refueling, on to Frankfurt in Germany. They would stay overnight in Frankfurt, again at the transient quarters. This time, Randy came down with a mild case of diarrhea. The VOQ provided a playpen for Randy to sleep in, but he didn't like that. The pen and the diarrhea made for a rough night, and with Randy not sleeping nobody else slept either. It was not his fault. Pepto-Bismol seemed to help a little, but the problem was still there the next day. Nevertheless, the Son's boarded a C-54 for Naples, Capadachino Airport the next day. AFSOUTH had assigned an officer to meet us on arrival and take us to the hotel that would be our temporary quarters until we could locate an apartment. The St. Elmo Hotel in the Vomero section of Naples was quite nice, and cer-

tainly adequate as a temporary base of operations. Our project officer contacted the Navy pharmacy and got a prescription for Randy that cleared up his diarrhea in short order.

Naples is situated in a huge, semi-circular ampi-theater, open to the south and the Bay of Naples. The climate would compare favorably with that of Southern California. If it were thought of as a football stadium, the hotel where the Sons were staying was located high in the upper deck, at the 50-yard line. Stepping out of the hotel and walking to his waiting staff car, Son could see the entire city and its environs laid out before him. Dating back to pre-biblical times, Naples was originally seven cities, separated from each other with defensive walls. The walls no longer function as defensive ramparts, but it is interesting to note that there are seven local dialects, roughly corresponding geographically to the old walls!

To his left he could see the storied volcanic mountain, Vesuvius. Looking to the right at his 10 o'clock position he could see the port and up-lying hills and green leafed orange groves of Sorrento.

Due south and across the bay, the Isle of Capri beckoned across the inky-blue Mediterranean. To the west he could see the Isle of Ischa. Thousands of years ago both were playpens for the Roman Emperors, Augustus, Agrippa, Antonius, Caesar and Caligula, the mad emperor - the one they called "Little Boots."

Today, they are still playpens for American and European tourists. At the foot of this ampitheater lay "The String of Pearls," the street that circumscribed the waterfront. In the western to north sections upscale, high-rise apartments elbow each other for space in the sun. It is a scene that is unbelievably rich in history. Some call it "the cradle of civilization." Today it is vibrantly alive, pulsing with the culture that is unique and Neapolitan.

The next day, Son took a staff car which the headquarters had sent to pick him up, and traveled through the teeming city of Naples, from the northern hills where the hotel was, through downtown to the water front, thence to the tunnel on the western side called "Piedi Di Grotta", or Foot Of The Cave. As they drove west along "The String of Pearls" the Bay of Naples was dotted with multi-colored sailboats and an occasional freighter, even an aircraft carrier belonging to the U.S. Sixth Fleet.

Son could not believe the noises of the city! Thousands of vehicles, 600 cc. Fiats and Vespa motor scooters, vied with each other for control of the streets. Large trucks that belched a particularly nasty and black diesel smoke, elbowed their way through the traffic. Horns honked incessantly, to be augmented with verbal histronics! The Italian police or Carbenieri stood on street corners in groups of two or three, talking animatedly while paying no attention to the chaos all around them.

"Che va!! - - -siamo patzzo!! Gniamo! Where the h - - - you going?! You're crazy!! Let's go!!"

These imprecations were accompanied with obscene gestures that only an Italian can make properly. Italians seemed to think that they could talk or honk their way through traffic!

Entering the Peidi Di Grotta tunnel, Son and his driver were plunged into smoky, eye-burning darkness. On bad days, the smoke can get so thick that headlights cannot penetrate it. The tunnel was built who knows how many hundreds of years ago. It has no lights and no ventilation. It is wide enough to provide for two lanes, more or less, each way. The cacophony of the Neapolitan street is magnified ten fold inside the tunnel. It is like being inside a huge oil drum, where everything echoes. Combining the sounds with the smoke and the darkness make a trip through the tunnel an experience to be remembered. Son would be making that trip twice each day for the next three years. It is the only connection between Naples and the villages of Bangoli and Puzzuoli. Puzzuoli, a small fishing village, was the home of Sophia Loren during her youth. Bangoli is the home for NATO headquarters for southern Europe. The Commander-in-Chief, Southern Command (CINCSOUTH)

has separate headquarters for land, sea and air forces reporting to him. Son's assignment was to Headquarters AIRSOUTH. In April 1955, General Patrick W. Timberlake became the commander. That headquarters, in turn, was responsible for two allied tactical air forces, Sixth ATAF, headquartered in Izmir, Turkey, and Fifth ATAF, headquartered in Aviano, Italy. Sixth ATAF was comprised of both Greek and Turkish air forces. Fifth ATAF contained only Italian Air Force units. In the event of war, the mission of these allied forces was to support the operations of the U.S. Sixth Fleet which was nuclear capable. It should be remembered that in the middle fifties, the United States and the Soviet Union were locked within the lethal embrace of the cold war, where the strategy being pursued by both sides was MAD (Mutual Assured Destruction). It was, incidentally, a strategy that worked!

CHAPTER 41
A New Job

Son signed in at the headquarters AIRSOUTH building where he would be working for the next three years. He met his new boss, Colonel Edwin R. Russell, a very friendly but correct, non-rated "Pointer." Col. Russell headed up the weapons shop in the directorate of operations. Son's job title was "Weapons Specialist." His job would be to develop operational weapons procedures and safety rules for the handling and delivery of all ordnance. Colonel Russell said that there was a lot of work to be done and that he was glad that Son was going to be "holding down that desk." "We need some expertise, Herman," said Russell. Col. Russell then took Son on a quick tour of the operations directorate within the headquarters, introducing him to at least two-dozen officers, some Greek, some Turkish and some American. He wouldn't remember their names the first time around, but later he would get to know all of them.

Colonel Russell asked Herman about his family and where they were staying. He told him that there was no hurry about getting to work. "The first order of business," he said, was to find an apartment and get his family settled. Then he could come to work with a clear head the Colonel said.

Colonel Russell took him to lunch at the Officers' Mess and introduced him to several more officers. Son's head was spinning. How was he going to remember all these names! The food was great, although nothing unusual. The only things that Son noticed were the white tablecloths and napkins and carafes of wine, one red, one white, at each table. After lunch, Russell told him to take the rest of the day off.

"I'm sure you've got a million things to do to start getting settled."

"Yes, thanks. I do. The first thing I want to do is buy a car. We sold our cars in the States. I can see that I've got to have wheels right away!"

"Yes, I can understand that. There is a GM-Opel dealer in Naples. If you want a new car, you might want to check with them."

"Thanks! Good idea. I'll check with them tomorrow. I hope that they have cars in stock."

"Don't bother to come in tomorrow, Herman. I know you'll be busy. Just keep me posted by calling in. M/SGT John Anderson, who is chief of our administrative section, will let me know how you're doing. Just call him. Call the motor pool section for a staff car to take you back to the hotel."

"Thanks again, Colonel. I really appreciate it. I'll call you tomorrow!"

Son saluted and left Colonel Russell's office. He went next door and talked with M/Sgt John Anderson, who was very helpful. John had been in Naples about 8 months, had a

family - his wife, Bertha and two children, a boy and a girl. He was already settled, so he had lots of tips and suggestions for Herman.

The next day, Herman and Arretta left Mary-Lynn and Randy with a nursery facility run by the hotel and approved by AFSOUTH. They caught a cab and went straight to the GM-Opel dealership. There they found just what they were looking for - a brand new 1955 Opel Cadet Station Wagon. Its 4-cylinder engine gave good mileage. The station wagon configuration was ideal for their family of four, with plenty of room for the kids, luggage, groceries or whatever. They bought it on the spot, paying for it with a personal check for $1,675.00, and drove it back to the hotel. The next day, they had to get Mary-Lynn back in school. She had already missed nearly two weeks during the travel from Phoenix. The U.S. Navy was responsible for all infrastructure facilities and tasks for the military in Naples, including a top-notch dependent school, providing elementary grades 1 through 8 plus four years of high school. They found out that the Navy ran school busses throughout the city and that M-L could catch the bus right in front of the hotel where they were staying!! Herman took Mary-Lynn to school and got her enrolled.

On the following Saturday, they decided to attempt a trip with their new Opel. The Navy Commissary, carrying a line of groceries and other items similar to a U.S. supermarket, was located at Capodachino Airport north east of the city. They got a street map of Naples and tried to figure the most direct route. Direct? There was no such thing! They asked the desk clerk at the hotel, showing him the map. Herman and Arretta, at this time could speak not a single word of Italian. The clerk's English was only fair. Together they pored over the map until Herman thought he understood how to get there. So, off they went. An hour later they were completely lost, deep in the bowels of downtown Naples. The streets were so confusing. Every street eventually ran into a piazza or traffic circle. There were no rules except that traffic circled the piazza in a counter-clockwise direction. Few streets were marked. The more Son tried to make his way toward the north east, the more entangled and confused he became. All attempts to ask directions from the locals were completely fruitless. No one, absolutely no one, spoke English. The Carbenieri, normally visible on street corners and piazzas, were not to be found. At one juncture, as the streets grew narrower and narrower, they ran into a crowd of scunizzi or street urchins. They crowed around the car so that Son could not move. They started beating on the sides of the car, yelling, "Tedeschi!! Tedeschi!!" This is the Italian word, Son found out, for German. They thought we were German because we were driving a German made Opel. If there is one thing that united Italians, it is their hatred of the Germans. Great! Son was afraid they were going to overturn the car, as they began rocking it. Finally, he put the car in gear and slowly but rentlessly pushed his way out of that knot of urchins. Eventually, they found their way to the outskirts of the city, and from there were able to pick up the main road leading to the airport. What a relief! Both Herman and Arretta vowed, right then, that they were going to learn to understand and speak Italian. On Sunday, they took the Opel out for another spin, this time down to the waterfront and the String of Pearls. At least here they could find their way. They also drove up into the western hills where the highrise apartment buildings were located. They negotiated twisting, switchback streets with names like Via Posillipo and Via Petarcha. Such lovely buildings they saw along these flower lined streets.

"Maybe we can find an apartment in one of these," said Son. "They must have beautiful views of the Bay and the Islands," said Arretta.

On Monday, they contacted the housing office, run by the Navy. An agent who was a native of Naples was assigned to them. They told her what they were looking for. It took nearly two weeks to find a suitable apartment. During that two weeks, Son thought, that they had looked at just about every apartment and villa in Naples. Either they were dumps

or they were too expensive. Finally, however, they located one that suited them. It was in a brand new highrise building that was just being completed. It was located at Numero 407 Via Posillipo, and it was gorgeous. Clean and brand new, it had three bedrooms, two baths and maid's quarters with bath. The floors were polished marble. Floor to ceiling glass doors led to a large balcony that faced the south and that offered a breathtaking view of everything!

"How much is it?" Son asked, afraid to hear the answer.

"160,000 Lire per month," was the answer. That, after taking into account the then current exchange rate, turned out to be about $300 per month. With their $165 per month extra housing allowance, that made it affordable.

"We'll take it!"

"Bene, bene!"

A one-year lease agreement was drawn up and signed. The Sons had a home. Momentarily, however, they didn't have any furniture. It was all packed up in wooden crates and was somewhere between Phoenix and the Port of Naples. A check with the transportation people indicated that it would be arriving in about 10 days! In the meantime they continued to live in the hotel.

Now that housing had been secured, Son felt that he had better get to work on his new job assignment. Col Russell gave Son a desk and told him that as a weapons specialist he would be responsible for developing and maintaining "stock pile to target sequence" procedures for all non-nuclear weapons (NATO forces were all non-nuclear, that capability being reserved solely for U.S. military forces). This included bombs, rockets, napalm and ammunition. The first emphasis, Russell said, was to examine current procedures and evaluate them for adequacy. He said that in his opinion they were very skimpy to non-existent. The next task, of course, would be to develop updated and upgraded procedures. Additionally, Colonel Russell pointed out, all NATO forces, including those from northern, central and southern Europe, had been directed by SACEUR (Supreme Commander, European Forces), always a U.S. four-star general or admiral, to coordinate and develop war plans with U.S. nuclear forces. Further, these joint plans were to be tested in SHAPE wide exercises on an annual basis.

Colonel Russell said, "In addition to your weapons procedures work, much of the work that you will be doing will be involved with helping to write the detailed operational plans for these exercises. From our perspective, Herman, the objective of these exercises in the southern region is to test how well the forces of Fifth and Sixth ATAFs support the nuclear operations of the Sixth Fleet."

"Wow! Sounds like a lot of things we have to track!"

"Yes, but I'm sure you'll get the hang of it quickly. Your branch chief, Lt. Colonel Al Hayduk, is not here today. He'll be back tomorrow and I'll introduce you. I know you will be able to call on him if you have problems. Also, you have an Italian Officer, Maggiore Guissipe DeNapoli, and a Turkish officer, Lt. Col. Feyan Erderk. You can draw on them for detailed knowledge about Italian and Turkish Air Force operations."

"I'll give it my best, sir!"

"I know you will! Now, let's see if we can get in to see General Young. He's U.S. Air Force, and is our Chief-of-Staff. I'd like for you to meet him."

With that, Colonel Russell picked up his phone and called the General's office. His secretary told Russell that he was tied up in meetings the rest of the afternoon. Russell set an appointment for the following Tuesday morning at 10:00. Then he told Son that he should check in with the 1141st SPACTRON Flight Section (Special Activities Squadron). That unit maintained the aircraft assigned to the headquarters, and scheduled flights as needed to support the headquarters. Col. Russell said that he noted that Son was qualified in the

C-47, which he said would be sure to please the Flight Section. They needed pilots who could qualify for an Air Transport Rating (pink card) necessary to command a flight with passengers.

"Boy, are we glad to see you!" said Captain Bill Shearin who headed up the Flight Section. "We're really short of qualified gooney pilots! I see from your Form 5 that you have over 800 hours in that old double-breasted cub! We'll get you checked out right away. I can tell you that you'll have lots of opportunity for trips. We fly to anyplace that our headquarters has business, Italian Air Force Bases, Greek and Turkish bases, and of course, frequent trips to Hq. SHAPE in Paris. We also go to Wiesbaden pretty regularly. That's where Hq. USAFE (United States Air Forces - Europe) is located, you know! They've got a great commissary and PX there."

"Yes, so I've heard!"

"WE even get occasional trips to London. Let me line up an IP (instructor pilot) to fly with you on Thursday. He'll give you a proficiency check and a check ride for your ATR card."

"Great! I'll make myself available. Just don't make it Tuesday. I've got an appointment to meet General Young. Until I get it done, Colonel Russell said that this was first priority."

"I'll give you a call."

On Friday, Son was scheduled for his C-47 proficiency check and ATR check. It all went off without a hitch. Shearin said he'd put Son on the board for passenger carrying trips and that he could expect to be scheduled regularly.

"That's fine with me, Bill. Call me anytime!"

In the days and months following, Herman began to develop an inventory of extant weapons procedures. Colonel Russell was right. There wasn't much in the way of formal standards and operating procedures. That meant that he had a huge project on his hands. For each weapons system, he had to develop a proposed S.O.P. Then it had to be coordinated through the hierarchy of the headquarters to get sign off approvals. Once a tentative approval was secured within AIRSOUTH headquarters, each procedure then had to be shipped out to the ATAF subordinate headquarters for their comments and/or approvals. Then and only then could a procedure be "chiseled in stone" and published as official AIRSOUTH doctrine. Although Son had done staff work at Luke where the approval of other departments was required, it was nothing like this. The time required to get anything done was beyond anything that he had experienced before. Working with officers of other nations, while interesting, was also frustrating. Although English was the official language and every officer assigned there was supposed to be proficient in English, the facts of the matter were that the language barrier was real. The normal bureaucratic red tape that is present in any large organization was therefore multiplied.

Son's frustration, however, was not without some positive outcomes. For one, he decided that he had to learn Italian. Although that would not entirely eliminate the language barrier it would help. For another, he decided that he had to take steps to further his formal college education. This was his first real staff job where he was "out of the cockpit." Flying, while still important, was not a primary duty; it was additional. Further, the Air Force had set an objective for 100% of the officer corps to have at least a bachelor's degree. Fortuitously, The University of Maryland had established an off campus program for military personnel based in the Naples area. Son investigated and signed up immediately for credit courses that would advance him toward a bachelor's degree in business. It was the beginning of a ten-year night school quest that would lead eventually to a Masters degree in Business before Son retired in 1968. Twelve hours of college level Italian was available. Son signed up for it, and happily, so did Arretta. They began attending classes at Bagnoli Post three nights per week.

Finally, the Sons were notified that their household goods were due to arrive at the Port of Naples soon. Presumably, when they were off-loaded from a ship they would be placed in a secure warehouse until delivery could be arranged.

Right?

Wrong!

On a Friday afternoon, in a pouring rain, a crane dropped crates onto the dock containing much of Son's worldly possessions. Because everybody went home on Friday afternoons, there the Son's crates stayed - in the pouring rain!

There is an old saying in the military about moving: "Three moves equals a fire." This experience proved the truth in that saying. Almost everything that wasn't wood or steel was ruined. Son knew that he would have to submit a claim for the damages immediately. He called the claims office. They arranged for a claims officer to meet the Sons at their apartment when the shipment was delivered. The next two days were spent in itemizing, cataloging, taking pictures and documenting everything. All of this had to be done in order to submit a claim. Eventually, they were paid for the damages. The dollar amount was not enough to cover cost of replacement. In addition, many of the items that were destroyed were irreplaceable. There were enough items, such as tables and chairs, bed frames, dishes and cooking utensils that were salvaged to allow the Sons to "set up camp" in their apartment. They found a skilled cabinetmaker who designed and built custom furniture so that eventually they had their apartment done to their liking.

As soon as they got settled in their new apartment, they interviewed and hired a full-time live in maid. Her name was Anna Falana, and she was a jewel. She was an original earth mother, in her forties, who spoke some English. The Son's tried to help her with her English, she tried to teach them Italian. Importantly, however, she was a good cook and knew how to shop the markets on the streets of Naples for fresh produce. She knew how to make her own pasta and her own homemade sauce from scratch! She also loved children, particularly Randy, who at that time was about 18 months old. Anna and Randy spent a lot of time playing together. It was soon apparent that Randy was bi-lingual! He spoke just as much Italian as he did English.

Anna Falana and friends

The next order of business was to find a ballet teacher for Mary-Lynn. Through the San Carlo Opera House the Sons were referred to Madam Regina Caroly who was M-L's teacher for the next three years. Madam Caroly had a great number of students, all from military families in Naples. She was a wonderful teacher from whom Mary-Lynn learned much.

CHAPTER 42
Europe And The Near East From The Flight Deck

Because of Son's ATR rating, which allowed him to carry passengers when flying the C-47 his services were in great demand. During the three years of his assignment to Naples he made numerous trips to places such as, Athens and Aroxos in Greece; Izmir, Ankara, Istanbul and Diyabakir in Turkey; the Islands of Crete and Malta; Tunis and, yes, Casablanca in North Africa; Paris, Frankfurt and Wiesbaden in Central Europe and even a trip to London. Most of the time the flying was routine but Son always enjoyed it. He particularly enjoyed the chances these trips afforded to see parts of the world and the way that indigenous peoples live. Every trip impressed upon him how fortunate he was to be an American citizen and to live in a country that enjoyed unique democratic freedoms.

Col. Russell
Son
Afsouth staff trip to Aroxos, Greece 1956

Diyabakir is located in far southeastern Turkey, near the border with Iraq. The population there is predominately Kurdish, populated by nomadic, sheep and goat herders. The economy is poor. Turkey maintains an air base there that is home to Turkish Air Force fighter wing. In the 1950 - 60 time period they were equipped with F-84-G Republic Thunderjets, an aircraft with which Son was quite familiar. Son took a group of 24 AFSOUTH staff officers there on a formal staff visit. Of course their coming was announced in advance and much anticipated by the Turkish Wing Commander.

Upon landing and turning onto the taxiway Son was directed to his parking area. It looked as though the entire base had turned out to greet them. There was a brass band. There was an honor guard of Turkish troops. Son pulled to a stop, following the "FOLLOW ME" jeep that had led him in. He shut his engines down and threw open his side window. He could hear the band. What a reception! The passenger door was opened and a stairway was trundled into position. From the flight deck Son looked out his side window and couldn't believe what he saw. A red carpet, they were actually rolling it out, leading from the reception committee to the stairway! The Wing Commander and his staff were waiting! As the visitors deplaned and walked down the carpet, salutes were exchanged all around. Then, whisked into waiting staff cars, Son and all his passengers, now in motorcade, were driven to the Officers Club for a reception and grand luncheon. There was a long table covered with a snowy white linen table cloth , napkins, china and silver. There were flowers and

carafes of wine. The table was sufficiently long to seat everyone including the Commander and his staff. Place cards at each seat told us where to sit. Proceedings began with a short welcoming speech by the Turkish Commander who spoke excellent English. He concluded his welcome with a toast to the visitors. We all raised our champagne glasses in response. Colonel Russell then toasted the Commander and his staff, after which everyone sat down. Then lunch was served. The first course was a bowl of a cold soup, somewhat like vichyssoise. There was a small, pinkish, round object about the size of a golf ball in the middle of the bowl. Son asked Colonel Erderk who was sitting next to him:

"Feyan, what is that thing in the middle of the soup?"

"That is a sheep's eye, Herman, It's a sign of admiration and respect when your host serves you a sheep's eye."

"I've never tried a sheep's eye. Do I have to eat it?"

"No, but it would be a sign of poor manners, even disrespect, if you didn't."

Son, along with all the visitors, ate their sheep's eyes.

After the soup, six more courses were served with more toasts and wine to wash it all down. In all the lunch took two and one-half hours. The visitors were then escorted to quarters to rest and relax so that they would be fresh for the staff inspection that was to begin the next morning. The details of the inspection, which went very well, were not important. The important thing was that the host and the visitors established a strong rapport and got along famously. On the trip back to Naples everyone commented on what a fine outfit the Turkish Commander had. Some even said that the sheep's eyes were not half bad.

Turkey is a land of contrasts. It is predominantly Islamic. But of all the predominantly Islamic countries in the Middle East, it is the most democratic. The others, Saudi Arabia, Iraq, Iran, Syria, Jordan, et. al., are tribal kingdoms. Because of Kemal Ataturk, Turkey stands today as the only Muslim nation in the Middle East that has a representative democracy. Still, there are things about Turkey that western democracies find abhorrent. Torture appears to be regularly used in police stations to force prisoners to confess, or give up information about illegal organizations. It is also used to intimidate detainees into becoming police informers, or simply to punish people who are believed to support illegal organizations. Torture methods in Turkey documented by Amnesty International include severe beatings, being stripped naked and blindfolded, hosing with pressurized ice-cold water, suspending by the arms or wrists bound behind the victim's back, electric shocks, beating the soles of the feet, death threats and sexual assault. But Turkey is trying hard to westernize. A little history is helpful in understanding a Turkish nation that is in transition.

This is what a web page on the internet has to say about Kemal Ataturk:

"Mustafa Kemal Atatürk, the founder of the Turkish Republic and its first President, stands as a towering figure of the 20th Century. Among the great leaders of history, few have achieved so much in so short period, transformed the life of a nation as decisively, and given such profound inspiration to the world at large.

"Emerging as a military hero at the Dardanelles in 1915, he became the charismatic leader of the Turkish national liberation struggle in 1919. He blazed across the world scene in the early 1920s as a triumphant commander who crushed the invaders of his country. Following a series of impressive victories against all odds, he led his nation to full independence. He put an end to the antiquated Ottoman dynasty whose tale had lasted more than six centuries - and created the Republic of Turkey in 1923, establishing a new government truly representative of the nation's will.

"As President for 15 years, until his death in 1938, Mustafa Kemal Atatürk introduced a broad range of swift and sweeping reforms - in the political, social, legal, economic, and cultural spheres - virtually unparalleled in any other country.

"His achievements in Turkey are an enduring monument to Atatürk. Emerging nations admire him as a pioneer of national liberation. The world honors his memory as a foremost peacemaker who upheld the principles of humanism and the vision of a united humanity. Tributes have been offered to him through the decades by such world statesmen as Lloyd George, Churchill, Roosevelt, Nehru, de Gaulle, Adenauer, Bourguiba, Nasser, Kennedy, and countless others. A White House statement, issued on the occasion of "The Atatürk Centennial" in 1981, pays homage to him as "a great leader in times of war and peace". It is fitting that there should be high praise for Atatürk, an extraordinary leader of modern times, who said in 1933: "I look to the world with an open heart full of pure feelings and friendship".[1]

The world might wish that other Arab nations establish similar reforms. They would go a long way toward reducing or eliminating the threat of world terrorism.

Still, Turkey is a backward nation in many ways. It is a poor nation by western standards. Standards of sanitation are worse than poor. They are almost non-existent. There is little refrigeration. Butcher shops hang their meats out in the open air, allowing flies to help themselves. Water supplies are all suspect. Fresh produce can be a source of cholera at the worst and a bad case of "the GI's" at best.

The history of the land that is now Turkey goes back to the time of Moses and Abraham, even before that. It is a gold mine for paelo-anthropologists. The remains of ancient civilizations are buried and scattered across the Turkish landscape and are clearly visible from the air. Most of these sites have not been explored. The site of Noah's Ark is reputed to be near Mt. Arat. To say that this land is the cradle of civilization is not an overstatement. The three major religions that are found here, Christianity, both Byzantine and orthodox, Judaism and Islam all have their roots in this ancient land.

On another staff trip to Ankara, the capital of Turkey, Son and his group were housed in a local hotel, supposedly a "five star" establishment. By this time, Son had learned to take a prophylactic dose of aureomycin and to carry chlorine tablets to disinfect drinking water. What he didn't anticipate, however, was what happened after he went to bed. When he pulled back the covers, everything looked normal. He got into bed and noted that the mattress made noises like it was filled with straw. That was no problem. He switched off the light and started to drift off to sleep, when suddenly he started scratching. Something was biting him! He jumped out of bed, switched on the light and saw two bed bugs scurrying over the edge of the mattress! Needless to say, he spent the rest of the night sitting in a chair! On his next trip to Turkey he added DDT to his TDY (temporary duty) kit!

"If one state existed on earth, Istanbul would be its capital." So said Napoleon. Again, taking from the internet, the following snippet about Istanbul is appropriate:

"A stay in Istanbul is not complete without a traditional and unforgettable boat excursion up the Bosphorus, that winding strait that separates Europe and Asia. Its shores offer a delightful mixture of past and present, grand splendor and simple beauty. This horn-shaped estuary divides European Istanbul from Asiatic, Byzantine Istanbul. Called "The Golden Horn" because of the way the setting sun turns the water to gold, one of the best natural harbors in the world, the Byzantine and ottoman navies and commercial shipping interests were centered there."[2]

They didn't have time for the boat trip, but:

"Absolutely the best lobster I have ever tasted," exclaimed Son, after he and his party had concluded a memorable meal at a fabulous restaurant, located right on the water's edge, where they could see the big ships going into and out of the Black Sea.

Son recalls another C-47 trip to Turkey that was memorable. Back at headquarters in Naples, he was scheduled for another Turkish trip, this time to Izmir, the headquarters for 6th ATAF. He was not involved in any official capacity other than that of "chauffeur." Of course, he was always glad to get out from behind his desk and get into the air. The Flight

Section had notified him of the trip, a couple of days hence. Lt. Col Al. Hayduk, his immediate boss, asked him if he could come along as co-pilot.

"Sure! Glad to have you, Al."

There was nothing particularly eventful on the trip. They arrived in Izmir, went to the Headquarters and signed in. They had dinner, at the club, but since there was no VOQ (Visiting Officer's Quarters) on base, they went into town to stay at a local hotel. Son and Hayduk had separate rooms. Son asked Al if he wanted to do anything, i.e., see the sights of Izmir.

"No, Herman, I have some personal business that I have to take care of that will take care of the rest of the evening."

"O.K." Al didn't seem to want to say anything more about his personal business so Son didn't ask any questions. After double locking his room door, he went to bed early.

About midnight there was a loud pounding on his door.

"Who is it!"

"Herman, this is Al. I have the Turkish police with me. I need to talk to you!"

What the. . .?? Son was almost afraid to open the door.

"Are you O.K., Al?"

"Yes, but I have to talk to you. The police want to ask you some questions!"

"Great," thought Son, as he got out of bed and went to the door. The Turkish police are not particularly subtle, and as already has been said, they have never heard of Miranda. "What kind of trouble is Al in, anyway," he thought.

Herman cracked the door slightly. He could see Al and he could also see that two somewhat menacing Turkish cops were escorting him.

"Let us in, Herman. It's O.K. You're not in trouble, I am."

"Well, I'm glad to hear that!"

With that, Son opened the door and let Al and his escort into his room.

"What's the story, Al?"

"A couple of months ago, I purchased and paid for 10 handmade Turkish rugs. I had to pay for them in advance or the rug dealer would not do business with me. He gave me a price that I couldn't refuse. He told me that it would take approximately two months to fill my order. "I will let you know when I have them," he told me. "Then, let me know when you can pick them up and I will arrange a truck to take the rugs to the airport. I can give you a good deal because I won't charge you any customs duty."

"I asked him if the police wouldn't get wind of it, but he assured me it would be O.K., so I went ahead with it. I didn't tell you Herman, because I thought that the less people that knew about it the better. When I went to his shop earlier this evening, everything seemed to be fine. The rugs were there, and they were beautiful. He said he had the truck ready. We loaded the rugs and proceeded to the airport. We were in the process of loading them on the airplane (Son's airplane) when a police car came speeding across the ramp. To make a long story short, they confiscated the rugs, impounded the airplane and were about ready to throw me in jail. They asked me if I was the pilot of the airplane and of course I told them that I wasn't. That's how you got involved."

"Oh? I'm involved?"

At this point, one of the cops asked Son if he was the pilot. He confirmed that he was, but that he didn't know anything about the rugs. Hayduk assured the cops that he had not told me about his intentions to load the rugs on the aircraft. With that, the cops decided that they would not impound Son's airplane. They would notify the Provost Marshall at 6th ATAF Headquarters of the incident and turn it over to him for disposition. Both Al and Son were ordered to report to the Provost in the morning. Al and the cops departed, and Son went back to bed but not to sleep. Obviously, the rug dealer had sandbagged Al. Moral: Don't trust a Turkish rug dealer, particularly if you are doing something sneaky!

"General Timberlake wants to see both of you," said the Provost (General Edward Timberlake was the brother of General Pat T., Commander of AIRSOUTH).

After close questioning by the Provost and General Timberlake, the General said that was convinced that Son was not involved. He said that he would take action to have Son's Airplane released so that they could return to Naples, but that action would be taken with AIRSOUTH to bring charges against Hayduk. The eventual cost to Al was the price of the rugs, which was considerable, the forfeiture of the rugs which remained in Turkey, and a severe letter of reprimand to be placed in his permanent file. He was lucky. He could have spent time in a Turkish jail. He could have been court-martialed, fined and demoted.

Conversation between Son and his co-pilot on the return trip was somewhat forced.

Months later, Son and his co-pilot, not Hayduk, were on a flight from Naples to Aroxis, Greece. It was a late afternoon takeoff. Flying time to Aroxis was estimated to be a little over two hours. The weather was overcast, with a solid deck of stratus clouds extending from about 3,000 up to 12 thousand feet. There was no icing reported in the clouds, but the weather office said that there was a possibility of isolated evening air mass thunderstorms, imbedded in the stratus. Soon after takeoff, they entered the cloud deck. There was no turbelence. They climbed to 8,000 feet and Son established an outbound track from the Naples VOR (radio navigational fix) He set up the autopilot. It was about as routine as reading the morning paper. Passing Mt. Etna, an active volcano on the Island of Sicily, which they couldn't see on this trip because of the clouds, they turned left and headed out across the Agean Sea toward Greece. It was still routine with the autopilot doing the flying. The co-pilot said to Son,

"I think 'stormy' must have been kidding. I don't see any air mass thunder bumpers, do you, Herm?"

"Well if they're embedded in this stratus layer we wouldn't be likely to see them, would we? It would be nice if we had forward-looking radar on this old gooney. Then we'd be able to see and avoid them."

"Yeah, that would be nice."

Not a minute later, it happened. They flew smack into the middle of just the kind of storm that the weatherman had predicted. Within seconds, the airplane was smacked with every meteorological phenomenon known to man - turbulence, torrential rain, hail, lightning and St. Elmo's fire. The turbulence was extreme, causing the accelerometer to swing from minus 2 gs to plus 4 gs. Son thought of the possibility of structural failure. The first thing that hit them was a sudden, violent updraft. Son immediately switched off the autopilot and grabbed the controls. Bill, the co-pilot switched on the passenger seat belt sign and hoped that none of the passengers had been thrown against the ceiling. The rate of climb indicator was reading 4,000 feet per minute up. The airspeed indicator bounced wildly from 120 to 190 knots. The attitude gyro tumbled, making it useless. Son had to rely on basic instruments, the turn needle, airspeed and rate of climb indicator. All he wanted to do was hold the aircraft in some semblance of a straight and level attitude. This was not easy with the turn indicator bouncing wildly from left to right to left.

"Bill, let's get the gear down!" Attempting to hold his altitude in the updraft, Son pulled the throttles back to idle and pushed forward on the control column. His airspeed built to 190 knots, way too much, particularly in severe turbulence. Extending the landing gear helped to slow them down. Even with these measures, their altitude went from 8,000 to almost 10,000 feet. Just as suddenly, however, they went from an updraft to a severe downdraft. Suddenly, the rate of climb indicator reversed itself, from 4,000 ft/min up to 4,000 ft/min down!

"Up gear, Bill!" Son increased the RPM and throttle settings to takeoff power, while watching the altimeter unwind from 9,000 down to 7,000 feet. Suddenly the torrential rain changed to hail, hammering the aircraft unmercifully. The sound of the hail hitting the

aircraft was deafening. Along with the hail came St. Elmo's fire. This phenomenon is caused by static electricity in the cloud, causing every raindrop or hail pellet to register on the windscreen like so much snow on a television set with no picture. Little snakes of blue-white fire danced out from the edges of the windscreen. Both propellers turned incandescent. This was a severe electrical storm. They could see the lightning flashes and hear the sharp "bang" of a nearby bolt. Herman and Bill were still holding on for dear life when, just as suddenly as they had flown into it, they flew out of it. Although they were still in the stratus clouds the turbulence, the rain and hail and the lightning stopped. They were in smooth air again! On landing at Aroxis, they examined the airplane. It had sustained significant damage from the hail. All the leading edge surfaces looked as though they had been abraded with a ball and peen hammer! There was also an electrical burn mark on the left wing tip where a lightning strike had made a direct hit. In fact, it did knock out the low frequency radio equipment. After a through check by the aircraft crew chief, it was determined that the airplane was still flyable. They returned to Naples the next day. Son had always had a healthy respect for thunderstorms. After this mission, thought Son, I'll add awe to respect!

Mt. Etna, located on the Island of Sicily, is one of the natural wonders of the world. Its cone towering to over 10,000 feet, it is a very active volcano, erupting on a regular basis. During a major eruption in 1955, which lasted for several weeks, Son took his C-47 to a point about 2,000 feet above and to the side of the cone where he could look down into the maw. It was a sight that he shall never forget. For anyone who does not believe that Earth is not a hot coal, fired by the nuclear forces of the universe, Son suggests a brief look into the innards of Etna when it is erupting. The volcanologists call them "pyroclastic flows," red-hot liquid rock that flows up from below in a fountain of fire and smoke. Etna even blows smoke rings, perfect circles of gas and cinder that are released from the bubbling cauldron. They can rise to an altitude of over 15,000 feet. Etna can be dangerous, however the frequency of its eruptions lends it a certain degree of predictability, and therefore safety. Mt. Vesuvius, located near Naples and rising over the remains of the ancient city of Pompeii, is also an active volcano. In 79 A.D. it buried the entire city of Pompeii in a major eruption, preserving the city's life in exquisite detail, as in a snapshot. Today it is still classified as active, it's last eruption having occurred in 1942.

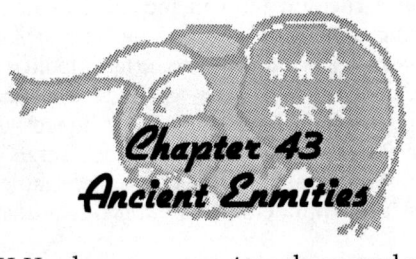

Chapter 43
Ancient Enmities

Back at AIRSOUTH Headquarters, now into the second year of his three-year tour, Son was working with the operational details of a SHAPE wide exercise called, "Operation Foxpaw." One of the main features of the exercise was to develop and demonstrate the role of NATO's conventionally armed air forces in the North, Central and Southern regions as supporting elements of U.S. nuclear armed forces, Army, Navy and Air Force. The details of this exercise were staggering in their complexity. The assumption was that The Soviet Union launched a major invasion of Western Europe, using their dominant land force to overwhelm NATO defenders. To stop this invasion, U.S. forces retaliated with nuclear weapons. NATO forces, in a supporting role and, armed conventionally, attacked appropriate targets not covered by U.S. forces. These targets, actually in SHAPE's war plans, were located throughout Europe in areas then behind the Iron Curtain - Hungary, Bulgaria, Romania, Czechoslovakia and Yugoslavia. Since these actual targets could not be attacked in peacetime, the artifice of "simulated" targets was used. Simulated targets for AIRSOUTH were located in Italy, Greece and Turkey. Each simulated target corresponded to an actual target in Europe. In order to demonstrate the unity and integrity of AIRSOUTH forces, it was decided to assign attack responsibility for simulated targets located in Italy to Greek Air Forces. Italian Air Forces attacked targets in Greece and the Turks flew against Greek targets. Oh yes, the Greeks also were scheduled to overfly Turkey. They were all just one big, happy family.

Son had already learned a little Balkan history. He knew that there was "bad blood" between the Greeks and the Turks, going back hundreds, even thousands of years. Currently, there was a major disagreement over what should be done about the Island of Crete. Then under British protection, Crete had a majority of Greeks, approximately 430,000. Turks, however, constituted a significant minority of approximately 95,000. In 1954, Greece proposed the union ("enosis") of the island of Cyprus with the Greek state, but the British refused. A guerilla group called EOKA (the National Organization of Cypriot Fighters) then began a campaign of civil disobedience and political violence on the island, in an effort to drive out the British. EOKA was led by George Grivas, a Cypriot-born former Greek army general identified with the anti-Communist forces in Greece during and after World War II. [1]

Son wondered about the wisdom of "Foxpaw" overflights as they were written into the exercise's operational plan.

Ten days before Operation Foxpaw was scheduled to begin, a bomb exploded at the Turkish consulate in Salonika, Greece. This sparked anti-Greek riots in Istanbul and Izmir,

and Turkey called for partitioning the island to safeguard the rights of the Turkish minority there.

Suddenly, the Greek and Turkish officers assigned to AIRSOUTH stopped talking with one another! "Foxpaw" was days away. There was no doubt that given the current state of affairs the overflights would be dangerous. Either the exercise would have to be cancelled or it would have to be re-written. To re-write it meant that all simulated target lists and target assignments would have to be changed. What a mess! Son and the entire Operations Directorate worked 18-hour days to make the changes and get a new operations plan distributed. They finished twenty-four hours before H-hour! Months later, the Greeks and the Turks were talking a little, but only when they had to!

Son briefed the Operations Division portion of the exercise plan to General Young, AIRSOUTH Chief of Staff, who complimented him and the Division for an outstanding job under pressure.

Chapter 44
Si Parla Italiano?

In the meantime, both Herman and Arretta were going back to school. They were enrolled in The University of Maryland's extension division classes, being held at Bagnoli Post. They both enjoyed Beginning Italian, taught by Il Proffessore Vecinzo Treversa. He was an excellent teacher. He later went to America and, at last check, was on the faculty at The University of California at Los Angeles. The inside joke at the Son household was that Herman studied Italian, but Arretta spoke it. She dealt with the people in the markets on the street who spoke a quite different version of Italian - Napolitano! Randy, now two and one-half years of age, was doing quite well with his Italian too, thank you! Anna, the maid, played with Randy and talked to him in local dialect which he picked up quickly.

Arretta's resolve to quit smoking, begun nearly a year earlier, played itself out one day. Herman, returning from work, unlocked the door to their apartment. Arretta came to the door to meet him and gave him a perfunctory kiss.

"Let's try that again," said Son. "Are you smoking again?"

"Yes, I'm afraid so."

"Why?"

"Well, you know we keep cigarettes in the apartment. I got nervous and I thought I would smoke just one."

"You know that won't work, don't you?"

"Yes. I'm sorry I started again. I'll try to quit again."

Son knew from her choice of words, saying that she would "try" to quit, that she wouldn't do it. Cigarettes were rationed at the commissary to one carton per adult per week. Even Americans who didn't smoke usually kept cigarettes to use for tips since they were much in demand by Italians. He was sorry that they had kept cigarettes in the apartment, making it easy for her to start again.

Arretta seemed to enjoy the Italian classes. In fact, she seemed to be doing much better with her anxieties in Italy than she did in Phoenix, even without the regular visits to see Dr. Bendheim. The agoraphobia problem was still there, however, anytime there was a demand to attend any kind of social function. Son tried to avoid these situations as much as possible but the excuses were wearing pretty thin.

Herman moved ahead with his plans to get his undergraduate degree. He enrolled in one or two courses each semester - Personnel Management, Military Policy, European History and Expository writing. At the rate he was going he figured it was going to take him about another 8 years. That seemed like a very long time, but he thought, "Where will I be eight years from now if I don't start?" He continued to work on it.

Chapter 45
Behind The Iron Curtain

The bombing of the Turkish Consulate in Salonika, while cause for some anxiety in Southern Europe, was relatively mild and of short duration. What happened the following year in Hungary, which was a satellite of the Soviet Union, was not. On October 23, 1956 in Jozsef (Joseph) Bem square, in Buda, Hungary a crowd of several hundred students took to the streets to protest the Soviet occupation. Protestors began shouting anti-Soviet slogans like "Ruszkik haza!" (Russians go home!) and began to read poems of Hungarian independence. One of the poems read was Sándor (Alexander) Petôfi's "Nemzeti Dal." It was this poem that had sparked the Hungarian revolution of 1848. Some people removed cutting tools from their coats and grabbed Hungarian flags with the Soviet symbol in it. They began cutting these seals out leaving the Hungarian flag with a gaping hole in the center. This is the reason that flags with a hole in the center would turn out to be the symbol of the revolution. The crowd that had begun as a few hundred people had now swelled into the tens of thousands. Clearly, Soviet rule was not tolerated by the masses.

In Naples, Son and the military organization of which he was a part took more than a passing interest. What, they wondered, would be the Soviet response. If the Soviets tolerated the revolution where would it lead? Could it be the precursor of a general crumbling of the Soviet empire and loss of its satellite states? On the other hand, if the Soviets crushed the revolution, which they clearly could, what should the position of western nations be? Should they stand up against such naked aggression or should they ignore it and pretend that it didn't happen? In the period from October through December 1956, Son experienced the events of the revolution as a stream of current events. In 2002 they have long since been written into history. From a historical perspective, the Hungarian revolution may be seen as a watershed event.

An article copyrighted in 1998 written by Zoltan Csipke, first generation son of Hungarian immigrants, provides a riveting account and analysis:

"To Western society, freedom has lost much of its meaning. The people of Western nations take their freedom for granted. They do not know what life would be like if they were to be stripped of their freedom. What is freedom? Is it the right to preach inane subject matter? Or is it the right to choose between two options? Freedom is none of these. Freedom, in its most basic form, is the right to think for oneself and to openly share ideas free of censorship with other people and not be subordinate to another nation or political entity. It is not surprising then that so many people have given their lives, so that their fellow people may bask in freedom. Why would people do such a thing? It is because without freedom, life is not worth living. Hungarians have long sought freedom, only to have it dissolve time and again. The events that unfolded from October to December of 1956 symbolized man's endless yearning for freedom. In it, an oppressed people rose up against their oppressors in a feat of such courage

that will not be challenged for some time. In the eyes of the Western nations, the revolution at first seemed an act of foolishness. Soon, they realized it was not. The freedom fighters of Hungary had risen because they could no longer stand the iron fist of communism. Their only goal was to free Hungary from foreign occupation." [1] (Zoltan Csipke)

Why did they revolt? Surely, it could not have been that bad. This is a view commonly embraced by the man in the street in the West. Maybe if it is ignored it will just go away. Unfortunately, it is also a view that was held by Western nations, but based on incorrect assumptions about Russian communism. After World War II Winston Churchill warned that the West was facing an expansionist Soviet Union and that if the West did not wake up, Europe would be divided into Eastern Europe under domination of the Soviet Union and a free and democratic Western Europe. Franklin Roosevelt failed to recognize Stalin for what he was. It was his blunder that allowed Stalin to subjugate the countries of Eastern Europe - East Germany, Poland, Czechoslovak, Yugoslavia, Hungary, Bulgaria and Albania.

Hungary as a whole was generally left undamaged by the German occupation. When the Russians arrived, they surrounded Pest and destroyed large areas of the city. Because the Germans had destroyed the bridges linking Buda and Pest, the Russians shelled Pest for six months until winter came and the Danube River could be crossed.

Soviet soldiers looted what remained undestroyed. All the wine and jewelry stores were plundered, thousands of homes ransacked, thousands killed, and thousands of women were raped, (Mikes 29). All in all, the Russians did a lot more damage in a few weeks than the Germans had in the past year. But most important, Hungary had been "liberated."

Josef Stalin appointed Mátyás "Little Stalin" Rákosi (born Mano Roth, he also hid in the Soviet Union between the two World Wars) to be the premier of the Peoples' Republic of Hungary. Under the rule of Rákosi/Stalin, Hungary was transformed into a satellite Soviet hell. If anyone spoke directly against the regime of Rákosi or Stalin, they were executed. If a person in a fit of rage damned Rákosi or any part of his regime to hell, they were arrested, falsely tried, convicted, and murdered. Before they were murdered, they were often tortured for weeks to months at a time. Prisoners were forced into their prison cells naked, without towels or anything to keep them warm. Inside a stone cell without heat they were left to bear the cold Hungarian winter, which often killed them. Well over ninety-five percent of the prisoners were in jail for political reasons. It was in this fear that the Hungarian people lived their daily lives."

Given these facts, it is little wonder that the Hungarian people revolted. During the early days of the revolution, the Hungarian army, ostensibly loyal to the regime, was an unknown factor. Would they remain loyal or would they switch sides? Truncating a lot of detail, they did switch sides. They ripped Soviet emblems off their uniforms. The revolution spread from its origins in Buda to the countryside. Eventually, Soviet tanks withdrew and it appeared that the revolution had succeeded. Again quoting from Csipke's account:

"Most of the events that took place in the few days of freedom were glorious. For the first time in over ten years, Hungarians could now walk down streets not having to fear the ÁVO (The Hungarian Secret Police). After the Soviet withdrawal, Hungary experienced freedom for the first time in over ten years. More than a dozen newspapers were started up which wrote the truth, not communist interpretations of it. Collection boxes were set up to help the widows, orphans and the other less fortunate. These boxes were left unattended on sidewalks and often were nearly overflowing with money, yet no one stole any of it. The stores, most of which had belonged to the communists, were not looted, even though the people were poor. It was for this reason that the revolution remained 'clean.'" [2]

Political prisoners were released from prisons. One of those was Cardinal Jozsef Mindszenty, Prince Primate of the Hungarian Catholic Church, who was imprisoned and tortured for years. His speeches motivated and inspired the people for a new beginning. He restored faith to a people denied of religion. He was the symbol of purity that the people

needed. At the Citadella, which overlooked the city, was the place where the Soviets had erected a monument for their "liberation" of Hungary. Several statues of Russian soldiers overlooked Budapest and were toppled by the freedom-fighters. Since the other statue was not of Soviet origin, and had originally been dedicated to István (Stephen) Horthy, the son of Miklós (Nicholas) Horthy, Hungary's regent between the World Wars, it was not toppled.

Imre Nagy, who became the first legally elected official in seventeen years, renounced the Warsaw Pact and declared Hungary a permanently neutral nation. He dissolved the one-party system and for the first time since 1946 multiple parties emerged. At first the people wanted a liberal communist government, but soon they wanted nothing to do with communism at all. Out of Nagy's cabinet three fourths were non-communists. Included in Nagy's cabinet was Colonel Maléter, the hero of the Killián Barracks. Nagy had promoted him to general and General Maléter was now Minister of Defense. With this act Nagy gained even more support. He repeatedly asked the Russians to leave. It took them a long time, but they finally did withdraw, or so it seemed, if only for a short time." (Csipke)

The Russians returned in force on November 2. This time they were well armed and they overwhelmed the Hungarian defenders. They captured Imre Nagy, removed him to Romania where in 1958, after months of torture he was executed. The revolution was over. What were its lessons? For one, it exposed the Soviet Union for the despotic regime that they really were. It also demonstrated that the world would not confront them directly. The world would object ostentatiously but it would not take direct action. The status quo in Eastern Europe would continue. In the Soviet Union the U.S. was seen as a paper tiger. While it held a nuclear big stick it did not have the stomach for non-nuclear confrontation. What would have happened if America had "put its money where its mouth was?" Would the Cuban Missile crisis have happened? What about Viet Nam, or the killing fields of Cambodia? Would the Soviet Union dared to defy an America that had demonstrated its will to act in defense of the Truman Doctrine? — most probably not. Will America ever learn?

At about the same time that the Hungarian Revolution was happening, another tense situation, centered around the Suez Canal, was developing. It was precipitated on July 26, 1956 when the Egyptian President, Gamal Abdel Nasser, nationalized the Suez Canal. Earlier, America and Great Britian had agreed with Egypt to finance the construction of the Aswan Dam. However the Soviet Union, using Czechoslovakia as a proxy, had been inserting itself into the middle East, by also promising help for Aswan. America and Great Britian withdrew their offer. This caused Nasser to seize the Suez Canal. He predicted that the tolls that he would charge would pay for the dam within five years. This gave Nasser a choke hold around a main oil supply artery. England and France feared the worst. Diplomatic efforts to solve the crisis got nowhere. England and France, in cooperation with Israel, then secretly prepared to take military action to regain control of the Canal, and if possible to topple Nasser. On Octobr 29, 1956, Israel invaded Egypt. England and France, as they had previously planned, demanded that Israel and Egypt withdraw all troops from the Canal. They announced that they would intervene to enforce a cease fire ordered by the United Nations. The Soviets, however, threatened to intervene. This, plus opposition at home, led to a cessation of British and French plans. Both nations withdrew on December 22, 1956 and Israeli forces withdrew in March, 1957.

Nasser emerged the victor and a hero for the cause of nationalism. Israel did regain shipping rights in the Straits of Tiran, however England and France lost most of their influence in the Middle East as a result of the episode. It marked an increase in the bipolarization of the cold war, with the Soviet Union and the United States emerging as the major powers. The Middle East was, is and probably always will be a barrel of snakes!

Chapter 46
The Beauty of Europe

With the passage of these two events - The Hungarian Revolution and the Suez Crisis - tensions in the region abated somewhat. U.S. and NATO forces came off their "hair trigger" alert and life returned to normal. Son returned his attention to the daily details of his job at AFSOUTH. University night classes were going well. There was plenty of flying, with repeat trips to Greece and Turkey as well as trips to Paris and Wiesbaden, Germany. The Alps, including Mt. Blanc at over 13,000 feet are among the most beautiful and rugged mountains in the world, snow capped for most of the year. They presented a barrier to direct flights from Naples central European destinations in the C-47 which was not pressurized. Passenger carrying flights, therefore, had to take the long way around, flying west over the Island of Corsica to Monaco and the Riviera to Marseilles, France, thence north to either Paris or north east into Germany. Such a flight presents some of the most beautiful scenery in the world. When the sun is shining and the Sea calm as it is most of the time, the waves of the Mediterranean reflect the sunlight in millions of diamonds. The sea itself is cobalt blue. Resorts along the coast are one picture postcard after another.

Trips to Wiesbaden and Lindsay AFB where Headquarters USAFE (U. S. Air Forces, Europe) are located usually meant a trip to the well stocked Commissary and Base Exchange. Son would shop for items that could not be had in Naples. As personal favors he would also try to buy and bring home items for friends.

Winter flying in Europe can be somewhat tricky, often featuring low ceilings and visibilities. Son was always careful not to stick his nose into any situation that he could not handle. He was a competent instrument pilot, however, and usually got through to his intended destination. One flight involved low ceiling and visibility on departure, not the destination. Son was the command pilot on a flight to Orly Field south of Paris, delivering AIRSOUTH and AFSOUTH staffers to a conference at Headquarters, SHAPE (Supreme Headquarters, Allied Powers, Europe). SHAPE is located at Fontainebleau south of Paris. The flight involved a two-day layover, so Son, not being directly involved in the conference, had an opportunity to see some of Paris. He sampled and developed a taste for escargot (snails roasted in garlic butter and served in the shell). French coffee wasn't bad either. His overall impressions: Paris is a beautiful city. Parisians are not. In general, they are aloof, brusque, even rude. Perhaps if he spoke French it would be better, he thought. Oh well, not to worry.

The return flight to Naples was scheduled to depart at 6:30 A.M. Son arrived at Base Operations at Orly at 5:00 A.M. to do his flight planning and check the weather. As soon as he checked the weather reports he spotted a potential problem. The air was clear, not a

cloud in the sky. The winds were calm, not a breath of air stirring. The temperature was only one degree above the dewpoint. The dewpoint is the temperature at which the air becomes 100% saturated, generally creating fog. It is possible for the temperature and the dewpoint to be the same if the air is absolutely calm. However, the slightest breath of air can trigger sudden fog formation. Commonly, that breath of air will occur as the sun comes up and creates uneven warming. It was still dark as Son filled out his flight plan. Hopefully, he would be able to take off before sunup and before the fog would come.

He got his passengers on board and started his engines just as the fog started to form. As long as he could get to the end of the takeoff runway he knew he would be able to do an instrument takeoff. He asked the control tower to provide a ramp vehicle to lead him to the runway. This was provided, and as he taxied out he followed the vehicle's flashing lights. That was all he could see as they proceeded down a long taxiway. Finally, arriving at the end of the runway, the ramp vehicle led him down the center stripe of the runway for a few yards,. Then, flashing his lights the ramp vehicle turned sharply to the right, leaving Son and his C-47 astride the center stripe. The control tower cleared him for takeoff. He went through his pre-takeoff checks, checked his instruments carefully and gripping the throttles with his right hand, smoothly opened them to takeoff power. Holding the runway heading precisely, he waited for the airplane to gain flying speed. He lifted the airplane off the ground.

"Gear up!"

"Gear up!"

The layer of dense fog that had formed was no more than 200 feet thick. Almost before the landing gear had retracted they popped out on top of a brilliant white blanket. There was no sign of the ground - except for one thing. Looking ahead and to his 10 o'clock position Son could see the dark silhouette of the Eiffel Tower poking through the brilliant white blanket! C'est magnifique!! Herman will never forget that view.

Chapter 47
Family Life In Naples

The longer Son and his family lived in Naples, the more they began to appreciate the rich and complex culture and history that surrounded them. With a history going back 3,000 years or more, one only had to look around to see the fingerprints of civilizations past, and to realize that modern Naples is a product of all its past - its languages, its arts, politics and wars. Over the centuries, Naples, and to varying degrees the rest of Italy, have come under the influence and/or domination of the Etruscans and the Romans. The Roman achievements in building the infrastructure and culture of the region are everywhere to be seen in the roads and architecture. After the dissolution of the Roman Empire, Naples came successively under the influence of the Goths, the Byzantine Greeks, the Normans, the Spanish and the French before Garibaldi finally unified the country in 1860. Each epoch left its mark. Great artists, such as Michaelangelo, Titian and Botticelli; the astronomer Copernicus; politician and statesman Machiavelli and the Medici family, all are a part of Italy today.

"Arretta, do you realize how much there is to see here, practically under our nose? Take a look at this travel guide. Within a two or three hour drive, at most, we could be at places like Sorrento, Mt. Vesuvius, Pompeii, Herculaneum, Caserta and Paestium. Paestium is an ancient city founded by the Achaens originating from Greece. It is thought to be over 2,000 years old. Then there is the Amalfi drive, across the peninsula from Sorrento. It is supposed to have some of the most spectacular scenery in the world.

"Here, let me read a couple of short paragraphs from this travel brochure." Son read aloud the following glowing words:

"Not all of paradise was lost. A dollop of it remains to be found again in Italy's Campania region, a region blessed with that most operatic of cities, Naples, with famous archeological sites, with islands floating in sun-dappled waters and coastal towns of shimmering beauty edging them.

"Capri, Ischia, and Procida are the sea-wreathed isles, and of these, islandophiles have always had a special love for Capri. Erstwhile pleasure dome to Roman emperors and still Italy's most glamorous seaside getaway, this craggy island is epic in its beauty. Its main town is a Moorish opera set of white houses, tiny squares, and narrow medieval alleyways, it cliffs the very embodiment of time; it has bougainvillea-shaded pathways overlooking the sea, magnificent grottoes. It has always been a stage that lesser mortals could share with the beautiful people, and even though today's summer scene resembles a stampede, the crowds are not enough to destroy Capri's special charm.

"Back on the mainland, Campania has the Sorrentine peninsula and the romantic towns of the Amalfi Coast. Connecting these towns is the Amalfi Drive, a cliff-hugging stretch of

road that tests one's faith in civil engineering as it snakes above rocky cliffs plunging into the sea. Erosion has contorted the rocks into mythological shapes and hollowed out grottoes where the air is turquoise and the water an icy blue. White villages, dripping with flowers, nestle in the coves or climb like vines up the steep terraced hills; small boats dot the blue below like brightly colored fish. The road must have a thousand turns, each with a different view, on its dizzying 69-km (43-mi) journey from Sorrento to Salerno. En route, it traverses some of the most drop-dead gorgeous real estate on earth.

"Don't forget the Isles of Capri (yes, they wrote a song about it), and Ischa. They're all practically in our back yard! It would be a crime not to visit them while we're here. Let's pack up the Opel with some picnic fare, pick a spot and make a day of it. We could cover one or two of these places per month. It would be good for Mary-Lynn. She's old enough to understand a lot of it. Randy is too young to fully appreciate the history, but he would enjoy being out with us, I'm sure."

". . .As long as I don't have to sit down in a restaurant. I get panicky in situations like that you know."

"Yes, I know. I think we can avoid most of that."

The next Saturday, they headed out in their little Opel, southeast down the coast highway from Naples, their destination: Sorrento and then up the steep mountain and through a long tunnel to the Amalfi drive. The weather was sunny and gorgeous, the Bay of Naples on their right was at its bluest best. Sorrento was even more beautiful and picturesque than advertised. They stopped near the docks and found a place on the pier where they could open their cooler and have their lunch. Then began the climb up the mountain. While Naples is built within a semi-circular amphitheater, Sorrento is a terraced city, simply clinging to the flat sides of the mountain. The terraces are planted with orange and olive trees. One could easily spend a week in Sorrento visiting its fishing village, its museums and churches. But the Sons wanted to cover as much ground as possible in one day. They set out up the mountain, negotiating the steep zig-zag streets. Finally through the town, they continued to climb. As they approached the top of the mountain they saw signs: "Aprete la Lucia - Grotto fa!" (Turn on your lights, tunnel ahead!). As they entered the tunnel Son saw immediately why the sign called for headlights. There were none in the tunnel. Although he couldn't be sure, it seemed that they were still climbing in the tunnel. It was over a mile in length. Finally, he could literally see "light at the end of the tunnel."

Just before they exited the tunnel, their headlights illuminated a sign that said to slow down to no more than 20 kph, followed by a big yellow arrow sign pointing to the left. It indicated a 90 degree left turn. The dot of light grew larger. Then they popped out of the tunnel into an immediate left turn.

"Oh, Herman, be careful!"

"Wow! Look at that!"

They were on a narrow, two-lane road now traveling southeast. It clung to the side of a vertical cliff. Thousands of feet below was the inky blue Mediterranean . The view was literally breathtaking. They followed the road through the towns of Posmano, Priano, Positano and , eventually, Amalfi.

"Look out!" Arretta yelled as a big Fiat tour bus careened toward them on the narrow road ahead. The driver was hugging the cliff, but it looked as though he was taking fully three quarters of the available road. There was no guard rail to Son's right. He aimed his Opel at the left side of the bus, missing it by inches!

"That's the way they drive in Italy!"

"Well, they're crazy!"

"Don't worry about it. They're used to it!"

"Really? Well, I'm not!"

After negotiating the next switchback, Son was driving west down the cliff face. This time he was on the inside, hugging the cliff as opposing traffic squeezed by him. The Amafi drive provides a good example of driving techniques in Italy. In America people have been known to go from Jeykll to Hyde when they get behind the steering wheel of an automobile, but it's nothing to the transformation that seems to seize Italians. They make liberal use of the horn, figuring, one supposes that blowing the horn gives them the right of way, particularly over two-wheeled donkey carts, pedestrians and chickens! Busses and trucks, of course, being bigger than other vehicles always have the right of way!

Son chuckled as he thought to himself, "Hold it gently!"

Amalfi was a charming place, nestled into the space between the cliffs and the seashore. Today, it caters to tourists. In centuries past, Amalfi was a burgeoning naval power on a par with Venice, Genoa and Pisa.

The Sons spent the rest of the day until late afternoon exploring the streets and shops of Amalfi. It was indeed a fascinating place. They could have spent a couple of days there easily and not seen everything there was to see.

"We should come back here. Let's make reservations at that cute pensione we saw. We could come early, sight see all day, then stay overnight and come back home the next day."

Rome, 1956

"Well, let's think about it," said Arretta.

There were many situations like that during the three years that the Sons were in Italy. There was so much to see. They would never be able to see it all. On other weekends they made trips to many of those places - Vesuivus, Pompeii and Herculaneum, Paestium, Ischa and Capri. They did stay overnight at a beautiful bed and breakfast pensione on Capri which gave them a chance to explore all the many delights of that island. Half the fun was in getting there. They took an excursion boat, big enough to carry 100 happy, vacationing people. There was music, Italian music, like "Funiculi, Funicula," "Come Back to Sorrento," "O Sole Mio," and "Volare!" The warm sea breezes, the music and the people all contributed to the holiday spirit.

They were intrigued by the Blue Grotto, and underwater cave located on the southern side of Capri. The entrance to the cave was by small boat. The boat would wait at the entrance until the sea ebbed sufficiently to allow it to dart quickly into the cave. Once inside, Son and his family were treated to a marvelous view. Light filtered into the cave from the direction of the entrance, which for a good part of the time was covered with water. The light gave the water a weird luminescence. It was a magical place, filled with strange rock formations and echoing sounds. When they were ready to leave, their boatman repeated the process that he used to enter the cave. He waited at the entrance until the water level dropped enough to open the entrance. He darted out and again they were back in the brilliant sunshine.

They made several one day trips to Rome, trying to take in a little of the city each time - the Coliseum, the plazas and churches and museums, the aqueducts and, of course, St. Peters, the epicenter of Roman Catholicism. The paintings by Michelangelo were awe-inspiring. They visited Florence and Pisa. They climbed to the top of the Leaning Tower. They took a three-day weekend to visit Venice. There they stood in the great square in front of the Palace of The Doges and the famous clock tower topped by the Lion of St. Mark. They fed the thousands of pigeons that get fat on the tidbits that they cadge from the tourists. They took a trip in a gondola through the smelly canals that comprise the streets in Venice. They glided under the famous "bridge of sighs", which arched between two buildings on opposite sides of the canal. The bridge gained its name from the sighs of prisoners

who were being transferred in shackles from the court where they had been sentenced back to their prison cells. They took a trip to the famous Murano Glass Factory and watched the glass blowers work their art in multi-colored molten glass.

During most of these trips, Arretta's anxieties seemed to be held in check. She seemed to get outside of herself in focusing on the many interesting things they were seeing. Why couldn't she do this at home and in social situations? Son wondered.

One spring, as Son recalls it was in 1956, Son decided that it would be interesting to take a two-week vacation in the outdoor camping mode. The little Opel had a luggage rack on top with plenty of room for a tent, sleeping bags, camp stove and other equipment. He ordered a full compliment from Speigel. When it came he arranged it on top of the Opel and found that, indeed, it did fit very well. They planned their trip for early August. They would stay at AGIP camp grounds which were located conveniently all over Europe. It would avoid hotels and restaurants which in the past had proven to be sources of anxiety for Arretta. Son was confident that it would be a lot of fun.

CHAPTER 48
Sampling The Outdoor Life

Son packed everything neatly atop the Opel, covered it with a waterproof tarp and cinched it down firmly. They picked a camp ground near Ravenna for the first night. Driving west, over the Appenines they picked up the costal highway. It was a beautiful drive, offering close-up views of the Adriatic Sea. They could almost see across to the opposite coast and Yugoslavia. They found the camp-ground, checked in and located their site. Everything went beautifully. In no time, Son had the tent deployed and secured with stakes and ropes. He set up the Coleman gas stove. Arretta, with assistance from Mary-Lynn and Randy, got the air mattresses inflated and sleeping bags set up. Son fired up the stove and they were ready to cook dinner.

"Wow!", everybody said. "All the comforts of home!"

Dinner was simple, consisting of some sautéed Spam, eggs and fried potatoes. The coffee pot worked to perfection. All of it was delicious. After cleanup they double checked everything in the tent and got ready for bed. The sleeping bags were snug and cozy. As they drifted off to sleep, Randy was heard to say,

"Daddy, I like this. This is fun!"

The next morning, they had breakfast, the menu being a repeat of last night's dinner, then they packed up and were on their way to their next destination. It was another AGIP camp ground near Lake Maggiore in the Italian Alps. This time, the routine of setting up camp went even more smoothly.

"What a blast! This is great," exclaimed Son.

Little did he know.

Sometime during the early morning hours it began to rain. Well, the tent was waterproof wasn't it? Yes, the top and sides of the tent were waterproofed and designed to shed most rain. The floor, however, was not designed to be submerged in water. Son had forgotten, or didn't know, how important it was to dig a trench around the upside walls of his tent. Consequently, when the rains came, they sluiced down the hill into the upside wall of their tent. They ran under the tent and up through the canvas floor!

"So much for camping out," said Arretta, her voice dripping with sarcasm.

Sleeping bags are not very comfortable when they are wet.

The rest of their vacation was in the conventional mode, no more camping out.

Their next stop was the General George S. Patton Rest Hotel in Garmisch-Partenkirchen, Bavaria. The trip from Lake Como took them up through the Alps and the Brenner Pass into Bavaria. The scenery was stunning.

At Garmisch they were close to Oberammergau, site of the annual Passion Play, and all things quaint. The Germans here have a penchant for painting all sorts of scenes, some

religious, some of mythical themes, on the end of their buildings, using them as giant canvases. Hitler's mountain hideout, sometimes referred to as "The Eagle's Nest," was not far away. Son and his family visited both places. At Oberammergau they bought Randy a Tyrolean outfit, consisting of lederhosen, sweater and hat complete with feathered headband. It made him look like a charming young mountain sheep herder.

Randal - Age 3

They went to visit the Eagles Nest. High up in the mountains east of Garmisch, they entered a long 1000 foot tunnel bored horizontally into the mountain. The tunnel terminated directly below the hideout. Riding an elevator, they ascended upward for another 1000 feet. They emerged at the foot of a large circular building with glass windows all around. Except for all the windows it was done in swiss chalet style. This is where Hitler and his mistress, Eva Braun, came on vacation. Looking out at the mountains spread out below it was easy to imagine, Hitler once stood here. Here, he must have felt that he was on top of the world, looking out on his beloved Bavaria. Now a primary tourist attraction, there were all kinds of items for sale - books, post cards, pins, beer mugs and other memorabilia. An attractive dining room faced the windows. The view was magnificent. The four Sons sat down to a relaxing lunch and watched an aerial demonstration put on by a flock of very large black crows as they soared, riding the wind currents, up to and over the roof, then back down and around the windows. Somehow, these large black birds seemed symbolically appropriate for such a place.

Fisherman on Bavarian Lake

Another snippet taken from Son's memory, involved a lake. He doesn't remember the name. They were returning from their trip to the Eagles Nest. They stopped at the eastern edge, in late afternoon merging into sunset, he remembers how the waters, almost glass smooth, changed colors from silver-blue to gold, to rose to orange-red. A lone fisherman in his boat was parked perhaps a hundred yards off shore. In slow motion, the fisherman reeled in his line, then brought it up over his shoulder and smoothly forward again, sending his lure out in front of him, creating circular ripples in the smooth surface as it landed. As it grew darker the boat and the fisherman were rendered in total silhouette. It was a scene of total peace and beauty.

Arretta, understandably, didn't want to camp out anymore. They decided that they would stay in hotels for the rest of the trip, even though that would mean a return to environments that seemed to cause Arretta to become anxious. Such was the case during their short stay at the General Patton hotel. Arretta would not, could not come to the dining room for meals. Son took Mary-Lynn and Randy with him for dinner in the dining room. They sat down. Son perused the menu and ordered for himself and Arretta, and then spoke to the waiter,

"Mrs. Son will not be able to join us. Could you please have her meal sent to her in room 307?"

"Of course, sir! That is not a problem!"

"Very well. Give us another minute and we'll order for my daughter and son."

"I'll check back with you in a few minutes."

When the waiter returned Son gave him orders for Mary-Lynn and Randy. Hearing soft music, he looked around to see a small combo with piano, clarinet, bass and rhythm section. It sounded good. The music seemed to fit his mood. He opened his left brain and

attuned his feelings to the music - *"Memories are Made of This.... One life. .one love. . memories are made of this."* Is this what they are made of .. feelings of sadness? No. They are made of much more than this. Son snapped out of his reverie and back to the here and now. But, he would remember. Son's brain had a funny way of creating associations between specific events and music. Later, hearing the music would always evoke the memory.

By this time, Son had used up almost a week of his two week leave. They wanted to see as much of the rest of Europe as possible. From Bavaria they traveled north through Germany into Belgium and Holland. Like children in a candy store, they wanted to see/buy it all, but there was not nearly enough time. Highlights of their memories included the great cities of Antwerp and Brussels and the canals and the windmills of Holland.

Arretta said, as they took an excursion boat along the canals,

"I'm taking pictures with my eyes. Then I close them and commit the scene to memory. I don't ever want to forget this place."

Neither did Son.

They took a large ferry boat up into Scandanavia, hoping eventually to get to Sweden before they would have to turn around and rush back to Italy. It quickly became apparent that they would not have time to see Sweden. They settled, instead, on Copenhagen, Denmark. There were more trips on the ferry boat. They found Copenhagen to be a story book place, straight out of a Hans Christian Andersen fantasy. They visited the famous Tivoli Gardens and the waterfront where they looked northward across the strait at Sweden, not more than twenty miles away - so close, and yet so far.

CHAPTER 49
The Chickenpox

Now it was time to head back home. They had hoped to have enough time for a west-ward detour into France, but time would not allow it. Americans who have not lived in Europe do not realize how compact it is. They are used to long distances between places, particularly in the West. All of Europe, on the other hand, can be fitted into the map of Texas. On the autostradas (freeways) where there is no speed limit normal cruising speeds average 80 - 90 mph. It is easy to get from one end of Europe to the other in a short time. Back in Bavaria, the Sons planned on two more days to make it home, figuring on taking one day to make it through the Alps into Northern Italy and a second day to drive down the Adriatic Coast and across to Naples. But Randy had developed a dry, persistent cough.

That night, in the motel, Herman said,

"Look! I think he's getting a rash!"

"Chickenpox?"

"Could be. We'd better hurry home."

By the next morning, it was apparent that not only Randy, but Mary-Lynn as well, had florid cases of the chickenpox. Neither had had it before. It was pretty obvious that that was what ailed them. They didn't want to subject them to another night on the road, so Son decided that he would just drive straight through from Garmish to Naples. It figured to be about an 18-hour trip.

As they left the General Patton Hotel at 6 A.M. Son set himself into "long range cruise control mode." He remembered the time in Korea when he flew an 8-hour mission in an F-51. They almost had to pull him out of the cockpit he was so stiff. This, he thought, is going to be a repeat performance. Stopping only for gas and a couple of stretches, they made it back to their apartment in Naples at 12 midnight. They slipped the key into the door at their apartment, fell inside, got both kids in bed and then they crashed.

What a trip, never to be forgotten.

Both kids had fevers, but there didn't seem that there was much to do for them. Aspirin was prohibited, since it could cause Reyes Syndrome. However, when Son checked with the Navy Pharmacy, they gave him a prescription for paracetamol, a non-aspirin medication to help with the fever, and a bottle of calomine lotion for the rash. Randy was not going to school, but Mary-Lynn was. School didn't start until the last week in August, otherwise she would have had to miss a week or ten days.

CHAPTER 50
Festas and Holidays

Italians in general and Neapolitans in particular have an attitude about work. Briefly stated, work is O.K., but it shouldn't be allowed to take over one's life. "Slow and easy wins the race," they say. This attitude reminded Son of what his Basic Flight instructor used to say: "Herman, hold it gently. Don't choke it!" The Italian single word for it is, domaini! Translation: "Don't worry, it will keep until tomorrow!" The average Italian gets up in the morning, has breakfast and goes to work, devoting himself until lunchtime, usually around noon. He then repairs to his home or other relaxing venue to have lunch. Usually taking at least a couple of hours, it is much more extensive than lunch in America which is either skipped entirely or taken on the run. During the two or more hours that Italians take for lunch there is plenty of time for emotive conversation, some good wine, a little food, some more wine and some more conversation. By the time they are through with this routine, they of course are in need of a nap - a siesta` they call it. Storefronts and offices will be closed from about 2:30 until perhaps 6:30. After this restorative time, they will go back to work, perhaps for another three or four hours. Finally, they will go home and have their third meal of the day, usually a very light supper. Son found that this attitude and practice was pervasive in Naples.

Soon after they arrived Son noted that his Headquarters office was always on some kind of extended holiday. The Italian word for it is "festa". He found out that his office observed all holidays, Italian holidays, Greek holidays, Turkish holidays and, yes, even American holidays! At least a third of the time the offices were closed. Son doesn't remember all of them, but a couple of Italian ones come to mind.

The beginning of the New Year is universally observed, and in Naples they observe it with a bang!

Son & his family
Naples, 1957

There are several occasions for the release of fireworks but the beginning of the New Year is of first importance. The festivities begin at midnight, the end of the old year. Neapolitans orchestrate their firework displays, as in a symphony! They have rhythm, structure and phrasing. Beginning with pianissimo, in rising crescendo to sforzanda! There are slow movements contrasting with rapid fire staccato. They carry an audience along on a rising tide of emotion to a climax featuring big flash bombs that rattle the windows in every building. The entire Neapolitan littoral provides the stage for these extravaganzas. Across the bay

one can see supporting choruses in the displays lighting the horizon from Sorrento, Capri and Ischa. If the Italians had devoted the amount of cordite and black powder expended in just one such display to attacking the Germans in World War II, they would have chased them over the Alps in disgrace! The Son's apartment was located high on Via Posillipo, in Northwestern Naples. From their balcony they had a complete view of the entire city and the Bay of Naples. The stroboscopic flashes lighted the entire city and the waters of the bay. Ten minutes into the show, everything was shrouded with smoke. It looked and sounded like war! That must have been the way Randy saw it for he was terrified. The explosions, more than the flashes, really scared him. They started watching on the outside balcony, but Arretta finally took him inside. He could still hear the explosions but they weren't quite so scary there. After about an hour of this pandemonium leading to a gigantic climax it was over. The quiet was deafening! Randy soon settled down and seemed to be none the worse for the experience.

Another Neapolitan holiday to remember is called Peidi Di Grotta, literally translated The Foot Of The Cave. Although it features fireworks too, it is nothing to compare with the New Year. It is a cross between Mardi Gras, Christmas and the New Year in America. Public buildings are covered with lights. That's Peidi Di Grotta. People by the thousands of thousands come out on the streets. Everybody has a great time. Imagine the entire waterfront crescent covered with lighted strings of pearls. Imagine every building in the city with its own individual light display, many of them animated and depicting various mythical characters. Imagine a holiday atmosphere similar to Mardi Gras. Neapolitans are enthusiastic and fun loving. They know how to have a good time, and during Peidi Di Grotta they do.

CHAPTER 51
A Change of Address

The apartment lease that the Sons signed on 407 Via Posillipo was for a period of one year. Toward the end of the lease period they were notified that if they wished to renew their lease that the rent would be increased by 20%. While they liked the apartment they objected to the increase. They decided to look for another location. Fortunately, they found another location that they liked even better than 407 Via Posillipo. 207 Via Petarcha was located in another high rise building on a street that was one terrace above Via Posillipo. In other words, the new apartment looked down on the old one. It offered about the same square footage. In addition, it was on the first floor, facing the street. It had a small side garden that was accessed off the master bedroom. A high iron perimeter fence made the garden a secure place for Randy to play. It was available for the same rent that they were paying. Of course they took it. After moving in they discovered some other nice features. They could walk out the front door to the sidewalk and street and talk to street vendors, giving them a chance to practice their Italian. There was "the vegetable man," "the knife sharpener," and "the organ player!" Yes, the organ player had a monkey on a leash! Randy was a hit with all of them as he spoke real neapolitano!

Son remembers many things about Naples with a special fondness. It is a polyglot city with a rich, multi-faceted culture. Its peoples span the spectrum of human experience - rich, poor, educated, ignorant and superstitious, honest, openly emotional and sometimes deceitful, even criminal. They are enthusiastic about life. The language of the streets in Naples, Neapolitano is an admixture of Italian, Greek, French, Spanish, Turkish and who knows what else is nothing like textbook Italian as spoken in northern Italy, particularly in Lombardy. The latter is the kind of Italian that Herman studied while taking college courses taught by Il Professore Vicenzo Traverza. Traverza was fluent in seven languages, including all of the ones that provided input to the street language of Naples. One evening in class he said,

"You think that there is only one Neapolitano dialect, do you? Well, let me tell you that there seven! In the beginning, Naples was not one city, but seven. There were seven distinct city-states, demarked by fortress-like walls. Each city had its own distinct dialect. The walls, though deteriorated over the centuries, still stand. The city has long since overrun them. But the differences in dialect that began in each of these localities still remain. They correspond roughly to the areas outlined by these old walls!"

He remembers the characters, most of them friends, one in particular not. His name was "Lucky" Luciano. Lucky lived a stones throw from where Son lived on Via Posillipo. He lived in a big villa located down the hill toward the waterfront. A big Mafia crime boss in

America, he was finally indicted, tried and convicted. He was sent to prison to serve a life sentence. He was deported in 1946 when Thomas E. Dewey, then New York Prosecuting Attorney and erstwhile presidential candidate running against Harry Truman, commuted his sentence.

The Italian government gave strict rules on Luciano's livelihood. He could venture no more than a few miles from Naples and had to tell them about any visitors from outside Italy. That was a rule he broke frequently. He still conducted business back in the states through runners and even the telephone. His friendship with Meyer Lansky began to sour in the late 1950s, because he felt Meyer was cutting him out on more lucrative deals back in the States. Regardless, Lucky remained a very rich man.[1]

Luciano lived his remaining years in Naples. In 1962, he was to meet with a Hollywood producer who was interested in doing his life story. Lucky met The Hollywood tycoon at Capodichino Airport. They shook hands. Luciano grimaced, his face contorted. He died on the spot of a massive heart attack. Finally, he got to return to America where he is buried in St. John's Cemetery in New York.

Anna Falana was the Son's wonderful live-in maid. She was the original earth mother, caring, friendly and outgoing with a natural love of life and everything in it, including babies and young children, homemaking including cooking, and teaching the Sons to speak some neapolitano. She could whip up a mean dish of homemade pasta, served with a sauce that could not be duplicated. She loved Randy. Anna, who was a devout Catholic, has no doubt gone on to her heavenly reward. After the Sons left Naples they wrote to her and she responded in Italian one time. Son still has that hand written letter. After more than 40 years it is difficult to understand all of it. One phrase, however, at the beginning of the letter is quite clear: "Come stai Randy?" She thought of him almost as a grandchild. Subsequent attempts to correspond with her were unsuccessful. She will be remembered always by Herman, Mary-Lynn and Randy.

Antonio (Tony) Sabatto was the building superintendent at 407 Via Posillipo. That single street address included three high-rise apartment buildings, under various stages of construction at the time the Sons lived there. When he was young, Tony went to America, living in New Jersey. There he got a college education with a degree in civil engineering. He was married for a number of years but had no children. His wife died and Tony returned to Naples. His English, and of course, his Italian were impeccable. More than once we relied upon him to translate for us when we had to discuss business matters with trades people, such as when we had custom furniture built for our apartment. He was completely honest. We learned that we could trust him implicitly.

Madam Regina Caroly was from Romania. She was a somewhat blowsy, promiscuous and overweight ballet master from the San Carlos Opera House. She was Mary-Lynn's first truly professional dance instructor. She came to our apartment to give private lessons. She organized and set up group instruction at the Opera House for several young girls who were part of the U.S. military community in Naples. She spoke good English but with a thick Romanian accent. She regaled us with

Mary Lynn, age 7

many, many interesting stories about her early life and her career in ballet. She was a major influence in Mary-Lynn's artistic development.

Master Sergeant John Anderson, his wife Bertha and his two children were salt-of-the-earth Americans, the kind that made us feel proud. John was the chief administrative clerk for the Operations Division where Son was assigned. He had risen through the ranks, by dint of hard work and study. When on duty he always maintained proper military courtesy, saluting when required and addressing Son formally as "Major Son" or "Sir!" Off duty, he and his family became personal friends. They offered their help in finding an apartment, going to the commissary, the hospital or anywhere else that was needed. Son found out that John maintained a "birthday file," listing the birthday of every person he knew. His hobby was sending a birthday card to all his friends. Herman thought, "Surely he won't continue to do that after we leave this assignment." He was wrong. John continued to send them to us, year after year, from 1956 until just shortly before he died, a victim of Alzeheimer's disease, in 1996. He did more than just sign and send them. The cards always contained handwritten, newsy notes of what was happening with him and his family. After he retired from the Air Force he went back to college, getting his degree in Education. After a career in teaching he went to work for the U.S. Postal Service, finally retiring from that job when he reached 65 years of age. As a famous TV personality would say, "John was all that - and a bag of chips!"

During the summer of 1957, Son and his family began thinking of going back to America. Son was hoping for a good line assignment in tactical air operations. He wanted to be assigned to a wing or an air division, hopefully in Tactical Air Command. If not that, then maybe he would be able to land an assignment in Air Defense Command. That would be nice. Headquarters, Air Defense Command was located in Colorado Springs. There should be some good jobs there and the Springs, located next door to The Air Force Academy, would be a great place to live. Arretta, not being the least sensitive to Air Force organization and culture or her husband's career needs, said:

"Maybe we could ask for Luke AFB at Phoenix again!"

"You don't understand, Arretta. After an overseas tour in which I came from Luke, the Air Force isn't about to send me back to the same place. I'm supposed to be a career officer. Presumably, they have some kind of career plan for me, and it doesn't involve doing the same thing over and over!"

"Well, you could try, and maybe if we got to Phoenix you could try to find a civilian job there and then resign."

"Oh sure!"

There was no point in talking with her about it. This time, Son would just let the chips fall. Whatever happened, he'd go with it.

They decided to sell their little Opel Kadet, great as it was in a European environment. It wasn't what they wanted when they got back to the States. Son heard about a Chrysler Dealership located in Ankara, Turkey that would take orders in Ankara for a new Chrysler to be delivered in New York for pickup on their arrival. Rumor had it that they would charge invoice plus $50. That seemed hard to believe. Checking it out, however, he found it to be true. He checked with the Flight Section and found that there was an upcoming staff trip to Ankara in a couple of weeks. He got Shearin to put him on the board for the flight. At the dealer he found he could get a brand new Chrysler Town and Country station wagon with full leather interior for only $4,600, delivered at the Chrysler dealer in New Jersey. He ordered it, giving the dealer a check for $100, and told him that he would give him a delivery date as soon as he received his stateside orders. "Wow!" thought Son. We can pick up the car in New Jersey and drive it to our new assignment.

Although it was later called a "dumb" satellite, it didn't strike most Americans that way when they first heard about Sputnik.

"History changed on October 4, 1957, when the Soviet Union successfully launched Sputnik I. The world's first artificial satellite was about the size of a basketball, weighed only 183 pounds, and took about 98 minutes to orbit the Earth on its elliptical path. That launch ushered in new political, military, technological, and scientific developments. While the Sputnik launch was a single event, it marked the start of the space age and the U.S.-U.S.S.R space race."[2]

In the context of the cold war struggle between the Soviet Union and the United States, everybody wondered what Sputnik would mean. But Son had his own "fish to fry." Now it was time to wait for assignment orders. Finally, they came. Surely enough, they were assigned to Headquarters, Air Defense Command at Colorado Springs. Son was shipping as a Weapons Officer which meant that he would probably be involved with some aspect of nuclear weapons. He knew that Air Defense Command fighter aircraft, such as the F89 Scorpion, the F101 Voodoo and the F102 and 106 were all nuclear capable. He didn't know too much about the armament and fire control systems of these airplanes but, he said, he'd learn.

Their orders called for them to travel first class to New York aboard the USS Constitution departing Naples on December 10, 1957. The trip was scheduled to take 7 days, putting them in front of The Statue of Liberty on December 17, 1957. They were excited.

"We'll be living pretty high off the hog," said Son. First Class, how about that!"

"High off the hog - what's that?"

"You're from Arizona, you wouldn't know. That's the Missouri farm boy in me."

"I see."

They sold their Kadet to an Army Master Sergeant for $850, not bad considering that they had driven it nearly 50,000 miles in the three years they lived in Naples.

On November 29, 1957, Ditta Giovanni Pagliga, s.r.l., Custom House Broker and Forwarding Agent, brought a big van to the Son's apartment. A crew of six people were ready to start packing all their household goods for shipment. For the next two days, under Arretta's watchful eye, they disassembled, wrapped and packed almost everything that the Sons owned, in all over 10,000 pounds. Then it was crated and loaded aboard the van. That was the last they would see of their things until well after they arrived in Colorado Springs. They said their goodbyes to Anna, their live-in maid who had become a part of the family.

"Anna, Stai Bene (Be good). We'll miss you. Scrive!"

"Si! Randy, mi amore!"

There were tears. All of the Sons loved Anna. If they could have brought her back to the States, at that point, they would have done so.

On December 1st, they moved out of their apartment and back into the St. Elmo Hotel. Now it was a matter of days before they would board the USS Constitution and be on their way home. They said "goodbyes" to General Young, Colonel Russell and Lt. Col. Hayduk.

"John, I hope you won't blame me for what happened that night in Izmir."

"Not at all. It wasn't your fault. I should have told you."

"Yes, but if you had, I would have told you not to try what you did on my airplane."

"That's why it wasn't your fault. Don't worry about me. I'll just have to live with that letter in my file."

"Well, good luck!'

"Thanks!"

Although they were not close personal friends, Son did respect and admire the two foreign officers in his office - Major Guisseppe Di Napoli of the Italian Army and Col Erderk of the Turkish Air Force.

"If either of you get a chance to come to America please get in touch. You have my permanent mailing address."

"Yes. We'll miss you, Herman," said Colonel Erderk.

"Si! Stai, Bene, Maggiore!"

"Grazie tanto!"

There was an exchange of salutes. Son turned and left. Although it didn't do anything positive for Son's career, it was, nevertheless, the end of a beautiful assignment.

CHAPTER 52
Arrivederci, Naples!

Aboard the USS Constitution, the Sons stood on deck as the big ship, making good a 4 P.M. departure slowly turned toward the southwest and pulled out of the harbor. Pointing between the islands Capri on the left and Ischa on the right the ship began the first leg of its journey back to America. As the Neapolitan skyline slowly receded off their port side they could see the two tall apartment buildings on Via Posillipo and Via Petraca where they had lived. They walked aft to the stern railing of the ship, now beginning to accelerate, and watched the white foam of its wake. Tomorrow morning they would stop briefly in Genoa then pass through the strait of Gibraltar into the Atlantic Ocean. The next stop after that would be the pier in Hoboken, NJ. They were experiencing a strange mixture of feelings - sadness on leaving a beautiful place that had really become "home," and anticipatory excitement and joy over what lay ahead.

Randy said, "I miss Anna."

"Yes, I know you do. She was a good friend to you wasn't she?"

"She played jacks with me and she taught me a lot of songs."

"Yes, I know. We recorded several of your songs and conversations with Anna on tape. I hope we'll be able to play all of them later to remind us of how nice she was."

"Well, we'll write to her," said Arretta.

The ship's sound system was playing Italian music in the background - " Arrivederci Roma."

"Close enough for government work," said Son.

Mary-Lynn said, "I wish Regina could come to America. I'll miss dancing for her."

They had dinner that evening in the first class dining room. The food was delicious and the service impeccable. Arretta had apparently chained her demons. She seemed relaxed and free from anxiety symptoms.

After dinner on the evening of the second day out of Naples, they went out on deck to watch the sunset. Suddenly several flying fish broke the surface, flying along inches above the water, darting like dragonflies. Then in another surprise, a group of dolphins pulled gracefully along side, barely breaking the surface, then diving back into the sea. They were like a fighter escort for our big ship. Later, after sunset, they could see the phosphorescent wake of the ship. This phenomenon is caused by microscopic marine life. Looking over the side of the ship, they could see millions of these little animals giving off pinpoints of light like so many stars. The sea was calm, the weather was perfect.

Son thought, "If I wasn't a pilot I'd like to command a big ship. The crew must feel a special affinity with the earth and sky."

In 1947, American Export Lines announced plans for three 30,000 ton liners for their New York to Italy service. When the order was placed with Bethlehem Steel, the number had been reduced to two ships, the first of which to be delivered was the Independence. Constitution, the second sister, entered service on June 6th, 1951, sailing from New York to Gibraltar, Naples and Genoa. At the time of delivery, they were the fastest American-built liners, achieving over 26 knots.

As dawn approached on the morning of December 17, 1957, the Constitution was positioned just outside New York Harbor. Ellis Island and The Statue of Liberty were becoming visible on the port side. How many thousands of people, Americans and immigrants alike, have looked at that scene and felt what Son and his family were feeling that morning? Over the next 90 minutes, in a cooperative effort between two tugboats and the Liner, Constitution eased in to her assigned pier in Hoboken. By mid-morning the Sons had debarked, went through customs, collected their luggage and in all the hubub found a taxi. Son gave them the address of the Chrysler dealership where they were to pick up their new Town and Country station wagon. It was an exciting time. They took delivery on their car with no trouble. It was getting late, but Son wanted to get out of town, find the New Jersey Turnpike and head west. He didn't care how far; he just wanted to get started. Colorado Springs, Colorado was more than 1,500 miles to the west.

The Chrysler was a dream automobile. Son couldn't believe he had purchased such a top of the line car for less than $5,000, even in 1957.

CHAPTER 53
Hello America

Arretta helped with the map reading as they threaded their way out of town. Son thought about the last time they were navigating their way through a strange city in that little German Opel in Naples. At least here, he hoped, he could find someone who could speak English if he got lost. This time, the navigation went smoothly. They found the Turnpike and headed west. The weather, however, was not going to cooperate. It began to snow. The temperature was about 30 degrees. A few big, fat flakes floated through the air. Then it got thicker. Within an hour, and just about dusk, it was sticking to the road, and it was getting slick. Son decided that the better part of valor would be to pull off the Pike and find a motel. They found a little mom-and-pop motel. It looked as though it hadn't been updated since Franklin Roosevelt was president. But it provided warm shelter, beds and bath. They'd get a fresh start in the morning. That's how their first day back in the USA ended.

The next day the snow had ended. Plows had cleared the roads. Back on the highway, their route took them westward through Pennsylvania and Amish country. They drove on through Ohio, Indiana, Illinois and Missouri. Herman had almost forgotten how lush and verdant the Missouri countryside was. He had written his parents before they left Naples that they would be driving through. He wanted to stop for a few days to visit and to give them a chance to know Mary-Lynn and Randy. He knew, however, that it would be a problem for Arretta.

"We won't stay long. Besides, there isn't anything for you to worry about. They're just plain people, no pretensions. They would really like to get to know you."

"I'm afraid I will panic. Please, can't you tell them we just won't have the time?"

"They'd know we were lying. Come on, even one day. Surely you can do that much!"

"I'll try, but it will probably make me sick."

"It'll make her sick!" Son thought to himself. "She really knows how to put me on the defensive and make me feel guilty for even asking."

He held his ground, however, and as they approached Warrensburg, MO, the little college town where his parents lived, he pulled off the interstate. Mama and Daddy were so excited and glad to see them. They were particularly glad to see Mary-Lynn and Randy, and they outdid themselves in being nice to Arretta. The nicer they were, however, the more nervous Arretta became. She behaved as if she were a witness in a court-room being cross examined by a prosecuting attorney. There was no reciprocal conversation. Mama and Daddy would ask about the trip, how she liked Naples and how Randy and Mary-Lynn liked it. Arretta would answer with curt, yes/no replies. Son tried to smooth things over,

but it didn't help. He was embarrassed. At Daddy's urging, they agreed to stay overnight, but Herman Franklin said that they would have to leave the next day in order to get to Colorado Springs on time. On their way to Kansas City the next morning, Son seethed with anger. He couldn't understand how Arretta could behave so rudely. The sad part of it was that there wasn't a thing that he could do about it. If he confronted Arretta it would only make things worse. She would turn it around and try to make him feel guilty for putting her in the situation in the first place.

Someplace west of Kansas City Arretta asked,

"When do we have to be in Colorado Springs? Do you think we would have time to spend a few days in Phoenix with my folks?"

"No."

Son couldn't understand why she always wanted to go see her parents when they had been such a clear source of her emotional dysfunction. It was strange.

CHAPTER 54
Our Mountain Greenery Home

The Sons arrived in Colorado Springs just before Christmas. In 1957, "The Springs," as it was colloquially called, was a beautiful little resort city, nestled in against the front range of the Rocky Mountains - population around 100,000. Snow capped Pike's Peak stood over 12,000 feet above sea level. But Colorado Springs itself was just over 6,000 feet, so the mountain didn't seem as tall as it actually was. As Son would learn later, the mountain and surrounding terrain exerted a strong modifying influence on the weather, particularly in the winter. Hard against the front range, it was also protected by the 8,000 foot Palmer Ridge, a feature that extended eastward into the high plains. The Ridge separated The Springs from Denver, which had an altitude of only a little more than 5,000 feet. The net effect of this was to protect The Springs. It has very light snow during most winters, and it is dry. Denver could be wet, stormy and snowy while The Springs would be protected in its little pocket. The only exception was when a large low pressure cell centered itself around Albuquerque. Lows have a counter-clockwise circulation. When conditions were right this weather pattern could pump large amounts of moisture into that little pocket formed by the front range and the Palmer Ridge. Overcast, low ceilings and bad weather at The Springs could result while Denver would be having good weather. This happened infrequently. On the day the Sons arrived, they came in from the south. The weather was clear and bright. Passing through Lamar and LaJunta, they followed U.S. Route 50 to Pueblo. There they tuned north on Highway 25. Passing through the little town of Fountain near the north entrance to Ft. Carson, Arretta said,

"This doesn't look very hospitable to me. Everything is brown. Don't they have any rain here?"

"Probably more than they have in Phoenix," Son said with just a touch of sarcasm.

They could see Pikes Peak and The Springs in the distance. Their plan was to find a motel for the short term. Then they'd look for an apartment that they could lease, hopefully, for no more than six months. Son figured they'd be there for at least three years. That would be long enough to make owning a home practical. Of course, they also had to think about schools. Mary-Lynn was in sixth grade when they left Naples, so they assumed she would pick up school at the same grade level. Randy was not quite five years old, so school was not an immediate requirement for him. However, he would be starting kindergarten in the fall. Son had five days before he had to sign in at Headquarters, Air Defense Command.

The day after they checked in at a Best Western Motel they went apartment hunting. They got some leads from the front desk at the motel that indicated plenty of choice in two, even three bedroom units. Most would lease on six-month contracts. They found exactly what they needed on the north side of the city. Warson School and Audobon elementary

school, both with excellent ratings were close by. Now they could develop their plans to build. There was no time to waste, however. It would probably take four to five months from signing of a contract to move-in. A quick reconnaissance of the city led them to conclude that they wanted to live on the north side, probably somewhere near the Austin Bluffs area. They found a builder who had some buildable lots in that area and contracted with him to build their house. They decided on an unpretentious three bedroom, two bath ranch with a full basement. The lot was beautifully located at 2313 Bennett Avenue, just off North Circle Drive. The house would face west, and would offer a beautiful view of Pikes Peak. Mary-Lynn could walk to Warson School where she would be entering the 7th grade. Randy would enroll in First Grade at Audubon School, not more than three blocks away.

CHAPTER 55
A New Job, But More Of The Same

Headquarters, Air Defense Command was located at Ent Air Force Base. The majority of Air Force Bases include airplanes and an airfield with runways - not so at Ent. It comprised a group of office buildings in downtown Colorado Springs. The Air Defense Command managed and provided Air Force assets to NORAD (The North American Air Defense Command) for their operational control in the defense of North America. In the late fifties - early sixties, USAF air defense bases were located generally across "the northern tier," that is, bases like Thule, Greenland, Griffis AFB, NY, Selfridge AFB, MI, Minot, ND and McChord AFB, WA. The fighter aircraft included the F89 Scorpion, F102 Delta Dagger, F101 Voodo and the F106 Delta Dart. All of these aircraft were capable of launching nuclear tipped missles. They were designed to counter the Soviet air-breathing threat. The dual threat during this time period was from Soviet long-range Bear bombers and from their long range nuclear missiles. Their routes of attack would have been across the north pole and Canada. Early detection was paramount, hence the "Dew Line" radars, deployed across the northern reaches of Canada, and BMEWS (Ballistic Missile Early Warning System) radar which could detect Soviet missiles early in their launch phase. The warning of a missile attack provided by BMEWS did not provide a direct defense against such an attack. It did, however, provide approximately 30 minutes advance warning, enough to allow bombers and Minuteman Missiles of the American Strategic Air Command to launch a deadly counter strike. This was the essence of the nuclear standoff called MAD, or Mutually Assured Destruction. Both sides knew that they could not initiate an attack that could disable a killing response from the other side. It was a successful strategy. For fifty years it prevented nuclear war.

Such a defense meant that U.S. and Canadian forces had to be able to respond within minutes of a warning. A portion of the fighter and bomber forces were placed on "strip alert," meaning that pilots were standing by and the aircraft were armed and ready to launch within 5 minutes.

Because nuclear weapons were involved, extreme precautions were required to insure against and accidental or inadvertent launch or detonation of such weapons. Detailed procedures, covering every aspect of nuclear weapons storage, handling, loading and launching were developed. These procedures provided the basis of rigorous training for all personnel having access to these weapons.

Son's assignment in Headquarters, Air Defense Command was within the Operations Directorate as a Weapons Officer. He, in coordination with Material and Maintenance Directorates, was responsible for developing and maintaining weapons handling proce-

dures. The Air Force established The Nuclear Weapons Systems Safety Group, reporting to the Nuclear Regulatory Commission. The purpose of the NWSSG, located at the Nuclear Weapons Laboratory at Sandia Base near Albuquerque, NM, was to develop and maintain so-called stock-pile to target handling procedures. There was a lot he had to learn about both the weapons and the aircraft that carried them. It took a lot of reading, a lot of questioning and attendance at a special school on nuclear weapons, but finally Son was appointed an Air Defense Command member of the NWSSG. This group met regularly to develop, approve and monitor safety rules and procedures for the handling and use of all nuclear weapons.

During the three years from 1958 to 1961, Son's professional duties focused on nuclear weaponry within the USAF Air Defense Command. His immediate boss was Colonel James B. Wilson. He and Jim got along well professionally. However, the old problem of Son's social activity within the military community reasserted itself. In two of the three O.E.R.'s (Officer Efficiency Reports) that Son received there were oblique statements about his, "lack of participation in the social life of the organization." Son made several attempts to encourage Arretta to join him as his "military wife." He was hopeful that the three years in Italy had given her an opportunity to gain some self confidence.

There was no change.

Soon after their arrival in Colorado Springs, Arretta began seeing Dr. S. F. Loder, a classical Freudian psychiatrist. The weekly visits at $25 each were a strain on the family budget. But, Son thought, if they help the cost is irrelevant. Again, Son asked Dr. Loder if it would help if he participated in the weekly sessions. Dr. Loder said, "No."

After his first O.E.R., Son talked with Col. Wilson, explaining the reason for his "social aloofness." Jim said that he understood. His next O.E.R. contained the same comments with an excuse. "Son's wife is ill and is receiving treatment."

Of course, that really helped.

CHAPTER 56
A House Becomes A Home

In June, 1958, the Sons were about ready to move into their new home. It had been a long six months living in a small apartment. Every day, as the home progressed toward completion, they would drive by to check on it. Finally, the day arrived and they moved in. It was great - three bedrooms, one and one-half baths, a one-car attached garage and a full basement. The combination living-dining room featured a big picture window that looked out to the west, framing snow-capped Pikes Peak in a perfect picture. All of this cost only $21,500! During the ensuing four years they put their personal stamp on it. Before the snow flew, Son worked hard to plant shrubs across the back lot line. They drove up into the mountains west of town and found two very small blue spruce trees that they dug up. Son carefully trans-planted them, one at the northeast corner of the house, the other at the northeast rear corner of their back yard. Just as he had done nearly ten years before, he built a brick barbecue pit. He also built a colorful, paneled privacy fence around the rear patio that was accessed from sliding glass doors off the dining room. When winter arrived, Son moved his home improvement projects indoors. The house had a full basement with rough-in plumbing for a bath. However, it was completely unfinished. Son set out to correct this. Months later, it sported another bedroom, a full bath and a family room. The ceiling was done in random perforated acoustic tile. The floor was finished with a cork patterned vinyl tile. Son spent every evening for nearly six months working on this project. When it was finally finished, it was a beautiful sight to behold! They moved their rattan furniture that they had acquired in Japan and their Zenith combination TV/Radio/Record Player into the basement. Mary-Lynn, fast becoming a teen-ager, took over the bedroom. For the rest of their time in the Springs, they enjoyed many hours in this down-stairs living area.

In September, 1958, Randy entered kindergarten at Audubon Elementary School, located only two blocks away from the Son's home at 2313 Bennett Avenue. There he thrived. Mary-Lynn went to Warson High School, only a block from their house in the other direction. She also found a good ballet teacher, a Mrs. Smythe, who was associated with the dance department at Colorado College. M-L was a good pupil. Mrs. Smythe placed her in several dance productions held at the college.

CHAPTER 57
There Are Those Who Have and Those Who Will

In March of 1960 Son had the only aircraft accident of his career. He got his flying time in T-33s, based at Peterson Field, located approximately 12 miles east of the Springs. Peterson was a dual use facility, functioning as the municipal airport and as a military base. Son and a fellow pilot scheduled a "round robin" training flight. Departing Peterson, then flying east to Goodman, Kansas, south to a navigational fix on the airway leading westward to Pueblo, Colorado. Finally, they would turn northward to return to Peterson. The flight was scheduled to take approximately one and one-half hours. The weather at the time of their departure was not really bad. There was a deck of broken clouds at about 1,500 feet, technically constituting a "ceiling." This did not pose a problem at takeoff. The forecast weather at their estimated time of return was approximately the same - broken to overcast at 1,500 to 1,000 feet. There was mention of light rime icing in the clouds. That could be a problem if it got heavier, but "stormy" said it wasn't likely. So off they went. The flight proceeded smoothly as planned, all the way to Pueblo, which was the navigational fix from which Son would initiate his penetration and approach to Peterson.

Earlier, the unique topography of Colorado Springs was mentioned. The area sits in a pocket, formed by the front range of the rockies immediately west of the Springs and the Palmer Ridge to the north. Most of the time this topography protects the Springs from more severe weather to the west and north. However, when an area of low pressure is situated to the south, it can, if moisture and temperature conditions are right create a northwesterly flow, pumping moisture laden clouds into the pocket and bringing with them, low ceilings and visibilities. Son was aware of this potential and he discussed it with the weather forecaster on duty. They decided that chances for worsening weather were low. While winds were from the southeast, they did not appear to be pumping enough moisture into the area to make things worse.

As Son approached the Pueblo VOR he received clearance for a GCA monitored ILS penetration and approach to Peterson. He also received the current weather report for Peterson - overcast with ceiling at 400 feet, visibility three quarters of a mile, moderate rime icing in the clouds. Son descended to 20,000 feet, the prescribed altitude to begin his penetration from the Pueblo VOR. At 20,000 he was flying just above the cloud deck.

"This is not going to be as easy as we thought it would be," Son said to his fellow pilot, occupying the back seat. As he passed over the VOR, he turned north to a heading of 350 degrees, extended his speed brakes , turned on his defrosters to full high, reduced power and began his descent. As soon as he entered the clouds his airplane started accumulating ice. It was more than moderate as reported. Within a minute, his windscreen had iced over despite the defrosters. Only a small hole on the left side of his canopy offered limited for-

ward visibility. He could see the ice building up on the wings. He knew that this would increase his stalling speed and therefore his minimum speed on approach. As he leveled off at 10,000 feet he slowed his airplane and extended the landing gear and flaps. He picked up the ILS localizer beam and began flying the indicators on his instrument panel to place his airplane on the glide slope and runway center line. As he slowed the airplane to about 135 KIAS it began to buffet as in a stall. He increased his speed to 140 knots which stopped the buffeting. But now he had a hot airplane. This was combined with a quartering 10 knot tailwind. Bottom line - he would be crossing the runway threshold at a ground speed of about 150 knots! Add a rain slick runway, only 8,500 feet long. Son quickly calculated that it would probably take every inch of the runway to get his airplane stopped. He would have to touch down on the numbers at the beginning of the runway. At a range of approximately one mile from touchdown, Son picked up the high intensity strobe lights. He could see the strobe through the small hole on the left side of his canopy that was not covered with ice. The animated ball of light appeared to be moving through the air, pointing to the centerline and the end of the runway. Son could see from the strobe lights that he was slightly to the right of the centerline. As the threshold lights loomed out of the fog, he eased back on the throttle. At that point the aircraft stalled and from an altitude of 50 feet or so came down hard on the pierced steel planking overrun, approximately 800 feet short of the runway threshold. They hit so hard that it drove the landing gear up through the wings. They slid to a stop just short of the end of the runway. Son opened the canopy and yelled at the other pilot to get out immediately. He was afraid of fire as the airplane still had nearly a half full load of fuel. He climbed out with his parachute still strapped on and ran for perhaps 50 feet before collapsing on the grass infield. It was then that he realized that he had been injured. His back felt as though someone had hit him with an axe! Both he and the other pilot had sustained compression fractures of their 5th lumbar vertebrae. Their injuries grounded both of them. A month later a formal accident board met to investigate the cause(s) of the accident and to render a report. The report was voluminous, taking over 150 pages, but the conclusion was inescapable. The primary cause was pilot error! This hurt Son's pride almost as much as his broken back. The report did find that icing and possible instrument error were contributing factors. That didn't make Son feel much better however. In nearly 8,000 hours of flying time he had never had an accident. He was placed on DNIF (duty not involving flying) for approximately two months until his back healed. After that, he took a proficiency check ride, got re-certified in the T-33 and "got back on the horse that threw him!"

CHAPTER 58
Man's Best Friend Comes to Live With Us

During that first summer in Colorado Springs both Mary-Lynn and Randy said they wanted a dog. The Sons found a breeder who specialized in miniature Shetland sheep dogs (shelties). That's how they met and fell in love with Golden Shadow of The Sun, known as Shadow for short. He was only eight weeks old when they brought him home. He was a handsome little thing with tan and white markings. All the family loved Shadow. He was exceptionally smart. Within a month he was house broken and never had an accident until shortly before his death nine years later from a brain tumor. During those nine years he was the most loveable and loving pet one could imagine. He trained easily on the leash, learning the standard commands of "sit," "stay," "come," "down," and "heel." He quickly developed a working vocabulary of several hundred words and would respond to complete sentences such as, "Shadow, where's Randy?" or "Take the ball to Daddy." When it was time to go outside, all that was needed was to say in conversational tones, "Shadow, would you like to go outside?" He would jump up and promptly head for the door. He was very protective and didn't take well to strangers unless someone in the family "Okay'd" them.

Bennett Avenue was a quiet, secure residential street. At least, that what the Sons thought. Randy loved to take Shadow for walks along the sidewalk that ran along the street in front of Son's house. So when he asked,

"Mother, can I take Shadow for a walk?" she said,

"Yes, Randy. Keep him on his leash and just stay on the sidewalk."

"I will. Come here, Shadow. Let's go for a walk!"

Shadow ran to Randy, jumping in anticipation, as he snapped the leash onto his collar. Out the front door they went. Minutes later, Son was outside in the back yard when he heard a great commotion, barking and yelping going on. He rushed around to the front of the house, just in time to see the aftermath. The neighbor living across the street and two houses down, kept a big German Shepherd dog in his back yard which was surrounded by a seven foot grape-stake fence. It should have been sufficient to contain the dog, but it wasn't. As the Shepherd heard Randy and Shadow, it scaled the fence and came after Shadow. With one leap, it seized Shadow by the head and throat! The big dog's jaws engulfed Shadow's entire head. Fortunately, the neighbor was in his back yard and saw the whole thing. He rushed out and pulled his dog off Shadow, but Shadow had sustained serious injury to his head and neck. Randy was terrified. The neighbor apologized, but his apology was hardly heard by Son whose primary concern was Randy, who had not been bitten but who was scared to death, and Shadow whose injuries required immediate attention by a veterinarian. Randy was crying, but he calmed down as they got Shadow into the car and took him to the vet. The vet said that Shadow was lucky. The injuries to his head

and neck were repairable. One deep cut was close to Shadow's left eye. Another fraction of an inch and it would have punctured his eye. The vet cleaned up and sutured Shadow's wounds and gave him an antibiotic shot. He made an appointment for follow-up care a week later.

Shadow, of course, received lots of tender, loving care from the Sons in the days that followed. The neighbor again apologized and said that he would take care of the vet's bill. He also promised that he would keep his dog on a chain when he was outside. In the weeks that followed, Shadow made a complete recovery. At least, it seemed so. Walks, now accompanied by Randy's father, resumed without further incident. Toward the end of his life, years later, he developed a brain tumor that resulted in seizures. Although it could not be proven, the Sons wondered if his injuries may have been a factor in the development of the tumor.

CHAPTER 59
The One-Year Sabbatical

In 1954 the Air Force announced a forward-looking policy that set an educational goal of at least a bachelor's degree for every commissioned officer. It established the Air Force Institute of Technology that offered ongoing, accredited undergraduate and post-graduate programs. There were a limited number of spaces available. Son applied for admission at AFIT, but was not accepted. The Air Force developed other programs in support of this policy, including one called, "Bootstrap." Under Bootstrap, the Air Force would pay for two-thirds of the cost in tuition and books for any college level course leading to a degree. Son took advantage of this program, beginning in Italy in 1954, enrolling in college courses offered through the University of Maryland. During the first three years of his assignment at ADC in Colorado Springs, he continued to pursue his bachelor's degree, taking several courses offered by the University of Colorado. By the end of 1961 he had accumulated approximately 75 semester hours of college credits. This made him eligible for a one-year sabbatical for the purpose of attending college full time to get his degree. To be eligible, he had to provide a letter from an accredited college or university, stating that he would be able to achieve the necessary credits within 12 months. Colorado College, located in the Springs, is a small, independent liberal arts college, ranking academically among the top schools of its size nationwide. Son talked to the Dean, Dr. Jones. He explained the Air Force program. After analyzing Sons prior credits, Dr. Jones worked out a program, calling for 45 semester hours, spanning courses in math, statistics, economics, money and banking, accounting and science. It was a very heavy course load, but Dr. Jones said that it could be done. Noting Son's 3.95 grade point average over the 75 hours of credits he had already amassed, he said he was confident that Son could handle the program. He wrote a letter outlining all of this and gave it to Son. He promptly applied to the Air Force for the sabbatical, attaching a copy of Dr. Jones letter, He was approved, and scheduled to begin his academic work beginning with the Spring, 1961 semester.

For the next twelve months, Son became a full time college student. His only military responsibility was to keep up with his flying time minimums under Air Force Regulation 60-16. That of course was easy. The school work, while exhilarating, took lots of effort. He told Arretta that while he would not be going to the office for the next twelve months, he would be working, just as though he had an eight to five job. Arretta was happy, because it meant another year in the Springs, which she had grown to love.

"We'll set up the small bedroom as your study. You can work there."

"O.K., but my primary work place is going to be the library at the college," Son said. I want to be able to focus 100% on my studies. I will have to do that, if I'm going to succeed."

Son bought a bicycle with a nice roomy front basket. Every morning except Sunday, he stashed his books in the basket, jumped on his bike and pedaled down to the college library. There, except for scheduled classes, he would spend the rest of the day studying.

During the following twelve months, Son logged the required 45 hours of credit with a 3.9 GPA. His only B was in Business Statistics. Math was always his most difficult subject. He was 39 years old at the time, and sat in classes with 19 and 20 year old kids. Most of those kids didn't have the motivation that Son had. They called him "the curve buster." Son hoped that compiling an outstanding academic record might help to offset some of the apparently unavoidable comments that were showing up in his O.E.R. file.

As the end of his sabbatical approached, he again began to wonder where his next assignment might be. He had just about given up on getting back into a tactical line assignment. He would just let the chips fall. Discussing the matter with Arretta, he told her to be prepared for a move.

Her response? "Can't you just resign? We have a house here and you could get a job. I really don't want to move again!"

"Arretta, I now have 19 years of active service. If I resigned now I would give up my retirement, all of it. You know very well that I have to have a minimum of 20 years active service to qualify for retirement. I'm not going to give that up, so forget it!"

CHAPTER 60
Another Backwater Assignment

When orders arrived in January, 1962, the Sons found out that they would be going to the Washington, D.C. area. His assignment was at the U.S. Army Engineers School in Fort Belvoir, Virginia, a few miles south of Washington and right next door to Mt. Vernon, George Washington's home. He would be the U.S. Air Force Liaison Officer to the Engineers School. His job: to teach courses at the school, explaining and illustrating the roles and mission of the United States Air Force. It was about as backwater an assignment as one could get for a career Air Force officer. All he could do was make the best of it.

As "Mr. Air Force" on the post, Son qualified for government quarters. They were assigned a rambling three-bedroom ranch at 407 Jadwin Loop. It was within walking distance from the main Engineers School academic building where Son would have his office. That was nice. The home itself was hard to describe. Built during World War I, it was entirely framed construction, had no air conditioning and steam heat. Perched on a hill, it had a big wrap-around deck overlooking big mature woods in back. Over the years, settling had caused floors and window frames to sag. Arretta said she would like to have some bookcases to fit around the windows in the living and dining rooms. Son went to the base hobby shop. It offered a beautiful wood working shop, complete with all the tools. There was an old fellow in charge who knew a lot about carpentry and cabinetry. Son prevailed upon him for some help in designing the bookcases. The problem was that in order to make them fit around the windows, they had to be built to compensate for the sagging building. In other words, they were not square! Son took careful measurements that the shop supervisor converted into plans. It took a couple of months working evenings. When Son finished the project, however, the cases fit perfectly. They almost made the house look "square."

When the leaves were off the trees there was a view of Dogue Creek and Mount Vernon below. The wrap-around deck was a great place to barbeque and have evening meals where the Sons could watch the squirrels and all kinds of birds.

Son's job assignment was ridiculously simple. He had to teach young combat engineers, career officers all, about the Air Force, its roles and mission. That, Son could recite in his sleep! Son took a look at his predecessor's course materials that consisted mainly of dry lecture outlines. He almost went to sleep reading them, so he knew that students would probably do the same. He built his program around good audio visuals including slides and films with some spectacular footage of air force planes and other equipment in action. He tied the Air Force mission in with the mission of the combat engineers. Staff Sergeant Cook, Son's enlisted assistant, said, "Major Son, you'll blow them away with all this stuff!" It turned out that Cook was correct. Colonel Clark, school Commandant set in on one of Son's classes and exclaimed, "I had no idea that the Air Force did all that!" Son thought,

"Surely, an Army Colonel would know that!" But he took the Colonel's comments as a compliment.

Family Decisions

There was a good elementary school on-post at Fort Belvoir. Randy enrolled there and did well during the three years Son and his family lived at Belvoir. The high school, however, did not offer the kind of curriculum that Mary-Lynn needed. Nor were there any good ballet schools in the area. For that reason, Mary-Lynn pleaded to be allowed to go to New York to study at the New York City ballet under George Ballanchine. Against his better judgement, Son agreed to let her attend for six months, but he was concerned about her academic education. Then Arretta found the The Washington School of Ballet. It offered an on-campus, accredited four-year high school program, combined with professional training in ballet. The school claims a long list of distinguished graduates such as Shirley McLain and Juielet Prowse. There was no doubt about the quality of the training. Still, M-L was only 16 years old. Son was concerned about this. Was she old enough to be allowed to leave home and be placed in a dormitory environment? Also, it would be expensive, but that was not the primary consideration. They would find the money somehow, if it were the right thing to do. Again he resisted, but Mary-Lynn and Arretta pleaded. Finally, he gave in and she enrolled at WSB.

It was while she was attending The Washington School of Ballet that she met Pfc Peter Hilton, a soldier stationed at nearby Ft. Leslie McNair. Eventually, they fell in love and when M-L graduated from high school, they were married and moved to San Jose, CA, Peter's home town. Both of them enrolled at San Jose State University. Shortly thereafter, Peter was sent to Viet Nam. In the meantime, M-L continued and eventually completed her college work. She went on to take a master's degree in dance anthropology from the University of Oregon.

George Washington University, The University of Maryland and American University all offered off-campus programs designed to help members of the military further their education. Son had just completed his B.A. degree with Colorado College. Now he had an opportunity to do graduate work. After checking the various programs he decided to go for a Master of Science in Business Administration that was offered by George Washington University. He could take all class work on base at Ft. Belvoir. The program would probably take two years to complete.

"Why not?" thought Son. So this is another backwater assignment. I might as well make the best of it. If the Air Force places a high value on education, maybe a post graduate degree will offset the backwater aspect of this assignment and help with my next promotion. Even if it doesn't, it will be valuable when I retire from military service."

He enrolled, was assigned a program advisor, and again found himself "hitting the books." His business degree had an area of concentration in organizational science. Its focus was on human behavior in "socio-technical systems." It asked: How to humans and technical systems interact? Does the design of technical systems affect human behavior? How do computers and human beings interact? Do humans behave differently in groups than they do individually? What are the group factors affecting behavior? What is leadership, and what is its function in system performance? How does leadership affect acceptance and/or resistance to change? What is the function of individual and group participation in organizational problem solving and decision-making? What are common leadership styles in business, and how can they be classified and analyzed? The course work involved classes in math, psychology, leadership and organizational communications. There were extensive research and writing assignments. Of course, there were a master's thesis and comprehensive exams, both oral and written. One project involved study of and a report on

a participative management style as practiced in a large corporation. Son chose to study The McCormick Tea and Spice Corporation, headquartered in Baltimore Maryland. He spent several weeks interviewing managers and supervisors at all levels of the company, and found that there was a close correlation between theory and practice.

Son enjoyed the course work, worked hard at assimilating its lessons and got top grades for his efforts. As usual his marks were straight "A"s except for the courses in mathematics. Two such courses were required - one in Linear Programming, involved working with simultaneous linear equations, sometimes called matrix algebra. It was a daunting course, but somehow, Son pulled a "B" out of it. Another, also difficult for Son, was Operations Research. It yielded another "B," everything else was "A.

Son did his master's thesis on "The Effect of Supersonic and Wide Bodied Aircraft on Transportation Systems in The United States." He began research at the start of his second year in the program. As he began to delve into current systems he found that in order to do a comprehensive study it was necessary to examine all modes of transportation, air, rail, highway and water. It was fortunate that he started his research when he did. He estimated at the beginning that it would take two to three months. As it turned out, he spent ten months. While Wide Bodied Aircraft were in the early stages of application, Supersonic Aircraft, with the minor exception of the Concorde, were not yet in service. Although design performance data, including such factors as speed, load carrying capacity and costs per ton and passenger seat mile were available there were no actual data on their application in the transportation system. The final thesis, completed in 1967 and comprising about 250 pages is on file at the George Washington University Library.

The last couple of months before scheduled graduation were spent in preparing for comprehensive examinations. The actual exams would take three days, two for written examinations and one devoted to oral defense of the thesis. At the end of this period, Son felt as though his brain were about to burst. When he asked his advisor what areas of program material he should concentrate his reviews on he was told that he should review "all of it!"

"What kind of questions should I expect?"

"Two thirds of the questions will be written essay-type, the rest will be multiple choice, objective questions. That's about all I can tell you."

"What will my oral exam cover? Will it be solely on my thesis?"

"No, it can cover anything you have studied during the program, but most likely the questions will focus on your thesis."

"Thanks!"

Eventually, the day for the beginning of his comprehensive exams arrived. By now, Son felt almost as nervous as he did that day he first soloed in the P-38. Dr. Wood, his advisor, told him, Just stay loose. You know the material and you'll do well. Good luck!"

There was a one week delay in reporting the results, during which Son felt on one day that he did well, and the next day he felt that he didn't. These feelings alternated with a great sense of relief. No matter what the outcome, he was glad to be able to get his nose out of a book!

"This must be what a woman feels after giving birth," thought Son.

Finally, the results arrived. He had passed! In fact he passed his comprehensives with flying colors.

Son was not able to attend his undergraduate graduation in Colorado Springs because he had already been transferred to the Washington, D.C. area. This time he would be able to put on the cap and gown and attend as a participant in a real college graduation ceremony! It was scheduled in June, 1967 on campus at George Washington University. He asked Arretta if she come to see him recognized for his achievement. She said that she couldn't, that it would make her nervous and possibly have a panic attack.

"O.K., I guess I understand."

His daughter, Mary-Lynn, who was attending The Washington School of Ballet, and her boy friend, Peter Hilton, were invited and did attend.

During his three-year stay at Ft. Belvoir Son still had to keep current in his flying skills. As required by Air Force regulations, he had to log 9 or 10 hours each month - some of it at night and some of it on instruments. He was attached to the flight section at Andrews Air Force Base, approximately 30 miles south-east of Washington, where he checked out in the T-33, a two-place jet trainer. Andrews is also the home of a special activities squadron. Its mission is to fly the President of the United States and his staff anywhere they need to fly. The squadron operates a small fleet of airplanes, including 3 Boeing 747s. When they are airborne, whichever one of these has the President aboard is known as "Air Force 1." All air activity except for emergencies is prohibited for one hour before and one hour after the President is scheduled to depart or to arrive. This can sometimes be inconvenient, but it is probably justified for security reasons.

CHAPTER 61
Where Were You When President Kennedy Was Shot?

In late October 1963, Son was ordered to Eglin Air Force Base, Florida to participate in a Tactical Air Command exercise that also involved elements of the U.S. Army. The exercise was to run for 10 days, and Son was assigned duty as an umpire. His job was to ensure that all participants observed the rules of the exercise and to "keep score," so that everything could be properly critiqued. Everything went as planned and Son even was able to go deep sea fishing in the Gulf of Mexico on Saturday, the day after the exercise had ended. He and three other officers chartered a boat. The Captain all but guaranteed that there were fish to be caught. The timing was right for King Mackerel and they were running strong, he said. The Cap'n was right! Son caught 8 big fish, weighing 20 to 30 pounds each. With four poles in the water they were pulling fish into the boat so fast they were hardly able to get them off the hooks and into iced lockers. When they returned to the dock, Son had his fish packed in dry ice and air expressed to his home address at Ft. Belvoir. It had been a good and interesting assignment and the fishing expedition was an exciting first time event for Son. Now he was ready to go home. He had his reservation and ticket on Delta Airlines with an early afternoon departure, giving him enough time to have lunch at the Eglin Officers' Club.

He was working on a club sandwich in the bar where the T.V. was turned on to something that did not command attention until the CBS announcer broke in with a NEWS ALERT. Son stopped eating in mid-bite.

"What's this?"

Walter Cronkite came on, slowly took off his glasses, balefully stared into the camera, announced in his most somber and lugubrious tones, "President Kennedy and Governor John Connolly have been cut down by assassin's bullets as they were riding in a motorcade in downtown Dallas. At this time we do not know if the President and the Governor are still alive."

This was an event equal to the attack on Pearl Harbor in its impact. Cronkite's announcement was a moment frozen in time. The TV picture of Cronkite, looking like a sad-eyed bloodhound that had just lost the scent, as he made the announcement will be forever burned into Son's memory.

Son left the rest of his lunch. His staff car driver came in to tell him that he was waiting outside. There was no radio in the staff car. The driver did not know that the President had been shot. There were a couple of questions, but Son couldn't answer the critical one:

"Is he dead?"

"I don't know. They didn't have any further details."

They rode the rest of the way to the airport in silence. There were a hundred questions racing through Son's mind: Who? Why? Was this the precursor to some other attack? At this moment, there was no way to know.

The scene at the airport was surreal, half travel bustle, half funerary wake. People were standing in small clumps. Heads shook slowly from side to side. The only TV's were located in bars and coffee shops. People were crowded around listening and looking at what by now was the only thing being broadcast.

Someone said, " He's dead. Half his brain, blown away! Connolly's still alive."

"Jackie's got blood all over her but she's not hurt!"

"Who did it . . do they know?"

"They think the shot(s) came from the book depository. Police are sealing off the building."

"Where's the Vice President?"

"They're locating him now. He's got to be sworn in."

"Oh, my God! Pray for us!"

There were only minutes remaining before Son had to board his aircraft. The last thing he heard was that the police were closing in on a suspect, who apparently had managed to escape the book depository and maybe was hiding in an adjacent theater.

On board the airplane, the Captain announced that they would monitor the breaking news and would keep everybody informed. There was no magazine reading, no other talk other than the terrible event and its possible consequences.

"Do you think the Soviets had anything to do with it?"

"Castro. He would love to get even with JFK for the Bay of Pigs."

"Maybe. How about the FBI?"

"A conspiracy? Oh, c'mon!"

These were the thoughts of people wherever they were at the beginning of an event that still haunts America. Air Force 1, now a funeral hearse, prepared to return to Washington with its tragic cargo - the dead President and his widow Jackie, Ladybird Johnson, and by now sworn in before take-off, the 36th President of the United States, Lyndon Baynes Johnson.

What would happen now? Time would tell.

Son arrived back at his home on Ft. Belvoir in early evening. The half-eaten club sandwich he had left on the table at Eglin was the last thing he had had. He was hungry. Arretta and the kids had finished dinner, so Son raided the frig and put together another sandwich. The TV was continuing to broadcast events in real time. The flickering, riveting story continued to play itself out. The authorities had captured the man who escaped the depository. His name was Lee Harvey Oswald. Details about him, who he was, where he came from, what his possible motives were, began to filter through. Was he a communist agent? A sympathizer? Or was he just a nut? Moreover, did he act alone or were there others? Operational elements of the U.S. military, including the Strategic and Tactical Air Commands, were placed on high alert, ready to respond if this was only the first event in a general attack on the United States.

Before Oswald was captured in the theater, he shot Officer Tippet, a sheriff's deputy who had tried to apprehend him. Captured, Oswald was brought the next day to the Dallas County Court House and booked for the murder of Tippet. On live TV, as he was being escorted from the court to jail with crowds of reporters surrounding him, a man rushed out of the crowd toward Oswald. At point blank range, and as Son and his family watched, the man fired two pistol shots into Oswald's stomach. Mortally wounded, Oswald slumped into the arms of the deputies escorting him. He was rushed to the hospital, but died shortly after arrival. His assassin was a man named Jack Ruby, a ne'er-do-well owner of a local

night club and strip joint. He apparently acted alone and out of revenge. He had an extensive police record but nothing beyond local petty crime. Ruby's actions raised more and more questions.

Answers to these and a million other questions, some satisfying some not, would come. A "thorough investigation" was being called for by every public figure. President Johnson promised a blue-ribbon commission to sit until answers were found. Later The Warren Commission, headed by Supreme Court Justice Earl Warren, eventually found that Oswald had acted alone, that there was no convincing evidence that there was more than one shooter and that there was no conspiracy. The voluminous final report of The Warren Commission did not satisfy, certainly did not put to rest all the questions. In fact, it raised new ones.

In the meantime, the outpouring of public grief and mourning continued. For the next three days there was nothing, nothing else to be seen on TV. On the day of the funeral, the cortege proceeded slowly down Pennsylvania Avenue on its final journey toward Arlington Cemetery. First came the flag-draped casket on a four-wheeled caisson that was pulled by a matched team of black horses. Following closely behind was a rider-less horse, a black stallion named Jack Black. The First Family, Jackie and her two children, Carolyn and John, came next. President Johnson, Lady Bird, members of the congress and the president's cabinet and representatives of other countries followed. The muffled, mournful beat of the funerary drums drifted through the air. Over this came the hushed, almost whispered and, Son thought, superfluous comments of the TV announcers.

John Fitzgerald Kennedy, the 35th President of The United States of America was laid to rest along with other heroes of the nation at Arlington. His widow lit the eternal flame next to the grave, and he was consigned to the ages.

Forty years later controversy over his assassination still simmers and questions still haunt us, the major one being, "Was there a conspiracy?" Could such a deed have been the work of a single deranged man? The answers to those questions may never be found:

". . . if you put the murdered President of the United States on one side of a scale and that wretched waif Oswald on the other side, it doesn't balance. You want to add something weightier to Oswald. It would invest the President's death with meaning, endowing him with martyrdom. He would have died for something. . . . A conspiracy would, of course, do the job nicely." [1]

So it goes . . .on and on. Since 1963, millions of words have been written and spoken about the event and the "facts" surrounding it. There is little feeling of closure. Speculation will probably never end.

The Legacy Of JFK

It is not the intent here to write extensively about our 35th President. Other more capable authors have written millions of words about him and his foreshortened administration. Nevertheless, his policies and actions had a profound impact upon our national defense establishment of which Son was a small part. Three events, in particular, need to be mentioned:

The first occurred in April, 1961 when 1500 CIA-trained anti-Castro expatriates attempted to invade Cuba. That the invasion failed is generally attributed to Kennedy's loss of nerve at the critical moment when he cancelled air strikes that were supposed to incapacitate Castro's air force. As a result, more than a hundred men were killed, the rest surrendered, and the Cuban exiles in America never forgave Kennedy for this "betrayal." This was JFK's first venture into foreign policy and the use of force to accomplish national aims. Soon he would be tested again. Fortunately, he was a fast learner.

In October 1962, the Cuban Missile Crisis, which lasted for 14 days, was the closest the world has come to nuclear war. The fate of the World was on the line in this high stakes game of Poker. This time would Kennedy be up to the task? In 1962 the Soviet Union was

desperately behind the U.S. in missile and warhead technology. They did not have the long-range missiles necessary to counter the U.S. Atlas and Titan missiles. How could the Soviets counter this threat? They installed nuclear missiles in Cuba, just 90 miles off the coast of the United States. Castro, still smarting from the Bay of Pigs, welcomed the chance to get even with the United States. U.S. reconnaissance flights showed the missile sites under construction and Soviet ships with missiles on board enroute to Cuba. U.S. armed forces went to their highest state of readiness. The nuclear long-range bombers of the U.S. Strategic Air Command went on airborne alert, ready to attack on command. Kennedy ordered a naval blockade to prevent any additional missiles or material from entering Cuba. Soviet field commanders in Cuba were authorized to use tactical nuclear weapons if invaded by the U.S. The fate of millions literally hinged upon the ability of two men, President John F. Kennedy and Premier Nikita Khrushchev, to reach a compromise. Kennedy demanded that Khrushchev withdraw his missiles, stating that the blockade would remain in place until withdrawal was begun. Khrushchev stated that he would withdraw in exchange for U.S. withdrawal of U.S. tactical range missiles based in Turkey. Kennedy ignored his request. Khrushchev, seeing that he was at a tactical disadvantage, finally folded his hand and began withdrawal. There is no doubt that both sides had their fingers on the nuclear button. It is a tribute to the bravery and courage of JFK that the crisis was resolved and the nuclear Rubicon was not crossed.

The third event had its roots deep within the recent history of South-East Asia. In the middle fifties, proxies often fought the long twilight struggle between Soviet communism and the West. North Korea and North Viet Nam were prime examples.

The Korean War, in which Son was an early participant, has yet to be formally concluded. The Soviet Union and Red China were both strongly involved in this war. If the U.S. had not intervened there would be no independent South Korea today. The war was fought to a stalemate that culminated in a tense cease-fire agreement, with both sides facing each other across a demilitarized zone along the 38th parallel. Some say that South Korea and its allies were not victorious. However, as a result of the war, South Korea retained its independence. Today it is a prosperous, democratic republic. U.S. participation in this war was based on treaty obligations arising at the end of World War Two. The U.S. position was and still is that free peoples should have the right of self-determination.

It was this basic principle that motivated early U.S. involvement in the conflict in Viet Nam. When the French decided in 1954 after their defeat at Dien-Bien-Phu to pull out of Indo-China, communism took root in North Viet Nam. Supported by the Soviets and Red China, they pushed aggressively on the Saigon government in South Viet Nam. To say that the South was democratic, would be stretching the point perhaps. However, they were strongly anti-communist. President Eisenhower announced U.S. support for South Viet Nam in 1954. Initial U.S. participation of South Viet Nam, and in support of the right to self-determination, was limited. In 1963 A small military advisory group of only about 15,000 troops, was deployed. It was hoped that the South would be able to prevail. However, in August, 1964, the scope of the war changed dramatically. The Tonkin Gulf incident triggered a string of events. Here, briefly, is what happened:

President Johnson's Message to Congress August 5, 1964

"Last night I announced to the American people that the North Vietnamese regime had conducted further deliberate attacks against U.S. naval vessels operating in international waters, and I had therefore directed air action against gunboats and supporting facilities used in these hostile operations. This air action has now been carried out with substantial damage to the boats and facilities. Two U.S. aircraft were lost in the action.

After consultation with the leaders of both parties in the Congress, I further announced a decision to ask the Congress for a resolution expressing the unity and determination of the United States in supporting freedom and in protecting peace in southeast Asia.

These latest actions of the North Vietnamese regime has given a new and grave turn to the already serious situation in southeast Asia. Our commitments in that area are well known to the Congress. They were first made in 1954 by President Eisenhower. They were further defined in the Southeast Asia Collective Defense Treaty approved by the Senate in February 1955.

This treaty with its accompanying protocol obligates the United States and other members to act in accordance with their constitutional processes to meet Communist aggression against any of the parties or protocol states.

Our policy in southeast Asia has been consistent and unchanged since 1954. I summarized it on June 2 in four simple propositions:

America keeps her word. Here as elsewhere, we must and shall honor our commitments.

The issue is the future of southeast Asia as a whole. A threat to any nation in that region is a threat to all, and a threat to us.

Our purpose is peace. We have no military, political, or territorial ambitions in the area.

This is not just a jungle war, but a struggle for freedom on every front of human activity. Our military and economic assistance to South Vietnam and Laos in particular has the purpose of helping these countries to repel aggression and strengthen their independence."[1]

But after years of fighting and more than 58,000 Americans killed, On April 29, 1975, America withdrew completely from Saigon, leaving the old non-communist capital and its former allies to fall to North Vietnamese tanks. Twenty-five years later in Ho Chi Minh City, the new name of Saigon, Vietnamese celebrated the anniversary of their victory over the United States and its South Vietnamese allies.

Why? Why was this allowed to happen?

American goals were lofty and principled to be sure, identical to the goals that we had during the Korean War. Then why did Viet Nam end in such a miserable, frustrating failure? The answers to that question are many and complex. They will not be dealt with here, except to say that we were defeated politically and were therefore not allowed to win militarily. The simplicity of this statement does not obviate its truth.

CHAPTER 62
The McNamara Years and
A Tour at The Puzzle Palace

During most of the Viet Nam years, the Department of Defense was "managed," not led - there is a difference — by a product of U.S. industry. He was a former president of the Ford Motor Company and was JFK's choice to become Secretary of Defense. His central belief was that every decision could be measured in terms of its "cost-effectiveness." Every decision has an "opportunity cost." That cost can be expressed in dollars. Also, every decision has an outcome. Outcomes can be expressed as tangible benefits. Therefore, every decision can be evaluated and compared in terms of its "cost/benefit." Such cost/benefit analysis can be applied to personnel as well as hardware. During his tenure, Robert Strange McNamara - yes, Strange was really his middle name — left his mark on U.S. defense policy and profoundly influenced the course of the war in Viet Nam.

Early in 1966, Son's tour with the United States Army and his assignment as Air Force Liaison Officer to the Army Engineer's School was coming to an end. The war in Viet Nam was gaining momentum. Was there an assignment opportunity there? - a benefit? Perhaps. Was there a cost? Definitely. For starters, he might get killed. He had to think about his family. Was it prophetic that Son was thinking this way, long before he knew much about Robert S. McNamara?

With little question, he could make his next assignment to Viet Nam a reality. Volunteers were being accepted. He could get back into the operational side of the Air Force. If he was ever going to be promoted to Colonel, he needed to make a change in direction. He would have his MSBA degree shortly. Now, if he could get some combat time in Nam, who knows, he might make "bird" yet. He was tempted. The more he thought about it, however, the more it came down to a career vs. family decision. His family situation was far from secure. If he took his family back to Phoenix and left them for a year there probably wouldn't be a family. He decided to explore the possibilities of another assignment in the Washington area. He had experience in weapons and in air defense. Surely there must be a job on the Air Staff in the Pentagon that could make use of his experience. He started making some contacts, which eventually led him to the Directorate of Studies and Analysis on the Air Staff. He talked with Colonel Marion Morphew who headed up the air defense section. Morphew told him he had an opening for a branch chief and that he would be glad to have him. Morphew made the request and the personnel wheels began to turn.

When the assignment came through and he told Arretta she was pleased. She liked the Washington area, and as long as there were no social demands, she was reasonably content. She figured, correctly, that there would be less demand of that kind when they moved

off post at Ft.Belvoir. Now they would have to find a house. They located a nice, three-bedroom split-level in Alexandria, Virginia, only about four miles southwest from the Pentagon. It was off Seminary Road in a nice residential area and it had the added benefit of being less than a mile from St. Stephens School for Boys. They had already decided that they would have to find a private school for Randy. The public schools were poor. School for M-L was already set. She was going to the Washington School for Ballet. Adding $4,000 per year tuition at St. Stephens to what they were already paying for M-L put a real crimp in the budget but it was worth it.

Son signed in at the Pentagon and got a more detailed briefing from Colonel Morphew on his new job. The Chief of the Directorate of Studies and Analysis was a two-star general with a background in the Strategic Air Command. General Kent reported directly to the Chief-of-Staff of the Air Force.

"Within the Pentagon, where all branches of the military services are represented, there has always been a struggle for primacy between them — Army, Navy, Air Force and Marines. Each service struggles to preserve or expand its share of the defense budget. Each attempts to define its role and/or mission and therefore budget share annually to the Secretary of Defense. Since the beginning of McNamara's reign, however, these struggles - more like battles - have intensified. As a result, General White, Chief of Staff of the Air Force, directed the establishment of our directorate. Our mission is to be chief advocate for the Air Force, to protect and defend our role and mission."

"Sounds political."

"It is. Your job will be to direct your group in conducting comparative cost/effectiveness studies on air defense weapons systems. You will look at system "A" versus system "B," maybe system "C." Or, you may look at combinations. First, you will examine them in terms of their effectiveness. What can they do against various threats? For example, how many bombers can they kill, and by extension, how many millions of lives can they save in U.S. cities. Second, you will want to look at the costs of these systems. How much will it cost for each system to develop, test, field and operate over a ten-year period? Then comes the pay-off. In terms of ten-year systems costs, stated in dollars, what is the cost per million of lives saved?!"

"Good grief!"

"I know! It sounds bizarre. But this is the kind of data that the Chief of the Air Force needs when he goes into the tank with the JCS."

"Tank?"

"That's what they call the situation room where the Joint Chiefs-of-Staff, Army, Navy, Air Force and Marines, meet and where these battles are fought. We have to give General White his ammunition."

"Boy, this is a long way from the cockpit, isn't it!"

"No doubt! It's a dirty job, but as they say, somebody's gotta do it!"

As Son got further into his job he found out that he would be playing games.

"Games?"

"Computer simulations. We have two big IBM 360 computers that give us the ability to simulate, for example, a fleet of Russian Bear long-range nuclear bombers flying over the North Pole and attacking major U.S. cities - New York, Washington, Chicago, Detroit, Los Angeles, San Francisco. If we offered no defense whatsoever, and based on what we know about their weapons and their accuracy, how many millions of casualties could we expect?"

"But why wouldn't we try to defend ourselves?"

"Of course, we would. But in order to measure the effectiveness of various systems of defense, we need to establish a zero-defense data base. Then when we deploy system "A,"

for example, we can measure its effectiveness, not only in terms of how many bombers it kills but how many millions of lives it saves!"

"Oh!"

"Then, we have to look at missile defenses. In fact, the most probable scenario involves a first wave missile attack, designed to knock out our ability to retaliate. They'll target our Atlas and Titan missile sites. The Bears will come later to mop up."

"What kind of missile defenses do we have?"

"Frankly, not much. There are few Nike sites, and something that the Army has, called SAM-D. We just have to field a total system that convinces the Russians that they cannot knock us out with a first punch."

"Seems to me that if the nuclear button gets pushed, both sides will die. No body wins."

"That's why they call it MAD - if you don't know, that stands for Mutually Assured Destruction. That's the essence of our strategy, and theirs too, for that matter. So far, it's worked."

"O.K., Colonel Morphew. I'll see if I can wrap my mind around all this arcane stuff. I may have a lot of questions to begin with."

"Sure. The guys in your branch will be glad to help. Don't feel shy about asking if there is something you don't understand."

"I won't."

Son began to "get his feet wet" in his new job. He had six talented officers reporting to him in his branch. Three of them were specialists in operations research, the application of advanced mathematical techniques to solve very complex problems. The other three were computer experts with knowledge and skills necessary to program and make the big IBM 360s do their bidding. Although Son had broad knowledge in both these areas, including nuclear weapons and their effects, he was far from expert. During his master's program at George Washington University he had taken courses, but that didn't make him a savant. Far from it, and he knew it. He knew what Colonel Morphew wanted and how it fit into the "big picture." He told his specialists that he would be depending upon them to keep him out of trouble, at least in the beginning. He asked for their cooperation and support and he got it.

As he got further and further into the details of his job, he began to feel like a character out of "Star Wars," maybe Cap'n Kirk. Dick Johnson, the senior operations research specialist, explained to Son what he was doing.

"This is a computer simulation to establish a base line, a point of departure for all the other simulations we will be doing. When we get through with this one, we should know pretty accurately what would happen if the Russkies jumped us from over the North Pole with their Bears and we didn't defend."

"Well, I've got a good idea what would happen - disaster!"

"Yes. But we need to know with a high degree of specificity. How many people would be killed or wounded. What would happen to our infrastructure, health care systems, our road and highways, railways, airports? What about utilities and communications? We can build a detailed model of these things, including population distributions, as they exist in North America and put them into the computer. They become the target data-base."

"Wow! Do we have that kind of information in the computer now?"

"We're about 75% complete. It's a big job. Some of the data is hard to come by. We've asked civil authorities. Some are more cooperative than others."

"I can imagine. Colonel M. tells me he wants to have this done by the end of next month. Can we do it?"

"I think so. We're waiting on data from Detroit and St. Louis now. They've both said that they will have it for us by the 15th."

"Once we have this information in hand, what then?"

"We attack the data base with 200 Bears - in the computer, of course! That's the assumed threat. We know what kind of weapons they carry, what their yield in megatons is and their delivery accuracy. We know what effects those weapons will have. They will create blast, heat and radiation. There will be physical destruction by blast. There will be firestorms. Last, but certainly not least, there will be lingering radiation. One part of our data-base is personnel distribution in each of our population centers. There will be millions upon millions of casualties, to say nothing about the physical damage to our infrastructure."

"That would kill us, wouldn't it?"

"Yes, almost certainly. But we don't and won't let that happen. We have to know what these numbers are, though, so that when we deploy various defensive weapons systems against the threat, what the savings will be."

"Savings?!"

"Yes - savings in millions of lives and trillions of dollars in infrastructure."

"Good grief, Charlie Brown!"

"Pretty strange, isn't it?"

"For sure."

Son continued to work with his small band of math and computer geniuses. After they completed construction of the target data-base they ran the 200 Bear, no-defense attack model against it. Run in 1967, the results of this simulation were classified TOP SECRET. As far as Son knows, they are still classified. They were mind-boggling, nevertheless. After establishing these no-defense results, a series of simulations were run, deploying various air defense weapons systems against the same 200-Bear threat. The raw numbers, stated in terms of casualties saved and millions of dollars of infrastructure damage avoided, were then blended with system costs. System costs included engineering and development, testing and deployment and 10 years of operating costs.

The analyses showed that A combination of F-106 and F-12 interceptors, augmented with SAM-D and Nike missiles were the most cost effective. Although the F-106 Delta Dart was deployed and became operational, the F-12 never reached full operational status. An air-defense version of the better known reconnaissance SR-71 Blackbird, only 6 F-12s were built for test purposes. Both the Blackbird and the F-12 were awesome airplanes. They normally operated at the fringes between the stratosphere and space at altitudes of up to 100,000 feet and speeds of Mach 3 (3,000 mph). The wings and control surfaces of the airplane were made of titanium and steel alloy to withstand the stresses of hypersonic flight. The F-12 was armed with three nuclear missiles and a special long-range Doppler radar that gave it the ability to search from above for low altitude targets that were hugging the earth to try to avoid radar detection. The mission profile called for F-12s to take off from northern tier bases located along the U.S.-Canadian border. They would climb northward at Mach 3 to 100,000 feet and begin Doppler scanning the terrain below. They would detect their targets, now coming at them head-on, at ranges in excess of 100 nautical miles. The F-12s would launch their nuclear missiles at ranges of up to 100 miles. The missiles would snap down to hit their targets with nuclear warheads. The effectiveness of the F-12 against the air breathing threat was phenomenal, near 100%.

Son's close friend from Korean War days, Major Joe Rogers, was doing most of the flight-testing of the F-12. He made several trips to the Pentagon to give the Air Defense Division input on F-12 capabilities.

"Hi, Joe! It's good to see you again!"

"Hi, Herm! How are you?"

"Great, but I wish I had your job and you had mine!"

"I'd do most anything for you, Herm, but not that!"

"Yeah, it's quite a step from flying Buckeye Blitz out of K-2 and what you are doing now."

"Well, they're both airplanes. The Twelve is a phenomenal bird though. It's kinda weird to look out and see the leading edge of the wings glowing cheery red from air friction. Never noticed that in the "Stang."

"Yeah, pretty amazing. But they couldn't have picked a better fighter pilot for the project than you, Joe."

"Thanks for your vote of confidence, Herm. "Preciate!"

CHAPTER 63
The Promotion Wars

During the months that followed Son continued working on the same assignment. The war in Southeast Asia continued to increase in scope and intensity. The U.S. commitment to the war expanded by the week. An intense air campaign was mounted, utilizing every type of airplane in the Air Force inventory. F-105 Thunder-streaks and F-4 Phantoms carried most of the offensive mission. One of the big problems was locating and identifying the enemy. The Viet Cong was extremely skillful in hiding and camouflaging their operations in the dense jungle terrain where much of the fighting was occurring. Even the venerable old C-47 was pressed into service as - of all things - a gunship! A 20 millimeter Gatlin Gun was mounted in the rear, looking out the side door. Since the airplane could loiter indefinitely over a target area, it could be called upon to deliver devastating firepower at a moment's notice. American troops on the ground loved it, giving it a nickname that stuck. They called the old gooney bird, "Puff The Magic Dragon!" The concept and the nickname became permanent. In later years, Puff, upgraded to a C-130 and equipped with even more lethal armament, became a staple in the Air Force arsenal.

As the mission and sortie load increased in Viet Nam the need for pilots to replace those who had completed their combat tour, normally 100 missions. Those returning from Nam with combat records were being favored for promotions. Son had just entered the "primary zone" for consideration for promotion to full colonel. However there were only a limited number of spaces (slots), no more than 250. Competing for this small quota were approximately 5,000 eligible Lieutenant Colonels - pretty small odds. Son knew that he had some good O.E.R's in his file. But he was also acutely aware that they contained some limiting remarks about his family situation and his lack of social participation. There was no doubt that those were negatives. However, there were other plus factors. He had an outstanding combat record in Korea. He had worked hard to get his undergraduate degree with honors and had gone on to obtain his MSBA from George Washington University. After he had been in the division for several months he talked with General Kent about his situation. He told General Kent that he realized that the competition would be tough but he hoped that his record might make him a contender.

"Yes, Colonel Son. I've seen your record and you have a lot of things going for you. You do have some negative remarks in your file. Whether they would be decisive or not is hard to say."

"Is there anything I could do to increase my chances?"

"Well, you could volunteer to go to Nam."

"I know. If it were not for my family situation, as I am sure you are aware, I would do it. I just don't feel I can leave my wife at this time. She needs my full support."

"I understand. There's probably not a lot we can do for this next board. They meet at Randolph in a couple of months. If past board actions are any indication, most of the available promotions will go to Nam returnees with combat experience. I'll ask Morphew to give you a special O.E.R. He can do that, based on your current work. I'll give it a "he-walks-on-water" endorsement. Then we'll just have to see."

"Yes sir. I'll appreciate your efforts very much. I understand that my chances are not good. And I have no quarrel with Nam people getting the lion's share. After all, they represent what the Air Force is all about, and they should be rewarded. But maybe I can sneak in on the bottom of the list!"

"We'll do what we can, Son."

"Yes sir!"

Another weakness in Son's file was the fact that although he had earned his college degrees he had not attended any of the professional officer schools of the Air Force - The Squadron Officer's Course, The Air Command and Staff College or the Air War College. Progress through at least through the ACSC was considered almost a prerequisite for promotion to Colonel. The Air War College was generally reserved for those with an inside track to general officer rank. Son thought about this. It was too late to do much to correct this. He discussed the problem with Colonel Morphew.

"What can you tell me about taking either the ACSC or the Air War College by correspondence?"

"Not a lot. I am sure you can't do the AWC by correspondence. It has to be on campus at the Air University at Maxwell AFB. I doubt if you can get the ACSC that way either. I do believe though that the Industrial College of The Armed Forces is available by correspondence."

"How does that compare? I don't know anything about it."

"It's normally given on campus at Ft. Leslie J. McNair, just across the way from us. It's considered to be at the same level as the AWC, however its focus is different from the AWC. It examines the industrial and economic component of our national defense posture. Sounds like an interesting program."

"Well, maybe I could do it by correspondence. Do you think it would make me any more "promotable?"

"It certainly couldn't hurt."

The next week, Son enrolled in the ICAF correspondence course. The registrar told him that he would get lesson units, including all books and printed materials, by mail, at a pace that would be determined by how fast he completed each unit. As soon as unit 1 had been completed, mailed in and graded, he would get a report card and the next unit. Most students complete the course in 6 to 9 months. The first unit dealt with the organization of the Department of Defense. For the first time, Son got a complete overview, and a better understanding of the interfaces between the military and civilian authorities. It took Son about two weeks to read all the materials and complete the self-administered test materials. He mailed them off to ICAF and within a matter of only a few days; he got his report card - overall 94%. The next unit dealt with the economy, how it works, what its strengths and vulnerabilities are and how it relates to the U.S. defense posture. Part of it is expressed in military capability. Perhaps the greater part, however, is expressed in our participation in world trade. The latter is an important part of our diplomatic strength in dealing with other countries throughout the world. Again, Son finished the unit in just over two weeks. Other units followed, dealing with such areas as communications, transportation, industrial and technological resources. In six months, he had finished the program and had received a certificate attesting to his completion of the program. The information was entered into his personnel records. Would it help get him promoted? Who knew?

Family Life in Alexandria

The Sons move off post from Ft. Belvoir to Alexandria caused two major changes in their lives. They had to find a home. That was relatively easy. The Washington metropolitan area has a highly transient population. Military, government and diplomatic personnel come and go with regularity. This fact creates and sustains a real estate market that is very fluid. There are always lots of homes to buy and lots of buyers and sellers in the market. They found a three-bedroom split level home for $41,500 that fit them perfectly. Three years later, when they left Washington, they rented their house for more than enough to cover their monthly mortgage payments. After renting the house for two years, the tenants bought it.

The second change involved a marginal public school system. It did not meet the standards that the Sons had established, especially for Randy. He had done very well while at Ft. Belvoir and they felt that it was important to find a school that would continue to challenge Randy. Fortunately, St. Stephens School for boys was located on Seminary Road, very close to the home that the Sons had purchased. They talked to the school superintendent who said, after administering entrance tests to Randy, that he was very well qualified. The tuition was expensive, however — $4,000 per year. In the 1960's, and on the salary of a Lieutenant Colonel, that was a lot of money. They looked at their budget, and with some scrimping, figured they could make it work. Randy was enrolled and attended there for the rest of Sons time in Washington.

CHAPTER 64
Getting to Work at The Pentagon

Most people have no idea how huge the Pentagon really is. It is, as its name implies, a five-sided, five story building built around five concentric rings with a large, five-sided courtyard in the center. It houses the Department of Defense, Headquarters for the Army, Navy, Air Force, Marines and the Coast Guard. It is full of generals, admirals and high-level civilians.

It is one of the world's largest office buildings. It is twice the size of the Merchandise Mart in Chicago, and has three times the floor space of the Empire State Building in New York. The National Capital could fit into any one of the five wedge-shaped sections. There are very few people throughout the United States who do not have some knowledge of the Pentagon. Many have followed news stories emanating from the defense establishment housed in this building.

The Pentagon is virtually a city in itself. Approximately 23,000 employees, both military and civilian, contribute to the planning and execution of the defense of our country. At any given time the permanent population is augmented by an average of 10,000 "visiting firemen," there to conduct business with various DOD offices. All of these people arrive daily from Washington, D.C. and its suburbs over approximately 30 miles of access highways, including express bus lanes and one of the newest subway systems in our country. They ride past 200 acres of lawn to park approximately 8,770 cars in 16 parking lots; climb 131 stairways or ride 19 escalators to reach offices that occupy 3,705,793 square feet. While in the building, they tell time by 4,200 clocks, drink from 691 water fountains, utilize 284 rest rooms, consume 4,500 cups of coffee, 1,700 pints of milk and 6,800 soft drinks prepared or served by a restaurant staff of 230 persons and dispensed in 1 dining room, 2 cafeterias, 6 snack bars, and an outdoor snack bar. The restaurant service is a privately run civilian operation under contract to the Pentagon. The main concourse even contains a shopping mall with major department stores. The concourse is the military crossroads of the world, where you are likely to run into someone you have served with in years past.

Son lived approximately 3-1/2 miles southwest of the Pentagon, in Alexandria, Virginia. His house was only a block off of Seminary Road. Every day he traveled the Shirley Highway, affectionately known by those who used it as "the world's longest parking lot!" If the weather was good, and if he got an early start, leaving home around 0600, he could plan on the journey taking about 1-1/2 hours. That would give him 30 minutes to walk the mile or so from where he parked his car in the south parking area to his office in 3C201. 3C201 meant that his office was located in the "C" ring (third one in toward the center) on the second floor, room number 201. Simple, huh?

One early December evening, Son caught the weather forecast on TV for the next day. It called for snow, starting around 0400, with accumulations of up to 4 inches. In the Washington area that meant that traffic would be all but paralyzed. Sometimes, in similar situations there would be announcements that government offices would be closed. This time there was no such announcement. He figured that if he was going to make it to his office he needed to start around 0500. It had already begun to snow when he turned out of his subdivision, north on Seminary Road and then onto the eastbound entry ramp to the Shirley. As he came down the ramp he could see that traffic was already starting to back up. It was too late to change his mind. He was committed. Bumper to bumper, traffic was crawling. The temperature was about 28 degrees, the snow was sticking and the road surface was slick. Cars would move forward a few feet then stop. Soon, they were loosing traction and over correcting by applying too much throttle, spinning their wheels furiously in an attempt to move forward. Cars started spinning out into the median strip between the east and westbound lanes. His car radio was no help. Traffic reports were all the same - gridlock all over town. There was nothing to do but continue and be patient. He was glad that he had nearly a full tank of gas. At 1130 he pulled into the south parking lot, made note of his parking location and began the long trek in the snow toward the main south entrance to the Pentagon. About half of the Division people had made it in. Already, they were talking about a go-home order. At 1230 a snow day was declared and everybody was told to go home! Back on the highway, bound for Seminary Road, Son endured the traffic again, finally arriving home slightly after 1700! If this sounds extreme to the reader, you can believe it, it was.

There were other problems. By 1966-67 the Viet Nam War had become a feverish political boil on the skin of the American public. Demonstrations, many of them violent, were common. The Pentagon and its workers comprised a natural target for many of the demonstrations. Because of this, Son and his fellow officers had to wear civilian clothes, not that that made much difference. The demonstrators would stake themselves out in the parking lots, particularly around the walkways leading to the south and east entrances to the building. They would build camp fires, litter, defecate and urinate on the grounds and generally make themselves obnoxious. Pentagon security people would sometimes arrest them, sometimes chase them away, but they always came back. Sometimes they would follow along beside those walking from their cars to work, shouting obscenities at them:

"Baby killers! Murderers! S - - -heads!"

Sometimes the demonstrators would throw things - beer cans, filled, but not with beer. Used condoms were a favorite. We were under strict orders not to retaliate. It wasn't easy.

Putting all this in context, this was volatile time in our nation's capital. Civil rights commanded almost as much attention on the front page of the Washington Post and other papers as did the war in Viet Nam. Martin Luther King and over a million people marched on Washington and camped out around the reflecting pool between the Washington Monument and the Capitol Building. Rioters put north Washington to the torch, burning down major portions of the city. These events, of course, were not directly linked to U.S. military forces, or even to what was going on in Viet Nam but it filled the air with tension.

CHAPTER 65
Sad Trip To Missouri

Early in March, 1967, Son got a telephone call from his sister, June, in Chicago. Mama was gravely ill in Warrensburg, MO. She had been in poor health for sometime, having undergone a mastectomy two years previously, she had steadily declined. Son took an emergency leave and flew to Warrensburg. Her doctor said she was suffering from congestive heart failure - fluid buildup around her lungs and heart. Chances for her eventual recovery were not good. She was in a state where she could go at any time. On the other hand, her doctor said, she could hang on for a month, maybe even eventually recover. Son was glad he was there. He got a chance to talk with his mother and tell her that he loved her. She told him how proud of him she was. He talked with his father. He seemed to accept the fact that Mama wouldn't last long. He said that he'd be O.K. living alone. His favorite sister, Stella, lived in Vienna, MO, not far away. She was a widow. He said he would spend some time with her and that everything would be all right. Son thought about the possibility of asking his father to come to Washington to live with them, but the more he thought about it the more he knew it wouldn't work out. Arretta would not be able to tolerate it. June said that if he decided he couldn't live alone, she would be glad to take care of him. Her three boys, Cal(18), Paul(15) and Craig(12), adored their grandpa.

"It would be no problem, Dankin," she said, using the childhood nickname for Son that she had used since they were kids. You know the boys love their grandpa. They'd take good care of him."

"Well, I think you know my family situation. I don't think it would work out."

"Yes, I understand completely."

"Well, let's play it by ear. Maybe Daddy will be all right by himself, as long as he can be in touch with Stella."

They left the potential problem unsolved. Son had only 5 days emergency leave and had to get back to Washington. June would stay on for a while and promised to keep "Dankin" updated.

Son had only been home a couple of days when he got the call from June. Mama had passed away in her sleep. She would be buried in the cemetery at New Hope Church, near the farm where she was born and the town of Marion, MO where she taught school as a young woman before she met Son's father. Many members of the Garnett family are buried there. June said the funeral would be the following Tuesday. Everything had been prearranged. Son told Arretta.

"I assume you'll be going back for the funeral?"

"I'll be going back? I certainly will be. I assumed you would come with me. Can't you come?"

"I couldn't do it. I'd panic."

"Why, for heaven's sake? Why? This last time - you could pay your respects. I know Daddy would appreciate it."

"I can't."

That was that. Son flew back to Warrensburg alone for the second time in a little over a week. The funeral was held at the mortuary in California, MO, near New Hope. In addition to his father, June and her husband Walt and his aunt Jane Keeran and her husband uncle Jolly were there. He told everybody that Arretta was ill and couldn't come. That was the truth.

The funeral cortege proceeded over country roads back to the old church, and Son, with a lump in his throat, stood beside the open grave in his Air Force uniform. A cold March wind was blowing as the minister began to pray: "Our father, which art in heaven, hallowed be thy name; thy kingdom come, thy will be done . . ." Son blinked back the tears. Mama was proud of her son and what he represented. He knew that. He thought about her life and what she had given to her family - their lives, their safety, their values and education. Yes, Mama was proud, proud of her children and what she had done. Now she could rest.

On the flight back, Son thought about Arretta and the fact that she had not joined him. He felt lingering resentment. Why couldn't she at least have put in an appearance - would that have been so difficult? The more he thought about it, however, the more he realized that Arretta really couldn't help it. Did he forgive her? Not completely. Not then, anyway.

He talked with Arretta some more about her problem, knowing that it wasn't something that she could solve by herself. She agreed. They found another psychiatrist, a Doctor Fodor, who although he was a Freudian, seemed to focus a little more on current behavior than her previous doctors. He said that he mixed traditional methods with newer approaches including cognitive analysis. This approach examines self-talk and how it influences feelings and therefore, behavior. After talking about it some more, they decided to give it a try, even though it put another strain on the budget. His approach did seem to help. Arretta seemed less up tight, more normal more of the time. She was taking a greater interest in her painting, which Son rightfully praised. This was encouraging. Wouldn't it be nice, thought Son, if after I retire and the pressure of military life and frequent moves is removed that we could live a "normal" life someplace? Son was already beginning to think of his alternatives if he didn't make "Bird" on the next promotion list. He knew that he could stay in for a full 30 years as a Lieutenant Colonel, and he knew also that if he didn't get promoted by this next board that his chances of ever making Colonel were next to none. Each additional year of active duty would result in a 2-1/2 % increase in his retired pay - not that much. He had a brand new MSBA degree and he was only 45 years old. His thinking was: If I don't get promoted, I should get out and get started on a second, civilian career. But, he'd cross that bridge when he came to it.

CHAPTER 66
Why Do They Call It The "Puzzle Palace?"

Back at the Pentagon, things continued to move in their complex, sometimes arcane way. The military services were dealing with two problems. They were fighting a strange and different kind of war in southeast Asia. Also, they were operating in a different political environment.

On the military side, it was a war fought against an enemy that was elusive, hard to find, one that moved and fought in the dark of night but that holed up and took cover during daylight hours. The Viet Cong were masters at hit and run guerilla tactics. This was completely different from the set piece battles of World War II. All branches of the military had a lot to learn, and they did. So, also, our political leaders had a lot to learn. I'm not sure that they did. In World War II, the military was given a clear mission with victory as the objective. For the first time, in Korea the military was told that it could not win, it could only strive for a stalemate. Time has proven that in the case of Korea stalemate did achieve our political objective - the defense of South Korea, which today is prosperous, democratic and free. In Viet Nam, however, the war was micro-managed. That war could have been won militarily and the Viet Cong defeated, if the military, particularly the U.S. Air Force, had been allowed to operate to its full capability. North Viet Nam could have been brought to its knees if the U.S. had been allowed to bomb critical, strategic targets - dams, hydroelectric facilities and other industrial targets. The politicians decided that we would not do that. The politicians also decided that we could not attack tactical supply lines along the Ho Chi Min Trail, the jugular artery that ran from Hanoi through Cambodia into South Viet Nam. Because they were in Cambodia they were off limits. Toward the end of the war, we did attack targets on the Ho Chi Min Trail, but by that time the damage had been done.

The U.S. Military was not defeated in Viet Nam. The U.S. was defeated politically. As the war dragged on, it lost the support of the American public. That led to the ultimate debacle when the last U.S. forces were ordered to evacuate the U.S. Embassy in Saigon, leaving South Viet Nam and Cambodia to the tender mercies of the communist North, and in the case of Cambodia, the murderous Pol Pot of the infamous killing fields. Millions of Cambodians were exterminated there. America had good reason to be ashamed. The bitter taste of this war still lingers in the American psyche.

In America, the military is always subordinate to the civil authority. There is no question about the wisdom of this arrangement. The civil authority must lead, but it should lead from a position of mutual trust and responsibility. In Viet Nam, the authority for decisions concerning tactical and strategic details of the war were, more often than not, made from the office of the Secretary of Defense. Instead of giving broad mission objectives and

guidance to the theater commanders and then letting them run the war to accomplish those objectives, SECDEF usurped the roles of the theater commanders. For example, SECDEF continually asked for "body counts," in other words numbers of enemy soldiers killed, as if this was a true indicator of military performance in the field. Theater commanders obliged, giving SECDEF what he wanted. It was doubtful, however, if the right questions were being asked.

All of this left the Pentagon in turmoil, as the four service branches and the Department of Defense tried to cope. There was much pulling and hauling, back and forth, about the "lessons" to be learned from Viet Nam. Much of it related to the central dynamic of Pentagon politics, the fight over "Roles and Missions." Roughly, the missions were: Ground Warfare, War In The Air and War at Sea.

The Army and the Marines squabbled over who had jurisdiction over amphibious operations. The Air Force and the Army argued about Close Air Support of ground combat operations. The Army wanted control of all close air support and they wanted it at army division level. Ideally, they wanted an air umbrella over them, 24/7. Their answer was helicopters, lots of them. The Air Force held that the Army's approach was wasteful, that helicopters were vulnerable to ground fire and that a more cost effective approach was to put Air Force fighter and fighter/bomber aircraft under Air Force control, where they could be used not only to provide close air support but could also be used in other combat roles critical to overall mission success. These roles included air superiority over the battlefield and interdiction of enemy supply lines. They also wrestled over who should be responsible for air defense, particularly as it pertained to the defense of North America. The Army philosophy for air defense focused on fixed point, ground to air missiles. The Air Force idea was to use long-range interceptors to destroy the air breathing threat over the Arctic Circle before it reached North America. The missile threat was to be countered with missiles designed to intercept and kill Soviet missiles early in their boost phase of flight. This of course required early launch detection, which would be provided by BMEWS (Ballistic Missile Early Warning System) radar scanning space with high-powered radars based at the Arctic Circle. The strategic offensive mission was also "up for grabs." During the fifties and sixties, the heart of America's strategic offensive capability was the long-range bomber force of the Strategic Air Command. Flying from bases in the U.S. and around the world, B-36s, B-52s and B-47s, all carrying nuclear weapons, were ready to launch against pre-selected targets within the Soviet Union at a moment's notice. While the Army and the Air Force argued, the Navy did not stand by passively. They saw the aircraft carrier and the nuclear-armed submarine as preferred instruments of war. The Air Force held that in the event of nuclear war carriers would be sitting ducks on a pond that would not last beyond the earliest phases of a nuclear war. The Navy held that while carriers might be somewhat vulnerable in a nuclear war, their use could be justified in conventional conflict, because they provided a unique ability to project American airpower quickly to hot spots around the world. As for the submarine, the Trident nuclear sub, carrying sixteen missiles, each capable of leveling a city, offered the advantages of stealth and survivability.

Into this environment came Robert S. (for Strange, really!) McNamara, Secretary of Defense, and his penchant for cost-effectiveness analysis. To secure his approval and consequent funding, a weapon system had to be based on an operational concept that could be proven and reduced to quantitative analysis. The winning system had to survive over other competing systems in terms of cost and effectiveness.

So said Mr. McNamara, "Figures don't lie."

Ah yes, but liars can certainly figure! Throw in a little intra-service politics and a tight defense budget into this mix and things can get bizarre. What would Cap'n Kirk have to say about all of this? One wonders.

CHAPTER 67
Promotions - Where Are They?

The Colonels' Promotion Board was scheduled to meet at Randolph AFB, TX in June. Son had done the best he could, he thought. He had a good O.E.R. file to which Colonel Morphew had added a special O.E.R., endorsed by General Kent. He had recently completed his MSBA at George Washington University and he had completed by correspondence the course work for the Industrial College of The Armed Forces. He had an outstanding combat record in the Korean War, although that, increasingly, came under the category of "Yes, but what have you done for the Air Force lately?" He was in the "primary zone," meaning that he had at least 5 years time in grade as a Lieutenant Colonel. The Air Force Times reported that there were approximately 5,000 Lieutenant Colonels in the zone, vying for no more than 250 spots for promotion to Colonel. Statistically, that meant he had a 20 to 1 chance of making it. Those were not very good odds, he thought. In addition, the Viet Nam factor had to be taken into account. The Air Force, rightly so, put a premium on Viet Nam combat experience. There was little doubt in Son's mind that this would further decrease his odds. It was not very encouraging, but still, he hoped. Sometimes, he felt like a very small cog in a very large, impersonal machine. Still, he had to "take care of the store," and do his daily job in the Air Defense Branch. He and his group of analysts continued to work on computer simulations using various air defense scenarios. They varied the threat. There was the Bear bombers only version, with numbers ranging from as low as 50 to a high of 500. There was a missile silo busting threat with Soviet SS-9 missiles launched first against our Atlas, Titian and Minute Man missile force, then followed up with bombers. They varied the defense, looking at fighter interceptors only and a mix of interceptors and surface-to-air missiles. They looked at the F-12, the most advanced, and also the most expensive, fighter in the U.S. inventory. They played game after game after game, each time reducing the results to numbers that could be displayed on a graph. Each graph purported to show ten-year system costs, stated in dollars, versus one or more criteria - i.e., lives saved, infrastructure damage avoided. The rationale behind each graph had to be explained in text that was sometimes mind-boggling. Son wondered, sometimes, how much good all of this effort was doing. He never saw or talked with the ultimate audience for his work, which was Robert S. McNamara, the president and the congress. General Kent told him, however, that their work was well received at SECDEF. Good. He was glad to hear that!

CHAPTER 68
Washington, D.C. - An Historic Place

When Son wasn't involved in the Pentagon with Cap'n Kirk and Starship Enterprise, he, Randy — by now nearly 14 years old and a ninth grader at St. Stephens School — and Arretta, took advantage of their surroundings. There were so many interesting places and things to see and do. The footprints and fingerprints of our nation's history were everywhere. There was the U.S. Capital and the halls of congress, The White House, Jefferson Memorial, Lincoln Memorial, Washington Monument, the U.S. Treasury and the Smithsonian Institution. Everything in Washington has historical significance, even the cherry trees surrounding the tidal basin. The plantings of cherry trees originated in 1912 as gift of friendship to the United States from the people of Japan. In Japan the flowering cherry tree or "Sakura", as it is called by the Japanese people, is one of the most exalted flowering plants. The beauty of the cherry blossom is a potent symbol equated with evanescence of human life and epitomizes the transformations Japanese culture has undergone through the ages.

Each of these places were full of fascinating things to see and learn about. To see the U.S. Constitution in the original, as it is displayed in the rotunda of the National Archives Building is truly awe inspiring. So, also, are all the other historic sites in the city. The Air and Space Museum in the Smithsonian covers the entire history of aviation from the Wright Brothers to space exploration. Son found that this was one activity that he, Randy and Arretta could enjoy together without having to confront Arretta's agoraphobia. They took advantage of that fact. Also, before they left Ft. Belvoir, Randy had shown promising musical talent. The Sons had a piano in their family room and Son taught Randy. He was a fast learner, going through the basics and quickly showing an interest in jazz and pop. He had a good sense of rhythm and did well on tunes like Henry Mancini's "Pink Panther." There were the usual squabbles however over the need to practice. Some of the resistance, Son felt, was normal teenage rebellion. Son found a good teacher in Alexandria, and for a while, Ran's practice habits seemed to improve. However resistance again appeared, and after protracted discussion in which Ran said he wanted to quit his father relented. If there was no motivation to practice there was little justification for him to continue. Certainly in other respects he was well motivated and an outstanding student.

CHAPTER 69
"Crunch" Time

May turned into June and Son anxiously awaited the results of the Colonels' Promotion Board. The list of winners was due to be released during the third week of June. Finally, the day arrived. Copies of the list were pinned to office bulletin boards all over the Pentagon. There was a quick clustering of anxious candidates and others who were just interested. Son elbowed his way in and looked at the list, several pages, beginning with "A"; Abercrombie, Adams, Allen,. . Dugan. . .Dugan?!!(I know him!) On to the next page, and the next, . Levy . . (Gene! He's in my group!) . . Mackie, Madison, Mertens . . .next page, Nast, Overby . . Sams. . .Silvius . .Soderman . . Sorensen?????

Soderman . . .Sor. . .???? Thomas.

Up until that moment, Son had hope. Now it was over. He had to talk to General Kent. He turned and started walking. On the way down the corridor back to his office he saw Gene Levy.

"Hi, Gene . .Congratulations! I'm glad you made it, you deserve it!"

"Thanks, Herm. I'm so sorry not to see your name on that list."

"That's the way it goes, I guess."

"Well, maybe next year?"

"Very doubtful. Once a bridesmaid, always a bridesmaid they say."

"Well, hang in there Herm. Maybe Kent can do something for you?"

"We'll find out, I guess. In the meantime, Colonel, I hope you don't mind working for a Lieutenant Colonel."

"I couldn't ask for a better boss, you know that, Herm!"

Son knew that wouldn't last long. Gene would be transferred soon to a better, more responsible job. The Air Force, rightly, wouldn't allow him to continue to report to Herm, who was now his junior officer.

CHAPTER 70
Last Flight

Shortly after Son found out that he had been passed over for promotion he reached his 45th birthday, and had to deal with another disappointment. Air Force regulation 60-16 requires that all pilots who have 5,000 or more hours of flying time (Son had 8,000) and are 45 and who are not in a primary cockpit job such as commander of a flying unit shall be relieved of their responsibility to maintain annual flying minimums. While no longer being required to fly, he would continue to receive flight pay. Son was not ready to quit flying, whether he was paid for it or not. That was not the issue. However, there was no getting around the regulation. He had to give up his time in the cockpit. On his last flight in a two-place, T-33 jet trainer, which he flew out of Andrews AFB, he was scheduled to fly with his friend, former subordinate and co-worker, Gene Levy, now Colonel Levy. They planned a flight from Andrews to Maxwell AFB near Montgomery, Alabama.

Son said to Gene, "Why don't you take the front seat to Maxwell. I'll take the front on the return flight?"

"No, Herm, you take it both ways. I know this is your last flight. I want you to fly it both ways. I'll just go along for the ride in the back seat."

"You sure?"

"Certainly. This is a special flight for you. I wouldn't have it any other way!"

"O.K., thanks Gene!"

They planned the flight in detail as always, including information on the route along the Federal Airways. Checkpoints, including radio frequencies call signs and ETAs (estimated times of arrival) were noted. Fuel remaining at each point was jotted down on a flight progress form that Son would attach to his knee clipboard. The weather forecasts in route and for destination were included.

He had done it so many times before. It was so routine. Yet, for Son that day was one that he wanted to remember because it marked the end of his active flying career, a career that had been a major part of his life for 25 years. As they rode the ramp vehicle out to their aircraft, Son's senses were cranked up to the maximum. He wanted to remember how everything sounded, smelled and looked. He took in the vista of the field, the ramp, its runways and the day-to-day activities that were a part of military flying. As he climbed up the ladder and eased himself down into the front cockpit he took special note of everything, the faint kerosene smell of the plane, the dull black of the instrument panel contrasted with the white phosphorescent instruments, the controls which he knew so well. He plugged and strapped himself in and when both he and Gene were ready, signaled the ground crew to turn on auxiliary electrical power, supplied by the ground power unit. His memory flashed back to that time in Japan, more than 17 years ago, when he went through the same routine

while preparing to take off on a combat mission to Korea. After they were airborne they climbed to their assigned altitude of 30 thousand feet while heading southeast, flying over the southern end of Chesapeake Bay. Off his left wing he could see Assateague Island where the wild ponies roam. They flew over tidewater country, Williamsburg, Richmond, New Port News. At the Naval Base there, he could see several ships tied up, including a big aircraft carrier. He didn't know which one, but looking at the flight deck from 30 thousand feet it didn't look very big - certainly not big enough for a Tomcat Fighter. Son was reminded of the comment of a navy pilot friend when asked what it was like to land a fighter on the deck of a carrier:

"Herman," he said, "have you ever tried to land into your garage without going through the wall?!"

There was Myrtle Beach AFB, currently home of an F-100 fighter wing. Son had landed there many times. Then they turned right to a heading of 210 degrees, pointing toward Maxwell.

Then he was in a canary yellow J-3 Cub, bouncing down a small grass field airport in Warrensburg, MO. One more bounce, the Cub flittered into the air and he was flying, this time for real, not just in his dreams!

The voice of the ATC controller snapped him back to reality. He wasn't flying a Cub but a T-33. ATC had penetration and approach instructions.

"Copy your instructions, ATC. Air Force 4637 is cleared to Maxwell Approach Control. Descend and maintain 8,000. .Over."

"Roger, Air Force 4637."

Minutes later, they were on the ground at Maxwell. In Operations, they filed their return flight plan and hit the snack bar for some lunch.

On the flight back to Andrews Air Force Base Son again focused his mind and senses on remembering what he knew was his last flight. He wanted to store those things in his memory. Ordinarily, the flight would have been routine. The weather was good, the aircraft performed perfectly and the flight plan unfolded as expected. Letdown from altitude, penetration and approach to Andrews went off without a hitch. On final approach and having been cleared to land, Son thought:

"This is closing the book on a major part of my life. I know I will miss it. I will miss the challenge, the sense of freedom and power. I will miss the beauty of the universe seen from a perspective that earthlings do not share - the infinitely variable kingdom of the sky; the sunrises, sunsets, clouds and storms that wash the world clean, at least for awhile. Yes, you've been to the edge of that sky, and now you're coming back for the last time. Remember. Remember. Remember."

The landing was perfect. "Grease job!" said Gene over the interphone.

"Thank you, Gene."

Since he would not be flying anymore, Son turned in all his flying personal equipment - his flight suits, jacket, boots, helmet and oxygen mask, everything except his knee clipboard, which contained the details of his last flight. He still has that clipboard.

The book was closed and put securely on Son's memory shelf.

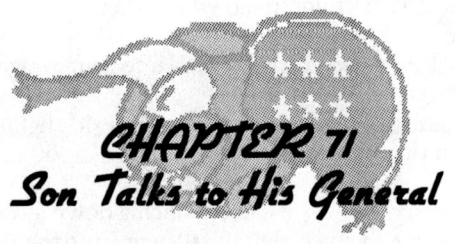

CHAPTER 71
Son Talks to His General

The Air Force promotion policy makes sense. It's called the "Up or Out" policy. It is aimed at selectively weeding out through forced retirement those officers who are not promoted after spending certain amounts of time in each grade. "Primary Zones" of eligibility, based on time in grade for each rank, are established. For example, Captains enter the primary zone for consideration to major after spending three years as a captain. Majors must have five years in grade to be eligible for promotion board consideration to lieutenant colonel. Lieutenant colonels with seven years time-in-grade become eligible to go before the colonels board. An officer may be promoted "below the zone," as Son was when he was promoted from captain to major with only 2 years time in grade. Such fast track promotions, however, are rare and are awarded only to outstanding candidates. The majority of all promotions are made from the pool of those who fall within their primary zones. When an officer moves into the primary zone for the next higher rank, a promotion board considers his record. The boards are given numerical quotas, generally less than the number of eligible officers within the zone. The ratio of eligibles to available "slots" gets higher at each step up the promotional ladder reflecting the increased competition at each step. If, during his first year of eligibility, an officer is promoted he is safe until he reaches the next primary eligibility zone. If he is passed over for promotion he will be considered again the following year. If he fails promotion the second time, he will be separated when he reaches the maximum allowable number of years of active service for his grade. While this may sound cruel, it achieves the Air Force objective of having an upwardly mobile officer corps and avoiding grade stagnation. Statistically, an officer's best chance of promotion occurs when he is considered the first time after reaching primary zone eligibility. If an officer is considered by the board but not selected for promotion he is "passed over." He will be considered a second time a year later but he will be looked on as a "stale doughnut" and his chances for promotion will be significantly reduced. On Son's first pass before the board he was one of approximately 5,000 eligible candidates from which the board could select only 250 for promotion to Colonel. These were not very good odds and they would almost certainly get worse during the following year.

Son considered his situation. He was 45 years old. He had just completed his Master's Degree in Business Administration at George Washington University. He had 26 years of active duty. If he did not get promoted he could stay until he reached 30 years of service, which would add 2 1/2% per year to his retirement pay. In 1968 dollars, instead of getting approximately $600 per month, his pay would increase to about $650 per month. In 4 more years, however, he would be almost 50 years old and he would be much less attractive in the civilian job market. Logically, he thought, he should retire now and get started on a

second career. He thought about his family situation too. Maybe civilian life would provide a more stable and secure environment for Arretta. Maybe they could open a new and more successful chapter in their relationship. With these facts firmly in mind he decided that he needed to talk to General Kent, the boss of the directorate. Aware of and observing protocol, he first asked permission of his immediate boss, Colonel Morphew.

"What do you want to talk to him about?"

"I think I want to retire, but I want to get his take on my situation first."

"Understandable, Herman. Go ahead. Just let me know how it went."

"Thanks, sir. I'll keep you posted."

Son then asked General Kent's secretary for an appointment.

"Tuesday, at 0900 will be fine, Colonel Son."

"Thank you. I'll be there."

General Kent was seated behind his desk and flanked with an American Flag to his left and a two-star flag to his right. Son marched smartly to a few feet in front of his desk, halted, came to attention and saluted.

Returning Son's salute, Kent said, "Sit down, Herman. I know what you want to talk about. I am very sorry not to see your name on the Colonels list."

"Sir, so am I, of course! Realistically, I knew the odds were not very good, but I thought that maybe, working for you, I could squeak through."

"Yes. I too thought that maybe we'd make it. You know that I gave you an exceptionally favorable endorsement on your last OER (Officer Efficiency Report)."

"I know, sir! And I thank you for those laudatory words. I appreciate your support."

"As you know, Herman, promotion boards are completely independent. I don't even know who was on the board. Independence and objectivity must be preserved at all costs."

"I understand completely, sir. I also agree with the board's actions in selecting the 250 officers for promotion that they did. They were all Viet Nam returnees with combat time in Nam. That's what the Air Force is all about, and there's no question that the board was correct in giving priority to them. I don't have a problem with that. My concern is, in the light of the board's action, about what I should do. Should I stay in and hope that I will succeed next year, or should I opt out now and get started on a civilian career? As you know, I have just completed my MSBA degree at George Washington University. I have also completed the course work by correspondence for the Industrial College of The Armed Forces. I wish I could believe that these actions will by themselves be enough to tip the scales in my favor with the next board, but I am highly skeptical. You know, sir, the odds this year were not very good. Next year the competition will be more intense. Every year that I stay in the Air Force will decrease my marketability in the civilian job market. I'll never be more valuable than I am right now." I think I should retire, but I'd like to know how you see it, sir."

"I know you're disappointed, Herman. So am I. Realistically, I knew that the odds were against it, but I hoped that your last couple of OERs and my endorsements would influence the board."

"But what should I do now?"

"You're a valuable part of this directorate, Herman. Colonel Morphew has kept me posted on the good work you have been doing on the Air Defense Weapons Tradeoff Study. I'd hate to lose you. It's up to you, of course, but if you want to stay, I'll continue to go to bat for you."

"Thank you, sir! I really appreciate your support. I know that you would do everything possible to advance my cause. But, I just don't know!"

"I know that under the circumstances this sounds less than candid, Herman. Maybe you won't believe it, but the Air Force needs you. You have experience that is invaluable."

"Yes, sir. That may be true. But if it is, why do I feel, right now, that the Air Force doesn't recognize that?"

"Herman, do you realize that only a small percentage of career officers make 0-6 (Colonel)? The pyramid narrows as you climb toward the top. Only a few can squeeze into the top of the pyramid. There are thousands of outstanding lieutenant colonels that will never make full colonel. That's just the way it is."

"Can I be frank, sir?"

"Of course."

"I have come to realize, too late I fear, that promotions to 0-6 and above depend not only on what you know but also on who you know. If I had had an opportunity to work for you or another general officer earlier in my career - someone willing to go to bat for me - perhaps it would have made a difference. I don't criticize this. It is internally and logically consistent. If we assume that the people of the top of the organization know the qualities, the knowledge, skills and the values that define organizational success, then they should be the gatekeepers who select those rising to the top of the organization. It follows that if one is to rise to the top, it behooves him/her to find a mentor early in his/her career. I know that I made mistakes along the way. I kept my head in the cockpit too long. I allowed myself to get sidetracked into backwater assignments - NATO and the U.S. Army, for example. I didn't worry about a mentor. Even though I did good work and got outstanding OERs it didn't carry enough weight."

"I can't argue with that."

"Well, sir, as some anonymous philosopher said, "We get too soon old, and too late smart! I'm going to sleep on it, but right now, I think I will be applying for retirement.""

"It's your call, Herman. I wish you'd stay, but whatever you decide, don't get your dauber down! You're too good an officer for that."

"Yes sir! Thank you for your time sir." With that, Son stood up, saluted smartly, about faced and left General Kent's office.

Back at his desk, Son started the paperwork on his retirement. It would have to go to the Chief of Staff of The Air Force for approval. On the way home that evening, he admitted to harboring some bitter feelings. He knew he was capable of performing at 0-6. His thoughts went back to key points in his career. He asked himself "what if????" questions:

"What if I had gone to Langley and TAC Headquarters, as originally planned, when I came home from Korea? That would have been a plum assignment that would have offered lots of opportunity. Perhaps I would have had a shot at a squadron or group command assignment. Who knows where it would have led? Instead I took a Training Command assignment and worked for a guy that I didn't get along with. That led to some negative OERs and a NATO assignment where I worked for a non-rated boss. But that's all water under the bridge. I can only work with the situation that I have now, and I know I'm making the right decision. I just hope General White will sign off on my request to retire."

The next day, Son completed a couple of forms that had to go with his application for retirement. He attached the standard cover and routing sheet to the package and gave it to Colonel Morphew, his immediate boss. Morphew knew it was coming.

"Well, I expected this, Herm. I wish I could change your mind. You've been a class act. I know that it doesn't seem fair that you were overlooked. Unfortunately, that's the way things work sometimes."

"Yes. I don't think there is anything anybody can do about it now. I know both you and General Kent would continue to push my case should I decide to stay, but I don't think it would make any difference."

"Herman, I'll endorse this with a 'Recommend favorable consideration.'"

Now all Son could do was wait. There was one other thing he could do. Assuming that his application would be approved, he needed to get started on finding a civilian job. He

fished out his resume', did some updating and editing and started mailing to a list of companies across the country. He didn't care about location. It could be east coast, west coast or anything in between.

Son had a resume', spanning 26 years, mostly military service. He had amassed nearly 8,000 hours in the air, was rated as a command pilot, had 107 combat missions in Korea, where he won the Distinguished Flying Cross and the Air Medal with 9 oak leafs. He realized, however, that would not cut much ice with a prospective employer. Accordingly, he down played his military experience except for leadership and organizational achievements. He highlighted his two business degrees, a B.A. in Business Administration and Banking from Colorado College in 1963, and a Master of Science in Business Administration from George Washington University, completed in 1966. His MSBA degree featured an area of concentration in organizational science and communication.

Son boiled down his 3-page resume into a one-page summary "teaser" letter paired with a recent wallet size black and white photo. His career objective was growth and a position where he could apply his knowledge and skills relating to organizational science. He was looking for a position where he could help a company develop its human assets and, in the long term, improve its "bottom line."

As he was developing a mailing list for his letter he got some disconcerting news.

The office secretary said, "Colonel Son, Colonel Morphew wants to see you."

"O.K.," thought Son. This is approval on my retirement application."

"Herman, you won't believe this! Your application has been rejected."

"What! Why?"

"Convenience of The Air Force."

"What does that mean! I know what it means, but why?"

"You'll have to read it, but the Air Force can always do this. You know that."

Son read through the endorsement from General White's office: "Request denied for convenience of the Air Force. Unless there are extenuating circumstances personnel requirements assessed by the war in Viet Nam preclude favorable action at this time."

"I hate this! Am I going to have to play the compassionate card again? I can do it! I can get a statement from Arretta's doctor. But if the Air Force can't promote me, why can't they just let me retire without having to go into all the personal, family reasons?"

Son took the package from Colonel Morphew. Now, his mind was made up. He had to get out. He called Dr. Fodor, Arretta's doctor, who gladly gave him a letter stating that there was a medical necessity for Colonel Son to retire in order to provide his wife with a stable environment.

He resubmitted his application. This time it was approved, but it left a bad taste. His retirement date would be 31 July, 1968. Son redirected his attention to his job hunt. He mailed over 150 letters. Most didn't answer. Of the thirty or so that did, most sent polite "we-have-reviewed-your-qualifications. . .and while impressive. . .blah, blah, blah, we-will-keep-your-application-on-file" responses. Three, however, produced encouraging responses, leading to on-site interviews. All, perhaps not surprisingly, were from aerospace companies: (1) Lockheed Corporation in Sunnyvale, CA, (2) Boeing Aircraft Company, Seattle, WA and McDonnell Aircraft Company, St. Louis, MO. He scheduled interviews and took 5 days leave to fly out for the interviews. All three offered interesting job opportunities. McDonnell in St. Louis, however, had the winning formula as far as Son was concerned. The position was as Manager of Career Development Programs, reporting to a director. The starting salary of $350 per week in 1968 dollars, while modest, seemed more than adequate to Son. His boss would be Dr. Robert W. Barclay, erudite, polished and very academic.

"Mr. Son, we have a great need here for programs dealing with organizational training in management skills. But even more important than that, I believe, is a need to develop

programs that will identify people in lower and middle management who have the potential for advancement. We then need to identify the knowledge and skills that they will require to qualify them for career advancement. It seems to me that your academic credentials when coupled with your military experience provide a unique fit for our position. How do you feel about it?"

Choosing his words carefully, Son said, "Yes, based on what you have told me, I believe I can make a positive contribution to the success of the organization. I like the idea of working with top level managers to identify the "comers" in the organization and to develop tailor made programs of development for them. If you agree, as it seems you do, that I should come aboard, what should be the next step?"

"I will have to develop a formal job offer covering the parameters of the job, starting salary and proposed starting date. I will need to get it approved by our corporate vice-president of personnel. This may take a day or two. You can expect to receive the offer by mail at your home probably within a week. Then the ball will be in your court!"

"Thank you, Dr. Barclay. I have enjoyed meeting you and other members of the McDonnell team. I will look forward to hearing from you soon!"

One week later there was a letter in Son's home mailbox in Alexandria, VA. It was from McDonnell Aircraft Company. Son opened it. His eyes took in the important words: ". . .as Manager, Career Development. . .starting salary of $350 per week. . .beginning not later than August 31. . .please signify your acceptance in writing on or before July 7." Hot diggity! St. Louis and McDonnell Aircraft Company it would be. He now had a good job in civilian life that would offer growth and opportunity. It fit his academic background and military experience. He would get off a letter of acceptance right away. He showed the letter to Arretta.

"Honey, it's St. Louis! It's the McDonnell offer, just as I told you. I'll be making $350 per week in addition to my retirement pay, no more moving. We can settle down. You won't have to worry about getting invitations to attend any "command performances." Isn't that great!"

"St. Louis? That's close to Warrensburg where your father lives, isn't it?"

"Yes, we can visit him once in awhile. He's 80 years old now, and he's alone. I'm sure he'll appreciate that we'll be closer now."

"Well, I'm not going to get involved. You can go see him by yourself."

Son had hoped for a more enthusiastic response than that. "But so be it," he thought. She'll like St. Louis once we get settled down. They would buy or build a home.

Then he thought, "Ooh, no! I can't accept the offer. Not now. Not as long as the Air Force denies my compassionate retirement request! But surely I'll have a response to that before July 7. Oh Please! They've got to approve it! I can't afford to miss this opportunity."

Back in his office at the Pentagon he had General Kent's administrative officer check with General White's office to see where his application was. It was on the Chief's desk. A reply should be forthcoming shortly. Shortly? How shortly? "Usually, within a couple or three days," said the admin officer. That was all Son could do. He couldn't go up to General White's office and demand that he act. All he could do was wait. Finally, just before the 4th of July holiday Son got his answer in a single word, "Approved." It bore General White's signature. He could retire effective 31 July, 1968. Son got his acceptance letter to McDonnell Aircraft off in the afternoon mail! The die was cast.

The ensuing weeks were taken up with checking out. He had to turn in his remaining personal equipment and process out through Bolling Air Force Base where all his personnel records were kept. The office planned and held a farewell lunch for him including all kinds of nice accolades and speeches. Son would hate to leave this group. They were all great people. It wouldn't be the first time that he had experienced those feelings, but perhaps it would be the last for awhile.

"It's been so long, since I've held you tight. .
Since I've said goodnight. .
It's been so long…"

"What? Why should that song start running through my head now?" He hadn't thought of that tune in years. It reminded him of the death of his maternal grandfather 30 years ago. Was it the finality, the severance of such a long and important relationship in his life? It was that funny quirk of his that associated certain pieces of music with important events in his life.

Forget it. Son had other work to do now. Most importantly he and Arretta had to dispose of their house at 1417 Juliana Place in Alexandria. They also had to make arrangements for shipping all their household effects to St. Louis. Thankfully, the Air Force would pay for that. He talked with Dr. Barclay by phone after enough time had elapsed to make sure that his acceptance had been received.

"Herman, we're so pleased that you'll be joining us!"

"Thank you, sir! We're looking forward to coming to St. Louis. I guess the first order of business will be finding a place to live. We're also concerned about school for our son. He's 14 now and will be starting his junior year in September."

"Of course. I don't think you'll have any problem with either of those concerns. There's plenty of good housing, and the schools here, particularly in the Parkway District of St. Louis County are outstanding."

"That's good to hear. As soon as we sell our house here in Alexandria and wrap up some final details here we'll be coming to St. Louis. I would expect we will arrive there sometime soon after mid-August."

The real estate market in the Washington area was almost like the major financial markets - highly liquid. Normally, real estate is not very liquid. But in this area that features a very large group of transients including military, diplomatic and political people, it is easy to buy and sell. If one wants to buy, simply find a house that fits, and offer the market price for it. If one wants to sell, put it on the market with an asking price somewhere close to market and it will sell quickly. It is like buying and selling stock on he NYSE. Son placed an ad in the local paper. Almost immediately the phone rang. Long story short: They found a buyer who was willing to pay the asking price, but because of a divorce, would not be able to close until after the divorce was final, probably not sooner than a year later. Although he was not an expert in real estate, Son suggested a lease-purchase arrangement. He had read about this in one of his college courses. Much later, he would learn about some of the complexities of real estate contracts. It would involve two contracts; (1) a lease for an agreed period of time at an agreed upon monthly rent; and (2) a sales contract for an agreed upon sales price and with a definite closing date. The buyer agreed with this approach and contracts were drawn up and signed requiring the buyer to pay $2,000 down and to rent for $450 per month for 18 months, then to buy for an agreed upon sales price of $41,500 ($3,500 more than the Sons had paid for it less than 3 years ago). (Reader: Please note. These prices are stated in 1968 dollars.) It sounded good. But what if. . .the lessee/buyer could not perform on either of the two contracts? What if they couldn't pay the monthly rent? What if they couldn't marshal the resources necessary to close on the second contract? These were important questions. However, the buyer seemed solid in all respects, and her legal imbroglio was understandable. She didn't want to assume legal title to the asset that the home represented until after her divorce was final.

The deal was closed at a local title company and the Sons arranged for movement of their household goods. It was time, perhaps for the last time, to break camp. Son knew that his decision to take the job at McDonnell would mean a major change in his life. That he understood. He had no inkling, however, that there would be changes more profound than just taking a new job. That would become apparent in due time.

CHAPTER 72
River City, Here We Come.

Toward the end of two days of summer driving across country, the Sons approached St. Louis. It was early August. As they passed through Belleville, Illinois they began to see the St. Louis skyline, dominated by the newly completed St. Louis Arch, the unique and beautiful architecture of Eero Saarinen, its soaring catenary curve framing the heart of the city skyline. Soon they were crossing the Poplar Street bridge across the Mississippi river, with the city skyline dominating the view to their right.

Son was excited. He was moving with his wife and 14 year old son, Randy, to the great "gateway to the west," St. Louis, situated on the banks of the Mississippi river.

Son thought of the many things about St. Louis that made it such an interesting and exciting place. It was the home of W.C. Handy, musician/composer of The St. Louis Blues. Scott Joplin, the creator of that deceptively simple piano style known as ragtime, lived composed and performed in St. Louis. In more modern times there was Miles Davis who did things with a jazz trumpet that place him among the greats. Also, there is Clarke Terry, now 84 years old and still active. He is another jazz original, famous for the style known as "bop." He created a unique musical style simply by moving the rhythmic emphasis from the last to the first beat of each measure. Other well known St. Lousians, past and present, include: Poet Eugene Field, Playwright Tennessee Williams, comedienne Phyllis Diller, Actress, Broadway star and expatriate Josephine Baker, sports personality Bob Costas, ballet star Katherine Dunham, actor Buddy Ebsen, Redd Fox, John Goodman, Betty Grable, Vincent Price, Al Hirshfield, Jack Buck, the voice of the St. Louis Cardinals, Ulysses S. Grant, and of course, Son's personal hero, Charles Lindbergh. all of them St. Louisians.

He would be working with a great aerospace corporation, McDonnell Aircraft Corporation. McDonnell manufactured the F-4 Phantom, at that time the world's best fighter plane. The company was also involved in a design competition for the follow on fighter to replace the F-4. They were also active in space technology, having produced the original Mercury spacecraft that carried John Glenn around the world. The next step into space, The Gemini project would soon be completed. It would feature a two-man space vehicle capable of sustained orbital space flight. Lots of exciting things were happening and Son was anxious to be a part of it.

They stayed at a Best Western Hotel their first night in St. Louis. The next morning, Herman called Dr. Barclay:

"Just checking in, Dr. Barclay . . .yes, we had a good trip."

"I know you will want to get settled, Herman. It may take some time to arrange for permanent housing, whether you decide to buy or to build. I might suggest that you check with the Red Carpet Inn. They offer efficiency apartments that are nice and reasonable,

much better than a regular motel. It's located on North Lindberg, only a few minutes from our office."

"Thanks. I'll certainly check that out."

"There's no immediate hurry to get to work, but if you'd like to drop by tomorrow morning, I'd like to introduce you around and then have lunch with you."

"Fine. What time would you like me to come?"

"Why don't you come in around 9 - 9:30. That'll give us time to chat awhile and meet some folks before lunch. Tell the security guard at the main gate who you are. I'll tell then to be expecting you. They'll provide an escort to bring you to my office."

" Great, Dr. Barclay! I'll be there."

As arranged, the next morning a security guard escorted Son to Dr. Barclay's office. "Wow," thought Son as he got into the staff car for the short ride to Building 1. "This has got to be a big change for me. Surely, McDonnell, on the cutting edge of aerospace technology, has also got to be on the cutting edge of business and organizational technology." This, as Son was about to find out, was not necessarily true. The techno structure at MAC was not nearly as advanced as their technical product.

Dr. Barclay introduced Son to the corporate vice-president for personnel, Mr. Robert Krone. Krone, Son noticed, spoke in short, clipped sentences. He gave he impression that he was pretty tightly wound. He was Dr Barclay's boss and Son would learn more, much more about him later. He met several other people who worked in the personnel depart- ment, all of whom he would get to know later. For now, they were a blur of faces and names. Then Dr. Barclay showed Son his desk, located in a private cubicle next to Barclay's. Next it was time for lunch at the executive's dining room. Reserved for division directors, vice presidents and above. Food choices were listed on a menu and there was white linen table service. "Pretty neat," Son thought. "I wonder where the poor people eat?" Actually, they (and they were not poor) ate in a spacious, neatly appointed cafeteria.

Suddenly, as he was about to sit down, Son saw someone at the next table that he knew from years ago.

"Irv! Is that you! I didn't know you were here. What are you doing?"

"I'm doing engineering test flying on the Phantom. Been here for a couple of years. What are you doing here?"

Son introduced his friend, Irv Burrows, to Dr. Barclay. "Irv, this is Dr. Barclay, my boss. Dr. Barclay, Irv Burrows. Perhaps you already know one another?"

"Yes, as a matter of fact, I know Irv well. He's one of our hottest test pilots!"

"Unbelievable. Irv and I have known each other for 15 years or so. In fact, he used to work for me at Luke Air Force Base when we were both in CCTAF flying F-84s."

"Well, it's good to see you again after all these years. Don't let me interrupt your lunch. I'm sure we'll be seeing each other often."

"Great, Herm. Good to see you!"

During lunch, Son met several other upper level managers, division chiefs and vice- presidents. The talk was all graceful small talk about Son's trip from Washington as well as numerous suggestions about where to live in St. Louis which Son found quite helpful. Of course, there was no grubby talk about the details of his new job. After lunch, Dr. Barclay suggested that Son check with the company housing office to get information on the hous- ing market.

"After you have talked with them, Herman, there is no need for you to stick around. I know that you will have lots of personal things to attend to, so if you would like, take the next two or three days off. Just let me know where I can contact you."

"Thank you, Dr. Barclay. I think we'll be staying at the Red Carpet. I'll give you a telephone number as soon as I can."

"Call me Bob, Herman."

"Thanks, Bob." With that, Son took his leave. He and Arretta would spend the next three days getting settled and starting their hunt for a house to buy.

But first things first, the Sons had to establish some roots. At the top of their priority list was to find or build a home. But where? St. Louis was a huge city, comprising over 2.5 million people in the greater metropolitan area. Top rated schools were most important. The consensus, after talking to many sources, reading real estate ads and driving through many areas, was that the Parkway School District was the best place to look. They finally settled on a small sub-division of modestly priced new homes located in the Parkway West School District. It was in a fast growing area, about 10 miles southwest from MAC and within a half-mile of a brand new high school. They choose a spacious 4-bedroom model that had a lot of style, a nice back yard and a rear entry 2-car garage. In 1968 dollars it was priced at $35,000. It seemed like a lot of money to the Sons, but they liked the neighborhood, the liked the school district and they liked the builder, Kemp Homes. They signed a contract and were told that they would be able to move into their new home by Thanksgiving! Things were definitely "looking up" for the Sons. The one-bedroom efficiency apartment at the Red Carpet Inn was cramped, with a small kitchen and living room. It was O.K., but as the weeks passed, it seemed to get smaller and smaller.

CHAPTER 73
From Military to Civilian Life

Son knew that he would miss the Air Force. After all, it had been a major part of his life for over 25 years. He would miss the camaraderie, the feeling of belonging to that great fraternity of fighter pilots. A part of his identity would always be in the great sweep of the skies. But Son also knew that life goes on and that as the years pass things change. He had prepared himself for this change with an advanced degree in business. He had also prepared himself emotionally, and he was looking forward to his new job at MAC. He told Arretta that this was the beginning of a new life for them.

"I think we picked just the right house for us, Arretta. We're going to really enjoy it. Let's turn over a new leaf. Let's make up our minds that for the next thirty or forty years, we're going to live each day to the fullest. I believe that Abraham Lincoln was right on when he said, 'Most folks are about as happy as they make up their minds to be.' Let's decide for ourselves that we're going to be happy. There are all kinds of things, all sorts of opportunities for us to seize. This is our chance. Let's grab the brass ring. O.K.?" Arretta's response, while not negative, was a long way from enthusiastic.

"I'll do the best I can, Sonny," she said. Son knew from her tone that a "but" was coming. "But you know that I can't go out in crowds and feel comfortable. If a panic attack hits me I just freeze."

"Yes, I know that's how it has been in the past. You've told me that you think that the stress of my being in the Air Force with all those moves and the social pressures contributed to your panic attacks. Isn't that right?"

"Yes, but. . ."

Son cut her off, feeling his anger beginning to rise. The endless "yes, butting" leading nowhere drove him to distraction. "Please. Don't give me another 'yes but'. I'm tired of it. You'll never have a better situation than the one we are about to begin. Can't you look at it positively?"

"I'll try. I just wish you could have found a job in Phoenix or at least closer."

"You know that I canvassed the job market. There weren't any jobs, at least none that I would have, in Phoenix. Besides, what does that have to do with being happy here, right here, right now?"

"I don't think you understand. ."

"Oh, I think I do. But if you're still having symptoms, let's get you another psychiatrist. Somehow, someway, somebody's got to know how to fix your problem. I don't want to spend the rest of our lives with this monkey riding our backs."

Their argument finally drug to an inconclusive close. They did decide, however, for find another doctor. Through a doctor's referral service they found Dr. Abrahamson, an-

other classical Freudian. By this time Son had some idea of the psychoanalytic approaches that would be used. He knew not to expect quick results. So it began: the weekly trips to see the doctor, the pills, the mood swings. Son didn't know what else to do. He tried to be supportive, but it was hard. In the meantime, he had a job that was demanding his attention.

The New Job Begins

Son checked in with Dr. Barclay on a Monday morning, following the few days he had taken to get his family situated, including the purchase of a new home. He was anxious to tell Bob all about it.

"Yes! We bought a new house. We're really excited about it. It won't be ready for several months, but Kemp has told us we should be able to move in by Thanksgiving."

"Where did you say it is?"

"Just south of Clayton Road and west of Woods Mill Road. It's in a brand new subdivision. We really like the area. We're also pleased with the Parkway School system. I think our son should thrive there."

"That's great, Herman. I'm glad for you, and I'm pleased that you got your personal situation secured so quickly. Now you can start your job with a clear head."

"I'm ready, Bob. From what you've told me, there is a pervasive need for training, specifically for middle managers in the basic concepts of management. From what you tell me, most managers in this category have come from strong technical backgrounds, but they have little or no training in managerial skills."

"Yes, Herman. Most of them manage their people using what I call a "my way or the highway" style of leadership. They get their orders from the next level above them and simply pass them down to their subordinates. Subordinates are generally not involved in making decisions. They simply carry them out." In fact, decision making at MAC, even on routine matters, is generally restricted to the highest levels of the organization.

"What you're describing is a "Theory X" style of management."

"Exactly! What we want to do is lead them to use a more participative style of leadership, one in which the manager involves his subordinates in problem solving, with decisions being pushed to the lowest level consistent with the tasks being performed."

"I have no problem with that, Bob. As you know, my MBA work involved an area of concentration on organizational behavior. I'm quite familiar with the work that Rensis Likert of the University of Michigan has done on participative management styles, sometimes called "Theory Y." How do we get started?"

"Good question, Herman. I have an answer. I have developed a 5-day management seminar that I call the Management Action Conference (acronym: MAC, of course). I have gotten commitments from department heads in engineering, manufacturing, quality control, flight test and security to select and send managers from their departments to the conference."

"Good. What will the conference cover?"

"I've structured it to cover the basic functions of a manager: Planning, Organizing, Motivating and Controlling. However, the details of what we will talk about, I want to come from the managers themselves. In other words, I want to demonstrate, through the managers themselves, how participative management works. We've got a conference scheduled starting next Monday. We've reserved meeting space at the Howard Johnson Motel on Dunn Road. I prefer to hold it off campus. Otherwise, managers will get phone calls from their departments. In this first conference, I'd like to have you sit in as a participant, so you can get a feel for the way it should go. After that, you can take over."

"Sounds great, Bob. You have already introduced me to my two management coordinators, George Chakides and Don Wylan. Will they be involved in the MAC?"

"Yes, they will, Herman. They will both be reporting to you, so this will be an opportunity to see them in action. I think you'll see that they are both very capable."

"Since I'm coming in from the outside, will there be any personal issues or resentments?"

"I don't think so, Herman, but it's perceptive of you to ask that question. I chose you to head the branch because of your qualifications, particularly your formal education. I wouldn't worry about George and Don. I think you'll find both of them to be cooperative. After next week's conference, you can use them in future conferences any way that you see fit."

"Well, I'm looking forward to next week. I know I'm going to learn a lot."

The following week, Son sat in as a participant in the conference. It was, indeed, a learning experience. There were 21 participants, including Son. The meeting room was arranged with a continuous U-shaped table with participants facing each other. Dr. Barclay stood at the top of the U, next to a large, plain flip chart. He began the conference by welcoming the participants. He then asked each participant to introduce himself by giving his name and department. He then asked an overhead question, directed to the group as a whole:

"Why do you think you are here?"

There was silence. Bob looked expectantly around the room, finally settling his gaze on one participant who seemed ready to speak:

"Bert, you seem to have some thoughts. Would you like to share them with the group?"

"Well, I guess so. I'm not sure why we're here, but I heard a rumor."

"Really? What would that be?"

"That if you're chosen to come to this meeting it means that you're too rough."

"Rough? In what way?"

"Well, you pound your fist on your desk. That's how you get your people to do what you tell them."

"I see. And what are we supposed to do in this conference?"

"Beats me. I guess you're supposed to teach us how to be more charming."

Everybody laughed at Bert's comment. Someone else volunteered that he had heard that the name for the seminar was "Charm School." Then Bob asked,

"Does anybody think that being 'charming' will make you a better manager?"

There was a lot of discussion, the general tenor of the comments being that "charm" didn't have much to do with being a manager, as they understood the term. Bob then led the discussion into an examination of the problems that they had as managers. Using the flip chart, he listed them as the participants brought them up. They developed a fairly extensive list, starting with Communications and including things like, Discipline, Absenteeism, Quality Control, Pay, Union problems, Cleanliness, Security and more. Bob then asked a key question:

"Do you think that we have enough collective brains in this room this morning to come up with some ideas on how some of these problems could be dealt with? If we could do that, do you think our time this week would be well spent?"

The answer, of course was "yes." Bob then developed a model for the management process. All managerial activities can be grouped into the following categories: (1) Planning, (2) Organizing, (3) Motivating, and (4) Controlling. The rest of the conference dealt with the list of problems that the participants had developed. Suggested actions and solutions were tied to the four managerial functions. Son was impressed with the way it all came together and with the high level of interest and participation. Both George Chakides and Don Wylan handled the leadership for parts of the seminar and did an excellent job. Son told both of them he was impressed. On Friday afternoon at the end of the seminar, Bob asked each participant to give some feedback in writing. "Just jot down your thoughts

about this week. What did you like, what didn't you like. Make it informal. With that, the conference was over. As each participant finished their critique, they turned it in and left.

That was the beginning for Son in his new job. He felt quite comfortable with what he had seen and heard and felt confident that he could handle the tasks. During the next year he scheduled and ran 40 MAC conferences. Over 800 middle level managers from across the entire company attended. The feedback that he got from participants was almost universally positive. If there was a negative component, it had to do with participants feeling that they wouldn't be able to practice the concepts that they had learned once they got back to the departments. Son was concerned about this, but at this point didn't know what to do. He would have to talk to Bob about it.

George and Don asked Son about the possibility of doing a similar program for first line supervisors, the foremen on the factory floor. Son thought that would be a good idea. He discussed it with Dr. Barclay who also supported the idea. Son suggested that they put together a 5-day program, similar to the MAC but tailored specifically to fit the unique problems faced by first line supervisors.

"We need to get some ideas from production management. What do they think the needs are? If we get the green light, they we should try a pilot program and see how it is received."

George and Don agreed to work together on putting a pilot program together. It was well received and resulted in the establishment of a regular schedule of a program called "Supervisory Skills. "It's too bad," thought Son, "that a program like this wasn't started 20 years ago. If it had, maybe we'd have middle level managers by now that were better managers."

CHAPTER 74
The New Home

Son was so absorbed in the details of his new job that time passed quickly. Almost before he knew it, completion of their new home approached. Soon, they would be able to move in and forsake the cramped quarters that they had occupied at the Red Carpet Inn. Since mid-September, Son had been driving his son to high school at Parkway West. It meant about 25 miles of extra driving in the morning, and the same thing in the afternoon. When they moved into their new home, bus service to the school would come right to their door. What a relief that would be!

The Monday before Thanksgiving, 1968, the day finally arrived. They signed all the closing papers, took on a new 1st mortgage and did a walk through inspection of their shiny new home. What a beauty it was. The moving van came the next day with their household goods that had been in storage since they left Washington. Now they could spread out and get organized. Ran could have his own room. There was room for an office/sewing room, a spacious master bedroom suite with private bath and a spare bedroom. The family room with fireplace adjoined the open kitchen. There were lots of windows. The house had a bright and open feel to it.

"What more could anyone ask for?" said Son. Even Arretta's normal reserve seemed to thaw. She liked it too. They unpacked the scores of cardboard boxes that the moving van delivered and slowly began to get their house turned into a home. Ran enrolled at brand new Parkway North High School as a junior and fit in immediately. He made friends easily with Dale Greenwood, who lived only a block away, and a likeable fellow named Ed (don't remember his last name). Son met the superintendent of the High School, Dr. Al Burr, and was impressed with his personality and attitude. Son assumed that this would be one area of their family life that would go smoothly. At least, he hoped it would. Ran's program involved him in the usual subjects for his level: math, history, English and biology. He particularly liked biology and his teacher in that class, a Ms. Melba James.

Soon, Christmas was approaching. The Christmas decorations came out of their boxes and they went hunting for a tree. They couldn't seem to find a cut tree that suited them. Finally they hit upon the idea of buying a live, balled, tree. That way they could have it not only for Christmas, but afterward they could plant it in the front yard. They had just the spot for it and after Christmas, Son dug a hole and planted the tree. (35 years later, the house, no longer owned by Son, and the tree, now 70 feet tall, are still there.) They bought Ran a new stereo for his room and several articles of personal clothing. Herman and Arretta exchanged gifts, but somehow, at least so Son felt, the usual spark wasn't there. Arretta acted like she wanted to be somewhere else.

Since the Sons had lost Shadow, their smart little Shetland sheep dog, they still grieved over his passing. Arretta loved Shadow. Son thought that maybe it would help counter her depression to get another dog. Without talking to Arretta he went to a breeder who specialized in Shetlands. There he found two beautiful little Shetland puppies. He immediately fell in love with them. He thought that surely Arretta would feel the same way. He brought them home and Arretta had a fit.

"Don't expect me to take care of them. They will need constant attention until they are house broken and trained, I simply won't do it! I won't be tied down to them. You'll just have to leave them in the garage when you are at work."

So that is what Son did. Every morning when he left for work he would put the two pups in the garage, making sure they had plenty of water and food. There they would stay until he came home at night, usually around 6:00 P.M. Naturally, they made a mess in the garage. That was no way to house train little puppies.

Besides being a voracious reader, consuming a couple of books per week, almost exclusively fiction, she had an abiding interest in painting. This pursuit, begun while the Sons were in Colorado, continued to demand her attention. Son encouraged her. It seemed to be the one thing that gave her an outlet for self-expression. He praised her work, though he was no expert in art.

"Arretta, I'm no expert, but some of the things you've done are good, I think. Why don't you see if you could get some of it exhibited?"

"Oh, I couldn't do that! It's not that good. Besides, if I had to go out in public I'd panic." Son knew that his wife had a terrible self-image. He also knew, from conversations that he had had with Arretta that most of her personality problems stemmed from her early childhood. That she had been abused seemed evident. Arretta would never reveal the details of that abuse.

"I don't think you would have to get involved with the public very much. Why don't you let me explore the possibilities a little?"

"Well, all right, but don't commit me to anything."

"Sure."

Son found out that there was a local artists group that was very active. They held small classes, critiqued their work and occasionally put on public exhibits. He met the secretary of the group, Leslie Herzog. She was a very personable, friendly woman. Son found out later that she was married to a research engineer who worked for Monsanto. Arno smoked a pipe, and was an expert in the design of LED (light emitting diode) displays. The pipe seemed to fit his somewhat laconic personality. It was also quite the opposite from his wife, Leslie. In addition to her interest in painting, she was an avid cross-country skier who was good enough to compete at the Olympic level for seniors. In spite of her athletic achievements, Son thought her personality might mesh well with Arretta's. She was outgoing but not overbearing. Son liked her and thought that their common interest in art would help Arretta emerge from her shyness. Leslie said that their group was holding a public exhibit in a couple of weeks at a nearby mall. She suggested that Arretta might want to show some of her work.

"Well, I'll ask her, Leslie. I'm not sure that she's ready to show, but maybe I can bring her by and you can meet and talk with her."

"That would be great, Herman. I'd love to meet your wife."

Leslie gave Son the information on the exhibit. He told Arretta, and wonder of wonders, she responded positively to it.

"Yes, I'd like to go," she said.

Arretta didn't show any of her paintings at that exhibit, but she and Leslie did seem to like each other. Later, after Leslie had seen and critiqued some of her paintings, she did agree to show some at the next association exhibit.

As spring blended into summer, family life at times seemed almost normal. Arretta seemed to be making slow but inconsistent progress with Dr. Abrahamson. Arretta announced, after one session, that Dr. A would like to talk with both of them.

"Really? That's great! I'll be glad to go with you. If I can help, you know that I want to, don't you?"

"Yes. But you don't need to be so enthusiastic. It makes me nervous to think of both of us talking with him together."

"Why?" Don't we both want to help you get over this?"

"I don't know. I just know that I'll be nervous."

"Well; I'll do what you and Dr. Aabrahamson decide "

A couple of weeks later, Son and Arretta sat in Dr. A's office. Short and chubby, and seated behind his desk, he smiled wanly at Herman and Arretta. He took off his glasses and began rubbing them with a tissue. After what seemed like a minute, he said:

"Who would like to start?"

Again, there was silence. Before the session, Son had decided that he was going to let Arretta lead the conversation. After a couple of minutes of aching, awkward silence, however, he volunteered:

"This is Arretta's session. . .I think. . .I'm here to help, but I'd like to hear something from her."

"Hmmmmm," mused the doctor.

Arretta sat frozen, not saying a word.

After more dead silence, Dr. A said, looking at Son:

"Why don't you tell us what the problem is, Mr. Son?"

Son spoke for several minutes. He was not sure how long. He tried to outline what he thought the problem was. He took care to say that he realized that it was a relationship problem, that both he and Arretta had ownership in it. He tried not to find fault or lay blame. Still, he could not avoid calling it as he saw it. Arretta was reclusive and pathologically shy. Her double bind style of communicating constantly put Son in the role of persecutor. This made Son angry. When he expressed his anger, Arretta would play the victim and lapse into pouting. She was giving a good demonstration of that behavior as Son spoke. Dr. A gently asked Arretta to respond, but didn't have much luck. In spite of himself, Son found himself carrying the conversation. At one point Son looked across the desk at Dr. A and noted that he was nodding off. "Oh, boy," thought Son, "this is hopeless!"

CHAPTER 75
Herman's Father Is In Trouble

One of the advantages of living in St. Louis was that Herman's elderly father lived in Warrensburg, MO, less than 200 miles away. Son wanted to drive up to see him on a weekend. He was concerned about his dad and didn't think he should be living alone, as he had been since losing his wife and Herman's mother. John Herman, however, said he was perfectly happy living by himself. He did seem to be doing fine. He made regular visits to see his favorite sister, Stella, who lived in Vienna, MO. They kept each other's spirits up. Stella, however, died of pancreatic cancer in 1969. That threw "Daddy" into a deep depression. Son called him regularly after that, and he seemed to be all right. However, Daddy's next-door neighbor called Herman one Saturday morning.

"Mr. Son, this is Bill Horn, your dad's neighbor. I am concerned about him. Newspapers and milk bottles are piling up on the front porch and I haven't seen him in several days. I know he's in the house. I see lights going on and off. The front door is locked and shades are drawn. I have knocked on the door but he won't answer. I think you might want to come up and check on him."

Oh yes, I will! Thank you so much for telling me. I have been concerned about him living by himself, but when I have talked to him by telephone he has said that he wants to stay there. Are you sure that he is in the house and that he is moving around?"

"Yes, yesterday when I knocked on the door he wouldn't answer it but he yelled for me to go away!"

"O.K., I'll be there this afternoon. It'll take me about four hours."

When he finished talking to the neighbor, Son turned to Arretta.

"Daddy is in trouble. We need to drive up to Warrensburg right away to see what's going on. Mr. Horn says he won't answer the door. He knows he's in the house and could answer, but he won't. There's something strange going on.

"Don't say 'we'. I'm not going. You can go by yourself, but I'm not going. I'd feel like a fool!"

"Well, you said it, I didn't!"

Son knew there was no point in arguing with her. Why she had to be so bull-headed about it he couldn't understand. But she was, and that was that.

Arriving in Warrensburg later that evening, he found the situation to be exactly as Mr. Horn had described it. Son knocked on the door loudly.

"Daddy, this is Herman Franklin. Open the door!"

He repeated the knocking and calling to his dad. Finally, the shade covering the front door window was slowly pulled aside. Daddy peered through the slit.

"Daddy, let me in. I need to talk with you!"

The elder Son slowly unlocked the door and opened it a few inches. Herman could see that he was in his pajamas. Herman pushed gently on the door.

"Daddy, come on. Let me in!"

"Herman Franklin? Get in here. Quick!"

Herman stepped inside. His dad seemed to be afraid of something.

"What's the matter, Daddy? What's wrong?"

"Herman Franklin, quick, close the door. Lock it! There are people across the street that are spying on me!"

"Awww, really, where?"

"They are looking over here from the upstairs window in that house across the street!:

"Who? Daddy."

"It's the FBI! I think they're going to arrest me!"

"Daddy, that's ridiculous. Why would the FBI want to arrest you? You haven't done anything."

"I think they found out that I made some mistakes on my Railroad Express receipts and they're coming after me!"

"Oh, that can't be, Daddy. Your books when you worked for the railroad were audited regularly, and you know that any clerical mistakes that you may have made were corrected. Besides, you've been retired for over 10 years now. Here, let's go into the kitchen and sit down. Got any coffee?"

"I think I've got some instant around somewhere."

"Sit down, daddy. I'll look. By the way, you look pretty spiffy in those PJs."

Daddy smiled a thin smile. The humor of Herman's remark was not lost on him, Son was glad to note. Emotionally, however, it was easy to see that his dad was a half-bubble off center. Son was no psychiatrist, but he recognized paranoid delusional behavior when he saw it. He continued his conversation with his dad as he looked for a jar of instant coffee in the cupboard.

"Here it is. I'll heat some water. Where's your tea kettle?"

Herman found the tea kettle and made some coffee, meanwhile watching his father. It was obvious that he could no longer live by himself.

"Daddy, how is your diet?"

"Oh, it's good."

"What did you have for breakfast this morning?'

"Bacon and oatmeal."

"And for dinner?"

"Oatmeal and bacon."

"Any vegetables?"

"Not many."

"Daddy, I think you ought to come to St. Louis for awhile, just for a visit."

"Oh, I don't think so. I'm doing okay by myself, and I don't want to trouble you and Arretta. Besides, I don't want to go outside. The FBI will see me."

"I know, Daddy. But don't worry about them. I'll protect you."

It took some more talking and reassuring, but Herman finally got him to agree. He packed a small suitcase. He got his father into his car and drove back to St. Louis. Herman didn't care what Arretta thought about it, Daddy was going to be staying with them, at least for awhile. It was late when they got back to St. Louis, so Herman put his father to bed in the guest bedroom. He knew that his father was an early riser, so he got up at five o'clock the next morning. His father was already awake and sitting on the edge of the bed, asking where he was.

"Daddy, you're in St. Louis in my home. You're safe here. Let's go have some breakfast."

"I'm not hungry. Let's go back to Warrensburg."

"Well, let's go have a cup of coffee anyway," said Herman, ignoring the request to go back home.

"Do you have any oatmeal?"

"Of course, Daddy. I'll fix some."

When the oatmeal was put before him he just looked at it. Son coaxed and cajoled. Finally, he ate a few bites. About that time, Arretta came into the kitchen, poured herself a cup of coffee, lit a cigarette and smiled perfunctorily at Daddy. It was clear that as far as she was concerned that Daddy wasn't welcome.

First priority with Herman was to get a medical checkup for his father. Dr. Abramson, Arretta's psychiatrist, said that physically he was in reasonable health for his age. However, it was apparent that he was suffering from paranoid delusions. He said that his condition could have been brought on by a combination of isolation and a severe deficiency in vitamins, particularly B vitamins. He prescribed a mild anti-depressant and a theraputic B-complex vitamin.

"I'd like to see him again in two weeks."

"Thank you, Dr. Abramson. I'll se up an appointment with your receptionist."

Within a matter of two or three days Herman could see that his father was coming out of his paranoia. Dr. Abramson was correct. He called Dr. Abramson and told him that his father seemed to be improving rapidly. The doctor said it wouldn't be necessary to come in again. Daddy's condition was apparently triggered by the death of Stella, his favorite sister. Living alone and poor diet exacerbated it. But now Son realized that he had another problem. Much as he wanted to have his father live with them, he knew Arretta wouldn't tolerate it. Without at least her passive cooperation he knew it wouldn't work. He called his sister, June, in Chicago and explained the situation. Herman will be forever grateful for her response. She understood perfectly that her brother couldn't take care of their father. She and her husband, Walt, had three young sons, Cal, 16; Paul, 14; and Craig, 11. Herman was afraid that that might pose a problem for June, but she said not to worry that, "the boys will love to have their grandpa living with them." The following weekend, June and Walt drove to St. Louis. Herman had already talked to his father about their coming, not saying anything about living arrangements. But when he saw his daughter he smiled. It was easy to see that he would be happy with them. John Herman Son moved permanently from his home in Warrensburg to Chicago to live with his daughter and her family. It was the right decision. He lived with them for the next 12 years until he passed away at 92. Herman is sure that a special crown is reserved for his sister and her family for the love and care that they gave.

CHAPTER 76
Work is a Saving Grace

Back at MAC, Son continued to get more deeply involved in his work. It was a saving grace, countering the frustration and anger that arose from his rapidly deteriorating relationship with his wife. Both the Management Action Conference and the course for first line supervisors were going well. He had scheduled and would conduct 40 MAC seminars and 25 classes for first line supervisors during the next year - an ambitious schedule. The end of course critiques from participants continued to rate both programs as outstanding. Still, Son wasn't satisfied. In face-to-face conversations with several graduates of his programs he found that although they felt that that they had gained valuable new insights into how to be better managers, most admitted that they couldn't practice the techniques that they had learned in the seminars.

"Why," asked Son?

"Because I would be a round peg in a square hole, that's why!"

"Do you mean that your boss or your subordinates won't let you apply what you've learned?"

"You got that right! We're a Theory X outfit, from Mr. Mac to the bottom! Your ideas are great but ain't no way I could practice what you taught us, Herman. My boss would kill me."

This "truth" was straight from the source. It was hard to take, but it confirmed Son's hunch, that what was really needed at MAC was a global cultural change. There were up to seven levels of management between Mr. Mac, as he was respectfully called, and a first line supervisor on the factory floor. Decision making in all but the most trivial was restricted to the highest level of the organization. Mr. Mac practiced micro management. He even edited the company newspaper called "The Spirit." A company joke had it that decision making at MAC was like gestation in elephants: it all takes place at a very high level and it takes forever for any kind of results.

All of this meant that working with several individual managers brought together in a brief seminar where they would learn how to be round pegs simply wasn't effective in the long run. When they got back into their departments they were pressured to become "square" again. It meant, instead, that change would have to be effected by working with departmental work groups. He had to get everybody in the group to accept the idea that "roundness" was better. How could he do this, Son wondered? He resolved to talk to his boss, Bob, about it. First, however, he wanted to discuss what he had learned with George Chakides and Don Wylan. Both George and Don agreed that team building was a good idea, but they were skeptical that he would ever get approval to develop such a program.

"You'll never sell it, Herman," said George. "I know what you are saying. We're doing very little with our seminars to change management style. I'm not sure it can be done."

"Then we are just wasting our time, is that right?"

"You could say that, Herman."

"Well, I can't hold still for that, George. The company is paying us good money to train their managers in ways to manage more effectively, but it's not working. It makes me feel like we're the house monkeys. We're just here for show. I'm going to talk to Bob about it."

"Bob will just 'tut..tut' you, tell you to relax and stop rocking the boat, said Don."

"We'll see," said Herman.

Bob had a DBA (doctor of business administration) and was very knowledgeable in his field. Surely, Son thought, he could talk to Bob and make his case that with team building he could make a difference. What he didn't fully appreciate was the rigidity of the organization and how fiercely it would resist change.

"Bob, I know this would work, if they would just give us a single department and let us work with them on a pilot program. If we could make it work, and I am sure we could, we could expand he program."

"I know you mean well, Herman," said Bob. "But you don't understand this company. There may come a time when we can push for more progressive things, but not now. If I took what you're proposing to Bob Krone he would run me out of his office! Krone is one of Mr. Mac's most fanatical "pilgrims." That's what Mr. Mac calls those who were with him when he founded the company. He is a true disciple of the MAC style. He gained his experience and whetted his philosophy in labor relations. He hates unions, sees them and employees as the enemy, and he sees employees as a commodity, not to be trusted, only to be driven. He is utterly convinced that management's job is to ride herd and crack the whip on the rabble. More than that, Herman, Krone has a mean streak. He can be vindictive toward those who oppose him."

Son took Bob's advice seriously. He thought he had better proceed with caution. However, didn't give up his idea. He had come to know the prevailing management style at MAC and it was atrocious. There were several unions at the company, the largest two being the Machinists and the Electrical Workers. Although the company followed the procedures prescribed by the Taft-Hartley Act in handling grievances, there was constant tension between the company and the unions. At contract renewal time strikes were a part of the routine. There had to be a better way. He would have to give it some more thought.

On the home front, Randal was doing well in school. He had completed his junior year and scored very high on his SAT. With Son's help, R. started looking for a college. He wanted a small, independent college with a reputation for high academic standards. Among the schools that he checked out were Knox College, Reed and Whitman College. During his senior year he made application for admission at all of them and was accepted at all. He would have to think hard about which one he would prefer. Dad was very proud. Son assumed that Arretta was proud also, but she seemed passive about it. He was concerned and wondered if the medications that Dr. Abramson had been giving her were depressing her. He spoke to the doctor about it. Dr. A. said that in recent months he had been aware of her tendency to slip into depression. That was why he had prescribed thorazine. Herman told Dr. A. that she seemed "unplugged", almost zombie-like. Dr. A. said he was considering ECT or electro-convulsive therapy. That seemed pretty radical to Son, but after discussing it further with both Arretta and her doctor, they decided to try it. She was admitted to St. Louis University Hospital for the treatment. Three days later she came home. Her mood did improve. There were no lows, nor were there any highs, just a sort of unnatural (at least for Arretta) middle ground. Of course, she continued seeing Dr. Abramson on an out patient basis, but there didn't seem to be much progress. Son was beginning to believe that a

full recovery wasn't to be. It was very frustrating because he simply didn't want to give up on her.

Paradoxically, whenever she talked about her father and wanting to go to Phoenix to take care of him her spirits brightened. She had recently talked by telephone to her mother, Mary. Mary said that "Dad", as she called her husband, Claude, was very weak. His emphysema was getting worse, and he wouldn't quit smoking.

"Dad really needs me," Arretta said. I'd like to fly out."

"What could you do? Isn't his condition chronic? He won't get better just because you're there."

"I can give him moral support. He needs that."

"Well, Ran and I need moral support too. How long would you want to be gone?"

"I don't know. I guess a couple of months at least."

"What about Dr. Abramson? Interruption of your care with him doesn't sound like a good idea to me."

"I'll be comfortable there. I won't have any problems."

"You do what you want, but I don't like it."

For the next two and one-half months, Arretta was gone. Her only contact with her husband and son were short letters and a couple of telephone calls.

CHAPTER 77
Randal and His Dad Have a Battle

Still concerned about Arretta's health and while he and Ran were living alone, another crisis arose with one of Randal's teachers at Parkway West High School. One of R's favorite courses was biology, and his favorite teacher was, of course, his biology teacher. Melba James was a competent teacher, well liked by all her students apparently. Randal had mentioned her several times to his dad. He said that he and one of his best friends, Dale Greenwood, really liked her not only for her knowledge of biology but her personal interest in the lives of her students. She had been telling them about a new, scientific approach to the life of the mind and spirit, and a new "scientific" way to remove emotional blocks that prevented one from achieving one's full potential.

"That sounds interesting, Ran. It almost sounds too good to be true. What do they call this method?"

"It's called 'Scientology', Dad It's a method that was developed by L. Ron Hubbard. He founded the Church of Scientology."

"Church? Really? I think I've heard about it. Seems that I read an article in the paper. I don't remember all the details, but as I recall the article didn't paint a very favorable picture. The gist of it was that Scientology was a scam, that they called themselves a "church" to avoid taxes that they would otherwise have had to pay on pretty substantial income that they derived from their members."

"I'm really interested in this, Dad. I want to learn more about it. They're offering an introductory seminar for only $50. That's reasonable, isn't it? Dale Greenwood is planning to go. I'd like to go too."

"Randy, I don't approve of this, at least not until I find out more about it. In the first place, I don't appreciate a teacher in our public school system proselytizing her students. She is a high school biology teacher, not a recruiter for some so-called religion."

"Aw, Dad! You don't understand. She's just trying to tell us about something that had helped her in her life and she wants us to know about it. It's only fifty bucks. If I don't like it, I can quit. Please?"

"Ran, for now, the answer is NO. But I'll look into it. I want to do some reading. I'll reconsider if it's warranted. I'll let you know what I find out."

After extensive research at the St. Louis County Library it was obvious to Son that Scientology was indeed a scam. In fact it was fraudulent, its claim of scientific removal of emotional blocks, called 'engrams', was pure hokum. They bring recruits, which they call "pre-clears," in for auditing sessions. From their own literature, they say that, "auditing is assisted by use of a religious artifact which helps the auditor to locate areas of spiritual distress or travail. This religious artifact is called an electro-psychometer. It is designed to

measure extremely low voltages and psyche. When the person holding the E-Meter electrodes (which look like a couple of beer cans) thinks a thought, looks at a picture, re-experiences an incident or shifts some part of the reactive mind, he is moving and changing actual mental mass and energy."[1]

Really?

Son had to admit that their business plan was clever. After attendance at a first level auditing session, acolytes are praised for their enthusiasm and insight. With such talent, they are told; they could go far in scientology, in fact, all the way to the top. But to do that, they will have to rid themselves of all those engrams. All that would be required would be attendance at a series of increasingly expensive auditing sessions. During these sessions participants would hold on to the "beer cans" which would be connected by wires to a metered black box. Eventually the acolyte would reach an emotional state called "clear" in which all en-grams would be removed. By that time they will have spent thousands of dollars. If they decide to quit, they and their family will be hounded. The "Church" will use any information that they may have collected to embarrass or blackmail the person.

Son concluded that The Church of Scientology was neither scientific nor religious in any traditional sense of those words. Neither could it be called psychotherapy, although they use some of the jargon of psychology. It was fraudulent, a financial and emotional rip-off.[2] Now, he would have to tell Randy. He knew that he was in for a battle. Although it frustrated him that Arretta was in Phoenix, in this case it was probably a good thing. If she were at home Son would have to deal with both of them. Arretta would use all her skills of manipulation to make him look like a bull-headed ape in his son's eyes. In any case, he wasn't looking forward to what he knew would be a confrontation.

"Ran, I've researched Scientology at the library and it hasn't changed my earlier conclusion. In fact, it has reinforced it. I simply can't allow you to get involved with them. More than that, I am going to talk to Dr. Al. Burr, your school superintendent, and tell him that I plan to file a formal complaint against Melba James."

"Aw, Dad, you're wrong. Scientology is straight-arrow! And please, don't get Melba in trouble. She doesn't deserve it!"

"We'll see what she deserves. It's Burr's responsibility to deal with her. I want him to know that one of his teachers is going over the line in proselytizing her students." But my answer to you is NO. I cannot allow you to get involved."

"Dad, this is spiritual. It's religious, and that's something I need. Because we've moved so often while you were in the Air Force, you've never given me a chance to learn anything about God. Mom can't help me and you won't! What can be wrong with me wanting to learn about religion and the spirit?"

Randal had a point. Son knew that the tempestuous relationship that he had with Randal's mother had impacted his son. He knew that his emotional development had suffered. Still, he was sure that Scientology was not the answer.

"No! That's it. End of discussion, Ran."

"Is it the money, Dad? If it is, I'll get the money on my own."

"No. It's certainly not the money. The answer is still NO!"

With that, Randal stomped out of the room, down the hall and into his bedroom. He slammed the door with enough force to rattle the windows. Within a minute he fired up his stereo, put on his record of "Ina Gadda Da Vida" by Iron Butterfly and turned up the volume all the way up. Son was sure the noise could be heard down the block. But he didn't tell his son to turn it down. He deserved the right to blow off his anger.

Son called the administrative office of Parkway West and asked for an appointment to see Dr. Burr. The secretary asked what the purpose of my appointment would be.

"It's a matter involving my son and one of his teachers."

The next morning at 9:00 a.m. Son walked into Dr. Burr's office. Dr. Burr was personable and very friendly, easy to talk with.

"Yes, Mr. Son. Please sit down. What can I do for you?"

"Thanks for seeing me, Dr. Burr. I'll get right to the point. I want to report a problem with one of your teachers. She is proselytizing, trying to get some of her students, including my son Randal, to get involved with the Church of Scientology. I know from what my son has told me that she has approached at least one other student besides my son. I hope you will agree with me, this is a flagrant violation of her role."

"Mr. Son, are you sure?"

"Most certainly. Randal has asked my permission to attend a beginner's class, they call it auditing, at the so-called Church. It is located on Lindell Boulevard downtown. I asked him where he had heard about Scientology and he told me that Ms. James had talked about it to him and several other members of her biology class. I told him that on the face of it I did not approve, but that I would research it and if I found reason to change my mind I would do so. However, the more I read about it, the more certain I became that my original stand was correct. Even if I approved of Scientology, however, I cannot agree with Ms James' usurpation. Her job is to teach biology."

"You said that your son told you that Ms. James had approached another student. Could you give me his name?"

"My son told me that his close friend, Dale Greenwood, also wants to get involved. He also told me that Dale's parents did not object. There may be other students involved, but I don't know this. I emphasize that this is only what my son told me. While I have no reason to doubt him, I do not have first hand knowledge."

"What you have told me is disturbing, Mr. Son. Of course, I will talk to Ms. James."

"Based on what I have told you, Dr. Burr, what is your position on this?"

"I believe that teachers need to be careful in what they say to students outside of their subject areas. I won't say that Ms. James shouldn't talk to students about anything outside of biology. She is, after all, a teacher, and to some degree should be a role model. However, I think that such things as ethics and religion, particularly if proselytizing for a particular sect is involved, should be off limits."

"Thank you. I appreciate your thoughts. I hate to intervene in this way, Dr. Burr. But I cannot abide what Ms. James is doing. I feel that I had to tell you."

"Rest assured, I will talk with Ms. James and I will get back to you with a report and my decision on corrective action."

"Thank you again. I will be waiting to hear from you."

With that, Son left Dr. Burr's office. He felt badly. This was not a win-win situation for anyone - not Randal, not Ms. James, Parkway High School or Son. Randal was in a blue funk for several days after. Son didn't try to talk to him anymore about it. He had already said what he had to say on the subject, and wasn't about to change his mind.

Days later, Son received a call from Dr. Burr. He said that after talking with Ms. James, he had concluded that she was indeed recruiting for Scientology. He told her that this behavior was a gross violation of her trust and that he would have to ask for her resignation. She left at the end of the semester. Years later, Son learned that she went deeper into Scientology, working at the "Church" full time and going for advanced levels of training. But she became disenchanted and tried to quit. The Church would not let her go, saying that she owed them a lot of money for the training she had received and that the only way she could discharge that debt would be to "work" it off. Eventually, after a lot of struggle, she did break free. She publicly denounced Scientology as a fraudulent scam. Son understands that years later she was reinstated by Parkway and resumed her teaching career.

Son hated the struggle that he had to go through with Randal. It depressed him. It made him question himself as a father. What could he have done to avoid the confrontation

that was forced upon him? In the short term there was probably nothing that he could have done short of caving in and giving his son his way. He was certain that this would have been a mistake. But perhaps there were things he could have done over the long term to have developed a closer relationship with his son. He was proud of Ran, proud of his talents, intelligence and academic achievements. He tried to encourage him at every opportunity. But was that enough? Maybe he fell short in just "hanging out," talking to him at his emotional level. Son thought that sometimes he related too much to Randal at an adult level. Maybe the high expectations that he had for and that he communicated to Ran put too much pressure on him. Maybe he should have just let him be a boy. Also, Son questioned the fact that Ran had not been exposed to any kind of religious training. There were reasons for that but the fact remained. The problem was further exacerbated by the dysfunctional relationship between Son and Arretta. When the three of them were together it was difficult for Son to maintain a close and stable relationship with Randal. Arretta was always part of the equation, and rarely if ever in a supportive way. Whenever Son attempted to talk to Arretta about this he got denial, pouting and a continuation of the same victim/persecutor/rescuer dynamic. When Arretta got back from Phoenix, Son told himself that he was going to have to bring this issue to a head. More combat. There were other problems with Randal and his girl friend, Debbie. For reasons of privacy, he will not go into them here. Suffice to say, however, they were serious. Herman was left to deal with them without his wife and Randal's mother. She was absent without leave. He hated it!

CHAPTER 78
Operation Bootstrap

Son felt stressed by the craziness of his family situation and his troubles with Arretta. Now there were problems at his job that also concerned him. He talked periodically with his boss, Bob Barclay, about trying a different strategy to affect change in managerial styles at MAC. He wanted to try at least a pilot program using the techniques of team building. Bob continued to say no, saying that starting such a program would be like throwing a cherry bomb into a henhouse.

Still searching for some way to be more effective, Son and his two assistants came up with a program to help upper level management identify their potential successors. Son found out that there were absolutely no formal plans or programs to identify "comers" and to groom them for promotional succession. In almost every case divisional vice presidents had been in their jobs for twenty or more years. "What would happen," Son asked, "if the vice president for manufacturing dropped dead of a heart attack? Do we know who would replace him? What knowledge or skills would he need to be able to step in and take over?"

"To be honest," said Bob, "we have no idea, at least not on paper."

"Don't you think we should have some idea?"

"Definitely."

"I'd like to put together a program that works with divisional VPs to identify one or more people in their divisions that have promotion potential. That would be step number one. Step two would be to develop a job profile for the VPs job, in terms of knowledge, skills and experience. Step three would be to assess candidates to determine their knowledge and skill levels and to identify gaps in their profiles that need to be addressed in order to prepare them for promotion. Step four would be to develop tailor made programs for each candidate that would aim to give the candidates the requisites for promotion. In other words, why not grow our own talent so that when the need arises knowledge and skills to fill the need will be available?"

"I think I could sell something like that. Why don't you, George and Don get to work on it and see what you can come up with? I'll be glad to interface with the VPs when we get to the point where we need to get them involved."

They went to work on designing the program. The more they got into it, the more excited they became. Short of being able to do team building, this offered some potential to affect change in the organization. It would be slow, working with individual managers, but if division VPs bought into it, it could work.

Meanwhile, a lot of things were going on at MAC. From its inception, McDonnell Aircraft was a frugally run company. Mr. Mac, as he was affectionately called, was a practicing Scotsman, tight fisted with a dollar. That fact, combined with lucrative contracts with the

Navy and Air Force for its successful fighters, pushed cash balances ever upward. This was not the case with some other airplane and defense contractors. Douglas Aircraft, based in Long Beach, CA, was a case in point. Douglas was a completely different company. First, MAC was a captive supplier to a captive customer, the Department of Defense, supplying 100% military product. Fixed price or cost plus contracts, negotiated with DoD, were the rule. Douglas, on the other hand, had many customers, each with unique needs. While they did sell to the military, their product mix was loaded toward civilian product. In their civilian product line they had many competitiors. This, plus the nature of their multiple markets, placed a premium on flexibility, fast reaction time and "sharp pencil" negotiation for contracts. Profit margins were slim. Whereas an organizational chart at MAC looked like a tall pine tree with seven or eight layers from top to bottom, Douglas' chart was flat, with no more than three layers from top to bottom. Critical decision making was pushed down, in some cases, to the sales executive who interfaced with the customer. The culture in the two companies could not have been more different. MAC was astute, rigid and by the numbers. Douglas was, in the words of one MAC executive, "loosey-goosey." In summary, MAC was an engineering oriented company. Douglas was a marketing oriented company. Those simple facts determined their quite different cultures.

Could an effective marriage be arranged between these two vastly different companies? Maybe. MAC held the whip hand with its large bank account. Douglas was skating on the edge of bankruptcy. Certainly, Douglas could use MAC's cash. But could they be happy in tandem? Long story short, they did merge. Actually, MAC bought Douglas. Thus began a long, sometimes tempestuous relationship. MAC's cash came with strings. The "strings" were in the form of demands that Douglas get its fiscal house in order. That was, apparently, no small order. The pulling and hauling between the two companies continues. However, the development of a strong corporate headquarters, has over the years, smoothed the edges of most conflicts.

In the meantime, Herman, George and Don continued to work on their manager development program, now called, "Operation Bootstrap." Don Wylan took charge of it and began step one: contacting divisional VPs to obtain a list of potential candidates.

While this was going on , they continued to run MAC and First Line Supervisor seminars. There was no doubt that they were busy. By now, since Son had joined the company, his department had provided training to nearly 3,000 people. The question in Son's mind, however, was how effective were they, really? He wondered when he thought of the nickname that MAC people used in referring to his department and its seminars: they called it "charm school." "We teach 'em how to be charming, but do we teach them how to run the company? I wonder?"

CHAPTER 79
A Downward Spiral

Just before school was out in the spring of 1969, Arretta wrote that she wanted Randal to join her in Phoenix. Ran said he would like to go so Son, still upset over his battle with Ran over Scientology, said "Yes, go ahead." Ran flew out to Phoenix to spend the summer. During the ensuing two months Son received one short, perfunctory letter from Arretta. He wrote back, asking Arreta when she would be coming back to St. Louis. In response, she called and shocked Son with a proposal that Randal stay in Phoenix. She said that her father was still ill and needed her presence. She missed Randy, she said. He could enroll for his senior year there and there'd be no need for him to come back to St. Louis. Son thought back to the argument they had had years before when he was in Japan and Arretta didn't want to come to join him.

"No! This has got to stop. Do you really expect me to agree with that! That's not right for any of us. You are, presumably, my wife. I refuse to conduct my marriage by mail or long distance. It's not right for Ran either. He's doing well in school here. He has friends. To uproot him again and put him in a school of strangers for his senior year would not be fair to him. I want you to come home. Now."

There was something in Son's upbringing that wouldn't let him admit that his marriage was a failure. He believed that divorce, if not a sin, represented a moral failure, and that it could be avoided in all but the most extreme cases. Both he and Arretta had invested half their lives at that point in their marriage. Even though there were problems, also there was joy and accomplishment. They had two children whom they had watched as they grew and matured. They had mutual experiences and memories of places they had lived and traveled to see. They had memories that would last the rest of their lives. But that was over balanced by the increasingly dysfunctional nature of their current relationship. Son felt that Arretta wasn't playing it straight with him. It kept him in a perpetual stage of anger and frustration. Her continuing agoraphobia made daily life difficult.

While tending to her father's needs, Arretta had mentioned Bob Bachman, whom she had dated when she was in high school. Bob was married and had three children by his wife, Ethel. At least that is what Arretta told him. Still, Bob had come at Arretta's request to fix a leak in their washing machine, to cut the grass and perform other chores. Son wouldn't have wondered about it, except in the context of his own unhappy relationship with Arretta. Still, he didn't accuse Arretta of any impropriety.

Reluctantly, she agreed. But back in St. Louis, she was like a wild bird in a cage, letting Son know by word and deed that she was unhappy, didn't like St. Louis, or for that matter, her husband. By now, Son wondered what was going on in Phoenix.

"Perhaps," thought Son, "I should give it one more chance. I won't give up! This time, I'm going to put the monkey on Arretta's back. I'm going to tell her that her unhappiness is her own fault, that it is the result of conscious decisions that she has made, and that she can change that if she so decides."

It didn't work. Every time Son pressured her to take more personal responsibility for her own happiness it resulted in another fight and ensuing days of silence between them. By now, Ran was well into his senior year at Parkway West High School. After surveying his options for college he decided that he wanted to go to Whitman College in Walla Walla, Washington. It certainly met all the academic as well as social characteristics that he wanted. He wrote Whitman, saying that he accepted their invitation to enroll in their freshman class in September. Ran began planning what he wanted to take with him. After some discussion it was decided that Son would rent a motor home and that they would combine a vacation with taking Randal to Whitman and dropping him off. After dropping Ran off at Whitman, Herman and Arretta would be alone together for the first time since Mary-Lynn was born. It would feel strange to focus on each other without any third parties.

"How will it work out?" Son wondered.

They drove east out of Washington into some of the most gorgeous country in America. From Kalispell, MT they climbed up north up the Sunrise Road. Herman snaked the big 28-foot Avro motor home around switchback turns all the way to the top, then over into Canada. They headed north to Calgary and from there turned west toward Vancouver, passing through Lake Louise. If anything competes with the American Rockies it is the Canadian Rockies. The scenery was awesome, so much so that Arretta almost forgot to hold onto her game face. Son tried to keep the conversation light and focused on the experience of the trip. It worked to a point. Arriving in Vancouver, they visited the beautiful formal gardens and bell towers there, and then took the ferry across to the U.S., landing at the point of the Olympic Peninsula. This area receives the highest annual rainfall of any place in the United States. The huge pine trees reflect this climatic profligacy. They soar hundreds of feet into the air and rival the California Redwoods in size. They did enjoy the experience, driving through the big trees, the dappled sunlight filtering through the overhanging branches, flashing bright and shadow onto their motor home. They drove south into Oregon and thence east through the Columbia River Gorge; there was more stupendous scenery. Out of Oregon, however, the country became less spectacular. Into Idaho and then Utah, it became arid and just one big, long interstate highway. The conversation faltered. Son turned on the radio, trying to find some upbeat music. But the freeze had set in. Arretta all but quit talking. She would respond to direct questions with one or two word answers, but that was about it. In retrospect, Son believes that she was planning then how she was going to ask for a divorce. It took another four months to come to fruition, but he was convinced that the planning started there. Arretta felt that now that the nest was empty there was no reason to keep the marriage together. Perhaps she was right.

CHAPTER 80
Adult Onset What???

After they arrived back in St. Louis, Son turned in the motor home, retrieved their two shelties from the kennel and went back to work. In some ways it was a relief. When he and Arretta were together the hostility between them was palpable. They made it through Christmas, though it wasn't much of a holiday. About this time, Son noticed that he was losing weight for no apparent reason. In fact he thought that he should be gaining, not losing. He had developed a sweet tooth. Every night before he would go to bed he would fix himself a big bowl of ice cream and top it off with syrup and/or nuts. He recognized much later that he was eating for emotional reasons. Ice cream was comfort food. When he first started to lose weight, however, he thought that perhaps his regular jogging stints were causing the weight loss. Again, he used the running as a way to compensate for stress and anger. When the pressure in his emotional boiler built up to a point, he would put on his running shoes and shorts and head out of the house. He would run until he was near exhaustion, returning home wet with sweat but with the anger dissipated.

"So what's going on?" Son thought. At this stage of his life, being only 48 years old and not having experienced any significant illness, he assumed that he was still the invulnerable fighter pilot. He put the thought that maybe there was something amiss out of his mind. It couldn't happen to him. Could it?

The problem didn't go away. He continued with his nightly bowl of ice cream. He noticed, however, that he was thirsty, even though he was consuming copious amounts of water. This was balanced by frequent urination. Still, Son kept his head in the sand. Finally, one morning he got up, went to the bathroom and switched on the light. Looking into the mirror he thought at first that someone had smeared something its surface. He could see his face but it was blurred. He wiped the mirror with a towel but it was obvious that the distortion wasn't in the mirror. It was in his eyes! He couldn't see his face clearly! "What's wrong?"

The doctor only took a minute to give him a preliminary diagnosis. "Mr. Son, your symptoms are classic. You have adult onset diabetes."

"Is that like sugar diabetes?"

"Yes, it is sometimes called that. It means that your body isn't manufacturing enough insulin to take care of the glucose in your blood or that you have developed a resistance to your own insulin. Either way, it means that concentrations of glucose in your blood have risen to dangerous levels."

"What do we do about it?"

"You told me that you have been losing weight. You need to lose some more. I will give you a diet for that, probably about 1800 calories a day, and no ice cream with chocolate syrup!"

"O.K. Will that take care of it, or do I need to take shots or medicine?"

"I am going to put you on an oral medication called Orinase. It is a pill that you take once a day. It will stimulate your pancreas to produce more insulin."

"What about my eyes, Doctor? I could hardly see well enough to drive here."

"I'll send you to an ophthalmologist for some temporary glasses. The problem with your eyes is caused by buildup of sugar crystals in the lenses of your eyes. Once we get your sugar back down your eyes should clear up."

"Wow! That's a relief."

"O.K., Mr. Son. Check back with me Wednesday and I'll have the results of your blood test, telling us how high your glucose levels were."

On Wednesday he called the doctor's office and found that his glucose number was over 500. Normal levels for a healthy non-diabetic should run from 80 to 120. That got Son's attention. He was determined to get that number down. For one thing, his eyes were driving him crazy. He had to get that cleared up!

The combination of diet, continued weight loss, exercise and medication worked. In a follow-up visit o his doctor, two weeks later, his blood sugar levels had fallen into the 130 range. At least, that's what a blood test showed on the day of his appointment. His doctor told him that the test number was encouraging. However, it represented only a snapshot; a single frame out of an entire movie. His appointment was just before lunch. The doctor said that his number would go up after a meal. A more accurate picture would be obtained by taking blood sugar readings two hours after each meal and to do it for a protracted period.

"That's the only way to get a true picture of how well you are doing."

"Well, I can't come in here three times per day. How can I check my sugar regularly?"

"You can use test strips to check for sugar in your urine. If your sugar gets over about 180, you will start to "spill" sugar in your kidneys and it will show up in a change in color from bright yellow to green on a test strip."

"But isn't a blood sugar of 180 too high? I thought you said that 80-120 was normal."

"Yes, that's right. But you may find it difficult to control your blood sugar levels that tightly. You are doing the right thing. Keep on your diet, exercise and medication and you'll probably do all right. Just use the test strips as an alarm bell. When color of the strip turns from yellow to green you will know that you have done something wrong. By the way, how are the glasses? Can you see any better?"

"Yes, a little. Things are still a little foggy though."

"Good. Just be patient. It should clear up entirely in a few weeks."

Son was learning the first elementary lessons about diabetes. The first lesson was that of acceptance. He had to get past the denial that he had in the beginning. Then he would have to learn how the disease presented itself in his body. He would find that it changed continuously in response to several variables such as the types and amounts of food he ate, the amount and types of exercise that he did, his medications and stress. He found that stress, particularly anger, would cause his sugar levels to rise, sometimes steeply. It was the beginning of a life-long process of learning; about his body and about the physiology and the psychology of his disease. As his doctor had advised, his vision gradually returned to normal and he was able to throw away his glasses.

Arretta's attitude about his diabetes was one of detached disinterest. When Son told her about it she didn't seem concerned or worried. He thought that was rather strange.

One day an interesting catalog, published by the community college, arrived in the mail. It contained a compilation of adult education course offerings. All were non-credit,

no exam kinds of courses, interesting but not particularly challenging from an academic point of view. A couple of art courses caught Son's eye. As he read the course descriptions he thought that they would be just right for Arretta. They would offer an opportunity for her to get out of the house, mingle with other adults who had a common interest and at the same time learn something that she would find useful in her artistic pursuits. The classes would meet at Parkway West, less than a mile from their house. Son thought, "I've got to convince her to take some of these things. She has the talent and this would give her a chance to display it in a non-competitive environment."

"Arretta, look at what came in today's mail. The community college is offering adult classes this summer, meeting at the high school. They have some courses that would be right down your alley. Look!"

He handed the catalog, with the art courses highlighted. She looked at them for a couple of minutes while Son looked at her, searching for some sign of reaction. After she read the descriptions she looked at Son with raised eyebrows as if to say, "So? Why do you think I would be interested?"

"I think you ought to sign up for either one or both of these courses. You'd enjoy them I know. You'd be right in your element. There are no exams to worry about. Why don't you call Leslie Herzog and ask her about it?"

"Oh, all right. I'll call Leslie. But I'm not promising to go."

Son dropped the subject, but a few days later Arretta said that she had talked to Leslie and that she had decided to try the course in art history.

"That's great, Arretta! I know you will enjoy it. When does it start?'

"July 15, for six weeks. It meets twice a week for a total of twelve times."

"O.K. I'll take you and pick you up so you won't have to worry about driving."

Son was elated. He thought that something like the adult programs offered by the community college would in the long run be more beneficial to Arretta than continued sessions with Dr. Abrahamson.

Son came home from work on the afternoon of the 15th, excited and ready to take Arretta to her first class. It started at 7:00 P.M.. As they sat down to dinner, Arretta was obviously nervous. He could understand that. He tried to handle it matter-of-factly. As they got up from the table, he told her that he would get out of his work clothes and be ready to drive her to the school in a few minutes.

"I've decided that I can't go."

"What! We've been talking about this for weeks. You talked to Leslie. You know it would be good for you, don't you?"

"It won't be good for me if I panic, and that's what I'll do, I know it!"

"You've decided ahead of time that you're going to panic! Why don't you decide instead that you will be relaxed and that you will have a good time? Picture yourself having a good time."

"It won't work. I'm not going that's all." She walked out of the kitchen and sat down on the couch in the family room. Son followed her, his anger rising, the muscles in his jaw flexing. He kept his voice down but it was full of pent up emotion.

"Arretta, I have run out of patience with you. During all these years, I have tried to understand you and your problems. I know that they have deep roots, and that much of your behavior is beyond your control. I find that hard to understand but I have accepted it. I think you know that. In fact, I think that you know that you can con me, make me do your bidding. I don't think that you've been honest with your doctors either. Well, I'm fed up! No more! No one can take charge of your life but you, and either you're not capable of doing it or you won't do it! Either way is unacceptable to me. I think you are an emotional slob! I can't go on living this way. Here we are, in the prime of our lives. Mary-Lynn is married and Randy is going to college. Our children have left our house. We have a full and I think

exciting life ahead of us. It's there for the taking, but if we don't take it whose fault is that?" Where you're concerned, I sometimes feel like I'm carrying a 300 pound sack of wet cement on my shoulders. I can't carry it any longer!"

Arretta sat on the couch in silence, her face a frozen mask. What was she thinking? What was she feeling? It was hard to tell, but this evening, Son didn't care. He went into the bedroom, changed to his running shorts and shoes and walked out into the street to jog: "one two, inhale, three, four five, exhale. Now, running gradually faster, he turned left down Clayton Road. That night he ran for 5 miles, coming home exhausted, physically and emotionally. He found Arretta, sitting up in bed, reading a paperback novel and smoking a cigarette. She had gone into a profound pout. She and Son did not talk to one another for several days. One thing was obvious. Their marriage, such as it was, was on the rocks. They both withdrew from each other. Son could not extend himself emotionally to his wife. It was too painful. Perhaps the same could be said of Arretta. This sorry state of affairs lasted until the following January, 1971 when Arretta announced that she had to go to Phoenix. Again, her father's emphysema had taken a turn for the worse, she said, and she had to be there. Son was left alone. Since he couldn't take care of the shelties, he called the breeder who offered to take them back and refund what Son had paid for them. 507 Rue Montand had turned from a home into just an address. Son went there every evening, to have something to eat, usually a frozen TV dinner. When that got tiresome, he would go out for a pizza or a hamburger. It was a lonely time for Son. Some of the time, he wished Arretta would come back. Some of the time he wished she wouldn't. He talked to her a couple of times by telephone, but the conversations were stiff, almost as if he were talking to a stranger. January crawled into February. Finally, on a Saturday morning, in early March it happened. The door bell rang. Son went to the front door and opened it. A strange man stood there with an envelope in his hand.

"Mr Son?"

"Yes?"

"This is for you. Please sign here," he said, as he gave Son the letter and a clipboard with a receipt form attached.

"Thank you."

Son closed the door, went back into the kitchen and sat down with the letter. He knew what it was before he opened it. It was legal notice from Arretta of her intent to file for divorce. An hour later, the mailman came. Son went to the box to retrieve the mail - a couple of bills, some junk mail and a letter from Arretta. In it she said that she hoped that Son would get the letter before getting notice from her attorney. Why she hoped that Son was at a loss to understand. However, she said that she had decided that she couldn't go on any longer and had therefore decided to contact an attorney. Mr. Larry Carp, she said would be contacting you shortly. She also said that her attorney had instructed her not to talk directly with Son, that all communications with her were suspended except through her attorney. Great.

Well, there it was; 28 years of effort, toil and trouble, ups and downs, hopes, joy, hurt and sadness, the stuff of life, Son guessed - all thrown in the trashcan. How did he feel? He didn't know. He was numb for the moment. What should he do next? Should he attempt to call her attorney, Carp? (Son thought what a loathsome and somehow appropriate name for a divorce attorney - a carp, a bottom feeding fish that frequents the muddy waters of the Mississippi). Over the weekend Son had time to think about it. What should he do? Should he contact Carp or should he get his own attorney?

The following Monday, Son went to work, still wondering what he should do. He sleepwalked through the day, somehow getting through it until five o'clock. Pulling out of the MAC parking lot, he headed south on Lindberg Boulevard, still thinking about every-

thing, his mind a jumble of thoughts and feelings. At the intersection of Lindberg and Clayton Road he eased into the right turn lane and waited for the light.

"I think I need a drink," he thought, as the light turned green. On the right side of the street about a hundred yards past the intersection was The Cupboard, then a famous Clayton watering hole. Son parked and walked into the bar. It was quiet at that time of the day, only a couple of customers seated at the bar. Son picked a stool, sat down and ordered a martini.

"Up with olives, please."

"You bet, general!"

All Son wanted to do was to sit quietly, relax a bit and think. He had taken a couple of sips of his drink when someone slid onto the stool immediately to his left.

"I see you are a martini man."

Son didn't really want to talk, but he acknowledged the stranger.

"Yeah."

"I'm a bourbon man myself. Just came from the court house. Need a couple of belts to relax after a day in court."

"You are a lawyer?"

"Yep."

"What kind?" Under the circumstances, he was mildly interested.

"Divorce. Just represented a guy whose ex was trying to roll him."

"Really? How do you defend somebody in a situation like that?"

"Well, it's kind of complicated, but you have to prove to the judge that either your client can't afford it or that the other party's claims are unjustified."

"Well, sure. I guess so." Son looked at the guy carefully. He was well dressed, wearing an expensive suit, crisp white shirt and conservative tie. He even noted that his shoes were shined. Then he ventured, "I don't know if I need a lawyer or not, but I just found out that my wife is suing me for divorce. I don't really want any legal battles. I just want to get it over with a minimum of legal pulling and hauling. I thought maybe I could just let the attorney that my wife retained handle the whole thing. Would that be wise?"

"No, it would not. I didn't get your name. My name is Herb Williams. Here's my card."

"Herman Son. Yeah, that's right, S-O-N. I know that's a weird last name."

"Well, it's easy to remember, anyway. But let me tell you, it would be a major mistake to let your wife's attorney handle everything. That would be letting the fox into the henhouse, Herman. By the way, who is your wife's attorney?"

"Larry Carp, I believe his name is. He has offices here in Clayton."

"Sure. I know Larry. He's a good attorney. You can be sure that he'll get everything he can for your wife That is why you need someone to represent you."

"Well, you say that you specialize in divorce. Would you consider representing me?"

"Of course I would."

That is how it began. Herman told Herb - by now they were on a first name basis - that he was a babe in the woods when it came to legal matters, so he would be depending on him to keep him out of trouble. Herb said that they should get started right away on building Herman's case.

"I have an office here in Clayton, on Carondelet, but I work out of my home most of the time. Why don't we meet there, say, tomorrow around 9:30 A.M.? Could you make yourself available then?"

"For something this important, no problem. Where do you live?"

Herb gave Herman his address. He lived in a good neighborhood in Town & Country. Son found his address on a street map and arrived there the next morning promptly at 9:30 A.M.. He rang the door-bell a couple of times and waited. He rang the bell a third time and was about to decide that there was no one home when someone turned the deadbolt lock. The door opened, and there stood Herb in his bathrobe.

"Come in, Herman."

"Am I too early? You did say 9:30 didn't you?"

"Nah, no problem, Herman. I was up late with another client last night, so I'm a little slow this morning. Come on in. Let's sit down here at the kitchen table."

Son sat down. He had a small leather folder in which he carried some bank statements and stock account reports. He didn't know what kind of information Herb would need. Herb had excused himself for a minute, apparently to go to the bathroom. When he returned he reached into a kitchen cabinet and pulled down a bottle of Jack Black, (Jack Daniels, Black Label) produced a good-sized water glass and poured into the glass until it was about half full. He popped a couple of ice cubes into the glass and took a long slow swig.

"There! That's better, he said. "Now we can get to work. O.K., Herman. Why don't you tell me the problem? Who wants the divorce?"

"I guess my wife does. She's the one who brought legal action."

"Yes, but what's your attitude about it. Did you ask her to sue you?"

"Absolutely not. I know our marriage was in terrible shape, but I didn't want to give up. I still think that we could work it out. But it "takes two to tango" I guess."

"Right. What was the cause for the action? Did you bring the petition that was served?"

"Here it is. I guess it says that there were irreconcilable differences."

"That's standard. Now the first thing we have to do is to compile a listing of all of your assets - bank and stock accounts, real estate, automobiles and any other assets."

They worked for the next couple of hours as Herb examined papers that Son produced. Herb made detailed notes, stopping now and then for another swallow of Jack Black. Son was a little concerned about that. He was not naive nor was he a teetotaler, but Herb's consumption seemed a bit excessive. He would find out later just how excessive it was. Also, Son would conclude, much later, that he was in no emotional shape to make sound decisions about his divorce and its outcome. He didn't know it at the time, but he was in severe financial jeopardy.

Son also found out that the so-called "wheels of justice" grind at a glacial pace. Herb took the financial information that Herman provided and presented it to Carp in the form of a deposition. That simple step took a couple of weeks. Carp then responded with a proposed settlement in the form of specific stipulations. Herb and Herman went over Arretta's proposal.. It was out of the question. She wanted all the proceeds from the sale of the house, half of the market value of their jointly owned stocks and half of all cash balances in bank accounts. She also wanted ownership of all of Son's life insurance, with Randal being specified as primary beneficiary in the event of Son's death. Son didn't object to Ran being named beneficiary as long as he was in college. That would insure that funds for him to complete college would be there in the event of Son's demise. He didn't like the idea of insurance policy ownership in Arretta's name, however. He hadn't even thought about it until the issue came up, but what would happen if he ever got married again? He would have no insurance. He and Herb discussed this and other items in the stipulations presented by Carp. Eventually, they went back with a counter proposal. This back and forth negotiation went on for a couple of months. At times, Son felt like he was getting rolled. He and Arretta too had worked hard to save and invest over the years and they had accumulated a modest nest egg. It looked as though this nest egg was about to be smashed. What Arretta didn't get the lawyers would. Son, of course, had to pay both lawyers. He was getting depressed over the whole thing. Truly, he did suffer from a situational depression. It was hard for him to sleep. He would doze off, sleep fitfully for perhaps an hour and then wake up. His brain would start rehashing all kinds of things: It was his fault; he should have been more understanding. He wondered what was going on in Phoenix with Bob Bachman? Did he do the right thing in hiring Williams as his attorney? At times he felt like

just giving up, telling Williams to give Arretta whatever she wanted. He just wanted the whole thing to be over.

In the middle of this legal scrum, Son came home one afternoon, and as he got out of his car and entered the house through the garage entry he heard the telephone ringing. He picked up the phone. There was a woman's voice on the line.

"Is Mrs. Son there?"

"No, she isn't here."

"Do you know when she will be home? I'd like to talk with her."

"I doubt that she will ever be here again."

"Really!" Her voice brightened. "I hope nothing has happened to her."

"Well, not exactly. We are in the process of getting a divorce. Mrs. Son is in Phoenix, and will probably be there until we get a court date. I don't know when that may be. May I ask, who is calling?"

"This is Leslie Herzog. I'm with the St. Louis County Artists' Association. I met you briefly at our last show."

"Oh sure, Leslie. I remember. I'm sorry. I didn't recognize your voice. Well, I could try to get a message to her, although that might be difficult. I have been constrained by my attorney from talking directly to Arretta during the divorce proceedings."

"Oh, I know! It must be very painful. I have a friend whose husband divorced her some years ago, and I know from what she told me that it was a sad thing to have to go through. But you know what? She got through it and now I think she feels that it all happened for the best. You will too, I'm sure."

"Well, thanks you for those thoughts. Right now, I don't feel very positive."

"Come to think of it, this friend of mine is a wonderful woman - smart, attractive, unattached and very outgoing. She's about your age, maybe a little younger. I could put you in touch with her if you'd be inclined."

"Oh, thanks, Leslie. I don't think so. Right now I'm not interested in dating."

"I understand. But I think you'll feel differently in a month or so. I'd really like for you to meet this woman, because I know you wouldn't be sorry. Could I call you in about a month?"

"I guess that would be O.K.," Son said reluctantly.

"I'll be in touch, Herman. Bye!"

Son hung up the phone, thinking "That's probably the last I'll hear from her." But a month later she called again.

CHAPTER 81
The Sons Go To Court

By the end of April 1972, Son vs. Son was ready to go to court. Their two attorneys had worked out the detailed stipulations of their divorce agreement. Financially, Son felt as if he had given away the store. Emotionally, he was also spent. He had almost reached the point of not caring - almost, but not quite. He had given Arretta almost everything she wanted in the way of assets and he had agreed to pay her $800 per month (in 1972 dollars) per month, half of it alimony and half child support. The child support was to run until Randal graduated from college. He had given up ownership of his insurance policies, although he would continue to pay the premiums on them. Their court date was set for Wednesday, May 15, 1972.

On Monday of the week that they were due in court, Arretta, accompanied by their daughter, Mary-Lynn, flew from Phoenix to St. Louis and registered to stay at the Holiday Inn in Clayton. Arretta called Herman in the afternoon and arranged to meet him at their house on Tuesday. Son waited for them to arrive, feeling like he was going to the Operating Room to have part of him removed, not just the physical but the emotional as well. Son wondered if there was an anesthetic for this kind of operation. When they arrived in a rental car, Son went to the door to let them in. They had not spoken to each other for nearly six months. Arretta was conciliatory, offering a kiss and a hug. Son responded with a strange admixture of feelings. Much to his disgust, he still felt the old physical attraction. At the same time, however, he felt distrust. It would never be the same. The kiss and hug were truncated and perfunctory.

"Sonny! You know I couldn't talk to you. My attorney. . . "

"Yeah, I know. So now what? You want to go through the house and pick out the items of furniture that you want to tag for shipment to Phoenix, is that it?"

"Yes."

Mary-Lynn was protective and somewhat apologetic. "Dad, you know I came just to give Mom some help and moral support?"

"Sure." Son thought. "Where's my moral support? Since I'm the bad guy, I guess I don't need any, huh?"

Arretta took most of the furniture, particularly in the living room and master bedroom. She took the dining room set, including the breakfront, dining room table and chairs. Basically, she left Son with a family room couch and a bed in which to sleep. Well, that was what they had agreed to, wasn't it?

They agreed to have dinner together at the hotel. Now that they were about to be divorced Arretta could apparently dine in a public place without panic. In fact, she seemed poised and relaxed. Her demons were apparently asleep. "Strange," thought Son.

Son asked her where she planned to live. After all, he had had no contact with her for months. "I've rented an apartment in Glendale. It's near the folk's house on Rovey. Bob is going to help me move in when the furniture arrives."

"That's nice," said Son, thinking about Bob. Ironic, but she still has to have a man to keep her afloat, doesn't she? He didn't want to get into that issue with Mary-Lynn there so he let it drop.

"This is all for the best," said Arretta. "We both need our freedom, and as Mary-Lynn has said, we are our own worst enemies."

"If you say so. I'll be listing the house next week. I've talked to an Ira Berry agent, who is going to come out and give me a market analysis. I guess I'll list it for whatever she thinks is appropriate unless you have some other idea."

"No, of course not. I guess just do whatever she suggests."

"That's what I plan to do."

The waiter came with the check for dinner. Son took out his wallet and started to pay. Arretta said, "Let me sign for it. We'll just put it on the room."

"O.K. That will be all right."

"Ah, such social grace," thought Son. "Is this the same woman who was my wife for 28 years?"

They said goodnight, and Son took his leave. "Well, to coin a phrase, "I'll see you in court!"

"Goodnight, Sonny."

This time there was no hug and kiss. It was just as well.

On Wednesday morning Son arrived in court and saw his attorney, already seated at the defense table. He sat next to him. Arretta and her attorney, Larry Carp, had not yet arrived.

In a few minutes, Arretta, accompanied by Carp, entered the courtroom and made their way to the plaintiff's table. The judge came in and seated himself behind his desk and the proceeding began. Son doesn't remember much of the details. It is something that he has mostly blocked from his memory. Arretta took the witness chair, and under Carp's questioning, established the basic facts, identifying herself as the aggrieved party and that she was asking the court to grant a divorce on the grounds of irreconcilable differences from her husband, Herman. The words ran together — blah, blah, blah. The judge asked the defense table for its response. Mr. Williams stood and said that there were no objections. It was over, almost before it began.

The next day, Mary-Lynn caught her flight for San Francisco. Herman had agreed to take Arretta to the airport for her flight back to Phoenix, for the last time. As the time came for boarding, they stood at the gate. They embraced for the last time and Son said goodbye to his ex-wife. His chin trembled. He couldn't help it. He watched as the 727 backed away from its gate. That was it. Goodbye.

Feelings of depression that night almost overwhelmed him. He felt like crying, but there were no tears. He slept fitfully, waking the next morning to an empty house. Maybe getting back to his work at MAC would help him snap out if it.

The next couple of weeks passed routinely. Work gave some structure to his life, eight to five. After that there wasn't much to focus his attention until the telephone rang:

CHAPTER 82
A New Life Begins

"Hi, Herman, this is Leslie! How are you?"

"Well, I guess. Our divorce was finalized a couple of weeks ago and I was pretty bummed out. I'm feeling a little better now."

"Good! You remember I told you about this wonderful friend of mine that I want you to meet? Well, I'd like to give you her name and telephone number and ask you to call her. I know you'd be delighted to meet her."

"You are some sales lady! I don't know, I guess I couldn't lose though, could I?"

"Certainly not, Herman! I think you will find that you have a lot in common. She loves music, she has three children. Her son is her youngest, a senior in high school. Her two older daughters are married. Most importantly, she is so outgoing and warm. I know you'd love her!"

"All-right Leslie! Who is she, and how do I contact her? Will she be expecting to hear from me, or is this a 'cold call'?"

"Oh, I'll tell her about you, don't worry! Her name is Marilyn Westlake. She's about 5' 1', blonde and cute as can be! I'll give you her work number. She is a decorator, working at a Sherwin-Williams Paint Store in Creve Coeur. You can call her anytime during working hours, including Saturday. She'll be expecting to hear from you."

"O.K., Leslie. You are some kind of cupid!"

"Herman I know you'll hug me for this! Bye!"

The next day Son thought, "Am I getting myself into a mess that I'm going to regret? Can I trust Leslie? Am I emotionally on the rebound? Can I trust myself?" All these questions ran through his mind as he toyed with the telephone. Finally, he picked it up and dialed. He could hear it ringing.

"Sherwin-Williams! May I help you?" said a musical, feminine voice.

"Yes, thank you. Is Marilyn Westlake there?"

"Speaking, may I help you?"

"My name is Herman Son. I believe we have a mutual friend, Leslie Herzog, who suggested that I call you."

"Oh yes, I know Leslie. She told me a little about you, and that you might be calling. I understand that you have just been divorced."

"Yes. You may not want to bother with me. Maybe you'll consider me a therapy case. But if you're willing to take a chance, I'd like to meet you."

"Yeah, I don't know you, do I? I would be taking a chance."

"That's true. And I don't know you either. I guess we'd both be taking a chance, wouldn't we?"

"I suppose so. Well, why don't you come into my store so I can get a look at you and you can get a look at me, and we can take it from there?"

"O.K. I guess I can find your store. You're located in Creve Coeur, right?"

"Yes. We're on North New Ballas Road, just south of Olive Boulevard."

Friday afternoon Son drove to the Sherwin-Williams store on North Ballas Road. There were a couple of customers in the store, one who was talking to the woman behind the counter. He looked at her closely. From Leslie's description he figured that she was Marilyn Westlake. Since she was busy it was natural for him to browse a bit. There were paint samples and wallpaper books and a display of paintbrushes to look at. As he busied himself checking the paintbrushes he was also busy checking her out.

" Not, bad at all," he thought. She seemed friendly in her interaction with the customer, but why wouldn't she. That was her job. He'd wait until he could speak with her directly. Finally the other two customers left. Son approached the counter:

"Marilyn?"

"Yes. Are you Herman?"

"Yes, I am. I'm glad to meet you, Marilyn."

After some small talk, Son decided to ask her for a date. "Marilyn, I'd like to get to know you better. How about a date for dinner, say, tomorrow night?"

"Yes, I would like to."

"Do you like Japanese food? I know a great restaurant in the Chase Park Plaza."

"Sure, that would be fine."

"O.K., how about 7:00. I'll pick you up at your home if that's agreeable, and if you will tell me where you live."

"That's fine."

"Well," Son thought, as he got back into his car and left Marilyn's store, "She's a pretty sharp gal; nice appearance, friendly and easy to talk to. I hope she didn't mind me spying on her in the store for a few minutes before I went up and introduced myself! So I've got a date for Sunday night dinner at the Mikado. I hope this will work out. The Mikado is supposed to be a nice place. It's bound to be good or it wouldn't be in the Chase Park Plaza. I haven't had a date in almost thirty years. I hope I'll know what to do. Should I bring her a gift? No, that would be ostentatious, I think. I'll just play it straight. How should I dress? Casual? Suit and/or tie? Think I'll just go for my grey flannel slacks and blue blazer with white shirt and tie. That would look nice Get your shoes shined and get a haircut. Get the car washed"

Son was excited. He had a real date!

Sunday evening Son drove past Marilyn's house quite early and without stopping, just to check it out and to make sure he wouldn't be late. "Hmmm, nice house, neat yard. This is Old Farm Estates. Don't know anything about it but the whole area looks nice. I'd guess the homes in here are in the $35 - $45 thousand price range. Know where it is now. I'll go get some gas and come back right at 7:00 on the dot."

He rang the doorbell. Marilyn answered promptly. She looked great and she was ready to go, tastefully dressed, her blonde hairdo was perfect as was her makeup. Nice perfume too, not too much!

Son said to himself, "Thank you, Leslie!"

On the way to the restaurant, Son asked, "Leslie tells me that you are interested in music. So am I! Tell me, what kind of music?"

"My parents were classical musicians, so naturally, I like classical. My father is a violinist. My mother plays the cello. Both played with the Toledo Symphony Orchestra and both taught privately. So, you see, I was immersed in Bach, Beethoven and Brahms. But I like almost any kind, as long as it's well done. I don't particularly like country, but other than that, count me in. I can't imagine a world without music. How about you?"

"Bingo! That's great, Marilyn. I, too, had classical music in my childhood. My mother wanted me to be a concert pianist. Nothing like aiming high, I guess! I did have twelve years of private piano, all classical. Like you, I grew up on Chopin, Litz, Rachmaninoff and Prokofiev. I made it to the National High School Music Contests a couple of years. My real musical love, though, is good jazz. I might be doing music professionally but for WWII, which gave me an opportunity to fly. That was great, but it interrupted my musical education. Leslie said that you sing. Tell me about that."

"I'm a Sweet Adeline, if you know what that is. I sing with a female barbershop chorus and I sing baritone with a quartet called the Impressions. You may be more familiar with the men's barbershop groups who belong to the Society for Preservation and Encouragement of Barbershop Quartet Singing in America! That's a mouthful, I know. But if you have ever heard a good barbershop chorus or quartet sing you'll know what I mean."

"Yes, I do know what you mean. I'm not too familiar with lady barbershoppers, but I'd like to know more."

"If you are serious, I'll take you to one of our chorus rehearsals."

"I'd like that."

They both spoke the common language of music. Son couldn't believe his good fortune. Arretta didn't dislike music, neither did she really appreciate it. Because of Mary-Lynn's interest in ballet, she was familiar with the musical accompaniment that went with the great works of ballet, but to her the music was secondary to the dance. Once the music went beyond the standard repertoire of ballet she lost interest. Not so, Son. Except for flying, the one thing that could command his attention and emotions was music. Marilyn said she liked all kinds. So did he. He remembered what Duke Ellington said,

"What is music to you? What would you be without music? Music is everything. Nature is music (cicadas in the tropical night). The sea is music, the wind is music. The rain drumming on the roof and the storm raging in the sky are music. Music is the oldest entity. The scope of music is immense and infinite. It is the 'esperanto' of the world."

Son didn't express this thought immediately to Marilyn. He didn't want to overplay his hand. He remembered a motto from his business training, particularly appropriate in selling situations: "K - I - S _ S - Keep it simple, stupid!"

"We meet in Kirkwood, at the Methodist church. We're getting ready for a big international competition next month to be held in Salt Lake City. As you probably know, rehearsals are not polished performances, but I could ask Betty Oliver, our director, if it would be all right for you to come."

"I wouldn't want to intrude."

"I'm sure it'd be O.K. I'll let you know."

"Great!"

CHAPTER 83
Some "Motherly" Advice

Stepping into the cool darkness of the Mikado, Son felt transported, almost as if he were in the restaurant in the Frank Lloyd Wright Hotel in Tokyo. Everything was understated. Teak and rice paper screens separated the reception area from the dining area. There were spare, almost symbolic watercolors of blue herons placed strategically on the walls. Son spoke to the matre d', who summoned a waitress, hair done tightly in a bun, her face powdered white and dressed in traditional silk kimono. She showed Son and his date to their table, secluded by the ever-present rice paper screens to afford privacy. Table? It was no more than a foot above the floor. The waitress asked them to take off their shoes. There was a pit under the table, affording room for diners to put their feet. They did take off their shoes. Then they sat down on cushions, putting their feet in the pit under the table.

"This is beautiful," exclaimed Marilyn. "Did you see those water colors when we came in?"

"Sure did. Also, did you notice the woven rice straw floor covering? Kind of made me feel at home - Japan that is. This is a beautiful place, isn't it? I hope that the food will be as good as the ambiance!" "STUPID!" thought Son. "Of course the food will be good! Why'd you have to make a remark like that! She'll think you've never been in a nice place like this!"

The waitress asked if they wanted tea. Yes, they did. It was green of course. She poured it, steaming, into small, shell thin cups from a small china teapot and left to return in moments with menus. Son recognized some of the items, but many he didn't. He knew the sukiyaki would be good.

"What looks good to you, Marilyn? Do you know anything about Japanese food?"

"Not really. They have a lot of fish dishes, don't they?"

"Yes, but I can't tell you much about them. I do know about sukiyaki. I've had that many times in Japan. It's pretty simple, but very good. The waitress prepares it in front of the diner, cooking it sometimes on a hibachi or charcoal stove. I don't know if they will use charcoal here or not. I doubt it for safety reasons. They'll probably use a sterno burner instead. It's a stir fry dish, really - thinly sliced beef, chopped green onions, mushrooms, squash or zucchini, tofu or bean curd, red pepper, sesame oil, soy sauce and sometimes a bit of sake or rice wine. It's served with rice, naturally. I think you would like that."

"Sounds good to me, Herman. Is that what you're going to have?"

"I think so. Would you like to try some sake to go with it? Very Japanese, you know?"

"It's not too strong, I hope?"

"Oh, no. It's made from rice and it's about the same as any kind of western wine."

The waitress came and took their orders. They both chose the sukiyaki. Son thought how lucky he was to be sitting there in that beautiful, intimate setting across that snowy

white tablecloth from such a beautiful and charming woman. Their conversation was easy and personal. Marilyn knew, of course, that Herman was newly divorced. On the other hand, it had been over four years since she and her first husband had divorced.

"What did you say your ex-wife's name was?"

"Arretta. That's a rather unusual name, isn't it?"

"Yes, I guess it is. She's in Phoenix now, I understand."

"That's right. She found an apartment near her folks home. But I really don't want to talk about her. I'd rather talk about you."

"I understand. But I have some "motherly" advice for you, Herman. You're just starting to date, and it's been a long time since you've been in that game, hasn't it?"

"Yes, I'd have to say so; almost 30 years."

"I know. I was married 24 years to my first husband. But I've been alone now for almost 5 years, and I can tell you a few things about the dating scene. Let me tell you that the woods are full of predatory females who are just looking for a handsome man like you! They'll be all over you, and if you're not careful you'll get swept off your feet before you realize it. Those women will all be sharpening their claws, just waiting for an opportunity to grab you! You're newly divorced and you are probably emotionally vulnerable. I don't say that as a criticism, just a fact based on my on experience. So, just be careful, O.K.?"

"Thank you for the compliment and thanks for the advice. I guess you're right. I probably am a sitting duck. One thing I know, though, is I don't want to get involved for a while. And above all, I don't want to repeat the mistake that I made in my first marriage."

" I didn't think I'd ever get divorced in my first marriage. We were married for 24 years and he left me for another woman with seven kids under twelve. I'll bet you thought you'd never get divorced either didn't you?"

"You are right. In part, that's the way I was brought up. My parents never divorced, and as far as I know they never even thought of it. One just didn't get divorced! Looking back on it, however, there were reasons why we couldn't stay together. I don't know why we were able to stay together as long as we did."

As they continued to talk, Herman felt himself relaxing. How did this woman do it? He had been so used to being guarded in talking to Arretta, always looking for the cross-up or booby trap in a conversation. Now in only a few minutes of talking with Marilyn, he felt completely at ease. "Careful," thought Son. "Don't get ahead of yourself. Just stay cool." Then he thought again. He wasn't being fair. She was open and transparent, and there was no reason that he couldn't be also. He didn't notice, of course, that Marilyn was secretly sharpening her claws, hidden from Son's view under the table. If she had an agenda, she certainly didn't divulge it.

As they continued to talk, the waitress returned with an assistant and set up the equipment for preparing their dinner. She lit the fire under the wok and added a small amount of oil. The meat and vegetables were attractively arranged on a large chop plate which she placed next to the wok. As the oil just started to smoke she added the thinly sliced beef, stirring it briefly until it turned from red to pink. Then she removed it and began adding the vegetables, one at a time while continuing to stir. She laced the veggie mixture with some soy sauce, a little sesame oil and a cup of sake. A cloud of fragrant steam arose from the wok.

"This is making me hungry," said Herman.

"Me too! It smells great, doesn't it?"

"Yep, you're going to enjoy this, I know."

While the vegetables were still crisp, she returned the seared meat to the wok and folded the whole mixture together. The dish was served on smaller chop plates decorated with Japanese motifs. Rice, kept warm in small, enameled, covered bowls, was served sepa-

rately. Another waitress brought the sake, kept warm in a small china bottle. She poured it into small, again, eggshell thin cups.

The waitresses bowed. One said something in Japanese.

Son said, "Well, I don't know how you say bon appetite in Japanese, but I know how to say thank you: Dom arigatto!" The waitresses smiled, almost tittered, and put their hands in front of their mouths. It's not polite to laugh with open mouth in formal conversation.

The waitresses bowed again and left, leaving Herman and Marilyn to enjoy their meal. "To our health and happiness," said Herman, as he raised his small cup of sake. Marilyn raised hers and they both took ceremonial sips. It was a wonderful meal that they both enjoyed.

Driving home, Herman turned west from Kingshighway to Highway 40. The lights of the city spread out before them. As they approached the Choteau overpass they could see an animated eagle, flying out of a huge, neon A, advertising the Anheuser-Busch brewery. It had been a St. Louis landmark for years.

"That's some sign, isn't it, Marilyn? I wonder how much electricity it takes to keep that eagle flying?"

"I don't have any idea," said Marilyn, laughing "but I'll bet it sells enough beer to pay for itself!"

"You're probably right. Between the brewery and the St. Louis Cardinals, Gussie Busch does well for himself, and St. Louis too, I guess. Do you follow the Cardinals?"

"Off and on. Toward the end of the season I do. I don't care for football. Guess I don't understand it, but I do love baseball."

"I think the Cards are in town next week, playing the Cubs or the Dodgers. I'm not sure which. Would you like to go to a game? I think they'll be playing at night."

"Oh, I'd enjoy that!"

"Let me check the schedule tomorrow and I'll call you at work. O.K.?"

"Sure."

"Great! She loves music and she likes baseball! Thank you again, Leslie!"

They pulled into the driveway at Marilyn's home, turned on the radio and tuned it to WSIE, the Edwardsville SIU FM station that played some nice jazz. At that moment a Duke Ellington arrangement of "Angel Eyes" was playing softly. They talked for several minutes and Marilyn said, "I'd better get in and get to bed. Have to work tomorrow, you know."

"Sure." Son got out of the car, went around and opened the door on Marilyn's side. At her front door he said, "Thank you for a wonderful evening, Marilyn. I really enjoyed being with you! May I give you a goodnight kiss?" With that, he bent over and kissed her, ever so expectantly. "Goodnight, Marilyn. I'll call you tomorrow."

"Goodnight, Herman. I enjoyed it too, very much."

"There is promise, there!" thought Son as he got into his car, turned the key in the ignition and slowly drove away. The next day, on the job at MAC, Son tried to concentrate on the details of his job, but his attention kept wandering. "Yes. There is promise there. She is one neat woman, so feminine, so poised, mannered and intelligent. She is so completely different from Arretta. I feel completely different around her. I don't feel that I have to be constantly on my guard. She's straight and completely open. I have to find out more about her. You're a long way from establishing a permanent relationship with another female, Herman. You just broke free from purgatory. Don't jump right back in it. Yes, I know, but with Marilyn I don't think I would be. Oh yeah? How do you know? I Don't! But I've got to find out." Thoughts continued to tumble through his brain until he remembered that he had to check on the baseball game at Busch. A quick phone call revealed that the Cards

were playing the Chicago Cubs on a three game stand, all night games, beginning next Tuesday.

"Marilyn?"

"Yes, Herman. That is you, isn't it?"

"Yes. I just checked with the Cardinals ticket office and found out that the Cubs will be in town for three straight nights starting next Tuesday. You said you like baseball. Would you like to go?"

"Oh, yes! That would be fun."

"I'll get tickets. How about next Wednesday? Bob Gibson is scheduled to pitch for the Cards, so it ought to be a great game. Night games start at 7:00. I guess we ought to get there around 6:30. How about picking you up at your house around a quarter to six? Would that rush you too much from work?"

"Okay, that's fine!"

"Great! I'll see you on Wednesday evening then!"

"Fine! I'll see you then!"

They concluded their conversation. Each was immersed in thoughts about the other. Herman thought, "This will show me a different side of Marilyn. I hope I will like her as much as I did the first time."

It was a really exciting game, which the Cardinals won 2 - 0, behind the superb pitching of Bob Gibson. Lou Brock got on base two times with a single and a walk. His second time on base he stole second and scored on a Ted Simmons double. They were excited not only by the game, but by each other. They laughed, they cheered, and they munched on hot dogs and had a really great time. Filing out of Busch Stadium with a crowd of over 40,000, they made their way to the parking garage across the street. Driving home through the heavy ballgame traffic, Son looked at Marilyn when the traffic stopped momentarily.

"Marilyn, would it offend you if I said that I like you very much? I'd like to see more of you."

"No, of course not!"

"I just don't want you to think I'm putting the arm on you. You've been so nice, and I want you to know how I feel. I'd like to see you some more. In fact, I have some more tickets, not to the ballgame but to the Planetarium. I haven't seen it, but I hear that they have a star show there that is out of this world, to coin a pun! Would you like to go and gaze at the stars with me?"

"Sounds like fun," she laughed!

"I have tickets for Friday's evening show, again at about 7:00. Okay?"

"Sure."

CHAPTER 84
The Vetting

Son was only 50 years old when he and Arretta divorced. He felt as though he were at least ten years older than that — depressed and angry. Now that he had found Marilyn Westlake he almost felt young again. His joy in being alive had returned and each morning he felt that surge of energy that he thought had left him. That evening in the main theater of the planetarium, he and Marilyn sat looking up at the Milky Way and a sky full of stars. It was wonderful. He slipped his arm around Marilyn's shoulders and gave a gentle hug. She snuggled back. It was hard to believe but, yes, life was wonderful again.

The rest of that summer of 1972 flew by. They continued to see each other two or three times a week. Herman met Marilyn's son, Robert and thought he was a great kid. Bob seemed to reciprocate. Marilyn obviously liked Herman and there was no doubt about his feelings for her. Herman thought, "Should I ask her to marry me? No! Not yet. You don't know her that well! Maybe you don't know yourself that well, either!" He was afraid of making a mistake. But the more he thought about it, the more certain he became that to not grab this opportunity might be the biggest mistake of all. Marilyn in the meantime was doing some checking of her own. She wanted to introduce Herman to her only and younger sister, Carol Burrows, and her husband George. They lived in Decatur, Illinois, not far from St. Louis. So, on a Friday after work, they drove to Decatur to spend the weekend with Carol and George. Herman was on his best behavior, wanting to make a good impression. But he needn't have worried. They thought Herman was the genuine article. That's what George said to Marilyn and Carol seconded him.

A week later Herman and Marilyn journeyed to Naperville, Illinois, a western suburb of Chicago. Marilyn and her family lived there before coming to St. Louis. Marilyn developed a special friendship with the Bennish family, Don and Marilyn, who lived next door. Don, better known as Skip, owned and operated a business which found buyers for dry cleaning establishments. Marilyn W. managed a store for Skip. They had two children, Geary and Dona, both adopted. The two Marilyns were really close, trusting each other completely. So it was important that Marilyn W. get some feedback from Marilyn B. on Herman. They had a great weekend visit, went out to dinner one evening and kibitzed as Skip did steaks on the back yard grill another evening. Skip and Herman found an area of common interest in flying. Skip had a Private Pilot's license and was really into building and flying scale model RC (radio controlled) airplanes. Everything went well until they were ready to leave for St. Louis and Herman lost his keys. Herman thought he had locked them in the trunk of his car. There was much frantic searching, checking of pockets and purse until the next door neighbor boy, came along and said, "You lookin' for the keys?

Here they are!" he said, pointing to the door lock on the driver's door! Oh yeah! Son's face was red. Still, he passed his test and has been a close friend of the Bennishes ever since.

Son still had to take care of some important details pertaining to his divorce. He and Arretta had decided that they would sell the house and split the proceeds after selling costs. He had already listed the house with Ira Berry Real Estate Company for $42,000. After paying a 6% commission and taxes that would yield enough to make a small profit. The house cost $35,000 when it was built. Son also had to liquidate their joint stock and savings accounts. Per their divorce agreement, Arretta was to get 50% of their net assets. So far, so good, but Son was required to pay out of his 50% both attorney's fees and all court costs. There was barely enough to cover it all. Son had been taken to the cleaners. In addition, he now also had an $800 monthly obligation that he had to pay Arretta for alimony and child support. Divorce is a lose-lose proposition, emotionally and financially. Nobody wins but the attorneys. At least, that is the way Son saw it. However, Son did have his freedom, and as the days passed, it gradually dawned on him that this was no small matter.

The house sold quickly for full list price, and the buyer wanted possession within 30 days. Suddenly, Son was confronted with looking for a place to live. Since Arretta had taken most of the furniture, there wasn't a lot in the way of personal possessions to worry about. He did, however, have to put a roof over his head. Since he was a bachelor who could live simply, he thought, why not look for a condominium, perhaps a small 2-bedroom somewhere near the McDonnell plant. He checked the classified ads and found exactly what he was looking for. It was a small unit in a complex called Granada located just south of I-270 and west of Hanley Road, advertised for sale by owner for only $21,500. Son called the number in the ad and made an appointment to see it. It was neat as could be and he bought it on the spot, including a practically new refrigerator and clothes washer and dryer. The fellow who owned it was an Ozark Airlines captain who was getting married. Closing was set for the end of the month, three weeks away.

After closing, Son rented a U-haul truck over the next weekend, and with the help of a couple of neighborhood teenage boys, got all his "stuff" loaded into the truck and moved. It took him another week or two to get everything back out of the boxes he had used to pack and to get the apartment looking reasonably well. Fortunately, Arretta had left one of the dining room sets that they owned - the old one - and he set that up in the dining area of the combination living room/dining room area. He had a small couch and occasional chair, which were just right for the small space. His stereo equipment fit nicely in the hutch of the dining room set. A small breakfast table with four chairs went into the kitchen. There was a handy gas grill located just off the kitchen on a small patio. Upstairs he took the larger of the two bedrooms and set up his double bed and nightstand. The other bedroom, for now, went bare. He took all the cardboard boxes, some half-empty and stacked them in the lower level. After doing this, there was barely room to get to the laundry area, furnace and hot water heater. After all of his handiwork, Son thought to himself:

"Nothing fancy, but not a bad bachelor pad, I'd say. Only thing it needs is a woman to appreciate it. I know! I'll invite Marilyn over for a home cooked meal! That'll be fun! Saturday, I'll invite her over to show off my new digs and plan a meal fit for a queen - a couple of Delmonico steaks, baked potatoes, a nice salad with something nice for dessert. He'd have to think about that. Wine? Maybe a nice Merlot that would go good with the steak! He went through his record collection to find some nice romantic music. Fortunately, Arretta didn't have any interest in his record collection. He'd have it all set up When Marilyn arrived the music would be playing, the lights would be turned down low and he'd have dinner ready to go on the grill."

When Herman called Marilyn to invite her to dinner she said, "Really? I didn't know you could cook too!"

"Of course I can cook. Nothing fancy, I'm a steak and potatoes man. Do you like steak? I do a great job with a Delmonico!"

"Sure. If you're that good, I want to see."

"Okay, I'll pick you up at home about 6:30."

"Great!"

Saturday arrived. Before Herman left to pick up Marilyn, he made sure everything in his condo was in readiness. The stereo was playing and the record changer was loaded with some nice romantic jazz. The lights were set. He even sprayed the condo with a nice spice air freshener. Marilyn was dressed neatly and casually. As always, she looked great.

"Marilyn, you look great! You always look like you just stepped out of an ad in Vanity Fair. How do you do it?"

"Thank you. I'm glad you think so."

The evening went beautifully. At least, Son thought it did. Marilyn seemed to be impressed. She said that she loved the music. It was obvious that Marilyn knew what she was talking about when it came to music. Son appreciated the fact that she seemed to like the same kinds of music that he did. Marilyn said that her steak was perfect. After dinner, he put the dishes in the dishwasher and straightened up the kitchen. He then asked her if she would like to see the rest of his condo. There wasn't much to show except two bedrooms upstairs and a basement area that was full of boxes.

"Would you like to see my bedrooms, said the spider to the fly? Really, I won't bite."

"Oh sir! Can I trust you?" said Marilyn with feigned concern.

At the conclusion of the tour she said that Herman's apartment was just what he needed, not too big, not too small, just right. It was an auspicious evening. When asked by a friend about his date, Son said, being ever the gentleman, that it was a great evening. Beyond that, he had nothing else to say.

By now, two months after they met, Son was aware that he had strong feelings for Marilyn. She was beautiful, intelligent, outgoing and openly honest. She had a highly developed sense of humor. Herman couldn't get over her outgoing honesty. What she said is what she meant. There were no hidden agendas to deal with, such as he had in his marriage to Arretta.

"Could I be falling in love? Son asked of himself. Yes. It is possible.

Still, he was cautious. "It's too soon. You're on the rebound. Remember, 'Love is Blind!' You could be making a big mistake."

Every time he saw Marilyn, three or four times a week, he felt close to her. He felt that he could trust her. He found out that she was an accomplished cook, no small talent. He liked her son, Bob, and Bob seemed to like him. The feeling of trust that he had was something that he never really had with Arretta. He began to ask himself if he should ask her to marry him. It was a big step. Before he took it, he wanted to be sure, as sure as one can be of such things. He analyzed their relationship. To him, it seemed straightforward and honest. Their chemistry when they were together was great. Still, Son knew that there was more to a good marriage than physical chemistry, important though that might be.

In September, Marilyn's parents, Harrington and Florence Gagnon, drove to St. Louis for a visit. Marilyn had talked with them by telephone and told them all about this "man" that she was excited about. Since her divorce from her first husband, over four years ago, they had worried about their daughter. Would she marry again? Would she pick the "right" man? They had to see for themselves. Herman was excited that they were coming. It would give him a chance to see what kind of parents Marilyn had. He had learned from his first marriage, that there is much to be learned about the spouse from the spouse's parents.

The first night of their stay, Marilyn planned a nice home cooked dinner - a roast, mashed potatoes, green beans and a salad. Of course she invited Herman. According to Marilyn, there was much cautionary advice from her mother about this "man," -"Herman

Son, did you say his name is? Is he Korean? That's a strange name. You've got to be very careful, you know. I'm not sure that when it comes to men that you are a very good judge!"

Marilyn said, "Just wait until you meet him. Then you can decide for yourself."

When Herman arrived, Marilyn introduced him. All except Marilyn sat down in the family room. She excused herself and went into the kitchen to attend to dinner preparations. What transpired during the next few minutes was a mutual interview, an exploration of Herman and another of Florence and Harrington by Herman. Herman wanted to find out as much as he could about them so he asked questions.

"Marilyn tells me that you live in Westlake, Ohio. She's told me a little, but what do you like about it?"

There were more questions: I understand both of you are musicians? What instruments do you play? You played with the Toledo Symphony? That must have been exciting. Do you keep up with your music since you retired? Harrington, I understand from Marilyn that both you and Florence teach? Florence teaches the cello? And you, of course, teach violin and collect them as well? I have an uncle in California who played with John Phillips Sousa. He's retired too, and he makes violins.

Son asked more questions, and he listened. He was enjoying talking to them. Florence was articulate and obviously very intelligent. Harrington, though not as verbose, seemed friendly and very much absorbed in his music. Herman made sure that he called him Harrington. Marilyn had warned him that Florence took umbrage whenever anyone called her husband, "Harry." He told Herman that he was a graduate of the Cleveland School of Music and that he loved playing with the symphony and teaching private students, but that he couldn't make enough money doing just that to support Florence, Marilyn and Carol. So during the depression he took a job selling vacuum cleaners with Sears and turned out to be one of their star salesmen. He worked at that job for thirty years, using it to provide for the material needs of his family. But music, he said, provided for the needs of the soul. He had brought his violin, and before the evening was out he would play. Son was impressed with his repertoire. He was well grounded in the classics. He also did humorous things like making his violin talk in a rendition of, "Mary Had a Little Lamb."

After a few minutes chatting with Herman in the family room, Florence excused herself: "I think I'll go see if there is something I can do to help Marilyn."

Florence sidled up to Marilyn, who was chopping something at on the counter and whispered, "Marilyn! Where did you find this man? He's wonderful! He likes music! And he's so handsome! How long has he been divorced?"

"Not long mother. Only a few months."

"Well, I can't imagine why anyone would want to divorce HIM! Has he asked you to marry him?"

"No, mother!"

"Well, if he asks you. . ."

"Mother, I don't know what may happen. I'm glad you like him. Right now we are seeing each other regularly. We like each other, but we're just letting things develop at their own pace. We're not in a hurry."

"Well, don't let him get away!"

The dinner and the rest of the evening went smoothly, except for one small detail. Herman produced a bottle of young Beaujolais, a light, dry red which he thought would go well with the dinner that Marilyn had prepared. He sampled it and pronounced it good. Then he poured for everybody.

"I hope you like this wine. It's dry, but not too dry, if you know what I mean. It's not sweet."

Harrington put his glass under his nose and smelled. "Smells okay," he pronounced, tentatively. Then he took a sip. He puckered his face as if he had bitten into a sour pickle! "Ouch," he exclaimed. That needs some sugar. Got any sugar?"

"Sugar!" said Marilyn. "You don't put sugar in a dry wine like that!"

"Well, I think some sugar would improve it."

"Okay, Daddy. If you must, here's the sugar bowl!"

Harrington put two heaping teaspoons of sugar into his glass, stirred it thoroughly and took another sip.

"There," he said without puckering. "That's much better!"

"Well, if he likes it, who am I to complain?" said Herman. Then to Marilyn he said, "Marilyn, this dinner looks great! I know it is going to taste every bit as good as it looks!"

"Yes, Marilyn is a pretty good cook. Did you know that she won the title of Mrs. America?"

"Yes, Harrington, she told me, and I'm not surprised at all. You have a very charming and intelligent daughter."

Florence said, "Marilyn, isn't he nice?"

"Yes, mother, of course he is." Then, turning to Herman, she said, "Thank you, dear."

During the rest of the dinner they chatted amiably about a number of things, including how Harrington got lost when he got to St. Louis. He took the I-270 beltway around the city in a counter clockwise direction as Marilyn had told him. But he didn't get off the beltway, turning west at Olive as he should have. Instead, he followed the beltway all the way to he south, finally exiting at Butler Hill Road, twenty miles to the south. After he got off the beltway he became hopelessly lost and had to call Marilyn. After finding out where he was, she gave him directions. This time he found Fourposter Court.

Florence also told Herman about how she met Harrington. She was engaged at the time to the son of a prominent political leader in Cleveland. Both sets of parents thought it was a great match. Florence, however, was lukewarm. Both she and Harrington were attending an orchestra rehearsal and there was a shortage of folding chairs. Harrington, followed by Florence, went to the basement to bring up some extra chairs, whereupon Harrington put his arm around Florence's waist, bent her backward and planted a smackeroo right on her mouth. That was the beginning. She broke her engagement to the son of the Cleveland scion and became engaged to Harrington.

The dinner was a great success. Herman was glad that he had he chance to meet Marilyn's parents. He got a good feel for their personalities, the kind of people that they were. As a result he checked off one more box in his mental checklist of things about Marilyn that were important to him. He was beginning to believe that Marilyn was the right woman for him and that he wanted to marry her. Florence and Harrington drove back to Cleveland. A few days later he sat in Marilyn's kitchen, telling her how much he enjoyed the dinner and meeting her parents.

CHAPTER 85
Decision Time

Marilyn said, "Well, let me tell you, you hit a home run! My mother thinks you are 'the cats pajamas!' Daddy likes you too."

"I'm glad that they liked me. If they didn't that would be a problem, wouldn't it?"

"Problem? In what way?"

"Well, if I asked you to marry me, I'd want their support."

"What? What did you say?

"I said that if I asked you to marry me, . . .would you?"

"Well, yes, I would. But we really haven't known each other very long, only about five months. That's awfully short, don't you think?"

"I don't know how I could know you any better if I knew you for a year or more. I think I know everything I need to know about you. Most importantly, I love you! I want to spend the rest of my life with you. What else do we need to know? I've told you about my life with Arretta before we were divorced. I know about your first marriage. I know your kids and I like them. I think they all like me. I feel very close to Bob. I don't see any problems, do you?"

"Well, no."

"Then you will?"

"Yes."

"Wonderful! When? When shall we do it?"

"You are in a hurry, aren't you?"

"I don't see any reason to delay. I know what I want. How does this sound? We could get married sometime after the New Year, say, February. And I could take you to England to visit your pen pal, Betty Hill and her husband, Burt. They live in Devon, don't they? I'll check on it, but I think MAC is scheduling a charter flight to England in March. That would be the perfect honeymoon!"

"Is that a promise?"

"Promise."

It was settled. They would be married on February 25, 1973. Herman gave Marilyn an engagement ring for Christmas and planning for the great event began in earnest. Herman had become a barbershopper when he joined the Suburban Chapter. Since Marilyn was a long time member of Sweet Adelines they decided to have a barbershop wedding! Marilyn asked The Tetrachords, a quartet from her chapter, that went on to become international champions, if they would be willing to sing at the wedding. They were glad to be part of the festivities. Herman asked Jerry Cohen from his chapter if his quartet would sing. They also agreed. Herman talked to the minister of the Methodist Church on Woods Mill Road in Ballwin and made all the arrangements including a reception, complete with wedding cake

and refreshments, in the church basement. Both Marilyn and Herman agreed to keep it simple and they really did try to limit the guest list. Nevertheless, it grew. Besides Marilyn's mother and father, there were other close family members: Herman's sister, June and her husband, Walter; Marilyn's sister, Carol, who agreed to be maid of honor, and husband George who agreed to be best man. Even Herman's elderly aunt, Jane and Uncle Jolly Keeran came from California, MO. There were Marilyn's three children, Holly, her husband, Paul, her daughter Amy, and son Bob. Daughter Carol and her husband Sian couldn't come because of the birth of their first child. Then the guest list expanded to include close friends, both Herman's and Marilyn's. There were the Bennishes from Chicago and Roger and Betty Oliver. Bob and Patricia (Pat) Inman were invited. There were Herman's associates at MAC, and all of their friends from barbershopping. It was getting to be an imposing list. How many friends did they have? It was hard to know where to make the cut. They couldn't invite everybody, much as they wished that they could. Finally, however, they arrived at a list and ordered invitations. They specified "no gifts," even though almost everybody ignored that order. One notable gift was season tickets to the Muny Opera from Herman's Barbershop chapter. R.S.V.P. responses indicated that there would be well over 180 guests. There was plenty of room at the church to accommodate that many, but both Herman and Marilyn wanted to have a party at Marilyn's house in addition to the church reception. Was there enough room for that? They decided to try it and ordered enough catered food for about 125 people.

"How strange and wonderful," thought Herman. "In the 28 years that I was married to Arretta we had practically no friends outside of my military friends. Now, since I have known Marilyn, we have hundreds of friends! I love it!"

CHAPTER 86
An Auspicious Occasion

As their special day approached Herman and Marilyn were excited. There were so many details to take care of, like getting a marriage license, renting a tuxedo for Herman and choosing a dress for Marilyn. She chose a beautiful pink number that still hangs in her closet. Carol, without talking to Marilyn, picked out a pale turquoise dress that went well with Marilyn's pink. Everything else was checked with members of the wedding party. They had a rehearsal and rehearsal dinner.

"So far, so good!" said Herman.

"I think we've thought of everything. I can hardly wait!"

"Me, too!"

The big day finally arrived. The church filled with guests, 189 of them to be exact! The wedding party was ready. Marilyn's and Herman's family members were seated. The organ began playing. Then the Tetrachords sang, "One Hand, One Heart" from Westside Story. Other than that, Herman doesn't remember what music was played, only that they defied convention by marching down the aisle together! Some of their friends said that they did it at "double time!" Following close behind came Marilyn's sister and maid of honor, Carol and her husband and best man George. The rest of the ceremony followed quickly.

"Herman, do you take Marilyn to be your wife, to have and to hold from this day forward. . . .?"

"I do!"

Marilyn, do you. . .?"

"I do!"

They exchanged rings. "You may kiss the bride," intoned the minister.

"May I present to you, Mr. and Mrs. Herman Son!"

It was done! Marilyn and Herman, both smiling broadly, walked back up the aisle toward the back of the church. The reception was great. There was cake and punch. There was friendship, laughter and joy. What else could one ask for? Not much. Herman wished that his two children could have been there, but for many reasons, including distance, it was not practical.

Everybody seemed genuinely happy for Herman and Marilyn. Of course it had been decided that Herman would move in with Marilyn. There was no way that the two of them could have fit comfortably into Herman's little two-bedroom condo. Herman had already sold his condo and was due to close on it within the next thirty days.

That evening they had a great party at the Son's home. Somehow well over one-hundred people crammed into their house. The revelry continued until the wee hours. Even

Aunt Jane at 84 was up for the party. About midnight, Uncle Jolly said he thought it was time for them to leave.

"It's gonna be a long drive back to California," he said.

"You're not leaving. You wouldn't get there before five in the morning! You're staying here," said Herman. Jane agreed. She said that there was no way that she would let Jolly drive that far at that time of night. They took the guest bedroom.

The next morning, Herman and Marilyn turned blissfully toward each other in bed. It was a wonderful beginning for a relationship that would last. At last account they have been married for nearly 31 years.

Our Wedding - 1973

Still together 25 years later

Meanwhile, Back On The Job

Although Herman had been going to work every morning, for the past couple of months his primary focus had been on his personal life. During that time he had to solve a lot of personal issues arising from his divorce. Herman tried to keep Bob Barclay, his immediate boss, apprised. He knew that Son had one foot in his job and the other foot in his personal affairs. He gave Herman the latitude that he needed. But now, it was time to redirect his attention to what was going on with his department and its mission. George Chakides and Don Wylan had continued to do yeoman work on putting on seminars and in working to develop their new management development program, "Bootstrap." Still, Herman felt that something more was needed to change the management culture. He thought that military organizations were big and bureaucratic. But he didn't fully appreciate the rigidities of large corporate hierarchies. In many ways, they were even more rigid. As soon as he got back from their honeymoon trip to England, he told George and Don, he wanted to brainstorm ideas on how they could get a team building program going.

"You're barking up the wrong tree. Krone would never ever allow something as revolutionary as that," said George.

"I agree," said Don.

"We'll see," said Herman.

CHAPTER 87
England, France and All That Jazz

Son checked with MAC's personal affairs office to see when the next scheduled charter flight to England. A BOAC 707 was scheduled to leave Lambert International Airport in St. Louis on May 10th, 1973, destination, Heathrow Airport in London. It would return 16 days later. There were still seats available, and of course Son booked tickets for himself and Marilyn. That evening when he returned home he told Marilyn the good news.

"Guess what! We're going to see Betty. Our flight leaves at 5 P.M., May 10th. We'll have 16 days. Isn't that great!"

Marilyn was overjoyed. She had already written Betty Hill, telling her of the possibility of a visit. Now she could confirm it.

"Oh, we'll have such a great time! There are so many things to see. I'd love to see some of London, and of course Devon and Cornwell in southern England are so beautiful."

"I'm going to check with the travel office at MAC and get all the information I can. We'll put together a trip to remember, won't we?"

They planned to spend four days in London. Must see items on their London agenda included Buckingham Palace, Royal Albert Hall, St. Paul's cathedral where British monarchs are entombed, The Royal Gardens, Trafalgar Square, London Bridge, Big Ben and the Tower of London, with all its grisly history, where Henry VIII beheaded his wives. They planned to sample some of London's night life. They wanted to take a river cruise down the Thames, seeing along they way such historical sites as: The RAF War Memorial, and Royal Festival Hall (Best acoustics in the world), The City of London School for boys, Sir Christopher Wren's house, and The London Fishmarket (known for its fresh fish and bad language!). They reserved a night to hear the legendary sax man, Zoot Sims, at Ronnie Scott's Jazz Club located in the heart of the Soho district.

Looking over their itinerary, Herman said, "Wow! We're really going to be going nonstop, if we get all of this done in four or five days. We could spend the whole 16 days in London and not run out of things to see and do. I don't think we want to do that. We have to budget some time to drive down to Devon and of course Exeter to visit Betty. I'd like to drive along the southern coast out to Land's End, too, wouldn't you?"

"As long as I get to see Betty I don't care what else we do. You be the judge, dear."

"Don't worry, we'll get that done, if nothing else, sweetheart!"

The next morning, Herman talked to MAC's travel office. He outlined what they wanted to do during their two-week stay. Driving south in a rental car, they would stop for a short visit with Herman's daughter, Mary-Lynn and her husband, Peter Hilton. Of course, they'd stop in Exeter to see Betty Hill, Marilyn's pen pal of over 50 years. They would stop in Plymouth, the port from which America's original colonists sailed on their epic journey.

The history of the original 13 colonies is a tangled tale indeed. There are many ways to view the events of that time and it is easy to think you understand. But no one knew where they were headed at the time and it could have ended up very different.

On the evening of May 10th, Marilyn's son, Bob, drove them to the Old Terminal at St. Louis/Lambert airport. Their BOAC 707, parked in front of the old terminal, was ready for boarding. The special charter flight cost $384 for both, round trip.

"This is so exciting!" said Marilyn. "I'm really going to see Betty Hill, after corresponding with her as my pen pal for all these years. I can't believe it!"

"You can believe it, Marilyn. We'll be on the ground at Kennedy for a short time and then we'll be underway for an overnight flight to London's Heathrow Airport."

At 7:43 P.M., St. Louis time, they were rolling down the runway at Lambert, lifting off for JFK Airport, where they would land two hours later. At 11:40 P.M. they were airborne again, this time flying eastward toward the sun.

"Go to sleep, Marilyn! There's nothing to see for a while. When you wake up, we'll be landing in London."

Herman grasped Marilyn's hand, turned toward her in his seat and went to sleep himself.

They arrived at Heathrow at 6:19 A.M., St. Louis time, but because of the time difference, it was just past noon, 12:19 P.M., in London. They passed through customs quickly and by 1:00 P.M. they were aboard a double-decker bus that took them through the cacophony of mid-afternoon London traffic to the Kensington Close Hotel where they had reservations. It was a neat hotel. There were towel warmers and London style wallpaper in their room. Marilyn snapped on the TV and was surprised at the brilliant, high-resolution picture. British TV had double the number of horizontal scan lines that U.S. TV used - what a difference! The main thing that they noticed, however, was the people, so smiling and friendly. Hungry after the long flight, they went to a lounge where sandwiches and tea were offered by a handsome Spanish waiter, who asked politely, "Tea for two?"

Back in their room, and feeling much better after the food, Marilyn called her friend, Betty Hill, at Exmouth School in Exeter, and Herman's daughter Mary-Lynn and her husband, Peter Hilton in Dorsett. Suffering from jet lag, they then went to bed and slept soundly for three hours. At 8:45 P.M. they were up and on their way to the Stratholan Room for dinner. Again, the staff was Spanish, including the Maitre d, Franco. Marilyn had Trifle for the first time and pronounced it delicious. Herman opted for bananas and cream. After dinner it was time to hail a cab for a ride to Ronnie Scott's Club to hear renowned jazz saxophonist, Zoot Simms, playing with the Alex Welsh Band. Herman had several of Simms albums in his collection at home.

They caught a cab back to the Kensington Close around mid-night where they met two chatty, friendly gentlemen in the lounge for a nightcap. So ended their first day in romantic London town.

Their second day, May 12th, was a busy one.

In a whirlwind of activity they visited Westminster Abbey where we were told a Man who was 153 years old was buried. According to records he was married at 80 for first time and had eleven children after that! Madame Tussaud's Wax Works was fascinating. At Buckingham Palace they saw the changing of the guard. They heard the stately tones of Big Ben as it chimed 2 P.M.! Poets' corner. Jewish Group - Ave Maria They took a trip on the Underground, got lost and met up with seven little girls on their birthday party. The weather that day? — 55 degree and sunny. Who said that it's always foggy in London? Not Herman and Marilyn! They continued their sight seeing at Trafalgar Square, famous for its statue of Lord Nelson and thousands of pigeons! Marilyn struck up a conversation with an elderly gentleman who was busily engaged in feeding the pigeons. The birds were flying up and landing on his shoulders and head, eagerly waiting to be fed. He told Marilyn that the pi-

geons belonged to the Queen, but that it was his responsibility to feed them. Without his help, he said, the pigeons would die and the Queen would hold him responsible so he took his duties very, very seriously.

They took a boat trip down the Thames River, taking in such sights as the Royal Naval Academy, The Queen's Summer Residence and the famous four-mast tall ship, The Cutty Sark. For riotous floral displays, the timing was perfect. Tulips, Roses and Azaleas in every color were everywhere, but none so beautiful as those at The Royal Gardens. They even found time to squeeze in a trip to The Tower of London where King Henry VIII imprisoned and often beheaded his wives and detractors. Of course, they saw nearby London Bridge.

The next day they arranged for a rental car, met Mary-Lynn, Herman's daughter, and her husband, Peter Hilton, and after some more sightseeing left for Longburton where Mary-Lynn and Peter lived. Driving in England was an adventure. All traffic stays on the left side of the road and all British cars have driver's wheel and controls on the right side. It took a little time, but soon Herman was driving their little four-cylinder Ford Escort with no problem. They stayed overnight with Peter and Mary-Lynn in a beautiful country estate which they were "baby-sitting" American owners. The Hiltons were most gracious hosts. The next day they took in the color and culture of the local area, talking with an old farmer next door about his cows and meeting the family dog, a pure bred basset hound named Henrietta. Sad of eye, long of ears and short of legs - that was Henrietta. Also, she didn't bark, she bayed, oh so mournfully! At a little village called Mulberry Bub they found an ancient little church dating from the sixteenth century, hardly big enough to hold fifty people. It housed an antique pipe organ, powered by foot pedals. Marilyn sat down and played it. It actually worked. Then it was on the road again, on the way to Exeter and Marilyn's long anticipated meeting with her pen pal, Betty Hill. Herman and Marilyn were overwhelmed with the Hill's hospitality. They couldn't have been more welcome if they had been family. They met Betty's mother, who at the time was in her eighties, as well as her husband Burt who worked for the main newspaper in Exeter. Burt was the perfect host, taking Marilyn and Herman in his car to Plymouth where they spent a day touring the city and its environs. They saw the docks from which the Pilgrims set sail for America in the fall of 1620. They had lunch at a Greek, yes Greek, restaurant, took in an art show and almost bought a beautiful painting.

What a beautiful trip it was turning out to be. The weather in Plymouth was the balmiest, with sunny skies and almost cloudless skies. It is strange how stereotypes color one's thinking. Thoughts about English weather conjure up cold and foggy days. But in Plymouth the Sons were treated to almost tropical weather. In fact, there are palm trees all up and down the southern coast of England.

On May 19th, the ninth day of their trip, Marilyn and Herman said goodbye to the Hills. It had been a wonderful visit. After a leisurely breakfast they climbed into their little Ford and headed for Newquay (pronounced "NEW - KEY") and Land's End on the southwestern coast of England. The drive along the southern coast of Cornwall was one picture post-card after another. There were charming small towns, narrow streets and white washed, thatched roof houses and shops. Tall palms, such as one might find in Florida or Southern California, abounded.

At Newquay, they had reservations at the Headlands Hotel, a huge red brick building with beautiful carpeting, sinks in the rooms instead of the bathroom, high 14-foot ceilings and a lovely dining room. After checking in and resting for a few minutes, Herman and Marilyn went to the dining room where the matre d' showed them to a table next to a large window. They looked out on an immense lawn that spread toward the rocks and ocean. They watched little bunnies playing on the grass as they sampled liver pate' to start their meal. The second course was halibut with a delicious hollandaise sauce served on hot dishes. Then came a layered salad, large enough for a meal in itself. Still the courses came: The fourth course was dressed crab. Finally there was desert. Marilyn had ice cream. Herman

opted for cheese. After dinner, in a lounge outside the bar, they drank coffee and listened to Simms and Watts - a drummer and electric organ — play pretty songs. They had friendly conversation with Mr. and Mrs. Turner from Torquay and Peter and Audrey Moss who upon learning that the Sons were newly weds, bought them a drink. They talked awhile and at around mid-night called it a day and went to bed.

The next morning they checked out of their hotel and headed back toward Longburton and Peter and Mary-Lynn's home. There was time, however, for a detour through The Moors, a highlands area of beautiful trees and gorgeous country.

"Look! There they are!" Marilyn exclaimed as she spotted some of the long-haired ponies for which the region is famous.

They did some shopping there. Marilyn bought a beautiful and colorful linen jacket and Herman found a handsome Harris Tweed sport coat. Then it was on to Longburton where they would have time for only a short visit and dinner with Peter and Mary-Lynn. They were scheduled to board the over night, cross-channel ferry to LeHavre, France, leaving from Southampton at 10:00 P.M. Peter said that it would take approximately one and one-half hours by car to reach Southampton, so at 7:30 they said goodbye to the Hiltons and pointed their little Ford south. After an all-night ride on the Ferry and a short train trip the next morning, they would have three days to spend in Paris! The Paris Air Show, internationally acclaimed, was in full swing. Herman hoped that they might at least spend a day there, so the schedule would be tight.

"Of course I'd like to take in the Paris Air Show, but I don't know if we'll be able to do it, Marilyn. We don't even have a hotel reservation. We want to visit the Louvre and see Notre` Dame. We'll just have to play it by ear," Herman said.

"Well, we'll do what we can," said Marilyn.

At the dock, they turned in their rental car and boarded the ferry, prepared for the all night trip. They would arrive in LeHavre at 6:30 next morning.

"Well, let's go up to the passengers' lounge and get comfortable. Maybe we can find some comfortable chairs and take a nap," said Herman.

As they walked into the lounge, crowded with passengers, a small world story was about to unfold. At the bar they struck up a conversation with a very British gentleman who, Herman noticed, was wearing a miniature set of pilots wings on his sport coat lapel. Stuart Morrison was a test pilot. He worked for Singer Products, Inc., and - guess what? - he and his American friend, Dennis Duncan from Pacific, Missouri were on their way to attend the Paris Air Show!

"Were you planning to take the rapid to Paris in the morning?" asked Stuart.

"Yes, that is our plan."

"Oh, and where are you staying in Paris?"

"Honestly, we don't know. We don't have reservations."

"Well, listen, why don't you come with us? My Jag is parked below deck. Dennis and I are staying at the Paix de Republique. Maybe we can get you a room there. If not, I'll talk to the clerk and we'll see if we can't get you a room nearby."

"Oh, that would be great! You're sure you don't mind us riding with you?'

"Not at all! It would be our pleasure!"

The next morning Herman and Marilyn were awake at 4:45. They had a continental breakfast at 6:00 and followed Morrison and Duncan to Morison's candy apple red Jaguar. Off the end of the boat, Stuart quickly found the autostrada and they were on their way at 150 km (110 mph) to Paris.

Herman and Marilyn were in the back seat. "How fast are we going," said Marilyn, noticing the landscape whizzing by.

Herman glanced over Morrison's shoulder. "About 100 to 110 mph, I'd say, said Herman"

"Don't they have speed limits in France?"

"Not on the freeways."

In a short time they were coming into the outskirts of Paris - lots of traffic, smelly busses, big elegant buildings. Morrison and Duncan were staying at the Paix Republique. Stewart asked the desk clerk to find a room for his two extra friends. He did, at the Hotel Paris France. It wasn't a five star establishment, but a room was a room! It was noisy and Marilyn was coming down with a case of dysentery. We got up early and went to the Louvre anyway - lots of big, depressing paintings. The saving grace, however, was the Mona Lisa, magnificently alone on the wall. Herman had taken his camera, but as they entered the museum, the guard told him that he could take his camera in, but that the use of flash was strictly prohibited. A check with his light meter showed Herman that without flash he could get the picture at F:2 and 1/4 second exposure. That would be hard to do without a tripod, he thought. But, nothing ventured, nothing gained, Herman stood in the middle of the room, and bracing himself and the camera carefully, squeezed off a shot.

"Well, I hope that will work," said Herman. "We won't know until we get home and develop the roll." Two weeks later, after they were home in St. Louis and had the roll developed and printed, they found that he had taken a perfect picture of the lady with the enigmatic smile.

They got lost, walking back from the Louvre to their hotel. By the time they got home, Marilyn had chills and aches.

"I don't feel very good, Herman. I hope this doesn't get any worse. Maybe if I lay down for awhile, I'll feel better."

They took a nap, which seemed to help Marilyn a little. Morrison and Duncan had asked them to have dinner with them so they did. It was a chance to get even with them for paying for everything on the trip from LeHavre.

Stewart said, "We'd like you to join us. We're supping at the Malliac Restaurant, one of my favorites in Paris. I think you will enjoy it."

"O.K., but only if you let us pay for dinner, Stewart."

"We'll see."

Dinner was, indeed, delightful. There is a difference between French and English cuisine! Dinner began with a marvelous aperitif, Les Crepe de la Tour, thin, thin pancake with cheese sauce and thinly sliced ham. The main course was Sole Miniere, grilled with butter, and of course, superlative French bread, wine and coffee. Eauf a la Neige was for dessert. It was a kind of pudding soup with beaten meringue on top, drizzled over with butterscotch sauce. The bill for four was 232 francs, which converted to only $64 dollars, a magnificent meal for the price. After dinner Herman and Marilyn begged off slumming. Marilyn didn't feel up to it. A good night's sleep at their hotel changed things. The next morning, Marilyn awoke feeling much better.

On May 24, 1973, they went to the Paris Air Show with Morrison and Duncan. They walked their legs off, seeing endless exhibits. Of course, an air show without flying would be no air show at all. McDonnell-Douglas demonstrated its DC-8 and Bob Hoover did unbelievable aerobatics with his Shrike. The Russians had a huge pavilion showing off their many scientific accomplishments including Sputnik, the first man-made object to be launched into orbit around the Earth. They were also very proud of their then new supersonic commercial airliner, the TU-144. It was scheduled to do a demonstration flight the next day. Tragically, toward the scheduled end of its flight it crashed. Herman and Marilyn stood agape, watching as it lurched out of control while turning on final approach. A huge pillar of black smoke marked the end of their SST aspirations.

Enjoyable as the Air Show was, however, the highlight of their Paris trip came that evening. They took a dinner cruise - Batteau Moche - down the Seine. It was a trip that they will never forget. As the glass-topped boat wended its way down that famous river, under bridges and through the heart of Paris on a spring evening they were treated to a

gourmet dinner that topped everything else. The table setting was gorgeous - white linen, silver place settings, candelabra; wine packed in ice, and lots of French bread, and appetizers they'd never seen. There was lobster with a butter sauce out of this world. Then there was Chateaubriande with roasted potatoes - delicious! Then waiters brought in flaming Baked Alaska. Everyone applauded. A harpist and accordionist provided just the right kind of music. People waved from the shore. The passengers/diners were from all over the world. Most spoke some English, including a Venezuelan couple seated at the next table. They were very nice to talk with. There was a Japanese tourist, complete with camera, who had too much of the good French wine. By the end of the cruise, he was barely able to get off the boat! It was a fitting end to their all too short Paris stay.

The next morning, May 25th, they left their hotel at 7:45. At Orly Airport they boarded a BEA flight at 9:30 bound for London.

Back in the Kensington Close Hotel, Herman and Marilyn prepared for the final three days of their trip. They called Peter and Mary-Lynn, who were staying with friends in London, and arranged to meet them that evening at The Players Theater. Marilyn made an appointment with the Hotel hairdresser, and this time the result was more to her liking than the one she had in Sherborne. That evening they had a great time at The Players. It was old time music hall stuff, corny but lots of fun. After the show they went to dinner and after a short, picture-taking walk along the Thames, said their good byes to Peter and Mary-Lynn.

May 26th was a real tourist day. It began with a cruise down the Thames. Among places they saw were: Westminster Bridge, Big Ben, The R.A.F. War Memorial, Royal Festival Hall (best acoustics in the world), Cleopatra's Needle, weighing 180 Tons, The City of London School for Boys, Black Friars Bridge, St. Paul's Cathedral, Sir Christopher Wren's house and The London Fish Market, known for fresh fish and bad language. At Tower Bridge there was the new Tower Hotel with 2,000 rooms. There was Princess Elizabeth's boat, now a restaurant, which was among 4,000 private boats that evacuated British soldiers from the beaches at Dunkirk during those dark days when Winston Churchill told the British people that all he could promise them was "blood, sweat and tears." There was Sir John's Wharf where Captain Kidd died, Dickens' House and Cuckold Point, where husbands dunked adulterous wives. Dead Man's Dock was so named for the thousands of skeletons found there in the aftermath of the Black Plague. There was the Royal Navy Station and Dock Yard where Sir Walter Raleigh put down his cape for queen Elizabeth. There was the Greenwich Observatory, marking the Zero Meridian, a reference point for navigators the world over. At Greenwich, Herman and Marilyn visited The Queen's House where Queen Elizabeth was born. They saw where Henry the VIII was born.

Back at the Hotel that evening, they dressed for dinner. Marilyn wore her "dragon lady" dress, looking like the character out of Terry and The Pirates." They went to Bess and Friends restaurant. Ate Escargot, steak in the best sauce ever, potatoes, green beans, French bread, pears with ice cream and chocolate sauce. To top off the evening they took the underground and a taxi to The Bulls Head and heard the Peter Ind Quintet - great jazz! It was a great evening.

On the 27th, they boarded their big, BOAC 707 charter jet for the long trip back home. There was a refueling and customs stop in Montreal before continuing on to St. Louis Lambert International Airport, where Bob and his then girlfriend, met them. They were home again after a glorious and memory laden trip. It was one that they would never forget.

Chapter 88
Fish Or Cut Bait Time at MAC

After their return from their honeymoon trip to England, the Sons settled down. Son was back on the job at MAC. Marilyn, who by then had changed jobs from Sherwin-Williams to Porter Paint, liked her job and a new boss. She had charge of the decorating department at Porter's store on Clayton Road. Still, the pay was not all that great. Marilyn's sister, Carol Burrows, lived in Decatur, IL with her husband George. George was owner and operator of a successful optical shop. Carol was a real estate agent for Masey Realtors, and was their star performer. During one visit to Decatur the dinner conversation revolved around Carol's experiences in selling real estate. Carol told Marilyn that she thought Marilyn would make a terrific real estate agent.

"You have such an outgoing personality," said Carol. "You know how to talk to people. All you would have to do to get started is go to school and get your license."

"What does that involve?"

"I don't know what the law says in Missouri, but here in Illinois we have to get 60 class room hours and then pass two tests. One is a national standardized test, the other is a state test which covers Illinois law. You wouldn't have any trouble passing. They will teach you everything you need to know to pass the test. And if you're any good at all, you could make three times as much money as they are paying you at Porter Paint."

"I don't know. It sounds sorta scary to me. What happens if I can't sell houses?"

"Well, you are paid on commission, usually around 1.5% to 2% of the sale price of the house. That means when you sell a $100,000 house you would get a commission check for $1,500 to $2,000. But it is true, that if you don't sell, you don't get paid! You wouldn't have any trouble though. If you sold five houses in a year you'd be making more money than you are now. And, it's so much fun! Every customer is different, and when you help them get what they want it's a real kick!"

After much discussion Marilyn said she would look into it. She contacted Gundaker Realtors and found out that they provided pre-license training. Long story short, she took the training, passed the test and became a licensed Gundaker Agent.

Meanwhile, Herman was dealing with major frustration in his job at MAC. He felt that his job at the company was to function as a change agent. He had the formal training, combined with organizational experience in the Air Force, to analyze the leadership styles within the company and to make recommendations for change. It was clear to Herman that the predominant management style at MAC was authoritarian. Bosses at all levels ruled with various combinations of fear and coercion. It was, to use an old phrase, "My way or the highway!" It was a toxic environment that took its toll on everyone who worked there.

Son had made several proposals for programs designed to improve management and leadership styles, but other than his regular 5-day seminars, his proposals were turned down.

All of this goaded Herman to take some decisive action. He wrote a letter, not to Dr. Bob Barclay his immediate boss, but to Nate Molinaro, Vice President for Personnel at McDonnell-Douglas. Herman knew that Bob Barclay would not support his ideas for change so he took the drastic step of going around Bob. This Son realized, was a serious breach of managerial etiquette. Nevertheless, he felt that it was the only way to get some resolution to his serious problem. The letter pointed out what Son saw as grievous mis-management. Further, the letter outlined a team building approach that should lead to changes in management style and climate throughout the company and suggested that, if they were not implemented, he could not be held responsible for the results. Son took the implied "My way or the highway" approach and turned it around, saying that if changes were not possible then he might really be ready to consider the highway! Long story short, although Son's ideas were sound, his approach to bringing them about was not very politic. Two days after Son wrote his letter Bob called him into his office to tell him that, "Mr. Molinaro wants to see you right away."

"Do you know what he wants?"

"No, do you?"

"Not exactly. He may want to talk to me about a memo that I sent."

"Memo?"

"I'll tell you about it after I talk with him," Son said evasively. Walking down the hall toward the V.P's office, he wondered what Nate's reaction would be. He was not very optimistic and, it turned out, he was correct.

Nate told Son he was fired.

"What makes you think you can vent your spleen on the company in this way? You know what our philosophy is and you should know that it's not about to change. You are telling us that we don't know what we're doing, and I am telling you, that we do! You'll be given two weeks pay, but I expect you to clear out your desk tomorrow. Under the circumstances, I feel that you no longer fit within the MAC team. Effective immediately, you are relieved of your position within the company. Do you understand?"

"Yes, I understand."

Son should have known better. He should have realized that the management climate at MAC could not be changed from his position within the company. For years he had been their house monkey and now he knew it. So ended nearly seven years with MAC. Son was sorry to see it end, not just for the loss in salary, but for the lost opportunity to work for change in a field that he loved. However, it was not to be.

CHAPTER 89
Of Friendships That Never Die

About half of the combat pilots who flew a full combat tour of one hundred or more missions in Korea survived (there's that guardian angel again). After the war, most remained on active duty, choosing to make a full career of the service. Son had decided, long before Korea, that he wanted a full career in The Air Force. There were many reasons for his decision. There was the camaraderie, travel to lands he had only read about, job security (In 1947 he was offered a regular commission), retirement, medical care and more. But the main reason that he wanted to stay in was that it offered a chance to fly - to do what he loved to do more than anything and get paid for doing it! This was his childhood dream, turned into reality. Most of those who were in the 8th Fighter Wing felt the same way.

There is no question that the group to which Son belongs represents some of the best people in The Air Force. Of the 500 or so officers that were assigned to the 8th during the period 1948 to 1953, a high percentage made it into "star country", that is, they made General rank.

After the war, they were all reassigned to various posts in the U.S. For the next thirty plus years they all went separate ways. Sometimes their paths would cross. Perhaps it would be in Europe. Maybe it would be at some base in the U.S. Perhaps Son would run in to an old friend in that most famous of military cross roads, The Pentagon. Wherever it happened to be, the conversation was predictable:

"Hey, Jim, know who I ran into the other day?"

"No, who?"

"Ray Lancaster!"

"No kiddin', what's he doing now? Last time I heard he had an F-86 squadron at Kirtland AFB."

"Yes, but he was here getting a brush-up on his French before being sent to Paris!"

"Paris? What's he going to be doing in Paris?"

"Air Attaché...he said he made the mistake of telling the Air Force that he could speak French!" Said all he knew was how to say, parlez vouz francias?"

"Doesn't that come under the heading of 'never volunteer?" He seemed pretty happy with the assignment though. He said Barb would love it. She is fluent in French."

"What are you doin', Herm?"

"I'm in the Directorate of Studies and Analysis. We're doing cost-benefit analysis, comparing the F-12 against the F-106 and other birds. Doing most of my flying with an IBM 360 computer! You know the name of the game today - cost/benefit analysis. We gotta show McNamara that we're getting the most bang for the buck with the F-12!"

"Sounds interesting."

"Well, some of it is. But you know what they say about bottle cap Colonels here. . .they're in charge of emptying the waste baskets!"

"Well, try to bear up! Good to see you again, Herm. I'm going back to Furstie tonight. Got another year over there I guess. Anyway, I'm lucky . . .I'm flying fighters!"

"You sure are! Good to see you again!"

And so it went, all over the world. There wasn't a one who didn't have the above conversation many times over. Somehow or another, they kept in touch.

CHAPTER 90
Our Life In Real Estate

In 1977, Marilyn left her job with Porter Paint Company to go into real estate. She went to school and obtained her real estate license in 1977. She worked exclusively in residential real estate. Herman, after leaving McDonnell-Douglas, was involved in free-lance business consulting work. He had a collaborative business relationship with a Cleveland based company, Professional Development, Incorporated, PDI, who provided him with business training materials and leads. Herman sold training packages to companies in all parts of the country and delivered on-site training. Client companies included many belonging to the Fortune 500.The training consisted of tailor made packages designed to meet a company's particular needs in the areas of sales, supervisory and management skills.

Herman also wrote and co-produced with PDI an eight part training video series called, "Organizational Transactions." It was based upon inter and intra-personal communications principles developed by well-known psychiatrist Dr. Eric Berne. His landmark book, *What Do You Say After You Say "Hello"* sets forth his basic theories, to wit: Man has three ego states that describe his persona and behavior. They are, as Berne labeled them, (1) Parent, (2) Adult, and (3) Child.[1] Drawing three circles, one above the other, can diagram individual persona. The top circle, (P), is Parent; The middle circle, (A), is Adult. The bottom circle, (C), is Child.

The Parent ego state is characterized by control. The behaviors can vary from authoritarian and critical to nurturing and supportive. They are automatic, non-thinking behaviors generally learned in one's childhood. They generally come into play in adult life in situations that involve children or child-like behaviors.[2]

The Adult ego state is the executive of the personality. It is the problem solver that ask dispassionately: who, what, when, and how? It is rational and deals with perceived reality in the environment.

The Child ego state is the seat of human emotion and feeling: love, hate, joy and sadness.[3]

Interpersonal communication between individuals can be described and diagrammed as exchanges between the ego states of individuals. Generally, an exchange between two persons will be functional and ongoing as long as the lines of communication are parallel. For example, Parent to Child is functional as long as the child responds back in an expected manner to the parent from his child ego state. Exchanges will become dysfunctional when the lines of communication are crossed.[4]

This book is not the appropriate place for a detailed exposition of Transactional Analysis. For the reader who is interested, reference should be made to Dr. Berne's book.

Unfortunately for Herman, the business relationship with PDI was flawed. Fees earned from companies who received training from Herman were billed and collected by PDI. Son's cut, an agreed upon 30% of the amount billed, was always late and sometimes missing. In the meantime, Herman's bills for travel, hotels, meals and other incidentals, not to mention expenses for maintaining his St. Louis office, continued to mount. He was barely able to keep up. Although he loved working with his client companies, something had to give. Discussions with PDI about their payment practices didn't produce any change. The constant travel was wearing thin, too. An old friend once told Herman that business travel is not the romantic whirl that some think it is.

"Sandusky, San Antonio and Lower Slobovia all look the same from inside a Ramada Inn, Herman," he said.

Marilyn was getting tired of the constant travel, too. "Herman, we've got to decide something. We can't continue to be married by long distance. I know you like your work, but I need to be with you. What do you think?"

"I agree with you, sweetheart. I wish there was someway to restrict my clients to St. Louis companies, but I don't think that's practical. I need to work with a national prospect list."

"Yes, Herman. But look at your travel expenses. Your last trip to New York cost you nearly $5,000. So you're making a lot of money. You're spending it just as fast as you make it."

"Sometimes, faster I know! PDI stiffs me for what they owe me, too. They're either late or short in their payments. I've talked to them, but it doesn't seem to do any good."

"Well, I have an idea."

"Good! That's what I need."

"Why don't you go into real estate?"

"Hadn't thought about that. Do you think I could do it?"

"Well, even though you don't have a license, you give me lots of advice on my deals. I think you'd be very good at it."

"How long would it take to get my license?"

"Talk to Gundaker's training department. They can tell you. I think you have to put in about 60 classroom hours before taking the exam."

They continued to discuss the situation in detail. The more they talked, the clearer it became to Herman that getting into real estate might be a good idea. He said to Marilyn:

"You know, Marilyn, what we have been going through is a perfect example of Adult to Adult problem solving as described by Dr. Berne in Transactional Analysis."

"Whatever! If it works for you, it works for me!"

Without dropping his relationship with PDI, Herman enrolled in real estate school and got his agent's license. In March of 1980, he took and sold his first listing.

"Hey, this is fun!" he exclaimed.

He went on to get more listings. He read a book on prospecting for listings that focused on For Sale by Owner properties (FSBO's). The general theme of the book: If you want to know where people are who need your services, just look in the classified section of your local newspaper under Homes for Sale by Owner. These folks advertise to the world that they want to sell. They are qualified prospects! Your job, as a real estate professional is to help them to: sell more quickly, for more money - bottom line - and with less hassle than if they attempt to do it themselves. After reading the Sunday Post Dispatch Classifieds, Herman picked a half-dozen properties that sounded good to him and tried the low-key, face-to-face techniques described in the book. They were client centered. They let the prospect describe the problem and the desired outcome. Herman offered suggested solutions, some of which the sellers could implement themselves. He stayed in touch and called back on a continuing once a week basis until he got the listing or the owner was successful in

selling it himself. Over time, his patience and helpful attitude was rewarded. Soon he was beginning to build an inventory of good listings. As unattached buyers came to look at his listings, he picked up many of them as clients. It took awhile, but gradually, his commission income began to grow.

He told PDI that he was terminating his relationship with them. They objected but Herman said that the relationship wasn't working for him and that he was closing his St. Louis office unless they could bring their accounts with him up to date. Although it was painful to admit failure, that's what it was. He couldn't make things go the way he wanted. He knew that if he was on his own he could make it go. Why didn't he try it? Maybe he was a little scared of doing it on his own.

CHAPTER 91
Salesmen Are Made, Not Born

These questions were revolving around in his mind when he received a telephone call from the training director at Carrier Corporation in Syracuse, NY. Bill Carpenter had attended one of Son's group sessions in New York several months prior.

"Herman, are you still working with PDI?"

"No. We have agreed to disagree. I haven't done anything with them for almost a year. I won't go into the reasons why. It didn't have anything to do with the quality of training I was providing."

"O.K. I know what kind of training you provide. It's the best. That's why I'm calling. We have a national distributor sales organization, all independent companies, that badly needs some basic sales training. Would you be interested in putting together something that you could deliver in two full training days - very basic - along the lines of, "Yesterday I couldn't spell s-a-l-e-s-m-a-n, today I ARE one?"

"That would be easy, Bill."

"I know you could do it. The companies that we've identified so far are located in Kansas City, Butte, Los Angeles, Lubbock, Ft.Worth, New Orleans, Miami, Atlanta, Alexandria, VA, Charleston, West Virginia, Wilks-Barre, Pittsburgh and Philadelphia, PA, and Detroit. I'm still working with seven or eight others that may want to come on board."

"When would you want to do this?"

"As soon as possible, probably starting the beginning of the year. Maybe you could schedule city "A" on Monday and Tuesday. Use Wednesday as a travel day and schedule city "B" on Thursday and Friday."

"Sure. That would work."

"O.K. Here's what I need from you: A proposal, detailing the kind of training, along with a detailed schedule for delivery, plus your turn-key bid price. You take care of everything, your travel, meals and lodging materials and fee."

"I'll need the other six or so cities before I can give you a definitive bid."

"Sure. I'll call you Monday or Tuesday."

"Great. I'll get to work on it right away so that when I get the other cities I can wrap it up quickly."

"Great, Herman! We'll talk next week."

As soon as he finished talking with Bill, Herman pulled out his calculator and started working up an estimated bid price. This time he would be working directly with the client company, not going through PDI. He was sure he could deliver a product to Carrier that would fit their budget and give him a reasonable profit. He figured $200 per hour for his classroom time, including all expenses, a reasonable fee in 1982. Each program would con-

sist of 12 hours of class time over two days. It looked like a total fee of around $45,000 for the entire program. That came to about $125 per person for 16 hours of classroom training. Considering travel and material costs, that seemed like a fair price.

Then he thought about Marilyn! I promised her I was through with traveling around the country. "I don't think she'll like this," he thought. That evening after dinner he broached the subject:

"Marilyn, I had an important telephone call this afternoon while you were out."

"Arretta is coming to live with us?"

"C'mon, I'm not kidding. It was a really important call. I talked to Bill Carpenter from the Carrier Corporation in Syracuse, NY. I met him when he attended that seminar we did in New York City. He's their corporate training director. He wants me to do some training for them at various cities around the country. I promised you I wasn't going to travel anymore, but this one is different."

"How so?"

"First of all, there will be no PDI in the loop. I'll be dealing directly with Carrier. They want me to go to 16 - to 18 cities to deliver a two-day seminar to each of their independent distributors. I worked out an itinerary. It would take about 8 weeks to do it."

"You'd be gone the whole time? I couldn't stand that!"

"I know. I'm in a quandary. They want me to give them a turn-key price including my time, materials and all travel expenses. I figured a rough price this afternoon at $45,000. Expenses wouldn't be more than about $15,000 by my estimate. That'd be a nice piece of change to collect."

"Could I come with you?"

"I didn't think you'd be open to that, but I don't know why you couldn't. You could be my executive assistant! Oh, that would be fun, wouldn't it? I won't know for sure until next week. Bill has to get back to me with the list of cities and I will give him a firm proposal."

"What about our real estate practice? We both have clients."

"I'll talk to Rich Hake in our office. I think he'd be willing to take charge of them for a 50/50 split on commissions. I know he'd take good care of them."

"O.K. by me, Herman, as long as I can go with you. Otherwise, I would object."

The following week, Herman firmed up details with Bill and they agreed upon a contract price of $45,000. The first seminar was scheduled for Kansas City, Mo on the last Monday in January, 1982. Herman made arrangements to purchase training materials from PDI and had them dropped shipped to each training site. The difference was that this time Herman was billing the client directly. Video tapes, player and monitor, however, Herman carried with him. He could not trust timely delivery to UPS or Federal Express. In those days the video was done on 3/4 inch tape and was shown of course on a 3/4 inch tape player. Add a monitor and there was a heavy load to be carried. Herman arranged and made reservations for meeting facilities at each location, generally at a hotel or motel where they would be staying.

Marilyn, in the middle of Christmas holidays, packed for a two-month trip. She did a fantastic job. It was not a simple task. In addition to both winter and spring clothing, Herman's medicine had to be packed. By this time he was insulin dependent so insulin and diabetic supplies sufficient to last two months had to be included. Diabetic meals were ordered for each flight. Finally, everything was in readiness and they were able to relax for a few days to enjoy Christmas.

It was January. On the Sunday of the scheduled departure, the day before they were to be in Kansas City to present their program, the weather, not surprisingly, decided to intervene. St. Louis was hit with a howling blizzard that started Saturday night. Sunday morning all roads were covered with 18 - 24 inches of snow. Herman called the airport at Lam-

bert. It was still operating. The problem was how to get to the airport. Just getting out of their subdivision was all but impossible. Marilyn called her son, Bob, who at that time worked for Evergreen Lawn service. He had a pickup truck with a snow blade on the front. He said he would get them to the airport and he did! They were off and running! Herman delivered the first two-day seminar to Carrier's Kansas City distributor and it was well received. On Wednesday, they departed by air to Rapid City, South Dakota where they rented a compact car and drove to Biddle, MT for a short visit with Marilyn's daughter, Holly, and her husband, Dick. Dick and his three brothers own and operate a 26,000 acre cattle ranch in southeastern Montana, along the Little Powder River. They planned to stay Wednesday and Thursday, leaving early Friday morning, to drive across the state to Butte, MT. Again, the best laid plans as the old Scotsman says, "aft gang aglye."

Somewhere, somehow, Herman came down with a severe case of food poisoning. Although he didn't blame Holly for it, he thought it might have come from a hot dog that he found in her refrigerator. He thought it would make a nice bedtime snack. Early Thursday morning He awoke with severe stomach pain, diarrhea and extreme nausea.

"Marilyn! My gut feels like I'm committing Hari Kari! Maybe I've got appendicitis!"

He was writhing in pain, seriously ill and in need of medical attention. Gillette, WY was the closest town with a hospital emergency room. Broadus, MT, about 25 miles north, did have a doctor. Dick said he would drive Herman to Broadus since that was the quickest way to get him the attention he needed. Dr. Bittemann, it turned out, was an ex-luftwaffe fighter pilot during WWII. A captain in the German Air Force, after the war he came to America and went to medical school. Herman was too sick to talk much, but he had to ask:

"What did you fly when you were in the Luftwaffe?"

"Messerschmitts."

"Really?"

"Ya, I did."

"And now you're a doctor?"

"Ya! das quite a yump, no?"

"Yeah, for sure! Well, I'm a retired fighter pilot too. I flew Mustangs. So take good care of me."

"Ya, I vill certainly!"

Dr. Bittemann was a general practitioner in a small country town. He did not have access to much in the way of technical equipment. He did the best he could for Herman, however. He ruled out appendicitis. He did a throat culture and told him that he appeared to have a bad case of salmonella poisoning. He prescribed an antibiotic and said that he would just have to tough it out.

The following Monday Herman was due to lead a two-day sales training seminar for The Carrier Corporation in Butte, MT. As he left Dr. Bittemann's office he was certainly in no condition to perform. All he could do was go back to Holly's home and hope that he would feel better. At the moment, he was miserable. There was no way that he could drive hundreds of miles across the state before Monday. Holly's husband, Dick, came up with an idea. Why not charter an airplane and fly to Butte?

"What? That would be expensive. Where would we find a charter service that would do it?"

"Herman," Dick said, "I know a commercial pilot who does that sort of thing. He has a Cessna 172 and he flies hunters all over the Montana and Wyoming. I don't think he would charge you too much. Besides, he's a friend of mine."

"What kind of pilot is he? You say he has a commercial license. Does he have an instrument rating?"

"Oh yes, I'm sure. I know he has a lot of time in the air. He uses his airplane to fly all over the west to Rodeos. Among other things, Johnny Morris is a six time world champion bareback rider, both broncs and bulls."

"Good grief! So he knows something about riding bulls. What does he know about flying? I guess he knows something about risk taking anyway, doesn't he? O.K., other than canceling the date I don't seem to have any other alternative. But what will I do with my rental car?"

"Don't worry about that, Herman. I can turn it in for you at Gillette."

"All right, go ahead and call him, Dick."

The arrangements were made. Morris would fly to the ranch Sunday Morning, land on the highway just north of Biddle. Dick would drive Herman and Marilyn, with luggage, to the appointed pickup spot and they would be on their way. Now all Herman had to do was get well. That, it turned out, was easier said than done. Herman lay down on the barca lounger at the Rumph ranch house. Marilyn covered him with a blanket.

"Honey, you look terrible. You haven't had anything to eat all day. Can I get you anything?"

"The thought of food gives me the shivers."

"O.K., your next pill is due in about 2 hours. Why don't you try to get some sleep?"

He slept fitfully. When he awoke, Marilyn gave him his pill and offered some clear chicken soup. It was hot. He sipped a little, but it didn't appeal to him. Waves of nausea swept over him and the very thought of food made him sick. But he made up his mind that he was not going to renege on his promise to Carrier. He had 48 hours to get better. Right then, his stomach was bloated like one of Dick's heifers after eating too many wild green onions.

By Saturday night there wasn't much improvement in Herman's condition. He still couldn't tolerate solid food, although he was able to handle chicken broth and hot tea. That was it.

"Herman, I don't see how you are going to be able to teach. You can hardly stand up," Marilyn said.

"I'll make it somehow. I'll tell them I'm sick. No sense in trying to fake that. I can keep my face time before the group to a minimum. I'll introduce each segment, show the appropriate videotape and then give them an exercise to do. The video and the exercises will take an hour each, more or less. During that time I'll go to our room and stretch out on the bed. Besides, by Monday I know I'll feel better."

"I hope you will. You're one miserable guy now though."

"I know, but I'll be all right. Just get me on Morris' airplane and we'll take it from there."

On Sunday morning everybody was awake by five o'clock. Holly wanted to give Herman some breakfast. What would he like? Nothing appealed to him. Finally he agreed to try a waffle, lightly buttered. He washed it down with some hot tea. It worked, at least for that moment. It didn't induce any nausea. Maybe things were getting a little better.

By six o'clock they were parked by the side of a long stretch of straight highway just north of Biddle. The eastern sky was just turning gray. The temperature was 20 degrees below zero, but the skies were clear. For that, Herman was thankful. He didn't relish the prospect of flying over mountains with elevations ranging up to more than 12,000 feet even in clear weather, much less if weather was a factor. Soon Morris and his 172 appeared, humming low along the horizon to the southwest. He flew north past them and then turned back southward, lining up with the narrow, two-lane highway. It wasn't much of a runway, but at that time of the morning there was no traffic. The 172 touched down lightly and taxied toward them, pulling up close to Dick's pickup. Morris cut the engine and hopped out. Dick, Herman and Marilyn got out of the pickup and shook hands with Johnny. He looked like he could ride broncos all right. He was short, muscular and compact looking not a little like "The Marlboro Man," wearing a cowboy hat and sheep lined leather coat. His weathered face bore the signs of long time exposure to the sun and wind.

"O.K., Herman. It's good to meetcha. Glad I can help you. We should have you there in good shape in a little over two hours."

The luggage was transferred from the pickup to the baggage compartment on the 172.

Johnny said, "Herman, I understand you're not feeling too well. We'll try to make it a smooth flight. Fortunately, the weather's good. Why don't you take the front seat next to me? Marilyn can ride in the rear seat, if that's O.K. with her."

"That'll be fine with me," said Marilyn. With that, they said goodbye to Dick and climbed aboard. Johnny started his engine and taxied north along the highway, back to the point where he touched down. The takeoff was uneventful. Johnny waggled his wings as he flew over Dick, waving and standing beside his pickup. They turned westward, setting a climbing on course of about 280 degrees. Johnny said they'd be cruising at 12,000 feet.

"Is that enough to clear all the mountains?" asked Herman.

"It'll work when we're on visual flight rules, said Johnny. "There are mountains along our course that go over 12,000. You'll be able to reach out and pick some pine needles. We'll be able to fly around them though."

"Good, let's do that!" said Herman, with just a trace of sarcasm.

Johnny was correct. As the flight progressed, the peaks of the mountains, pristine with snow, got close all right. Herman thought about the outside air temperature, probably hovering around 35 - 40 below zero. He hoped that the Cessna's continental engine would keep humming. A forced landing in those mountains would be fatal. The scenery awed Marilyn. Good, thought Herman. He would have enjoyed it also if he had felt better. He was still sick, so he just slouched down in his seat and tried to forget his discomfort. The altitude added to his gas pains. The flight took a little over two hours. As they approached the municipal airport at Butte, Johnny contacted the control tower and asked for landing instructions. Landing was toward the south, using runway 17. Among the useful information conveyed by the tower, was the current temperature: It was 47 degrees below zero, Fahrenheit! It was too cold to snow, but previous accumulation made the runway slick. It was no problem for Johnny, however. There was plenty of room for the 172, which didn't need a long runway. A courtesy van from the Best Western Motel awaited them. Herman had made reservations there for the seminar. As they walked from the plane to the van the snow underfoot squeaked and crackled like cornflakes. Yes, it was cold.

Herman wrote Johnny a check for $235 to cover the cost of the flight. "Good job, Johnny," Herman said. "I wish I didn't feel so bad, I would have really enjoyed it!"

Checking in at the motel, Herman made sure that the meeting room for his seminar had been reserved. After settling in to their room, they ordered room service and had a light lunch. Herman tried to eat but it was all but impossible. Tea and dry toast was about all he could keep down. That night he slept fitfully. The next morning at 7:00 A.M., with Marilyn's help, he got the meeting room set. Tables had already been arranged in a U-shape configuration. They set up the television and tape machine, and distributed 25 packages of material, one at each chair. Everything was ready. The seminar was to begin at 9:00 A.M.

"You look a little green behind the gills, Herman. Do you think you can make it?"

"I'll make it, but I'll have to tell them that I'm ill," Herman said. "I hope they'll understand. Oh. . .I almost forgot. We need coffee and rolls for our mid-morning break."

"Maybe you can have some too," said Marilyn.

"Yuuck! I don't think so!"

Bypassing some of the gory details, Herman, with help from Marilyn, managed to struggle through the two day seminar. At the end of the program, he apologized, telling the 25 attendees that he hoped they would excuse his lack luster performance. They all said they understood and said that they enjoyed the program and appreciated his effort.

Wednesday morning Herman and Marilyn were back in the air again. This time they flew Continental Airlines, destination Los Angeles, a bit more substantial than Johnny Morris

and his Cessna 172. Herman's intestinal tract was still doing slow rolls, but the pain had subsided a little. Marilyn's sister, Carol, and her husband George, lived in Mission Viejo, about 50 miles south of LA, so they got a chance for a short visit. Thursday and Friday they met with their Carrier sales group. This time, Herman was able to stand up and the seminar went very well. Their next date was in Lubbock, TX, the following Monday. They had a long weekend, which they spent with Carol and George. By Sunday, Herman was almost fully recovered. It was hard for him to grasp how that little salmonella bug could have made him so sick. How ironic it was that a doctor who was an ex-Luftwaffe pilot who had flown Me-109s should have treated him, a WWII fighter pilot, in a Montana cow town. In a different time frame they could have been shooting at each other. "Small world," thought Son.

The rest of their multi-city tour fell into a rhythm: arrive on Sunday for a two day seminar; travel on Wednesday to the next city; deliver another two-day presentation; have Saturday and Sunday off, then repeat the process. After Lubbock, they visited New Orleans, Atlanta, Wilks-Barre and Pittsburgh PA, Charleston and Alexandria, West Virginia, Mobile, AL, Miami/Key West, Detroit, MI and Philadelphia, PA. They got great satisfaction out of working with the Carrier sales people. They were all very responsive and appreciative of the training. During the time between seminars, Herman and Marilyn also got an opportunity to be tourists.

Of course, they enjoyed New Orleans, particularly the cuisine at Antoine's. They also took the opportunity to hear the fabulous and historic Preservation Hall Jazz Band where they heard Dixieland at its foot tapping best. Toward the end of their tour, A weekend in Miami gave them enough time to rent a car and drive over the long 7-mile causeway to Key West, and to visit Sloppy Joe's Bar, favorite watering hole for sometime resident and American novelist Ernest Hemmingway. An interesting sidelight there was the tetra dactyl (six toed) cats that frequented the bar. Herman and Marilyn were told that the cats were direct descendents of cats that Hemmingway brought with him from Havana where he had lived for some time. The weather in Miami was warm and soothing. Herman had by then fully recovered from his gastric distress. He and Marilyn remember well an Italian restaurant, Alfonso's, next to their hotel. The chef, also the owner, turned out a creamy fettuccine Alfredo, with just the right amount of parmesan, that was beyond delicious. Alfonso personally served tables and, after ceremoniously announcing that kisses from the ladies were part of the tariff, generously bestowed enthusiastic bacci (kisses) on all the female diners. They had Alfredo with kisses, every night for dinner.

"This is not good for my waistline," said Marilyn. "We've got to watch our calories."

"O.K., I will watch them as our waiter brings them to our table," said Herman. "This is too good to pass up."

The next stop was Atlanta, where it was still warm. That was not to last, however. A frigid spring ice storm hit town the evening of their arrival. The next morning they woke to a winter wonderland. Everything was sheathed in clear and sparkling ice! Trees sagged or broke under the heavy accumulation. The view out their hotel window was magical, but the roads were all but undriveable. Their seminar was a little late getting started that morning as their participants struggled with the monumental traffic problems caused by the ice. Atlanta is a historic town with much to see and do. However they didn't do a lot because of the weather. The Toy Museum, nationally renowned, was nearby so they were able to see it. The museum's collection of thousands of dolls was fascinating. By the end of the seminar, the ice had melted and spring had returned. On February 25, Marilyn and Herman observed their 9th anniversary, going to dinner at The Boston Sea Party, a wonderful place, where the waiter ceremoniously tied bibs on them so they wouldn't get the drawn butter sauce that came with the lobster on their nice clothes. Herman ordered a bottle of Pouille Fuisse wine to go with the lobster. After dinner they went to E.J's, a well known jazz club, for some good music.

On their way back to the hotel, Marilyn observed:

"We've been dining like Henry VIII for almost two months now. My clothes are beginning to pinch. When we get home, we're going to have to go on a diet."

"No doubt! But not just yet, O.K.?"

"I suppose."

On Wednesday, the weather had moderated. They left for their next city, Wilks-Barre, PA. Their seminar was scheduled at The Woodlands Resort in a mountainous park-like setting. Snow was on the ground. After Atlanta, they just did the seminar, had dinner in the hotel and went to bed early.

Pittsburgh, their next stop, was the home of Jerry and Marty Worth and their family, more former Fourposter Court neighbors. A Phd metallurgical engineer, Jerry, chief engineer for U.S. Steel, had to move from St. Louis to Pittsburgh when he got promoted. Of course, Herman and Marilyn arranged to have dinner with them.

Charleston, West Virginia followed Pittsburgh. Again, they were close to relatives. Marilyn's youngest daughter, Carol, and her husband Stan Hassebrock lived in Huntington, less than 100 miles from Charleston. Another visit was in order. Stan managed a Ramada Inn in Southpoint, Ohio. It was great to see them again, especially grandson, 7-year old Todd, the apple of his father's eye. Already, Todd knew the motel business from top to bottom. He could explain everything his dad was doing in running the motel.

On March 14, Herman and Marilyn took their leave of the Hassebrocks and flew to Alexandria, VA. This had been Herman's home town in the middle sixties when he was stationed at the Pentagon. He knew about its early American history and he felt right at home there. Mount Vernon, George Washington's home, is located only a few miles south. Herman and Marilyn arranged to meet and have dinner with their next door neighbors from St. Louis, Steve and Darlene Kuhlman. Steve was a flight test engineer for McDonnell Aircraft who was working on the F-15 fighter. His job took him for an extended assignment to Pautexant River Naval Air Station.

"Where should we meet?" asked Marilyn, talking by telephone with Darlene. Darlene suggested that Gadsby's Tavern would be a good place.

"O.K., let's try it. That sounds like fun."

During the period 1796 to 1808, Mr. Gadsby's establishment was a center of political, business, and social life in early Alexandria. The tavern was the setting for dancing assemblies, theatrical and musical performances, and meetings of local organizations. George Washington enjoyed the hospitality provided by tavern keepers and twice attended the annual Birthnight Ball held in his honor. Other prominent patrons included John Adams, Thomas Jefferson, James Madison, and the Marquis de Lafayette.

The waiters and waitresses dressed their historic parts, all in colonial style clothes. The décor was authentic in every aspect. Herman and Marilyn met the Kuhlman's and had a wonderful evening with them. On another night they met and had dinner with Marilyn's old friends from her high school days in Cleveland, the Settlemeyers. They took a tour through the Naval Gun Factory, prominent in America's wars since the Revolution.

Then it was time to fly south again, this time to Mobile, AL. Mobile lies west of New Orleans, fronting to the Gulf of Mexico. It is a major port and has many of the characteristics of New Orleans - the climate, the southern culture. It also has a place called Bellingrath Gardens, rivaled only, perhaps, by the formal gardens of Queen Elizabeth's palace grounds in London. The azaleas were in riotous bloom at Bellingrath. Mr. Bellingrath founded the gardens in 1909. At the time, he worked for the railroad and saved his money, some of which he invested in a risky little soft drink company called "Coca-Cola." When he quit the railroad his stock was on its way to the moon. He held on tight. The rest, as they say, "is history."

CHAPTER 92
A Shocking Surprise

Then came Detroit on March 2nd: It was cold — 30 degrees with snow. A surprise other than the weather awaited them there. They had reservations at the Ramada Inn in Southfield, a big 9-story motel located across the street from a large shopping center in Northwest Detroit. The hotel advertised an indoor pool, gift shop, a nice restaurant and an impressive disco bar called "Scandals" with lights in the floor and neat furniture. Scandals offered free hor d'oeuvres and live music from 5 to 8 p.m.

They were tired and a bit frayed from all the days of travel and teaching. "One more time," Herman said, as they hoisted their luggage from the courtesy van onto the hotel luggage cart. "We're getting close to the end. Won't you be glad, Marilyn?"

"Will I ever! I'm getting a little homesick for Fourposter Court!"

As they pushed their luggage cart toward the front desk, they heard the music coming from Scandals. Looking in, they could see that it was coming from a small grand piano at the corner of the dance floor. A small bar wrapped around the piano. A modest sign, placed on an easel near the door advertised the free hors d'oeuvres and the name of the piano artist, Bob Milne.

"Never heard of him," said Herman. "But he sounds pretty good! Let's check in, go to our room and freshen up a bit, then come back here and take in some of that and their free hors d'ouvres before dinner."

"Sounds good to me," said Marilyn

A half hour later as they entered the lounge the music was still playing. "That guy's good isn't he? There are some seats at the piano. Why don't you go over there and sit down? I'll go over to the bar and order us a couple of drinks and join you."

"Herman!" Marilyn said, gripping his shoulder: "That man sitting there by himself, listening to the piano - Look! Do you know who that is? That's Bob. . .Bob Westlake!"

"What! Are you sure?"

"Of course, I'm sure. I was married to him for 24 years!"

Marilyn had not seen Bob, written or talked to him since their divorce in 1968. He now lived in Tonawanda, NY, and worked as a salesman for the Benrus Watch Company. Herman, of course, had never met Bob, although he had seen many pictures of him in Marilyn's photo albums.

Taking a second look, Herman said, "I can't believe it, but I think you're right! That IS Bob! What do you want to do?"

"Well, I've got to speak to him. Let me stand here a minute until my heart stops beating so hard. Go order the drinks, then come over."

"Okay."

Marilyn thought to herself as she walked toward the piano bar. "I want to stay calm and make this a positive encounter."

Extending her hand to Bob she said:

"I guess they call this fate."

Taking Marilyn's hand and holding it, Bob said, "Hello?"

Marilyn waited for some sign from Bob that he recognized her. Finally, he said, "I know I should know you, but. . . . ."

Marilyn said, "I guess you should. We were married a long time."

The piano player hit a dissonant chord that sounded like he had dropped his music book on the keys. Bob jerked and said,

"I knew this would happen some day!"

"Yes, it should have happened when you were in St. Charles to visit our son and his wife."

"I didn't know how you'd feel about it, so I stayed away."

Herman brought the drinks. Marilyn introduced him and everything went beautifully. Bob introduced them to the piano player, Bob Milne, whom he seemed to know quite well:

"This is the lady I was married to for 24 years." He went on to explain that it was a chance meeting after 14 years. He said that it was Marilyn's glasses that kept him from recognizing her. They talked about their kids and their trip. Marilyn said that she wished that she had their trip pictures in her purse.

Herman said, "I can go get them."

Bob said, "Why not bring them tomorrow night. You have to hear Bob Milne who will be playing here again."

Herman and Marilyn excused themselves and went to dinner in the hotel restaurant. After they had ordered, Bob came in also.

"Why don't you join us," said Herman.

Later, in a letter to her daughter, Carol, Marilyn wrote:

"Bob seemed eager to join us for dinner. The conversation went very well and left me with the feeling that it was a positive encounter I'd hoped for. I was extremely proud of Herman who just did and said everything right. I must admit, I was proud of myself too in this rather dramatic interlude. I hope tonight will be comfortable for all of us."

Marilyn told Bob that he should not be afraid to stay in touch with his children. Holly, in particular, felt hurt by Bob's lack of communication. "Call them, write to them, go see them," she said. "They want to stay in touch with you, but it's your call, Bob."

Bob said he appreciated the advice and would act upon it. They had dinner together again the next night. Again, the conversation went well. Bob seemed to have lost the sense of embarrassment that he felt the night before. They talked at great length about their kids. When they said goodnight Bob said that he would be in touch. As they went to their room, Marilyn and Herman looked at each other with a mixture of disbelief and amazement.

Herman said, "How could this have happened? Bob didn't know we were coming here. Certainly, you haven't been in touch with him. . . .have you??"

"Of course not! You know me better than that. I would have no reason to contact him!"

"I believe you, really, I do! But it's such an improbable scenario. What are the odds that you and I would be staying at one of millions of motels in a city over a thousand miles from our home and that your ex-husband, from whom you have been divorced for nearly fifteen years, and who lives in New York, and with whom you have had no contact since your divorce would cross paths with us in this way? It's more probable that we would be struck by lightning! This is the small world story that tops them all!"

"I know! I can't believe it either."

"Well, I'm glad it happened anyway. You've said many times that you couldn't understand why Bob had broken off all communication with his kids. I think you got him straightened out on that score. Holly, Carol and Bob will be glad to hear from him again."

"Yes, particularly Holly, and Carol, too. I don't know about Bob though. He was twelve years old when we were divorced, and he was hurt more than our girls. I think he still has a lot of anger and feelings of abandonment."

"Well, we'll just have to wait and see."

With that they went to bed.

Hello Again, St. Louis

Soon it would be time to return to St. Louis. Herman and Marilyn had one more city to cover, the city of "brotherly love," Philadelphia. The Carrier Seminar there went well. By now, Herman could replicate it in his sleep. Feedback from the participants was positive. During their off time they took in the historic places in Philadelphia, Independence Hall, The Liberty Bell, and of course the Art Museum where Rocky Balboa trained by climbing the long steps approaching the entry. To be honest, Son felt like he had been following Rocky up those long stairs. He was bushed.

As they got on the airplane for the flight back to St. Louis the next day, Son told Marilyn he didn't feel good:

"Hon, I feel like I am coming down with something. Feel achy, like maybe I have a fever."

Marilyn put her cool hand on his forehead and said, "I think you do have a slight temp. Well, we'll be home shortly and we'll check it out if it persists."

"O.K. I'll try to catch some snooze when we get settled on the airplane."

Even though he felt a little rocky, Herman wanted to talk about their trip. "It's been an exciting two months, hasn't it, dear?"

"It certainly has! I wouldn't have missed it for the world. I'm glad to be going home though. I think we need a breather."

"I agree. Think I'll take a little snooze now. Wake me if they want to bring us anything to eat besides peanuts." With that Herman jostled a pillow under his head and went to sleep.

Later that evening, they collected their luggage, caught a cab and minutes later, let themselves into their home on Fourposter Court. They found some canned soup in the cupboard, heated it and had it before collapsing into bed. It was a trip well done.

CHAPTER 93
Aches and Headaches

Saturday morning, their first day home, Herman awoke with a bad headache and a deep, persistent cough. Marilyn took his temperature. It was 105 degrees, obviously indicating that something was wrong. The question was, what was it? They called Dr. Feldman's office, their regular family general practitioner. Of course, his office was closed on Saturday. A call to his answering service eventually produced a call from the good doctor. After Marilyn related Herman's symptoms to him he said he would see them in his office in half an hour. After the usual checking with stethoscope and tongue depressor, he ordered a chest x-ray. Herman dutifully went down the hall, stood in front of the machine and had his x-ray. Then he went back to Dr. Feldman's waiting room. Sitting there with Marilyn, awaiting some word from Dr. Feldman, he was surprised when Dr. Feldman poked his head out his office door to tell him that he would have to go back to the x-ray room. "They didn't get the picture they wanted," he said. Herman went back for a retake. After reading the second x-ray, Dr. Feldman said he wanted to admit Herman to the hospital because he was concerned that he might have pneumonia. There was a suspicious spot on the upper left lobe of Herman's lung. He wasn't sure it was pneumonia but because of his high fever, he wanted to have him in the hospital where more definitive diagnosis could be done. He would call ahead to Jewish Hospital and arrange for Herman's admittance. Marilyn drove him to the hospital where he stayed for four long days. During the first 48 hours his fever continued to run high - 104 to 105 degrees. He felt terrible. Marilyn said, "Can't you give him something to make him more comfortable?" The resident doctor said that Dr. Feldman said that he didn't want any palliative medication until a clear diagnosis could be made. Through the process of elimination they ruled out pneumonia. It wasn't that. Further tests indicated it wasn't tularemia (rabbit fever), anthrax or mesothelioma. Finally, they said that Herman had Legionnaire's disease! Legionnaire's disease? How could that be? Apparently, it is caused by bacteria that commonly grow in large-scale air conditioning systems that use water in their condensation units. Certainly, during their long trip, there had been ample opportunity for exposure, and after his run-in with salmonella food poisoning Herman's immune system may have been somewhat weakened. The good news was that now that they had a diagnosis, treatment could begin. He was put on a regime of heavy anti-biotics and quickly his fever broke. Within 24 hours he felt much better. After four days in the hospital, Dr. Feldman said he was cleared to go home.

The next day, Marilyn said that she had something she wanted to tell Herman. "Do you remember when Dr. Feldman sent you back to X-ray for a retake?"

"Yes. What about it?"

"While you were gone, Dr. Feldman told me that he thought that you had lung cancer, but that I was not to tell you. That's why he wanted to put you in the hospital."

"What! Why wouldn't he want me to know if that is what he thought? I'm angry! He had no right to lay that on you and ask you not to tell me!"

"Well, I was upset. But I thought I had better not say anything to you if he thought that would be the right thing to do."

"Why would that be the right thing to do? Number one - I had every right to know; number two - if he didn't want me to know, he had no right to lay that on you and swear you to secrecy. I don't know where he learned his ethics, but I don't agree with them! Beginning now, he is no longer our family doctor!"

The next day, Herman began the search for another doctor. His good friend and neighbor, Dr. Roman Patrick, recommended that he talk with Dr. Squireteri, a good general practitioner with offices in North St. Louis County. It turned out that Dr. Squireteri was exactly what Dr. Patrick said he was - a good general practitioner. He was not an endocrinologist or diabetic specialist. That was what Herman really needed - more about that later. After some routine blood tests, Dr. Squireteri increased Herman's insulin dosage schedule.

"This should keep your blood glucose levels a little closer to normal than what you were doing with your previous doctor. Unless you have problems, let's schedule you for a follow-up visit in, say, six months." With that decision, Herman began a relationship with Dr. Squireteri that lasted for four years. Herman did not do well on the increased insulin dosage, however. He was plagued with not infrequent episodes of low blood sugar, some progressing into insulin shock. For those who have no knowledge, it will suffice to say that insulin shock, caused by insulin-induced hypoglycemia, is scary. Loss of control of muscles and speech sometimes gives the appearance of drunkenness, or seizures. This understandably, upset Marilyn. She didn't think that Herman was getting the right medical advice and care. Finally, she decided to do something about it. She talked to a nurse acquaintance who gave her the name of an endocrinologist that she said was really good. His name was Dr. Norman Fishman. Marilyn called and got an appointment for Herman. As it turned out, it was a life saving decision. Herman has been with Dr. Fishman ever since, and it has turned his life around.

By the summer of 1985, things were going smoothly for the Sons. The real estate market was hot. Both Herman and Marilyn were licensed realtors, working with Gundaker Realtors, Better Homes & Gardens. Gordon Gundaker and his partner, Don Williams, had founded the company in 1969. Since inception, the firm had enjoyed accelerated growth. By 1985 it was the largest real estate company in Missouri. Both Herman and Marilyn had their brief cases full of client folders. Both sellers and buyers abounded. In April, 1984 they attended the Better Homes and Gardens National Convention. Held in New Orleans, LA, N'awleans, as natives call it, is one of the greatest tourist towns in America. Sometimes called "The Big Easy," it is one of the greatest tourist/party towns in the country. For four days they had a wonderful time. They sampled the night-life on Bourbon Street. They listened to great jazz music, including The Preservation Hall Jazz Band, trumpeter extraordinaire Al Hirt and Dixieland jazz clarinetist Pete Fountain. They dined at Anthony's and The Commodore restaurants. They took a riverboat cruise. Oh yes. During the day they attended some very educational and helpful seminars, all aimed at helping them be more effective agents. Returning home to St. Louis, both Marilyn and Herman were busy with their clients. They tried to pool their clients and work together but it didn't work. They weren't in competition with each other, but they had different styles of working. They decided that it was best for them to work separately. That was fine. At night they would often compare notes, but each of them retained responsibility for their own clients.

Herman's practice involved both residential and commercial work. Marilyn preferred to work with buyers. She had great empathy and terrific listening skills. She knew how to gain the buyer's trust and confidence. She also knew how to zero in on what kind of home the buyer needed and wanted.

CHAPTER 94
Enter Now, A Time Machine

In August, 1985, seventeen years after Son had retired from active duty, he came home from his real estate office to find Marilyn sorting through and opening the day's mail.

"Herman, look at this. It's from somebody in the 8th Fighter Wing - Don Miller - you'd better open it."

Don Miller? He was one of Herman's friends from his gunnery instructor days at Ajo, Arizona, even before he went to Japan and joined the 8th. "What could he be writing me about," Son wondered.

"Look!" he exclaimed as he read the letter, "they're planning a reunion. They want us to get together in Las Vegas next year. Miller and Homer Hansen, who was in the 36th and retired with two-stars, are offering to organize it and make all the arrangements for a four day bash! They want to include all of us who were members of the 8th Wing from 1950 through 1951. That would cover all of us who were there when the war began. Wow! We gotta go to that!"

"We? I don't know anybody in the Eighth Fighter Group or Wing or whatever. What would I do, talk airplanes with a bunch of guys I don't even know?"

"No. The wives are invited too. I've told you about the women of the 8th haven't I? Most of us had our wives and families with us when the war began. They are a special bunch of ladies and from their common experience they have a special bond. Arretta and Mary-Lynn were there too, you know. Arretta didn't get to know them but it wasn't their fault. They were as nice and friendly a group of women as you would ever want to know. Dottie Price-Victory is the widow of our Wing Commander, Colonel Jack Price. She is the matriarch of the group, a stately lady and someone you would love. She's in her eighties now and she'd love you like a daughter! Arretta didn't get to know these women because of her agoraphobia. They'd take you in as though you were an original, I know! It would give you an opportunity to know something more about my life in the Air Force before I ever met you." It'd be a great trip, too, Las Vegas is party town, USA, you know! There would be lots of things to do and see. Whatta ya think?"

"Well, you do make it sound inviting."

"Then it's a deal. I'll write Don and tell him to include us in."

Thus began an 8th Fighter Wing tradition. Since 1986, reunions have been held on even numbered years. All of them have been memorable. Guys and gals who hadn't see each other for decades pick up their relationships as though they had never been apart. Marilyn, as I had assured her, was taken in as though she were a charter member. She has gotten to know the wives and their husbands.

Since 1986, there have been reunions every other year, three times in Las Vegas, in Scottsdale, Arizona, Fort Worth, TX, San Antonio, TX, Colorado Springs, CO, Dayton, OH

and St. Louis, MO. Herman and Marilyn hosted the event in St. Louis. All of them were smashing successes. A half-century has taken its toll of course. Both Don Miller and Homer Hansen have passed on. So has Bob (Romeo) McCrystal, who entertained us all. He wrote, played on his guitar and sang such songs as, "Itazuke Tower", "Air Force 109," and "Beside a Guinea Waterfall." Big Jack Price, our Wing Commander, is gone, survived by his widow, Dorothy. "Honey Bucket" Bob Wayne is gone. So is Bill Samways. This is by no means a complete list. As the years flow by the ranks of the 8th Fighter Wing are thinning, but the bonds of brotherhood that were forged so long ago are strong as ever. Our next reunion is tentatively scheduled for the fall of 2004 in the San Francisco area. Vince Clarke, a 35th squadron stalwart and dyed-in-the-wool fighter pilot, has agreed to be the project officer. He will be assisted by Jack Krout, another Black Panther with impeccable credentials. We hope that this tradition continues until there are only two of us left and that we are able to get together to toast one of the finest groups of men and women in the military service. As the years go by, these events are shining pearls in our string of memories.

CHAPTER 95
Memories and A Eulogy

During the summer of 1996, my daughter moved from San Francisco, where she had lived for nearly twenty years, to Palm Springs, California. A major reason for the move was that she had become estranged from her mother. Marilyn and I had a trip to Southern California already planned. Marilyn's sister, Carol Burrows, and her husband, George, live in Mission Viejo, California. We hadn't seen Carol in two years George was felled by a major stroke shortly after our last visit. Today, he is almost a complete invalid. During this time, Carol had been taking care of George's every need. We really wanted to see both of them, and give Carol some moral support.

Since Mary-Lynn had moved to Palm Springs, only 75 miles east, it was easy to include a stop there to see her. We talked about the problems that she had been having with her mother. Basically, they were the same problems that I had had with her when we were married, and that my son had endured earlier.

When Arretta left Walla Walla, WA, where she had spent the previous ten years ma-nipulating my Son, Randal, into taking care of her, she moved to San Francisco to be near Mary-Lynn. Same song . .third verse (I was the first). Her main manipulative tool was guilt. She was a master in applying it to her victims to get what she wanted. First, she would use her considerable charm to soften up her target, subtly suggesting, after she sensed that you were ready, that she needed "this" or "that". "Why not?," thought the victim. "I can do that for her." Then, when the victim had done her bidding, she would deliver "the cross up."

She would say, "That's not right! How could you be so stupid?! . . .or words to that effect. The victim, who was expecting, perhaps, some token of appreciation, would, first, feel hurt and confused. To him or herself, the thought would be: "I didn't misunderstand her! I was only trying to help! Why is she treating me that way?" The hurt and confusion would give way to anger. When Arretta was confronted, she would react with recrimina-tions and pouting. How can you treat your mother this way?" All of this was designed to make the victim feel GUILTY!! After an appropriate "rest period," it would be time to start the game all over again: .first, charm, then, "I need your help," followed by the victim's willing response. The next move in the game was the cross up, followed by the victims hurt and confusion turning to anger. Then came the coup de grace. Make the victim feel guilty again! Around and around and around it went!!

How long could anyone with a shred of self-respect put up with this? Don't answer too quickly. It may very well depend on the relationship. If that person is your mother or your wife, for whom you also have feelings of love and affection, you may put up with it longer than you might think. The situation was much more complex than can be described

in these short few paragraphs. She had a whole basket full of neurotic behaviors. She was agoraphobic, subject to panic attacks particularly when going out of her house. She could not attend social functions of any sort . . .rough if her husband also happens to be a career military officer. This led to a number of heated arguments until Son realized the causes, which were complex and deep rooted. Even so, I felt a simmering anger and resentment toward her. My military personnel files contain several OER's (Officer Effectiveness Reports) that questioned my promotability. I didn't participate socially with my fellow officers. Separated by 25-plus years from that situation, I have wondered why I did put up with it for so many years. But, when I was in the middle of it, I was confused too. Answers as to what to do were not clear or apparent. I had my two children to consider in addition to myself. I thought I could help her or change her, and I tried desperately to do that. Wrong. There was no changing her. Only she could do that. I hoped she would, with the help of several different psychiatrists, get a handle on the problem and make some changes, for the children, for herself and for me. It never happened. Some anonymous psychiatrist (not one who had treated Arretta) said that, "The difference between a neurotic and a psychotic is that the neurotic builds castles in the air, but the psychotic lives in them." Arretta spent most of her time "building castles." Occasionally, she would take up temporary residence in one or another of her creations, but never for long. On rare occasions she would stop building castles completely, and come down into what the rest of us perceived as "the real world." Those times were wonderful, but they were few and far between.

So, after both of our children were "out of the nest", Arretta and I drifted apart. She went to Phoenix, on the face of it to take care of her Dad who was ill with advanced emphysema. After she had been there for about a month, I received a letter from her and, on the same day, a subpoena from the St. Louis County Sheriff's Office. I was being sued for divorce.

Divorce is never easy. I felt the full range of emotions, hurt, anger, guilt and depression. After receiving legal notice, Arretta broke off all communication. I could only talk to her lawyer, a gentleman of the bar appropriately named Larry Carp. In the ensuing game of legal 'Gotcha," I learned a few things about divorce and attorneys. The lessons were painful and expensive. After getting home from work, I handled my frustration by putting on my running shorts and shoes and running until I was exhausted. There was a track at John F. Kennedy High School, about a mile from the house. I would run down the hill to the track, and then do two or three miles. One day I felt like an overheated steam boiler. The pressure inside of me was at the point of exploding. I thought:

"Here I am, fifty years old. I have an Air Force retirement and a good job at McDonnell-Douglas. We have a nice home. Now we should be at the beginning of our 'Golden Years.' Why can't we live out this time in our lives with happiness and tranquility?" The more I thought about it, the angrier I became. I ran until I could run no more. Then, I collapsed on the infield grass of the track and cried until there were no more tears left to cry. In about three months, we were divorced.

I met the attorney who handled my case at a place called the Cupboard in Clayton, Mo. He was sitting on the next bar stool. Appropriately enough, he turned out to be an alcoholic. When I would go see him to confer, he always asked me to meet him at his home. He would say, "I haven't had any breakfast yet. Hold on a minute. He would go to a cabinet, haul down a bottle of Jack Black Bourbon, and pour himself half a water glass, pop a couple of ice cubs in it and say, after a couple of swallows, "There, that better!"

We got through the negotiations, but somehow, I had the feeling that I was being rolled.

I found out a year later that this unscrupulous and unethical attorney was playing both ends against the middle. He had rolled me. My son told me a year later that Mr. H.W., my attorney who I thought was in my corner, made two or three trips to Phoenix to talk to

— Arretta!

Why???

He told her that she would be getting "a sizeable settlement" from the divorce, and he convinced her, actually to invest $10,000 in a limited partnership venture that he was organizing to build and operate a cocktail lounge and nightclub in South St. Louis County!!! She never saw a dime's worth of return from her investment. I was told later, by another attorney that I probably had grounds to sue him for malpractice, and that if I won could have him disbarred. But, he also told me that it would be expensive, and that if I did get a judgment against him, that I might still be a long way from collecting anything. I marked that one up in my little black book of experience. Never trust anyone who is going to handle your personal affairs, unless you know them very, very well! And don't pick them up over a drink at a bar.

It would have been rougher, much rougher than it was if I hadn't met Marilyn shortly after we were divorced.

During the ensuing twenty years, give or take a year, I know that Arretta continued building and alternately living in her castles. I know this from reports that I received from both my son and daughter.

When Mary-Lynn finally decided that she had to get away from her mother, it was an agonizing choice. It took great, great courage for her to take charge of her own life and set out on a new and to a great extent unknown course. She too, went through the same emotions that I did 25 years earlier. She was alternately extremely angry, guilty and depressed. She was also afraid — afraid of dealing with these powerful emotions and afraid for herself. What was going to happen to her?

I asked my daughter, "What else could you have done to help your mother?"

"I did everything I could. Every time I tried to help her, it was always wrong. I would bring her breakfast in bed, and figuratively if not literally, get the plate thrown in my face!"

"Then do you think that you were a good daughter?"

"Yes. But I felt so guilty for having left her. Perhaps if . . ."

"Mary-Lynn, Please...I may not know much, but in this situation I am an expert. I played all those games with your mother even before you were born. As the years passed, the games became more complex and intense. We were like George and Martha, played by Richard Burton and Elizabeth Taylor in, 'Who's Afraid of Virginia Wolff.' They both recognized, in the end, what they were doing to each other, but they couldn't/wouldn't quit. As Virginia said, both sadly and sarcastically, toward the end of the movie, 'Poor George . . .Poor Martha. . .' So let me tell you clearly, from where I stand today, you were beyond question the best daughter that you were allowed to be. You couldn't have been a better daughter, and you have absolutely no reason to feel guilty. Now, your only concern must be getting on with your own life."

I hoped that what I had to say during that visit was helpful.

Months after we had returned to St. Louis, my telephone rang. It was Mary-Lynn. It was the middle of October, so I thought that perhaps she was calling to wish me a Happy Birthday. But as soon as she started to speak, I knew something was wrong.

"Dad, Arretta died," she blurted.

"What! No. When?"

"I found out just this morning. There was a message on my answering machine from the Marin County Coroner. When I called him, he told me that they had found her in her apartment, dead from an apparent heart attack. According to him, she had been dead for approximately five days."

"Mary-Lynn, are you OK?"

"I'm feeling terribly guilty. Depressed!"

"Mary-Lynn, listen to me. I know that you feel pain and grief. That's normal. Accept it. You can work through that. But don't feel guilty. As I told you when we visited you, you have no reason to feel guilty. Reject the guilt!"

"OK, Dad. You're right."

Finally, they hung up the telephone.

Son sat in his office, staring at the wall. For all these years since their divorce, he had not seen or talked with Arretta. "Arretta gone??? It can't be," he thought. Their relationship was a book that he had closed and put away on the shelf. Now the book was down from the shelf. He began examining its pages.

He thought about her life and its early promise, then how so much of it was wasted, trying to deal with her personal demons, fighting her husband, and manipulating everybody. Finally, there was her tragic death, alone and isolated from those who had cared for her. He blinked back the tears, continuing to stare. He thought about their first date, so many, many years ago. Then, from somewhere in the shadows in the back of his mind a vision came into focus. They were at the Adams Hotel in Phoenix. The darkened dance floor was crowded to overflowing with young cadets and their dates. The red and yellow juke box poured forth the rhythms of Glenn Miller's big band. Tex Beneke was on the lyric: "I've got the world on a string:

"Got the string around my finger
What a life!. .What a world!. . .I'm in love."

The music ended, and another song began, as Son and his date, Arretta Webb, edged their way onto the crowded dance floor and joined the swaying dancers. They were small talking, as the Juke began another number. Someone else apparently liked Glenn Miller. Son wasn't a very good dancer, but as the music swelled, he gathered Arretta in his arms and began to move to the music:

That Old Black Magic's got me in it's spell
That Old Black Magic that you know so well
Those icy fingers up and down my spine
The same old witchcraft when your eyes meet mine...
Then down and down I go, round and round I go
In a spin, loving the spin I'm in...
Under that Old Black Magic called love...

The scene faded, and was replaced by another. There was no office wall, only the fuzzy picture, coming into focus.

Look. . .over in the corner. . .a dimly lighted room. . .there's Old Hoagy, illuminated by a single yellow spot light. He is seated on a piano bench, hunched over the keyboard of an old upright. He turns toward the audience . . . flashes a crooked grin. His pale yellow shirt is open to the second button. Wide, maroon suspenders ride over his prominent collarbones. A nondescript tie, casually knotted, hangs loosely around his neck. A smoldering cigarette is perched precariously on the left side of his lower lip, the smoke curling up into his eyes, making him blink. A snap-brim fedora is pushed back on his head. He takes a last, long drag on the cigarette, and stubs the butt in an ashtray above the keyboard. Tentatively, his fingers wander up and down the keyboard. Then, in that slow southern drawl that was unique to Hoagy he says, "When I wrote this, I had no idea it would be so popular," With that, he caressed some preliminary chords from the piano, finally settling in to the familiar melody. Son, seated in the audience, leaned forward, listening intently. Hoagy sang a sad song of love lost:

"Sometimes I wonder why I spend these lonely nights
Dreaming of a song... The melody haunts my reverie,
And I am once again with you...
When our love was new, and each kiss an inspiration,...
But that was long ago, and now my consolation
Is in the stardust of a song...
Beside a garden wall, when stars are bright

You are in my arms
The nightingale tells his fairy tale,
Of paradise where roses grew
Tho' I dream in vain,...
In my heart it will remain
My stardust melody
The melody of love's refrain."

The music faded. The vision disappeared back into the shadows of Son's mind. He sat there shaking. After awhile, he turned to his computer, turned it on and pulled out the keyboard tray. He wished that his children were there, not thousands of miles away. He had to express his feelings about his first wife and their mother. He began to tap out his thoughts.

Dear Mary-Lynn and Randy -

Imprisoned by a destructive life script and assailed by her own implacable demons, Arretta fought all her life for psychological survival. The energies that were required for this struggle left her precious little resource to devote to maintenance of relationships with others. All her life she tried but was never able to develop normal friendships, much less strong and healthy relationships with those she cared most about - her husband and her children. She was starved for affection and approval and we tried to give it to her. She took our love, at first given freely and unconditionally. But try as she might, what she gave back was transformed and corrupted. Eventually, she alienated all of us.

She did the best she could with what she had. Like a play in three acts, however, her life began, developed and proceeded inexorably to its tragic and predictable conclusion:

ACT I

In the beginning, there was hope and excitement. In the fall of 1943 I was a young cadet, just past my 21st birthday, when I first met Arretta. It was on a blind date, arranged by a cadet friend. His name was Pete Webb, strangely coincidental, but no relation to Arretta. He had a date with Dolores Bachman (familiar name? -- she was the sister of Bob). Pete asked if I would like to double-date with him, Dolores and her friend.

"Sure", I said.

Tall and willowy, with shoulder length auburn hair, full lips and a shy smile, Arretta captivated me almost immediately. The electricity was almost overwhelming. That night, we went to a dark and inviting cocktail lounge at the Adams Hotel in Phoenix. It was crowded with cadets and their dates. We had drinks, cuddled in a booth, and danced on an overcrowded dance floor to 40's big band music on a five plays for a quarter, kaleidoscopic, red and yellow jukebox. I asked her for another date. Curtain for the first act here.

ACT II

Our life together began routinely enough. WWII, with all its perils and uncertainties provided a backdrop, but we were in love and were not concerned about "what if" kinds of questions. We were married in the base chapel at Williams Air Force Base by Army Chaplain Arlie McDaniel on March 16, 1944. In a simple ceremony, attended by Claude and Mary Webb and Dolores Bachman, our life together was joined.

Our first home was in a wartime FHA housing project in Ajo, Arizona, where we rented a small one-bedroom apartment for $32 per month. I shall truncate a mass of detail - enough for a book or two, really - by saying that very soon it became apparent to me that Arretta was marching to a different drummer. To say the least, I was confused, often hurt by her double-bind (damned if you do, damned if you don't) style of communication. Gradually, as I came to know more of her background, I began to realize that she was setting me up emotionally, trying to put her father Claude's face on me (During A's childhood, her father was a drunk, a philanderer and wife beater). It didn't fit me, but that didn't keep her from trying. I kept trying, trying to love her, trying to get her to love me in return. In her defense, I did get love in return, but it was often booby-trapped, set to explode in my face without

warning. Four psychiatrists and many years later, I came to understand the nature of her internal demons, to understand that much if not most of her behavior was compulsive and beyond her conscious control.

During this period, beginning in March, 1947, when you were born, Mary-Lynn, and ending in the fall of 1970 when you left for Whitman, Randy, we were involved in parenting both of you. We did our imperfect best to love and guide you. In retrospect, I know that our troubled relationship damaged our ability to function as ideal parents. It's one of the major regrets of my life. I could talk a lot about that, and perhaps sometime I will, but for now I want to stay focused on Arretta.

As I said, I gradually came to understand the demons that Arretta did battle with on a daily basis. But understanding didn't make it any easier to live with her. Neither did understanding her convey any power to change her. Change, if ever possible, would have had to come from within her. By now, I had retired and we had moved to St. Louis. I had a good job with McDonnell-Douglas. I hoped that we could enjoy our "golden years" together. There was no more moving around, no more separation, at least there shouldn't have been. Perhaps, now that the pressure of service life was removed, she would change.

The change I had hoped for never came. The demons won. There was nothing left to hold us together. We were divorced in June of 1972.

ACT III

After the divorce, Arretta moved to Phoenix, presumably to live on her own. Since I left the theater at the end of Act II, my knowledge of subsequent events is limited. Given the plot of the play, and what I have learned from both of you, however, its resolution and conclusion seem clear. Arretta was psychologically crippled, incapable of living on her own. When I first met Arretta she was dating Bob Bachman in high school. Bob had subsequently married and had three children. But, somehow, some way Bob was elected to keep her afloat. There are some details of a sub-plot here to which I am not privy, like what happened to Bob's first marriage, and when did it happen? But I digress. After Bob's passing, the scene moved to Walla Walla.— You were now elected, Randy. Since you are already familiar with this part of the play, there's no need for me to speculate the details. After several years in Walla Walla, she alienated herself again. It was time to move on, this time to San Francisco, and you, Mary-Lynn, where the destructive process of alienation continued. When you had had enough, you moved to Palm Springs. She was finally, irrevocably alone. Then, came the news of her passing. The final curtain came down.

Since hearing about Arretta's death, I have had many thoughts about her, and about the four of us. In thinking about Arretta's life, as my wife, ex-wife and mother to you, I have a strange admixture of feelings; sadness, anger, frustration, even love. With all the honesty I can muster, I have tried to express some of these feelings in this letter to you, my children. Although it paints a dark, dark picture of your mother in many ways, I hope that you can see a few rays of light. She was an intelligent, sensitive woman, and occasionally, when the demons were asleep, her true self would emerge. The contrast was so stark and startling that I sometimes wondered if I was talking to someone else. She was charming, witty and full of life. Then, without warning the demons would return. Therein lay the tragedy. In her own strange and distorted way, Arretta loved me. She loved you. She traveled life's highway as best she knew how.

The problem was that the garbled road map she used kept sending her down the wrong paths.

Now the demons are deprived of their host, and her spirit, the one we all sought and loved, is finally free.

Godspeed, Arretta. We love you.

Love,

DAD

CHAPTER 96
A Trip to Remember

In mid-April, 1994, Marilyn and I packed a few things and jumped into our Caddie for a short, uneventful (we thought) drive to Dayton, Ohio to attend our biennial reunion with our friends of the 8th Fighter Wing. Good place for the get-together, we thought. Wright-Patterson AFB was nearby, with its supreme Air Force Museum. Dayton is rich in the history of flight. It was in Dayton that the Wright Brothers, Orville and Wilbur, had their historic bicycle shop where they conceived and built the original bi-plane that flew at Kitty Hawk. There is a memorial garden, next to the AF museum, that memorializes most of the combat outfits of the Air Force, dating back to World War I. We headed east, across the Mississippi River departing our home at a comfortable 0930 or so. Picking up I-64 east-bound we continued to Effingham, Il., where it was time to stop for gas and lunch. Thirty minutes later, with a full tank and full stomachs, we headed out again. Ahhhh, so comfortable, and so nice with the CD player giving out with some nice, cool jazz sounds. The cruise control was set on 65 mph (honest!). I was driving. Marilyn was in the front passenger seat. She had gotten up early to pack, and her eyelids began to get heavy.

I said, "Why don't you adjust the seat back and take a little nap"

"Maybe I will."

Sometime later, with a suddenness that cannot be described, I was jolted by the sound of tall grass, whipping along the underside of our car. Panic!! I attempted desperately to get back on the road.

Too late! Over the side we went, skidding down a 70-foot embankment, finally to come to a stop against a barbed wire fence at the bottom! Fortunately, we didn't roll. Fortunately, also, we were spotted by a couple of friendly truckers who radioed for help. A tow truck pulled us out, we had the car checked for damage, which was minor, and we were on our way again, wide awake this time! Do we believe in Guardian Angels? You bet we do!

We checked in at the hotel, none the worse for our experience.

We were in Dayton for the entire weekend, touring the Air Force Museum where some of M's uncle, Charles Hubbell's paintings are on display. Mr. Hubbell is the world's foremost aviation artist. H. said it was good to visit old friends and be a young mustang pilot again, if only in his imagination! We also toured Carillon Historical Park where we saw Orville and Wilbur Wright's first plane, as well as antique autos, bicycles, motorcycles and trains.

It was, as usual, a great reunion, except that during the previous year we had lost Colonel Don Miller to pancreatic cancer. Don was one of the original organizers of our reunion, and a great friend. I had known Don from my first year out of flying school in 1944.

We were both stationed at Ajo, Arizona where we taught gunnery to young cadets. Don met his future wife, Martha Schultz, in Ajo. They were together throughout Don's entire career in the Air Force and reared four children. Sadly, however, Martha succumbed the same year to leukemia. Both Don and Martha will be sorely missed.

Before the reunion, we had heard from Whit Samways, who told us that they were planning on being with us in Dayton, "if Bill is up to it." We didn't know it at the time, but he had been diagnosed with myeloma, a malignancy affecting the bone marrow. When we saw them, there was no hint of Bill's illness. Although he seemed a little thin, he was in great spirits, and we had a wonderful visit. In late Fall, 1995, we received a letter from Whit, telling us about his cancer. He died in late April, 1996, almost a year from the last time we had seen him. Ray Lancaster, my Squadron Commander, and close friend to both of us, called from Stephenville, Texas to tell us of Bill's passing. Ray said that Bill's family was planning a memorial service at Bill and Whit's home near Irvine, California, on May 11th. Coincidentally, we were planning a trip to nearby Mission Viejo to see Marilyn's sister and her husband, George, as well as my daughter, who lives in Palm Springs. I wrote Whit, expressing our grief and sympathy. My letter to her is quoted below:

3 May, 1996
Dear Whit,
We received your letter of April 24, telling us of Bill's passing. I think our letters passed each other in the mail. We first learned the sad news from Ray Lancaster who called us when we were out and left a message on our telephone answering machine. Marilyn then wrote, expressing our sympathy and feelings of sadness. I am sure she did it better than I.

I wish we could be there for the memorial on May 11. I think Marilyn told you in her letter that we have planned a trip to California to visit her sister, Carol, and husband George, arriving there on May 19. You and Bill will be in our thoughts and prayers on the 11th. If I could be there I would like to have given a eulogy in person, but since we won't be, I would like to express my thoughts about Bill in writing, and ask you or some member of your family to read them for me. Could you?

I first met Bill Samways when he joined our squadron, the 35th Black Panthers, in Japan. It was in early Spring, 1950, only months before the start of the Korean War. I was a flight leader in our squadron, and Bill was our new squadron Commander. I knew almost immediately that there was something about this man that set him apart. Was it his self-assured confidence? His easy smile? His sense of humor? Yes, it was all of those qualities, but there was something more about Bill that I was to learn in the months ahead.

As the flight leader of A Flight, I drew the assignment of taking Bill up for his first area orientation flight. It was to be a proficiency check in the F80C Shooting Star, newly assigned to our squadron, as well as an area orientation flight. Everything went smoothly through formation takeoff with Bill tucked tightly in on my right wing, through climb out to altitude. Beginning with easy turns, we toured the local flying area, as I pointed out landmarks, the location of other military installations and so on. As I turned, both into and away from Bill, I noticed that he stayed tightly on my right wing. Most Lieutenant Colonels I knew up to this point couldn't fly that well. So I steepened my turns, pulling them tight and reversing direction rapidly. Still, there was Bill, just where he had been. I led him through loops and rolls, and still he stayed, like dancers locked in a tango, painted to my canopy, as though we were joined at the wing tips. Back on the ground, I congratulated him on his obvious flying abilities. Bill's typically self-effacing comment was: "You made it easy for me. You were so smooth I couldn't help but follow you."

Later, during the War, I had occasion to fly on Bill's wing in combat. Bill made it easy for me, just as he had said that I made it easy for him. He flew with a combination of power

and grace and positive aggressiveness that made him easy to follow — the mark of a great leader in the air.

He had those same qualities on the ground. Always, Bill Samways could be counted upon to do the right thing, make the difficult call and always, always to follow through on his promises. He never asked his pilots to do anything that he wouldn't do himself. He had a kind of flinty integrity that was rare, even in those days, much less in today's make-the-rules-as-you-go-along society. At the same time, he was so easy to know, to talk to. To use a modern phrase, he was "user friendly."

As I continued to live and work with Bill, I discovered another quality — compassion. At the end of a mission, he and the three other pilots in his flight (I was not among them that day) piled into the carryall ramp vehicle that brought them back to the squadron area. I was in the squadron ready room as Bill burst in, tears of rage streaming down his cheeks. He threw his helmet against the opposite wall in frustration, expressing his grief for one of our pilots whose crash he witnessed in Korea. As I remember, I think the pilot that was lost that day was Al Munkres, a member of our wing staff who was attached to us for flying duty. I remember because several wives, living at Kasuga, talked about "the three blue nosed airplanes (normally, there were four airplanes in a flight) that flew over the edge of the apartments where all of the married officers and their families lived. The word spread quickly, "Somebody in the 35th didn't come home!"

I have never forgotten those days and months in Japan when I worked and lived and flew with Bill Samways. In all my 26 subsequent years of service I never met another that measured up to the standard of excellence by which he lived. . .never another that was the man he was. If unique means one of a kind, that was Bill.

After Japan, our paths went in different directions, and unfortunately I never had another opportunity to serve with him again. I met Whit, his wonderful wife, in Japan, but never got the chance to know any of his children. I know that he must have been a great father as well as strong and loving husband. Late in life, we met again at the 1990 reunion of 8th Fighter Wing. Our friendship and feeling of mutual respect was renewed, strong as ever. Upon meeting my second wife, Marilyn, whom he did not know in Japan, Marilyn said to him, "Herman has told me all about you. He said that you were, without question, the best fighter pilot he ever knew." "Oh, not true," said Bill in typical Samways fashion, "Your husband is the best!"

In closing, it seems appropriate in Bill's honor to quote the famous poem, "High Flight", by John Gillespie Magee, Jr.:

"Oh, I have slipped the surly bonds of earth
And danced the skies on laughter-silvered wings;
Sunward I've climbed, and joined the tumbling mirth
Of sun-split clouds — and done a hundred things
You have not dreamed of — wheeled and soared and swung
High in the sunlit silence. Hov'ring there,
I've chased the shouting wind along, and flung
My eager craft through footless halls of air.
Up, up the long, delirious, burning blue
I've topped the windswept heights with easy grace
Where never lark, or even eagle flew.
And, while with silent, lifting mind I've trod
The high untrespassed sanctity of space,
Put out my hand, and touched the face of God."

Fly fast, Bill Samways! Fly high, fly high, dear friend ..... we'll miss you!
Herman Son
Lt. Col. USAF (ret)

Former flight leader, A flight, 35th Fighter Squadron
P.S. Whit, we'd like to see you when we come to California the week of May 19th. We'll call you when we get settled at Carol's home. Again, we will be thinking of you and Bill on May 11th.   H.S.

During our California trip, I called Whit from George and Carol's home. I asked if it would be all right to drop by for a visit. Whit was most gracious. She said, "By all means! How about tomorrow afternoon?"

"Great! What time?"

"Two O'clock?"

"We'll look forward to it!"

Whit Samways is a strong woman. She is, maybe, even stronger than was Bill. She was obviously, still grieving. But she reached out her hand, and welcomed us into her home. Bill and Whit bought 3 acres of prime, orange grove, California land, located at the end of a blind canyon, soon after coming home from Korea.

CHAPTER 97
The Media And The Military

In the middle of the morning Herman came home from the weekly sales meeting at his Gundaker Realtors' office. It was the middle of September, 1999. As he turned the key to the kitchen door entry and opened the door, he could hear the answering machine beeping. There was nothing unusual about that. Being in real estate, his home phone almost always had messages waiting. He noted that there were five messages, nothing unusual. He pressed the button to retrieve the messages, expecting routine business calls. The first message, however, jolted him to full attention.

"Mr. Son, this is Charles Hanley of the Associated Press in New York. I am researching a piece on the Korean War. I understand that you were a pilot in the 35th Fighter Squadron and that you were flying missions during the month of July, 1950. Please call me at 212-555-1551."

"What? What could that be about?" Herman quickly figured that Hanley had been rummaging through old mission reports, on file in the archives of the Air University at Maxwell AFB, AL. How else would he know when Herman and his flight mates were flying in Korea?

Herman called him and found out that he was following a lead that came from an ex-army soldier named Edward Dailey who had "confessed" to Tom Brokaw of NBC News. He claimed that he was a machine gunner with the rank of sergeant who was assigned to the 24th Division during the early phases of the war when U.S. forces were being overwhelmed by superior numbers of North Korean Army troops. In an overwrought, fifty years after the fact "mea culpa" he told Brokaw that on orders from his superiors he machine gunned Korean civilians who had been herded into a spot under a railroad bridge at a place called No Gun Ri. Edward Daley, the ex-soldier, told Brokaw that he was consumed with guilt and had to "get it off his chest." Brokaw bought Daley's story, hook line and sinker, and took Dailey with him on a dramatic journey back to the villages in the vicinity of No Gun Ri, where there were tearful confessions to relatives of those whom he had allegedly killed. There were hugs all around and of course lots of six o'clock news video footage. Smelling blood in the water and a sensational story in the making, the Associated Press jumped on the story. Hanley headed up a group of four or five investigative reporters who went baying after the story.

Hanley confirmed that he had, in fact, researched individual mission reports that had been archived at the Air University. He told Herman that he was contacting other members of his squadron, Bob (Smiley) Hall, Bob DeWald, Al Wimer, Ray White, Jim Tidwell and Herman's squadron commander, Ray Lancaster. He asked pointed questions:

"Were you in the air on July 26, 1950, in the vicinity of No Gun Ri?"

"Vicinity? I'm not sure that I was."

"Did you ever attack innocent civilians?"

Son began to feel like a witness for the defense under cross-examination by the prosecuting attorney. He decided that he would answer Hanley's questions truthfully. First of all, he had nothing to hide. But he realized that journalists with an axe to grind can make snow white look like a wicked stepmother. It would not be wise to lie. But neither did he have to give anything to Hanley beyond minimal yes/no answers.

"Not to the best of my knowledge."

"Did you ever shoot at people dressed in traditional Korean white clothing?"

"Yes."

"Then how can you say that you did not attack civilians?"

"It is quite possible that I attacked people dressed in civilian garb. That is not to say that they were in fact civilians or that they were not hostile."

"How did you know what targets to attack?"

"We were under control of a forward air controller stationed with the army on the ground."

"Did this controller ever tell you to attack civilians?"

"I can't answer that."

"Why not?"

"Because North Korean soldiers disguised as civilians often intermixed with Korean refugees and used this tactic to infiltrate our lines of defense. To the best of my knowledge, the army never asked us to fire on civilians. Our policy was to avoid civilian targets."

"But if you say that you fired on people wearing civilian white clothing, how can you say that you did not fire on civilians?"

"A North Korean soldier can wear white clothing. That does not make him a civilian. We had to go on the instructions we received from forward air controllers. From ground soldier's point of view, if they were receiving hostile fire from those dressed as civilians, they were considered hostile and could be attacked."

This line of questioning went on for 30 minutes. At the conclusion of the interview, Hanley said that he wanted to do face-to-face interviews with "several members of the 35th" and that these interviews could be scheduled either in New York or in each pilot's hometown. He said we would receive further information about these interviews. He was planning to release the story in late December, Hanley said, and that he would be notifying Herman before release.

Herman immediately called his old boss, Col. Ray Lancaster, who lived in Stephenville, TX. Ray confirmed that he had also been contacted by Hanley and would probably be doing further interviews with him.

On 29 December, 1999, The Associated Press released the story to international media. Hanley sent Son a copy of the full text of the article by e-mail. While some of it was factual, particularly where Son and other 35th pilots were quoted, the overall tone of the article was accusatory. A layman reader would conclude after reading it those American pilots were trigger-happy cowboys who shot first and asked questions later. That afternoon, while Son was still digesting the article, he received a phone call from Steve Jankowski, a prominent local TV newsman from Channel 5. He wanted to come to Herman's house and do an interview.

"Herman, I'd like to come to your house if that would be convenient."

"Sure, why not? When would you like to come?"

"I'd like to come out now. It will take me about 30 minutes."

"O.K., I guess. Come ahead." Herman told Marilyn they were coming. She busied herself with putting away the newspapers and straightening pillows on the family room couch.

She also checked her 35mm camera. She wanted to make sure that she had film in the camera!

Mr. Jankowski and his camera crew arrived shortly after his phone call. He was the essence of courtesy and professionalism. Cameras were set up in Son's family room, lights were set and adjusted and Jankowski's interview began. It continued for nearly 45 minutes. Questions ranged from those establishing Son's experience and credentials and his overall role in the Korean War to specifics concerning the alleged massacre of "innocent" civilians at No Gun Ri. Son had ample opportunity to respond. There were no "when did you stop beating your wife?" kinds of questions. Still, Son was a bit suspicious, realizing that 45 minutes of video tape would be boiled down to no more than a five minute segment on the six o'clock news. With this kind of latitude, it is possible to make Sister Teresa look like an axe murderer. He would just have to wait and see how Jankowski handled it.

This is what he said in an e-mail sent to Ray right after Jankowski left:

"Well, Ray. . .Channel 5 has come and gone, I've been interviewed and will appear on tonight's 10 o'clock local news, and all my friends, military and otherwise, will be watching.

"Now that my adrenaline has stopped pumping I think I am back in control. . .not that I was ever NOT in control. It's just that when they ask you "when did you stop beating your wife" questions, you have to be extremely careful.

"I THINK it went fairly well. Steve Jankowski, the local tv news guy, was pretty nice. But we'll see how he treats the 45 minutes of video that they shot in our living room this afternoon. He asked me questions like, 'Can you be sure that during your attacks that you didn't kill 'innocent' civilians?' I told him that I felt that that was a naive question. There was no way, considering all the circumstances, that I could know that for certain.. I told him that our policy, clearly stated down through the chain of command, was that under no circumstances were we to attack targets that were identified as civilians. I invoked your name a couple of times on that."

"He asked me another question, however, that came at me like a big, fat softball pitch. He said, 'In retrospect, why do you think that all this happened?' Short answer: It was because we were unprepared, under trained, and undermanned. The match, however, that touched off the conflagration was a statement made by Dean Acheson, U.S. Secretary of State, speaking before the UN. He said, paraphrased, that South Korea was not within the legitimate U.S sphere of influence. He drew a line from Alaska, through Japan and to the Phillipines.[1] A couple of days later, North Korea attacked. "Draw your own conclusions," I said.

"Jankowski promised me a copy of the video. We'll see. If I get it, you'll be the first to see it after me.

"I have also re-read the A.P. article. Sensationalist. It reminds me of what an 8th Grade social science study group, taught by a 22 year old rookie teacher, might come up with. It was about what I expected.

"Also got a call from a guy in D.C. who was with the Korean press. Obviously Korean, but seemed pretty nice. One of several points that I made with him was that without U.S. airpower, S. Korea would have been overwhelmed. Gone. Kaput!! He agreed.

"Anyway, it's been an interesting day, to say the least. Let me know if anyone calls. I would expect that they will.

Cheers,

Herm"

That evening, Channel 5 carried a five-minute segment of Jankowski's interview. To his credit, he did a straight job of reporting without spin. Herman's thoughts came across as he intended them. The next day at the office and later at the health club where he works out he was asked about the broadcast. Many people had not seen the original AP article.

For several days, the questions continued. Most gathered that because Son was quoted in the AP story that he had participated in the "massacre." Once a negative story comes out, accurate or not, an impression is created that is difficult to change. Also, as other print media picked up on the original story, ambiguities contained in the AP version were glossed over, leading readers to jump to negative conclusions. The more Son thought about it the angrier he became. He decided to write a letter to the Post Dispatch that had carried the article in full:

"St. Louis Post Dispatch
Letters to The Editor:
"I was a fighter pilot who actively participated in the Korean War. I flew my first mission on June 26, 1950, the day the war began. I was quoted in a recent article appearing in the Post Dispatch concerning The Air War and civilian casualties While the quotes were accurate, the general tone of the article was, in my opinion, sensationalist. By implication, it was accusatory. It did not give an accurate picture of the Korean War, how it started and what it was all about. Because it will be "yesterday's news," I realize that this letter even if published will do little to correct the overall negative impression conveyed by the article. That's too bad.

"Yesterday, I talked to a "civilian" friend of mine who wanted to know more, so I thought I should at least try to set the record straight. This is what I said to "Bob." Perhaps other readers might be interested as well:

'Bob. ... What the newspaper story leaves unsaid is that "war is hell." Bluntly stated, the military's job is to kill people and break things. It's a dirty, thankless job that is usually required because our diplomacy has failed — but somebody has to do it. There is no doubt that if we hadn't done it that summer in 1950, today there would be only one Korea — monolithic, communist, dirt poor and dangerous. There would be no free, democratic and prosperous South Korea. What we did was to put out a fire. Simply put, the fire was caused because America was unprepared. Also, there were the inept public statements made by Dean Acheson, U.S. Secretary of State. In mid-June, speaking before the UN General Assembly and contrary to our formal treaty with South Korea he said, paraphrased, that South Korea was not within our legitimate sphere of interest in the Pacific. This amounted to a public repudiation of our treaty with South Korea! Only days later, Kim Il Sung's forces attacked and the war was on. I had no control over any of that. Then I had a job to do, which my fellow pilots and I did to the best of our abilities under incredibly difficult conditions. . I have no regrets and make no apologies for my part in that war.'

"Perhaps if our politicians and diplomats realized how important their words are on the world stage, and that to be effective their words must be backed up by credible military force, we would have fewer wars to fight. At the beginning of the new millennium, one would think that those lessons would have been learned. I see little in today's events, however, to convince me that they have.

"When the time comes to fight, as inevitably it will, let us at least remember that occasionally some eggs have to be cracked to make an omelet.

Herman Son"

Hanley and his team of reporters were rewarded for their efforts with the Pulitzer Prize for investigative journalism, giving the story an important imprimatur. Almost immediately the Pentagon and the South Korean Government announced that they would be investigating the circumstances surrounding the alleged incident. An Army Lieutenant Colonel and an Air Force Major came to St. Louis. They sat in Son's kitchen, interviewing him for over three hours, going over maps of the area and corroborating details from mission reports. Their tentative conclusion was that Contour Red flight, Son's group of fighters, were not involved in attacks on civilians at No Gun Ri on 26 July, 1950.

Soon after the Pulitzer award, AP's story came under attack. In May, both U.S. News & World Report (5/22/00) and Stars & Stripes (5/11/00), a newspaper that covers military affairs, published long articles taking aim at the accuracy of the report. The U.S. News piece claimed to "raise substantial doubts" about the scoop—even placing the word "massacre" in quotes in the headline.

U.S. News' Joseph Galloway re-interviewed the veterans who had spoken to AP, picking out discrepancies and gray areas in their stories. Galloway also obtained military records showing that Edward Daily was not at No Gun Ri at the time of the incident—in fact, he was not even a member of the Army unit that was there. Morning report records obtained from archives showed that he was not a machine gunner but a motor pool mechanic with the rank of Pfc not Sergeant. At the time of the incident he was repairing army jeeps at the port of Po Huang, 85 miles from No Gun Ri. Other documents purported to show that some of the other veterans had also been absent from the site of the massacre at the time of the incident. Dailey, sensing that his castle in the air was about to collapse, checked into a veterans' hospital in West Virginia suffering from "emotional disturbances." He was unavailable for further comment.

Did Hanley and his reporting team give up their Pulitzer Prize? Of course not.

After expenditure of over $2 million tax dollars to investigate this 53 year old incident, what are the lessons to be learned from this series of events?

* Most importantly, the American media, including printed as well and television, play a critical role in the defense our country. They play on the emotions and perceptions of the American public. One of the basic tenets of our defense philosophy is that the support and understanding of the American public is necessary for any military operation. Without civil support military operations cannot long continue. The validity of this assertion is borne out in our Viet Nam experience. In that war, we were not defeated militarily, we were defeated politically. Whether or not one agrees with the premises of that war, one has to agree that the media played a crucial role in shaping public opinion about the war. That means that the press has a huge responsibility to get it right. They need to remember whose side they are on.

* The military has nothing to fear from accurate, factual reporting.

* Both the American public and the military have everything to fear from inaccurate, politically slanted and agenda driven reporting. This kind of reporting has been used all too often to discredit the military and to drive a wedge between our troops and those they serve.

* The responsibility for good reporting is shared equally between the government, the press and the public. Each has a job to do. Government must communicate as fully as possible within the limits of security. The press needs to strive for objective reporting. An example of this was the reporting provided by reporters imbedded with tactical units in the initial phases of the Iraq war that toppled Saddam Hussein's regime. The public must learn to listen critically and separate fact from opinion. They need to interpret individual news stories within the framework of a larger strategy as it impacts our nation's security.

CHAPTER 98
Tidbits, Truisms and Conclusions

Over the years certain phrases, quotations and pithy comments have lodged in my brain. At various stages of my life some of them have helped me understand. Herewith is a partial list:

● *"Attitude is everything. - Everything is perception."* Anon

● *"You can go a long way with a smile and a soft word. You can go a lot farther with a smile, a soft word and a gun."* Al Capone. NOTE: This may sound cynical, but my life experiences have confirmed it. POWER exists. There is no escaping it. It is an ingredient in every relationship, individual or collective. Per se, and until it is specifically applied, it is amoral. HOW it is used or not used determines its morality.

● In a recent survey of high school seniors, only 11% could answer the question: :"What happened at Auschwitz?" *"Those who will not learn history are doomed to repeat it."* Winston Churchill.

● *"In flying, airspeed and altitude are a pilot's best friends. They are interchangeable; one can be exchanged for the other. Never run out of both at the same time."* Anon.

● When man in his technological prowess gets too full of himself he should consider the miracle of humming birds. With unique wing structure and outstanding pectorals, they can do things no human pilot can do. I have concluded this while watching them out my kitchen window. - Herman Son

● "Always hold it gently." My basic flight instructor. He was talking about the stick, of course!

● "You can't love anyone more than you love yourself." - Anon. How true!

● "All diplomacy issues from the barrel of a gun " Mao Tze Tung. Another realist.

● "Always have an alternate airport (plan, solution)." - Anon

● "Most folks are about as happy as they make up their minds to be. " Abraham Lincoln.

● Freedom is God's priceless gift. Our country and its success are founded upon it. It must be defended at all costs. Herman Son.

● "Do not try to understand so that you can believe; believe so that you can understand. It's called "faith." There is a time and a place for it." Anon.

● Music is the universal language of the universe. - Herman Son

● Life is a mystery. Enjoy it while you can. - Herman Son.

● I am one of Freedom's children.

Epilogue and Conclusions

In 1996, I found a site on the Internet, The Korean War Project (http:/ www.koreanwar.org) that contained a searchable database listing all the casualties of the war. These are organized by branch of service, unit, date and circumstances of death. I found the names of two of my friends, flightmates who were lost during the war. They were Leon Pollard and Pat Gilliam. I left e-mail memorial statements at the site for each of them. This is what I said about Leon (Billy) Pollard:

"Leon was a member of my flight, and was lost while returning from a mission. We were in heavy clouds, flying tight formation when Leon, apparently experiencing extreme vertigo, lost contact with us. It is presumed that he crashed into the Sea of Japan. God be with you, Leon, You gave your life for a noble cause."

I said this about Pat Gilliam:

" I lost two members of my flight during the time I was flying combat missions in Korea (26 June - 30 September, 1950.) Pat was one. 'Pat', as we knew him, had only recently joined my flight, coming to our Squadron from the ZI. He was a young West Point graduate, smart, very likeable and with great potential. We were flying P-51 Mustangs, on a mission out of Taegu Airfield. Pat's airplane was hit by ground fire while we were attacking a truck convoy, approximately 25 mils north of Taegu. His prop governor quit working and his prop ran way. We headed back to the south, but it became apparent that we wouldn't make it. As he lost airspeed and altitude, I pulled alongside and told him to get out. I watched as he jettisoned his canopy and stood up in the seat. His airplane nosed over into a dive. I was still yelling for him to get out when he hit the ground. I think of Pat often. He was every inch a professional. I have a couple of pictures of him in my squadron yearbook if anyone is interested."

I subsequently was contacted by e-mail by relatives of both men who thanked me for letting them know the circumstances of Leon and Pat's deaths. Ben Smith, now living in Denver, wrote me:

"I was a boyhood friend of Pat in Petersburg, VA and had not known the particulars of his crash until reading Capt. Herman Son's remembrance just recently. Pat, from an old Virginia family, was an all-around good guy and of his many fine qualities the word 'honorable' first comes to mind. I remember late Spring and early Summer of 1944, as our high school days were coming to an end and his friends were becoming eligible for WWII military service. Pat was about to enter West Point. He ruefully told us we would be seeing action and 'getting medals' while he was attending school. As it turned out, some of us did see action in WWII or Korea, but Pat was the only KIA casualty from our group of friends. He left a big void in our midst.

I left Petersburg more than 45 years ago and now live in Denver, but I hope Pat's remaining relatives and friends will see Capt. Son's moving remembrance to a fine man."

Jan Pollard Thomas, Leon's half-sister, did not know of the circumstances of Leon's death until she contacted me by e-mail after seeing my remembrance. We exchanged many e-mails as I told her what I knew about her brother. She wrote this moving remembrance for Leon (Billy). I have her permission to use it in full:

Billy's Box

"In June of 1950, the Korean War began. A young man on the brink of life had joined the Air Force after participating in the Army in the latter part of World War Two. He didn't get too far in his Army career because the war ended, he was sent home and discharged. This young man was determined, however, determined and courageous. He came back to Texas, graduated from A & M, and then joined the Air Force as a First Lieutenant. He flew F-80s, a jet-type aircraft. He was a member of the 35th Fighter Bomber Squadron, the Black Panthers.

On visits home he met a fiesty young woman named Bobby. She knew the minute she went out with him that he was 'the one' and apparently these feelings were mutual, as he soon asked her to marry him. They became engaged over the phone during an early morning overseas call. By the time she got to the post office an hour later, she was congratulated three times on her impending marriage. In a small town in those days, those overseas calls were 'monitored' by operators.

Billy was training in Itazuke Japan when the Korean conflict began, so he was one of the first to go. In turbulent monsoon weather, Billy's plane went down over the Sea of Japan on July 9th, 1950. Though a rescue was sent out immediately, no remains were found. He was declared MIA at first but soon was reclassified as a loss.

Billy left behind a mother, a father, a stepmother, three half-brothers, one half-sister, and one broken-hearted fiancee. The eleven year old brother was the only one of his siblings old enough to have any memories and Billy was his hero. It was a tough time. Billy's stepmother, though only a few years his senior, had grown to love him and always said he was the smartest and most handsome of all the children in the family. There is no telling what this young man may have accomplished.

Today there is not much left of Billy; only a small box with a few reminders[is left, and we call it] - Billy's Box. The contents are comprised [sic] of a few newspaper clippings, some pictures, and a couple of letters including one who went to flight school with Billy. This man also perished in the war just a few months later. The pictures are of a very handsome young man in a uniform and some slides photographed by Billy himself. One of those slides is taken from his cockpit with his helmet on the dash. Today that picture seems far more ironic, I'm sure, than when he took it. And sad.

Billy's name was Leon Waddell Pollard, Jr., I am Jan Pollard Thomas, a second half-sister born to Billy three years after his death. When the Iraq War broke out this year [2003], these feelings of wanting to know more about Billy resurfaced. In May, I met a man who was wearing a Korean War Veteran's hat and explained to him my story of having lost a brother to this war. He told me he'd been a pilot, too, and was sorry for my loss. I thanked him for his kindness and service to our country.

Remarkably, through the magic of the Internet, my family has found both Billy's flight commander on that fateful day and his fiancee. Fifty three years later, I've begun to know a brother I never had the opportunity to meet. We won't forget you, Billy. We won't forget."

Jan Pollard Thomas
September 14th, 2003

Jan's words speak for themselves.

As I conclude my story in early 2005, I think of Billy and Pat. They were typical of the fine young men who flew in defense of freedom and democracy during the Korean War.

There were hundreds, even thousands, like them. Because of their efforts, South Korea is free and democratic today. They were heroes.

Who are today's heroes? September 11, 2001 changed everything. We are again at war - potentially, World War III. Our protagonists are the forces of extreme Islamo-fascism. It is a strange war, unlike any we have fought before. It is a war that calls for new strategies and tactics. It is a global war that may last for generations. But we cannot flag because it is a war that we must win. There is no other acceptable alternative. Winning calls for focused and measured application of all our resources - economic, industrial, educational, military and diplomatic. Who are the heroes of this strange war? They are not overpaid rock stars that make teens scream with delight. They are not movie idols or steroid-hooked sports figures. Although they remain an essential part of our society, traditional media such as television, newspapers and news magazines don't rate very high on my "hero scale" either. Media credibility has been questioned too many times. The talking heads of the mainstream press need to get the facts right, that's all - no spin. They need to remember which country gave them the First Amendment freedoms they now enjoy, and whether gambling against the constitutional structure which allows the individual not only to hold a bias but to freely express that bias is in their - and our - best interests. The real heroes are our cops, our firemen and our homeland security workers who keep our streets and homeland safe and secure. Our real heroes are our committed volunteer military service people - our soldiers, sailors and airmen who daily put their very lives on the line. They fight for our country. They endure indescribable hardships and privations. They fight for freedom and democracy all over the world. We owe them our respect and gratitude. In many ways, our future is in their hands. Let us give them what they need - materially, spiritually and emotionally.

I also think, at this time, of the things that have made my life meaningful. Two words come to mind - love and freedom.

Love transcends everything.

I love flying. That has been a central theme of this book.

I love my Squadron mates, the one upon whom I depended for my very life while they also depended upon me for theirs.

I love my wife, Marilyn, who has been my soulmate for more than 32 years. She has literally saved my life.

I love my family, my sons and daughters, my grandchildren and great-grandchildren.

I love America and the core value upon which it depends - freedom.

I love freedom. Without it we would have no country. Today, freedom is on the march. Every place it is extended is a place in which the threat of terrorism is diminished. Every place it is constrained becomes a danger point.

Finally, I love life. The reasons why are in this book.

Frank says:
"This guy has had quite a run, hasn't he? I think I'll listen in on his conclusions."

Now, in this third quarter of my eighty-second year, with another spring approaching, I reflect on my life and my reasons for writing this book. They haven't changed. I hope, first of all, that my children will read it. What they glean from these pages is entirely up to them, but they should realize that my accounts of my life are my best efforts to remember what happened. I hope that my friends, acquaintances and others may read it and in the process, learn something about me.

Because human memory is by nature subjective and fallible, I make no claim for verifiable accuracy. I can only say that the images and feelings that I have dredged up are clear to me. Have I dredged up everything? Hardly. I am a fallible human being with my share of closet skeletons that, for my own reasons, shall remain in the closet. Take it or leave it for what it is.

It has been a great trip, full of things that make life what it has been, full of friends and family, exciting, interesting, challenging, frustrating, occasionally boring and yes, worth doing again. Don't I wish? But I know my time draws nearer. How many moments, days, weeks, months or years do I have? Only God knows that. Right now, I can only say that I am not ready to check out. So for now, I will take a rain check on that day when I must say, "So long."

Herman Son
Contour Red Leader

Footnotes

Chapter 3

1. Acheson, Dean *Present At The Creation: My Years At the State Department* (New York, W. W. Norton, Inc. 1969), pages 354-357. The speech, given before the National Press Club on January 12, 1950, is widely believed to have been instrumental in triggering the Korean War.

Chapter 21

1. Ambrose, Stephen *The Wild Blue Yonder* (New York, Simon and Schuster) pp 69, 74-75

Chapter 25

1. Ambrose, Stephen *Citizen Soldier* (New York, Simon and Schuster) pp27-55. This is a hair-raising account of combat during the early days after D-Day and the battle for Europe.

2. Bradley, James *Flyboys* http://www.eyewitnesstohistory.com/vodday.htm, p 83

Chapter 36

1. Berne, Eric, *What Do You Say After You Say 'Hello'* (New York, Grove Press) pp 31-32. Script Theory posits that man's life follows a plan somewhat like a three-act play with a beginning, middle and end. Knowing the first act, one can predict the second and final acts.

Chapter 37

1. Decelleration Project, www.regulus-missile.com. Used with permission of Nick T. Spark.

Chapter 42

1. Csipke, Zoltan *The Hungarian Revolution of 1956 and How it Affected the World*, http://www.bolted.net/zoltan/1956.htm A riveting account of the revolution and what happened when the Soviets returned to crush it.

2. Ataturk, Kemal *Founder of the Turkish Republic* http://www.turkishnews.com/Ataturk

Chapter 43

1. Solstrin, Eric (ed.) *Cyprus, A Country Study*, 4th Edition (Washington, DC, Federal Research Division, Library of Congress) pp 30-31

Chapter 45

1. Csipke, Zoltan Ibid.

Chapter 51

1. Luciano, Lucky. Personal anecdote from speaker. This was common street knowledge in Naples at the time author lived here.

2. NASA, *The History of Sputnik*, http://www.nq.nasa.gov/office/pao/History/sputnik/

Chapter 61

1. Johnson, Lyndon B. *Address to Congress, August 5, 1964. The President reports on the Tonkin Gulf incident* http://www.vale.edu/lawweb/avalon/tonkin-g.htm

Chapter 77

1. Hubbard, L. Ron Dianetics, the Modern Science of Mental Health (Los Angeles, Bridge Publications) pp 1-24

2. Fisher, Harvey J. *Dianetic Theory, an Experimental Evaluation – 1953*

3. Alack, John *A Piece of Blue Sky: Scientology, Dianetics and L. Ron Hubbard, Exposed* (New York, Carol Publishing) pp.1-6

Chapter 90

1. Berne, Eric *What Do You Say After You Say 'Hello'?* pp. 11-12

2. Loc cit.

3. Ibid, pp. 19-21

4. Ibid, pp. 16

Chapter 97

1. Acheson, Dean *My Years at the State Department*, pp. 354-357

Bibliography

Dean Acheson My Years at the State Department
W. W. Norton, New York, NY 1969.

John Alack A Piece of Blue Sky: Scientology, Dianetics and L Ron Hubbard, Exposed
Carol Publishing Group: New York, NY

Stephen Ambrose The Wild Blue Yonder
Simon and Schuster: New York, NY

Kemal Ataturk Founder of the Turkish Empire http://www.turkishnews.com/Ataturk

Eric Berne What Do You Say After You Say 'Hello'? New York, NY: Grove Press

James Bradley Flyboys http://www.eyewitnesstohistory.com/vodday.htm

Zoltan Csipke The Hungarian Revolution of 1956 and How It Affected The World http://www.bolted.net/zoltan/1956.htm

Harvey J. Fisher Dianetic Theory, an Experimental Evaluation – 1953
David Cecare, 1999

L. Ron Hubbard Dianetics: The Modern Science of Mental Health
Bridge Publications, Inc., Los Angeles, CA

Lyndon B. Johnson Address to Congress, August 5, 1964. The President reports on the Tonkin Gulf incident
http://www.yale.edu/lawweb/avalon/tonkin-g.htm

Give Us Your E-Pinion!

JMT Publications prides itself on releasing quality products from novice writers with great potential. Our authors would love to hear from you - the reader - and get your feedback on this book. Potential readers benefit from your words as well, and if you help one of them to make a decision, you can get paid for your reviews.

Simply log on to the website, http://www.epinions.com and establish an account. Then, look for *Eagle Dreams* in the Books category. If they don't happen to list it (it takes a while new publications to be listed), start a Reviews page for it! Then, write your heart out. We cherish all good reviews, of course, but we respect your honest opinions.

If you're really enthusiastic, please add your comments and reviews to the *Eagle Dreams* listings at Amazon.com and Alibris.com. Once again, we appreciate your purchase of our product and your opinion.

Do You Have A Story To Tell?

JMT Publications is always seekiing quality manuscripts from authors who choose to self-publish. We can facilitate the publishing process quickly and easily for you, and take your manuscript from initial preparation all the way through printing and bindery. We even obtain the copyright and list your book with the Library of Congress for you! If you have a manuscript in process or completed and would like more information on how JMT can put YOUR words into print, please complete this form and return to: **JMT Publications, PO Box 64, Shirley, Indiana 47384** or visit our website (http://jmtpubs.tripod.com) and fill out our **Quick Quote** form on-line .

Name _____

Mailing Address _____

City, State, Zip _____

E-mail address _____

☐ I have a manuscript in process

☐ I have a completed manuscript and am ready to publish

☐ I have already self-published a book and want help in marketing it.